MODERN FICTION

MODERN FICTION

BY

DOROTHY BREWSTER

ASSISTANT PROFESSOR OF ENGLISH

COLUMBIA UNIVERSITY

AND

ANGUS BURRELL

ASSISTANT PROFESSOR OF ENGLISH

COLUMBIA UNIVERSITY

NEW YORK: MORNINGSIDE HEIGHTS

COLUMBIA UNIVERSITY PRESS

1934

FOREWORD

OF the essays in this volume the following have already appeared, either in part or in full, in the present authors' *Dead Reckonings in Fiction* (Longmans, Green and Co., 1924) and *Adventure or Experience* (Columbia University Press, 1930) : those on Gissing, Dostoevsky, Conrad, May Sinclair, Virginia Woolf, Lawrence, and three novels by Maugham, Bennett, and Mann. They have been carefully revised and brought up to date. Chapters I, VIII, X, XI, XII, XIII, XIV, and XV are entirely new, with the exception of two sections in Chapter XIV on Chekhov and Katherine Mansfield, reprinted from *Dead Reckonings;* three or four pages in the last chapter, reprinted from *Adventure or Experience;* and a few pages in Chapter I and Chapter XIV, taken from articles written by the authors and published in the magazine *MS*.

The work has grown out of courses in modern fiction—American, English, and European—given by the authors, for some years past, at Columbia University; and they wish to acknowledge here their great debt to the students in these courses. Class discussions and papers have developed and clarified their own personal points of view in ways that will be made evident in some of the following pages.

The book is intended for readers interested in matching up their own opinions with those of other critically minded people; and for readers who have encountered difficulties in finding their way among the fascinating but confusing experiments in modern fiction, and who wish to learn how to make their own appraisals. There is obviously no attempt to survey the entire vast field of the fiction written in the last half century in Europe and America, but there is an attempt to make the choice of novels and authors a representative one, and to illustrate a fruitful method of critical approach and evaluation.

Some of the chapters were written in collaboration. Others were written entirely by one or the other of the authors, and such chapters are signed.

A. B.
D. B.

Columbia University
in the City of New York
September 1, 1934

CONTENTS

MODERN FICTION

I

PERSPECTIVES

TEN years ago the authors of the following essays published *Dead Reckonings in Fiction,* a volume concerned with modern fiction and the questions involved in its evaluation. They felt at the time uncertain about critical standards, distrusting the old accepted formulas, and curious but unconvinced about new theories—rather at sea, in fact. Hence their choice of a nautical title, "dead reckoning" being a way of navigating without sights when the sky is overcast or the horizon blurred. Five years later they supplemented this volume with *Adventure or Experience,* containing several more essays similar in point of view and method to those in the earlier book, and including a chapter exploring—with the aid of two or three hundred students who had reflected and commented upon their own reading experience—the reader's relation to fiction.

The authors felt that this relation was usually neglected in the search for standards, or limited to the individual critic's experience, or made the subject of guesses so unsupported by evidence as to be valueless. The readers who helped them in this exploring expedition were students in university courses; they were of both sexes, of ages ranging from eighteen to sixty, and of many occupations and social conditions. It was no easy matter to draw forth these rather intimate expressions, because most adults who are taking college courses have acquired definite notions of what they ought to think about books, and a set of neat phrases embodying their opinions. They feel bound to appreciate what is "good"—morally or esthetically, the two often being pleasantly confused—and to give reasons. So they talk easily of convincing and unreal characters, well-built plots, local color, atmosphere, the significance of the author's message, and so on. One praises and another damns the same book; it is both good and bad on the same counts. And these sharply diverse judgments are couched in a technical jargon that students have been taught to use by teachers, critics, and reviewers. In their diversity they parallel the bewildering contradictions we are familiar with in current reviewing. Under the stereotyped formulas lurk intimate personal responses. Some special experience has made a book intellectually or emotionally accessible; or some unrealized prejudice inhibits sympathetic understanding; or some deep-buried complex makes the reader love or hate the book with a fervor he cannot explain, but can only feebly rationalize.

To give a simple illustration of the difficulty of getting behind the convenient formulas: there was an intelligent young man in a university course whose education, interrupted by the War, had left in his mind a débris of critical phrases which he automatically drew upon when asked his opinion of a novel. He picked out Jack London's *Valley of the Moon* as the "best" story he had ever read, and spoke of its consistent characters and well-constructed plot. But it took a couple of weeks to discover why he *really* liked the book.

Last summer [he ultimately wrote], when recovering from an accident, I sat out in the park while a young lady read the story aloud. A cool breeze ruffled the leaves of the trees, the birds sang, the flowers were in bloom, and the lady had a voice that was pleasant to hear. Rowboats floated on the lagoon nearby, and further off I could see tennis players hopping about after a little ball. I liked the book for the struggles of the hero. I'm very fond of struggles, provided they are someone else's. The tennis players, the boaters, the children playing tag, the motorists, and the hero of the book—all were struggling. So I was very happy. It really is a good book, though.

So the circumstances under which one happens to read a book may account for the impression it makes. That sounds utterly obvious, but it is often ignored or forgotten when the reader turns critic. A nurse, taking a correspondence course in fiction, judged the subject matter of Henry James's *The Ambassadors* trivial, unconnected with the "roots of things"; and the novel, therefore, without significance. A few questions brought out the fact that she had read it when on duty in the psychopathic ward of the hospital:

Strether's complicated brainstorms over Chad's morals were frequently interrupted by the would-be suicide who tried to tear the bandages from the throat he had failed to cut efficiently; and there was a slender pale-faced woman of forty who ceaselessly washed her hands.

All this variety of the "real" made what she called James's delicate flicking of butterflies from petals seem artificial and absurd. To another woman in the course James's novel was deeply significant; she emerged from it refreshed and happy; it was like having a lamp brought into the room where one has been trying to spell out a book in the twilight. But it happened that she had just passed through a pronounced change of attitude towards life; James had made the nature and stages of such an experience clear to her; he was profoundly satisfying because he pictured men and women in the throes of facing about.

One could easily confront more involved but equally contradictory estimates of *The Ambassadors* from professional critics. What influenced them? Possibly nothing more recondite than such relatively accidental circumstances as were at work in the case of these students. But critics, unlike students, do not have to submit to the rôle of victims in a Socratic dialogue. The "detachment" of their pronouncements goes unchallenged.

Socrates may however have to call Dr. Freud into consultation. Something more difficult to get at than accidental circumstances may be controlling one's response to a novel. Psychoanalysts assure us that we cannot discover our own complexes. They tell us that if we are fascinated by a writer who has a certain psychosis, we ourselves probably share that psychosis, and that is why the release he has achieved for himself through his art gives us also satisfaction. Or if we feel intense dislike of a book or a character, it is due to some obsession, unsuspected by us until we are challenged—and then we deny it with fervor. A young man criticized Sudermann's *Dame Care* as a third-rate novel, but could muster few reasons for his opinion that stood up under questioning. It finally came out that he hated the portrayal of Paul's father, a combination of fool and villain; and presently he realized that his attitude to the book was determined by the similarity between Paul's father and his own. Then he warmed to a resentful defense of his father. Why did he hate Sudermann's portrayal so intensely? Because he loved his father? Or because he had secretly passed the same judgment on him that Sudermann passes on Paul's father and resented being made aware of the fact? Or possibly because he suspected that he resembled his father and hated that thought? Here there is merely guesswork without the active coöperation of Freud or some other analyst. But at least the young man's confidence in the soundness of his judgment of *Dame Care* was shaken, and it was worth while to shake it, for he was going to be a librarian; he would be asked to give advice to readers, and the dogmatic assurance of his first attitude would have turned aside possible readers of a fine novel.

His confusion about himself and *Dame Care* is in interesting contrast with the clarity of a Chinese student, who preferred it above all other novels on a reading list, and knew why: it supported his own inherited conception of life.

It has a theme, and the theme is that extreme sacrifice is necessary in order to attain any great object. It has much the same
theme that most of our Chinese novels have. They are predom-
inantly ethical in tone. The hero is always made to undergo all
kinds of hardships and sometimes death to attain his object.
That object might be the salvation of other persons, the better-
ment of society, the rescue of one's family, or the elevation of
one's nation. *Dame Care* develops its theme adequately: every
scene contains some misfortune for the hero.

This clarity may not take us far on the road to an esthetic
evaluation of the novel. But if more critics tried to be as
honest with themselves as the Chinese youth, there would be
less smoke and confusion in the field of criticism.

To justify oneself, or to have one's point of view justified,
is more permanently satisfying than merely to escape into
an imaginary self and more congenial surroundings. Inten-
tionally or not, readers reveal how this or that novel has
made their own actions seem reasonable or inevitable, their
own temperaments interesting or excusable; has made it
more possible or more delightful for them to live with themselves. Writing of Philip, the hero of Maugham's *Of Human
Bondage,* a young man confesses:

He lives for me because our experiences and thoughts parallel
in many instances. His ceaseless groping for his niche in life and
a satisfactory career lead him into several experiments which I
have already attempted: I have left college because I believed
it would not lead me to any adequate occupation in after life;
I have studied art in Paris and discovered my mistake; I have
played with the idea of a number of careers and discovered that
my enthusiasm exhausted itself in planning and expectation,
just as Philip's did about going into the Church. The fact that
Philip survived so many failures and finally discovered a path
of comparative contentment makes me less hopeless on my own
account.

Philip is one of the most consoling of heroes; he makes so
many false starts, suffers so often what the world calls failure;

and yet his failures are made to appear to the intimate view justified and valuable.

Proportionate to our satisfaction in the book that vindicates us is our violent and often obscure resentment of the book that topples over some carefully built structure in which we were living comfortably. A social-service worker, enthusiastic for her vocation, took a course in fiction while waiting to marry an engineer whose work was to be in a coal-mining town. There would be plenty of wretched people there on whom she expected to try out some of the pet theories she had learned at college. Her social-service inclinations dated back (so she suspected) to early reading of the Pollyanna books, *Mrs. Wiggs of the Cabbage Patch,* and other stories that dealt with broken-down lives, prostitution, desertion, and poor orphans. Her favorite fiction in the course handled situations and people that needed the services of a social-service expert: novels by Galsworthy, Hardy, George Eliot. "I love to diagnose in fiction from any chapter 3 on." But when the Russian novelists came on the scene, she had a severe shock. She felt only hatred and contempt for all the characters in *The Brothers Karamazov;* she loathed Gorky and shuddered at the very mention of murder, insanity, gendarme. She was able to endure *War and Peace* only by firmly regarding it as a sociological treatise against war. Now one would have thought that some of the people in these Russian novels so needed the help of a social-service worker that her spirit would have soared to meet the challenge. Possibly the trouble was this: she felt equal, with the equipment of her theories, to a Galsworthy or a Hardy problem. But the Russians plunged their characters into distresses so unfamiliar and probed so deeply into predicaments she had never imagined that she felt unable to cope with them, and defended herself by hating them.

A novel may, without our being conscious of it, revive

emotions that belong to almost forgotten experiences. We like or dislike it in consequence, but shrink from the task of reopening the trail into the past, and content ourselves with what we fancy to be a disinterested judgment. One reader found *The Growth of the Soil* beautiful and *Pelle the Conqueror* sordid and distasteful, but she realized upon reflection that these opinions had much more to do with her own early childhood emotions than with the merits of the two novels. Hamsun re-created for her certain magical summers when she was six or seven, and played on her uncle's New England farm, gathering checkerberries by the pond, lying in the pine grove among the ferns, chasing the squirrels, "helping" with the ploughing and the butter-making—spending long, unlagging days in investigation, excitement, and peace. The children of Isak became, as she read, her brother and herself, and the novel gave her back the simple pleasures, the tranquil New England countryside, and her "unity with life." But *Pelle the Conqueror* was another story. There was coarseness on that Danish farm that she liked to think was quite absent from her New England environment; it marred for her the idealized memory. And the labor struggle stirred up an old terror:

The word "strike" recalls to my mind my mother's face as the riot call sounded in Lawrence one Friday in 1912. My father, one of the local mill officials, powerless to accede to the demands of the strikers, yet convinced of the justice of their cause, felt nevertheless that his duty was to do all he could to guard mill property from destruction. Every Thursday night for the whole course of the strike, he slept in the office. Mother's fears and those of us children used to reach their climax Friday morning when the time came for him to return for breakfast. He refused to carry arms. One morning he did not come, and had the bomb that was found later in his building actually exploded, the result on his family could scarcely have been worse. I remember the militia encamped in the basement of the mill, the soldiers forcing us to move on in the streets, the broken streetcar windows, the soup kitchens, my hungry schoolmates, many of them fed in our home, and over and over again my father's face. Nexö's picture of economic complexities is too well drawn. Unless I can act, I would rather not consider it.

But she no longer dismissed the novel as "sordid."

The discussion thus far of the reader's relation with the novel has stressed some of the very personal considerations that must be recognized and dealt with before the neat categories of criticism can be used or discarded with intelligence. Virginia Woolf [1] declares it to be our first task in reading a novel to master the author's perspective. A prior task is surely to be aware of our own, though it may be argued that we often become aware of our own only as we are confronted with another. But as the experiences quoted above indicate, we can go much further than we usually take the trouble to do in mastering our own perspective. Then we can climb on the novelist's shoulders, as Mrs. Woolf directs, and

gaze through his eyes until we, too, understand in what order he ranges the large common objects upon which novelists are fated to gaze: man and men; behind them Nature; and above them that power which for convenience and brevity we may call God . . . It would seem to be true that people who live cheek by jowl and breathe the same air vary enormously in their sense of proportion; to one the human being is vast, the tree minute; to the other, trees are huge and human beings insignificant little objects in the background. So, in spite of the text-books, writers may live at the same time and yet see nothing the same size . . . It is in their perspective that they are different . . . But here many difficulties arise. For we have our own vision of the world; we have made it from our own experience and prejudices, and it is therefore bound up with our own vanities and loves. It is impossible not to feel injured and insulted if tricks are played and our private harmony is upset . . . But the great writer— the Hardy or the Proust—goes on his way regardless of the rights of private property; by the sweat of his brow he brings order from chaos; he plants his tree there and his man here; he makes the figure of his deity remote or present as he wills. In master-pieces—books, that is, where the vision is clear and order has been achieved—he inflicts his own perspective upon us so severely that as often as not we suffer agonies—our vanity is injured because our own order is upset; we are afraid because the old supports are being wrenched from us; and we are bored—for what pleasure or amusement can be plucked from a brand new idea? Yet from anger, fear, and boredom a rare and lasting pleasure is sometimes born.

Mastering a novelist's perspective is not wholly an affair of reading his books intelligently, with an attention freed, so far as we can manage it, from confusing personal bias, that is, with our own perspective mastered. It may involve going behind the work to the man and trying to discover from what experiences he has developed his vision of the world. We have opened up the question of the reader's relation to the novel. What of the author's relation with his work? In this enterprise one meets with formidable difficulties and with the disapproval on this or that ground of many distinguished philosophers and critics and artists. For example, the German writer, Hermann Hesse, discussing "Imaginative Writing and Criticism" in *This Quarter* (September, 1931), attacks the amateurish literary criticism that inquires into works of literature in the manner Freud employs in his investigation of dreams and other unconscious mental content. Such criticism analyzes on the basis of his available works a writer's complexes and pet images and diagnoses him as belonging to one category or another of neurotics.

What is most distinctive in human attainments is converted back into unformed matter. Nothing is made of the still noteworthy phenomenon that out of the very same substance from which the neurotic Mr. Jones had brought forth no more than a nervous belly-ache, a rare individual here and there has fashioned superb works of art.

Hesse reminds us of the extreme delicacy, intricacy, and elusiveness of the actual process of psychoanalysis; the time, patience, and pains required; the cunning with which the origins of complexes hide from the analyst. And yet on the basis of nothing but the work left by a dead artist, these amateurs pretend to expose his complexes. "The patient is dead, a test of accuracy is not to be feared, and so the yarn is spun."

One may sympathize with Hesse's remonstrances, and yet retain a keen interest in these nefarious performances. A group of amateur psychoanalysts criticized an essay by a woman none of them knew except very casually; it was a charming essay, they all agreed, but betrayed the author as a repressed old maid; out of the emotions belonging to that state came the reflections and the imagery. The essay was one of the ordered daydreams called art. A dream may be very significant to an analyst, but one dream is only one bit of evidence, needing the support of countless other bits. Even granted the repressions of the old maid: why out of these repressions came a charming reverie instead of some eccentric pattern of neurotic behavior?

In the present state of our knowledge there is no satisfactory answer to questions like that. Consider such an artist as Strindberg, who all his life displayed bewildering contradictions and an emotional instability that took him to the border—if not for a season over it—of insanity. They say he had an Oedipus complex, probably an organ inferiority besides, and maybe other difficulties that make him a case for each and all of the leading schools of psychoanalysis. There are volumes upon volumes of his own confessions to work with. We go to see his tragedy, *The Father*, and reflect that if ever a man had a rare assortment of complexes, he had. But we don't know why his emotional fixation upon his mother, and his inveterate tendency to seek the mother in marriage, and then to hate and fear her and imagine he was being drained of his vitality and persecuted by her—why all that turned into a swift, logical, hair-raising drama, instead of a full-blown case of paranoia, as it has with other men, and almost did with him a few years later—and this in spite of the "release" afforded by *The Father*. We resort to guesses. Perhaps if he had not been infuriated by Ibsen's *Doll's House,* he would not have transmuted his marital miseries into a play. But there, happily, was that woman-worshiping Norwegian for a target to shoot at and thus make Strindberg believe he was fighting the devils outside instead of the devils within.

Strindberg was generous to the future psychoanalysts. His startling flashes of insight into himself point the way; and he poured forth the stuff of which his tormented life was made, sublimated and unsublimated, in confessions, dramas, novels, stories, paintings, furious controversial articles. He has not yet been neatly pigeonholed, just because the evidence is too abundant. But speculation, amateur and expert, continues. One cannot see *The Father* without being teased by the problem: what on earth or in hell did this man go through that made him conceive so insanely lucid a horror? And when we find this pattern of warfare, this death grapple of love and hate, this obsession with guilt, in drama after drama—fantastic shifting nightmares or plays as swiftly and brutally conducted as a prejudged criminal process—we are impelled to go behind the plays to the man. We can't help it, and we will use—*pace* Hermann Hesse—any instruments of exploration modern speculation puts into our hands. Nor shall we worry overmuch about what we are doing to Strindberg; he invited it by the clamor of his confessions and quarrels and by his own zest in vivisection.

Throw Strindberg to the wolves then; he was used to it; he must even have liked it. But what of the reserved and reticent artists, the decently impersonal, who make no scandal in their lives and no confidences in diaries and autobiographies? There is Turgenev, a model of the restrained and objective artist, in theory and practice. No one who reads more than two or three of his novels fails to notice a plot-pattern that has been summed up: how Jack did not get Jill—or, it might be added, anything else—a pattern of frustration. Each novel in turn is delicately convincing; yes, we agree, in this case, so it would have turned out. After four or five novels, we begin to wonder at the melancholy recurrence, but decide that, since Turgenev is so conscientiously objective an artist, his pattern of frustration and sadness was simply that of the Russia of his day. We remind ourselves of the heavy oppression which prevailed in Russia, the lack of outlets for the active and gifted, the indecision of the Russian temperament —the Russian Hamlet. But decades after Turgenev's death, letters and documents are made accessible by a Soviet government not made up of Hamlets, and Mr. Yarmolinsky orders all the material into a biography of Turgenev, in which he indulges discreetly the modern fancy for psychoanalysis. From the study emerges the picture of Turgenev's emotional bondage to two women: the tyrannical mother, and the contentedly married opera singer, Mme. Viardot, whom Turgenev worshiped until his death, forced to take what consolation he could from sitting on the edge of another man's nest. The mother was passionate but not lovable; Mme. Viardot was lovable but not passionate; and Turgenev, involved with the two of them, was about as defeated in his emotional life as one could well be. It was just a nice, quiet, steady, prolonged, wistful frustration; and he knew, as his biographer says, no fulfillment save in his art, where he loved to portray aspects of the thing he suffered from.

Why, out of having his young affection abused and his mature passion defeated, should come *The Nest of Nobles* and *Smoke,* instead of asthma, for instance? (Though Marcel

Proust's career shows how a complex is equal to producing both asthma and art in the same person; you may sublimate your complexes in fifteen volumes and have enough left over for your asthma.) Again we resort to guesswork. The mother who in her possessive hunger exploited her son and weakened his will passed on to him her own gift for vivid expression and close observation, and encouraged his writing—thus ironically putting it into his power to do her full justice in his portraits of detestable women serf-owners modeled after her. And Mme. Viardot, whose response to his love was so unsatisfying, drew him into circles in Paris where literary craftsmen like Flaubert discussed theories of objectivity in art that influenced his writing. And Russia had eager, socially minded critics who dinned it into the ears of this easily persuaded man, this "soft pear" of a man, that his duty was to serve the future of Russia by recording and interpreting the significant movements and the emerging types of character. No one, even after Mr. Yarmolinsky's fine study, would consider that all of Turgenev's complexes had been tracked to their secret source. But at least our impression of the Russian Hamlet is qualified, for we realize how much Turgenev's personal drama counted in the apparently impersonal portrayal of those heroes with their incapacity to make decisions.

The Hamlet-like Russian and the Christ-like Russian and the mystically minded Russian peasant are, one now suspects, much more closely related to the emotional conflicts of Turgenev and Dostoevsky and Tolstoy than to the actualities of the ordinary Russian temperament. Yet these notions of what is typically Russian have in recent years been among the serious obstacles to our understanding the Russian situation. Great artists may be very unsafe guides to the emotional constitution, the characteristic attitudes, the intellectual outlook of the race they belong to. It is the best-sellers in fiction, the books of the moment, that best reflect the stock responses, the current sentimentalities and prejudices, the daydreams and aspirations of the majority. In some cases a great writer has proved to be a prophet and forerunner, and the way he thought and felt has come in time to be characteristic of his countrymen. "Where I stood ten years ago," said Ibsen, "there now stands a compact majority," and added, "but I am not there any longer." This is more likely to happen in the realm of ideas; in feeling, the great writer may always remain peculiar. Birth or circumstance has given him some twist that his art is being used unconsciously to straighten out.

Why concern ourselves with these peculiarities that perhaps we can never be sure of diagnosing accurately—the patient, as Hermann Hesse says, being dead, and much of the needed evidence unobtainable? Suppose a person comes to you to talk about a situation that involves you both. He interprets it in a certain light, explains the motives of the people mixed up in it, and advises you how to act. If it comes to your knowledge that this person has certain persistent difficulties in his intimate relationships, or that he has a greater gift than most people of convincing himself of the truth of what he desires to believe, or that he suffers from some fear, or has a tendency, however slight, toward hysteria or melancholia or paranoia, or that his sex interests are of the less accepted variety, you will certainly consider these interesting symptoms in trying to decide how straight he sees the thing you are both concerned with. How far can you trust his interpretation? How much allowance should you make for distortion of vision?

So with artists, especially with novelists and dramatists. They are peculiarly busy with the same things we are: people and their motives and their actions, the interpretation of experience, the ordering of the confusion life presents. Whether we are aware of it or not, we are influenced by their interpretation. Thus it becomes much more than the indulgence of idle curiosity to find out about the novelist what we should want to know about the friend. André Gide explains his choice of narrative method in *The Counterfeiters:* "I wish to have its events narrated from different angles by the actors on whom the events have some influence; I wish these events as they tell them to appear slightly distorted; a certain interest results for the reader from the fact that he has to rectify the distortion; the story requires his collaboration." The reading of the great novelists calls for a similar effort at rectification and adjustment of perspective. We must know, if possible—guess, if we can't know—why each saw life as he did; and place his viewpoint in relation to those of all the others who subtly color our interpretation of experience. We must do this for our own guidance in a hazardous world.

In thus relating an author to his work, we do not pretend to be explaining its esthetic content. *Remembrance of Things Past* and *Fathers and Sons* remain to be evalued in terms other than the mother fixations of Proust and Turgenev. We hope to escape falling into the reductive fallacy of isolating some one constituent of a work of art, and reducing the work to the terms of this isolated element. After we have discussed certain novels, novelettes, and stories, and their authors, in the following chapters, we shall turn again to theorizing and try to make our critical theory clear in the light of our practice. But in the discussion of a specific work of fiction, we intend to take account of "the human conditions under which it was brought into being," and "the human consequences it engenders in actual life experience." For "when artistic objects are separated from both conditions of origin and operation in experience, a wall is built around them that renders almost opaque their general significance, with which esthetic theory deals." [2]

II

GEORGE GISSING:
RELEASE THROUGH FICTION?

GEORGE GISSING is now remembered chiefly for his gloomy realistic novel, *New Grub Street;* and for his famous long essay, *The Private Papers of Henry Ryecroft,* in which he wistfully contrasts the life he has lived with a life he wished he might have had, and generally unburdens his soul in reflections about his own unhappy temperament in conflict with a not too friendly age. A third book should be mentioned—*By the Ionian Sea,* an account of a visit to Southern Italy. If to these three books, we add two more—*Charles Dickens,* a critical appreciation, and *Veranilda,* an historical romance of the Roman-Gothic conflicts of the sixth century, we suggest at once the scope of Gissing's interests and achievements.

In this list we have mentioned only one novel, *New Grub Street.* But George Gissing spent most of his life writing novels, and, if we exclude *Veranilda,* all of them present recurring themes. Some of these recurrent patterns are: first, the vicissitudes of young men with good minds and no money, their resentful attitude towards society, their eventual compromise or failure; second, either an absurdly sentimental overevaluation of women, or the most vindictive and unjust underevaluation; third, heroes exhibiting flights from sex adjustments (often very cleverly rationalized) or flights into sex relationships that are usually disastrous.

There is nothing very remarkable in the fact that a novelist should deal with money—or the lack of it—and with love. Most novelists do. But in many novels the problems involved are accepted as being wholly the problems of the characters.

In George Gissing's world we feel that the heroes are often merely the protagonists for Gissing's own problems. This is to say that Gissing is a betrayingly autobiographical novelist (which is generally conceded); and this is only another way of saying that Gissing is an imperfect novelist, in that he never quite succeeds in presenting his characters with the objectivity that makes the reader believe in these people as living their own lives in their own world—propelled by their own inner natures. Virginia Woolf has quite justly said: "For Gissing is one of those imperfect novelists through whose books one sees the life of the author faintly covered by the lives of fictitious people . . . With such writers we establish a personal rather than an artistic relationship." And it is this "personal" relationship that we are trying to make clear in this chapter. Moreover, Mr. A. C. Gissing, a son of the author, writes in the Preface to *Selections, Autobiographical and Imaginative:* "There is no writer of fiction, that I know of, whose works are fuller of autobiographical material than are those of my father, or whose characters throw more light upon various aspects of their author's mind."

In a sense it is true that all fiction is nourished upon the writer's own conflicts. But there are some novelists whose characters walk off on legs of their own and flourish with a life distinctly theirs. Such novelists get so completely outside their material as to throw their work off into a realm where it moves in an orbit of its own. Arnold Bennett does precisely this in his great novel, *The Old Wives' Tale*. With such a novel there is usually no desire on the reader's part to explore the possible relationship between the author and his characters. One feels that Constance and Sophia Baines are completely realized in their own world; that in a sense they have no concern whatever with Arnold Bennett and that, still in a sense, he has nothing further to do with them. This seems to be true even of such obviously autobiographical novels as *The Way of All Flesh* and *Mary Olivier*. But there are other novels that tease us constantly with hints of below-the-surface adhesions, that are not wholly free of their creators. If we could trace the relationship we should understand better both the man and his books. George Gissing and his novels belong particularly in this latter category.

It is almost impossible to think of Gissing's work without reflecting about the man himself; and of this is generated a drama beyond the events of the stories. In Conrad, the part played by sea and ships; the lawyers and the inns-of-court in Galsworthy; patients and hospitals in Chekhov's universe— in such obvious correspondence between creator and creation there is no resonance of this additional drama. In Gissing's world the correspondence is something more obsessional, less clearly understood, more persistently presented, and charged always with resentment or the ostentation of despair. And hence to some critics he is a "whining" moralist rather than an artist redeemed through creation. Even in his finest novel, *New Grub Street,* in which Gissing is most clearly the creative artist, he is not fully redeemed by this creation. But here more than elsewhere he manages to endow his characters with lives of their own, to set them up in their proper spheres and rights, quite apart from anything that is obviously autobiographical, or that would make them seem mere functions of Gissing's own psychic disturbances.

The theme has to do with the conflict between the old and the new orders in the world of journalism as exemplified in three of the central characters. Harold Biffen and Edward Reardon represent the older school, men of good sound training, each with gifts in writing, but gifts for which there is very little market. Gissing says of them: "From the familiar point of view these men were worthless; view them in possible relation to a humane order of society, and they are admirable citizens." They have "kindly and imaginative virtues." But "the sum of their faults was their inability to earn money." Biffen, true to his temperament and to his ideals, had come near to perishing of hunger when he was completing a novel. In opposition to these men is Jasper Milvain, energetic, compromising, flashy, without integrity, and none too handsomely endowed with gifts, who yet makes himself easily at home in the real world and has considerable earning power.

These men compete not only in the world of professional letters, but in the world of love and domestic happiness as well. Reardon's wife, Amy, bears with her incompetent husband for a number of years, and eventually leaves him for Jasper Milvain, who marries her, in part, for the money she inherits.

That is only a very brief outline of the central problem. There are many other well-drawn characters, notably Alfred Yule, his daughter Marian, and the journalist Whelpdale. The point to be stressed here is that these characters are very effective creations—real, understandable, and credible. They are not happy people; they are for the most part fighting a losing battle (all except Milvain, whom we despise for the way he takes towards success); and you feel they will go under. The mood of the book is monotonously sad. These people experience frustration and poverty and nearly all the blows that assail the human spirit. And Gissing gives the reader no relief; unpityingly he follows through these sad, unhappy lives.

The gray tone is relieved once in the book, and very interestingly, when Gissing has a chance to incorporate a subject that he really enjoyed writing about. He himself, when in Greece, had seen a marvellous sunset over Athens, and he lets his character Whelpdale describe it.

The sun's rays showed themselves first in a strangely beautiful way, striking from behind the seaward hills through the pass that leads to Eleusis, and so gleaming on the nearer slopes of Aigaleos, making the clefts black and the rounded parts of the mountain wonderfully brilliant with golden colour . . . then the sun itself sank into the open patch of sky and shot glory in every direction; broadening beams smote upwards over the dark clouds, and made them a lurid yellow. To the left of the sun, the gulf of Aegina was all golden mist, the islands floating in it vaguely. To the right, over black Salamis, lay delicate strips of pale blue—indescribably pale and delicate . . . I turned eastward, and there to my astonishment was a magnificent rainbow, a perfect semicircle, stretching from the foot of Parnes to that of Hymettus, framing Athens and its hills, which grew brighter and brighter—the brightness for which there is no name among colours. Hymettus was of a soft misty warmth, a something tending to purple, its ridges marked by exquisitely soft and indefinite shadows, the rainbow coming right down in front. The Acropolis simply glowed and blazed. As the sun descended all these colours grew richer and warmer; for the moment the landscape was nearly crimson. Then suddenly the sun passed into the lower stratum of cloud, and the splendour died almost at once, except that there remained the northern half of the rainbow, which had become double. In the west, the clouds were still glorious for a time; there were two shaped like great expanded wings, edged with refulgence.

Though it is not nearly so true of *New Grub Street* as it is unmistakably true of his other novels, that about them linger many intimations of their creator's mortality, it must be said that Gissing never wholly transcended his turmoil and his misery. No straightforward, honest, or illuminating biography of Gissing exists. Those of his letters that have been published are obviously but a selection; and these selected letters are filled with surface preoccupations, and not with direct revelation of the inner man. It is in his fiction that we find Gissing both revealing and betraying himself, and it is to his fiction that we find ourselves turning for a truer account of the man himself. In doing this we must be clearly aware that characters in novels are after all *fiction*. But with Gissing it was only under this merciful veil of *fiction* that he was ever able to break through his reticent and evasive self and betray the trouble and misery of his own heart. Again, to quote Virginia Woolf, we approach such writers as Gissing

through their lives as much as through their work, and when we take up Gissing's letters, which have character but little wit and no brilliance to illumine them, we feel that we are filling in a design which we began to trace out when we read *Demos* and *New Grub Street* and *The Nether World*.

If we knew nothing and could discover nothing about the life of George Gissing and had only the novels reputed to be by a man of that name, we should presently be driven to invent a biography. Why did he write long, remorseless, humorless studies of the poor people in the slums of London when obviously he hated all the circumstances of their lives and in his heart seems to have hated them too? One doesn't ask why Dickens wrote about similar people—he liked them. Nor does one question Zola's motive; so clearly his desire was to be a "scientific" reformer. But why do Gissing's young men consistently experience frustration or tragedy because they have no money and can find no way of taking the places in society that they believe their minds entitle them to take? And why Gissing's sentimental or vindictive treatment of women? Let us look first at the few facts of the man's life before we go on to seek further and more enlightening personal evidence from his books.

George Gissing was born in 1857 in the little town of Wakefield in northern England. He attended the grammar school there and because of precocious work was given a scholarship to study at Owens College, now the University of Manchester. After about three years in Owens College, Gissing left. He had involved himself in a difficulty that wrecked his academic career, and the reverberations of this experience were to torture him in guilt and humiliation throughout his life.

It is unfortunate that we have no more authentic account of Gissing's difficulties than that offered in Mr. Morley Roberts's *Private Life of Henry Maitland,* the book generally acknowledged to be a veiled biography of George Gissing. But when Mr. Roberts is dealing with the event which is so very important in any presentation of Gissing, we may assume that he would be most careful not to exaggerate the account either in the direction of exculpation or of censure. So it seems safe to accept his statement as a pretty faithful record of the facts. This experience at Owens College offers a clue to much of the writer's work and to the man's behavior; and the account is here quoted in full:

During that time in 1876, we students at Moorhampton College were much disturbed by a series of thefts in the common room, and from a locker room in which we kept our books and papers and our overcoats. Books disappeared unaccountably and so did coats. Money was taken from the pockets of coats left in the room, and nobody knew who was to blame for this. Naturally enough we suspected a porter or one of the lower staff, but we were wrong. Without our knowledge the college authorities set a detective to discover who was to blame. One day I went into the common room, and standing in front of the fire found a man, a young fellow about my age, called Sarle, with whom I frequently played chess—he was afterward president of the chess club at Oxford—and he said to me: "Have you heard the news?" "What news?" I asked. "Your friend, Henry Maitland, has been stealing those things that we have lost," he said. And when he said it I very nearly struck him, for it seemed a gross and incredible slander. But unfortunately it was true, and at that very moment Maitland was in gaol.[3]

That Gissing was caught in these petty pilferings and that he served a sentence seem to be unrefuted. And these further details, also taken from Mr. Roberts's book, are offered straightforwardly here as explanatory of George Gissing. The only possible interest these facts can have is to help us account for the morbidity that dogged his life, and out of which, doubtless, his fiction was destined in large part to arise. The facts that led up to this exposure and sentence are these: the young man was lonely and he fell in love with a girl with whom he had picked up an acquaintance. It is quite possible the story is true, that to keep the girl off the streets he took this money to buy her a sewing machine. When he had served his sentence, friends, among them one or two of his professors, helped him to get away to America. He spent some time in Boston, then he went on to Chicago, where he was driven to supporting himself by writing fiction for the Sunday edition of the *Chicago Tribune*.

Much of this period of his life is to be found recorded as the experience of the journalist Whelpdale in *New Grub Street*. He was assisted by a casual acquaintance in a restaurant to get back to Europe. But before returning to England he spent some months in Germany. When he did return to England he married the girl. His domestic life was extremely unfortunate; finally he was forced to live apart from this alcoholic wife. After her death he married again. It would seem that this girl was illiterate and bad tempered. From the evidence of his letters, this marriage was as hopeless as the first. Gissing explained to those of his friends who tried to dissuade him from this marriage that he was insufferably lonely. Most likely what one of the characters in *New Grub Street* says is what Gissing himself felt: "the time had come when he could not do without a wife . . . Educated girls have a pronounced distaste for London garrets; not one in fifty thousand would share poverty with the brightest genius ever born . . . there is nothing to it but to look below one's level, and be grateful to the untaught woman who has pity on one's loneliness."

Gissing's latter days were spent with a French woman who

had come to see him about translating *New Grub Street*.
They lived in France, the last few months of his life in St.
Jean de Luz, where Gissing died in 1904.

Most people are not made to feel the heavy hand of society. They are guided by common sense, prudence, luck, as
you will. They may waken for a few moments from time to
time to the realization that they are part of the conventional
social pattern, and even if they are impelled to protest, their
very habit of caution restrains them. But Gissing very early
felt this hand. With his youthful misstep he and society
came into flagrant conflict. The penalty itself was severe
enough, but the evil consequences to a man of Gissing's
shrinking sensitiveness were much worse. It was with fear
quiveringly upon him that Gissing found himself back in
London, with the beast of Demos to be propitiated. It takes
more courage than most young men have to defy what in
their hearts they fear. Shelley could do it, but Shelley had,
along with the courage of his innate guilelessness, the security
of birth and money. Gissing had neither birth—rather the
profound consciousness of low birth—nor had he any money.
He professed a great sympathy for the downtrodden. He felt
himself to be one of them; and to raise the masses was in a
sense to raise himself.

In a letter of 1880, Gissing wrote:

I mean to bring home to people the ghastly condition (material,
mental, and moral) of our poor classes, to show the hideous injustice of our whole system of society, to give light upon the
plan of altering it, and above all, to preach an enthusiasm for
just and high *ideals* in this age of unmitigated egotism and
"shop." I shall never write a book which does not keep all these
ends in view.

By such a "credo of realism" he tried to make himself believe
that he loved the people. He wrote *Workers in the Dawn*,

The Nether World, Demos. Yet as he grew older and gained security, he dared to be more true to himself, he was more and more outspoken, until his final outburst of indignation in the *Ryecroft* papers:

I am no friend of the people. As a force, by which the tenor of the time is conditioned, they inspire me with distrust, with fear; as a visible multitude, they make me shrink aloof, and often move me to abhorrence. For the greater part of my life, the people signified to me the London crowd, and no phrase of temperate meaning would utter my thoughts of them under that aspect. . . Every instinct of my being is anti-democratic, and I dread to think of what our England may become when Demos rules irresistibly.

This was in 1903. He writes again in the same book:

The truth is that I have never learnt to regard myself as a "member of society." For me there have always been two entities—myself and the world—and the normal relation between these two has been hostile. Am I not still a lonely man, as far as ever from forming part of the social order? . . . And to think that at one time I called myself a socialist, a communist, anything you like of the revolutionary kind. Not for long, to be sure, and I suspect that there was always something in me that scoffed when my lips uttered such things.

Gissing's early fiction was a kind of propitiation of society; his middle work comes to be a form of revenge against society; when he is writing the books he loves most to write, he forgets society. And only then does he cease to express resentment or defiance through the stories of those young men of humble birth, good minds, but no money, who have been hurt by life—another name for established society; and who in their attempt to rise above their origins are monotonously frustrated by what appears to be an external obstacle. But this frustration, on closer observation, is clearly seen to result from some inner defect of character. Gissing himself seems only late in life to have been aware that the blame for his isolation did not belong to society alone, that he had brought his house down upon himself. Each time that there was a chance for Gissing to emerge from the self-imposed withdrawal from society, he would—as if fearing to be in the presence of people—forestall, by some such act as his second marriage, the attempts of friends to rescue him from his anguish and his despair. He clung always to the conviction that he had been too severely punished. Decent society had flung him out and he had landed in the midst of the London herd. If he would exist he must make some concession, some adjustment to the social scheme. The one thing he could do to resolve his conflict, is just what he did: he took his own equipment and withdrew to record the scene. He was in this way less harassed by the crowd.

When Gissing was twenty-five he published his first novel, *Workers in the Dawn* (1880). Mr. Austin Harrison (*Nineteenth Century,* September, 1906) points out that the hero, Arthur Golding, is a conscious autobiographical portrait of the author. This book is very hard to come by and for that reason the story is given here. And Miss May Yates in her admirable little book *George Gissing, an Appreciation,* says: "Arthur Golding is the first of those dubitative characters, rich in confessional interest, with whom Gissing is continually preoccupied. All the characters in this book reflect the inner discords and contemporary mental conflicts of the author."

Into Whitecross Street on this Saturday night in which the book begins comes Parson Edward Norman to visit his old friend Arthur Golding. He arrives in time to see Golding die. (Golding had robbed his employers, suffered the punishment for his crime, and had managed to kill himself with drink.) Parson Norman makes arrangements to call the next day for the little son, Arthur, about ten years old. He takes the child to the country to be brought up there with his daughter Helen. Arthur runs away and comes back to White-cross Street, where he gets a job guiding the fake blind man. There he meets Michael Rumball the bird seller, and Ned Quirk the potato man. All these are obviously modeled after Dickens, but they have their own peculiar power: if Dickens was wont to soften the lines, Gissing was not. These people are not in the slightest relieved by humor; they are stark and terrible when they are wicked; when they are good, they are not quite so wholly good as Dickens makes some of his people, and are therefore somewhat truer. Among the other characters are Mrs. Clinkseales and her daughter Lizzie, and Mr. Tolladay, printer, who comes to be Arthur's kind employer, friend, and foster father. Helen Norman comes into the book later, as do Gilbert Gresham, Edward Norman's friend, Maud, Gresham's daughter, and Orlando Whiffle, Norman's curate, very pedantic and very foolish. Maud marries for money, lives abroad, has a great many domestic battles, and finally shoots her husband. After Arthur has gone to the bad in a socially acceptable way, he keeps up appearances by becoming the lover of Maud. Under the tutelage and the sweet forbearance of Tolladay (a rather William Morris workshop hero), he comes to be a good deal of a prig. He studies painting with Gresham, an established artist, and Gresham comes to be very jealous of him. Into the plot at this moment is thrown the complicating factor of Pastor Norman's having made Gresham the guardian of Arthur Golding's legacy.

In all conventional novels, Arthur should have nearly married Maud Gresham, and finally married Helen Norman. But this is the sort of happy ending that filled Gissing with gloom. Temperamentally he couldn't have turned his novel in that way. Projecting his own misery upon the universe, Gissing was convinced that people were never happy, and so

how could you give a novel a happy ending and expect it to
be true? Helen, who, now that her father is dead, is wealthy,
leaves the Greshams' house to study in Germany. She is
deeply interested in social-service work; this, you feel, is
her way of hiding the fact that she loves Arthur. This Arthur
senses, and as soon as he is convinced that it is true, and as
soon also as he feels that he is perhaps in love with Helen,
he perversely marries Carrie Mitchell. Carrie is illiterate, but
pretty. She soon takes to drink and leaves Arthur, though
periodically she returns to him. Either she comes herself, or
Arthur receives calls from some of her friends who try to
blackmail him. When Carrie discovers that the other "ladies
of the house" are doing this, she comes and makes a rather
fine statement to Arthur of her innocence. In one scene she
tells him that she can't live with him again, that she isn't
fit to live with him, and the implication is clear that it is
because she has contracted a physical taint. All this part of
the novel, which incidentally is presented with much power
of conviction, reminds one constantly of *Of Human Bondage;* chiefly of that scene where Philip Carey sees Mildred
walking about the Piccadilly streets. Arthur gets a peculiar
kind of inverted pleasure in confessing to Helen Norman
that he is married, and in telling her the kind of woman
Carrie is. Helen urges him to go out and bring Carrie back.
Arthur goes out to look for Carrie and induce her to return.
He thinks he sees her walking about Piccadilly. She doesn't
come back. When Arthur sees the futility of his life, he
migrates to the United States, and at Niagara Falls, lured
or propelled by his own miseries, jumps into the maelstrom.
The fact is very melodramatic, to be sure, but the portrayal
of Arthur's mental state preceding the event, the cumulative
effect of the analysis of Arthur, makes the conclusion of the
book more moving than one would expect.

Probably the most interesting and yet the most false part

of the novel is Chapter XIV, called "Mind Growth," in which Gissing appears to publish the diary that Helen Norman has kept during her stay in Germany. It is filled with literary and historical allusions, with considerations of problems of philosophy and of sociology and politics. It is Gissing himself, more than Helen Norman. It sounds absurd to read it for a portrayal of Helen, so obviously is it Gissing's own. All the while it sets up this irritating incongruity, and ends in blurring the impression of Helen.

And yet this is very characteristic. In much of his work he seems to identify himself with some one of the women in his books. Mr. Seccombe says of him:

The distinctive qualities of Gissing at the time of his setting forth were a scholarly style, rather fastidious and academic in its restraint, and the personal discontent, slightly morbid, of a self-conscious student who finds himself in the position of a sensitive woman in a crowd.

Gissing spent the greater part of his time thinking about himself. In his novels, when he is supposedly writing about other people, he is really writing his own history. This mechanism is made clear in a letter from Schopenhauer to Goethe, dated November 11, 1815:

Every work has its origin in a happy thought, and the latter gives the joy of conception; the birth, however, the carrying out, is, in my own case at least, not without pain; for then I stand before my own soul, like an inexorable judge before a prisoner lying on the rack, and make it answer until there is nothing left to ask. Almost all the errors and unutterable follies of which doctrines and philosophies are so full seem to me to spring from a lack of this probity. The truth was not found, not because it was unsought, but because the intention always was to find again instead some preconceived opinion or other, or at least not to wound some favourite idea, and with that aim in view subterfuges had to be employed against both other people and the thinker himself. It is the courage of making a clean breast of it in face of every question that makes the philosopher. He must be like Sophocles' Oedipus, who, seeking enlightenment concerning his terrible fate, pursues his indefatigable enquiry, even when he divines that appalling horror awaits him in the answer. But most of us carry in our hearts the Jocasta, who begs Oedipus for God's sake not to enquire further; and we give way to her and that is the reason why philosophy stands where it does.

This is the reason not only why philosophy stands where it does, but the reason, moreover, why in Gissing's novels, though perpetually absorbed with Gissing's own conflicts, there is never probity, clarification, and release.

We shall turn now to one of Gissing's earliest novels, *Isabel Clarendon,* and we shall assume a close correspondence between the young author and Bernard Kingcote, the hero. The theme is one that Gissing used very often. Gissing was twenty-nine when he wrote this book; the hero is about the same age. The outline of the story follows—again given here because of the scarcity of the book:

Bernard Kingcote, with a small fund, retires from London's hard commercial life to the country. There he meets a scholar clergyman and his wife. The two men find their chief delight in making careful textual readings in Shakespeare. The great lady of the countryside is Isabel Clarendon, an attractive and well-to-do widow. In her home is Ada Warren, illegitimate daughter of Mr. Clarendon, who spends most of her days in the library. Ada is clever, intellectually rather precocious; she is also morose and crotchety. Bernard Kingcote meets these people. He convinces himself he is in love with Isabel. He is both attracted and repelled by Isabel's wealth and social position. Isabel really seems to be in love with Bernard; eventually she is really in love with him. At the moment when there is a possibility of Bernard and Isabel finding a life of happiness together, the worthless husband of Kingcote's sister dies, leaving the sister destitute. Bernard listens to the Jocasta in his heart. He seems actually glad of his escape from Isabel. He goes to London to live with his sister Mary. Isabel tries to get him back, but, buoyed up by his formal puritanical conscience, he resists. He enjoys his own nobility and his suffering. And Isabel marries a man she has known and respected for years. The story ends with a final interview between Bernard and Isabel, in which with dignity and with passion she pleads with him not to be afraid of his love for her. He seems still to believe that he loves her; but he finds it difficult to convince himself. He gives her up and goes back to his sister in Camden Town.

In the book there is considerable narrative power; the form of the novel is well managed. At the same time, there is a stilted, sophomoric quality, especially in the obviously "literary," monotonous sentences. All the external scenery seems very trumped up—the garden at night, the nightingale singing. Worse than this, the people remain, for the most part, paper people. It is true that at moments, they come to life, as, for example, when Kingcote paces the London streets, fighting with his own evil fate; or when Isabel, ill, sends for and receives Kingcote. Much of the talk and behavior of Ada Warren is also lifelike. But these episodes are only sporadic resurrections of a group of people that might, by a writer of greater fictional power, have been infused with the life of inner necessity.

The book makes quite clear the besetting sin of Gissing: he is absurdly glorifying woman, making himself as a writer quite sentimentally ridiculous, and so, one feels, protesting too much sentimental Victorian masculinity—obviously because he did not actually possess it; or else he is belittling woman in a bitter and vindictive and ferocious way that even the worst of his women seems not to deserve. As might be expected, the best parts of this novel are those which deal with the brother and sister working out their lives in Camden Town, because these are the victimized people with whom Gissing can most sympathetically identify himself. One feels convinced that Kingcote could have married Isabel, got a job, and supported his sister Mary from a distance.

But Gissing imposes his own frustrations upon his hero. He loved the crucifixion. Withdrawing thus from Isabel, and seeking refuge in his life with his sister Mary, Kingcote evaded the necessity of living up to the demands of a husband to one of Isabel's social class. And there is a definite kind of Gissing pride revealed; it was easier for Kingcote to live with a sister he was supporting than to feel he was marrying "a lady with money."

Isabel Clarendon (1886) is generally admitted to be the most autobiographical of all his books. The novel is further enlightening because it contains rather full delineations of the hero's parents, likenesses which seem to be drawn from Gissing's father and mother.

Let this description, then, of Mr. Kingcote, stand for Gissing's father. He was

not a man of strong character, though he possessed considerable ability in various directions; his temperament was impulsive, imaginative, affectionate; he was wholly ruled by his wife . . . the children appeared to stand apart from their parents; to be thrown very much upon their own resources . . . Mrs. Kingcote [let her stand for Gissing's mother], though behaving to them with all motherly care, did not win their love, neither appeared to miss it.

For Mrs. Kingcote, external facts of life sufficed—details of housekeeping. In the story, she had run off and married, chiefly, it would appear, to have a house of her own to rule and regulate.

There are a few quotations from the novel bearing upon Bernard Kingcote himself that are worth giving.

In Kingcote there existed his father's intellectual and emotional qualities, together with a certain stiffness of moral attitude derived from his mother. His prejudices were intense, their character being determined by the refinement and idealism of his nature. An enemy would have called him offensively aristocratic; only malicious ignorance could have accused him of snobbishness . . . His was an essentially feminine nature . . . Few men surpassed Bernard Kingcote in ingenious refinement of self-torture.

His "was not the face of a man at ease with his own heart, or with the circumstances amid which his life had fallen." He wanted to be free: "from sights and sounds which disgust me, from the contiguity of mean and hateful people, from suggestions which make life hideous; free to live with my fancies, and in the thoughts of men I love." "One ambition there is which has ruled my life: a high one. I have wished to win a woman's love."

The early parts of the novel *Born in Exile* are probably the most autobiographical passages to be found in Gissing's work. The later life of the hero, Godwin Peak, departs in its outer aspects from Gissing's, but the spirit and tone are very similar. There is a very fine chapter in the novel which tells how an uncle opens "Peak's Dining and Refreshment Rooms" directly opposite the college where his nephew was a student. To Godwin this blatant and insensitive advertising of their relation to trade is a bitter humiliation, and he leaves college because he is unable to endure the constant reminder of his humble origins. Godwin is a gifted and promising student. His shame and morbid pride permit the restaurant to wreck his academic career—just as Gissing's career was wrecked by the shameful episode of the theft. Godwin proceeds to London and works at journalism. Then he meets the daughter of one of his old professors, and with a desire to win this girl, he violates all his intellectual convictions and enters upon a career in the ministry. He believes that to be ordained will increase his social stature.

and thus he will be able to marry the girl. His religious and social hypocrisies are exposed, and he loses himself in the whirlpool of London life, more than ever an exile and an alien.

Gissing's treatment of women in his novels is most revealing of his own character. In *Thyrza* there is a sentimental idealization of a marriage, and one finds it almost necessary to believe that this is a retelling of the facts of his own first marriage, idealized to happiness. Of the character Elgar, in *The Emancipated,* Gissing says that he "couldn't read the marriage column in a newspaper without feeling a distinct jealousy of all the male creatures there mentioned." Yet later in the same book we find the following, which is just as truly Gissing:

How many wives and husbands love each other? Not one pair in five thousand. In the average pair . . . there is not only mutual criticism, but something even of mutual dislike. That makes love impossible. Habit takes its place.

Gissing is not Dostoevsky, and, clouded as Gissing was by his romantic, sentimental attitude toward women, he could never see life with the realistic clarity of Dostoevsky and know how inextricably hatred and love are bound together. Gissing had read Dostoevsky, and he might have gained something of the Russian writer's vision of love, if he had not himself been so penitentially involved in love adventures. As an incorrigible romantic Gissing loved to build both castles and dungeons in Spain—each in its way caricaturing reality. Yet it was characteristic of him at the same time to view his "dungeons" as true and to despise the other romantics who wrote precisely as he did. In his novel, *The Odd Women*—without doubt the gloomiest and most depressing of all his books—he has Rhoda Nun say, writing his own death warrant:

If every novelist could be strangled and thrown into the sea, we should have some chance of reforming women. The girl's nature was corrupted with sentimentality, like that of all but every woman who is intelligent enough to read what is called the best fiction, but not intelligent enough to understand its vice. Love—love—love; a sickening sameness of vulgarity. What is more vulgar than the ideal of novelists? They won't represent the actual world; it would be too dull for their readers. In real life, how many men and women *fall in love?* Not one in every ten thousand, I am convinced. Not one married pair in ten thousand have felt for each other as two or three couples do in *every* novel. There is the sexual instinct, of course, but that is quite a different thing; the novelists daren't talk about that. The paltry creatures daren't tell the one truth that would be profitable. The result is that women imagine themselves noble and glorious when they are most near the animals.

As a novelist, Gissing never came to terms with himself. Though always turning inward, he was like a squirrel in a cage, doing dizzy circles around himself as futile gymnastics of escape. The growth and development of George Meredith, brilliantly suggested by André Maurois in his *Aspects of Biography,* was not possible for George Gissing. M. Maurois says that Meredith was a snob, and he wrote *Evan Harrington* and overcame his snobbishness; he was an egoist, and he wrote *The Egoist* and conquered that vice, and so on. If this is at all true of Gissing, it is only very slightly true; for by temperament and early conditioning Gissing seems to have been a man of much greater rifts in character than Meredith, and of much less decisive will.

It was in the cloistered life of the scholar that he would have known greater happiness; there he would have found the best occasion for his gifts. His humiliation at college and the subsequent scar that he bore throughout his life closed to him the possibility of any such career. Yet he knew many modern languages—German, Spanish, Italian, French—and he had for Greek and Latin and archeology a passion that, given a chance, would have carried him far. His fiction was to him an irritation, something to be done that he might not starve. To escape this irritation, he studied constantly, especially history, and when finally the leisure did come, he wrote books nearer to his keenest desire: *By the Ionian Sea,* the *Ryecroft* papers, *Veranilda.* Moreover if it had not been for a ferocious and damaging pride, Gissing would have been helped to work that he loved by friends and acquaintances who appreciated his splendid equipment for scholarship. But he was cursed not only with this pride, but with domestic miseries; and these, with his shrinking sensitiveness and his raw social wounds that sent him deeper and deeper into retirement, made inevitable the life he lived.

He read and dreamed himself into the past, and the result of this faithful and illuminated dreaming is to be found in *Veranilda.* When he visited southern Italy, he was himself something of a spirit of a vanished age, and he was very happy in that brief experience. He confesses: "Every man has his intellectual desire; mine is to escape life as I know it and dream myself into that old world which was the imaginative delight of my boyhood." And it is true that all through Gissing's life of turmoil, ill-health, and despair, he was able by the power of this imaginative daydreaming, by his love of history and the classics, to find a little repose.

A year or two before he died he wrote, in the *Ryecroft* papers:

For of myself it might be said that whatever folly is possible to a moneyless man, that folly I have at one time or another committed. Within my nature there seemed to be no faculty of rational self-guidance. Boy and man, I blundered into every ditch and bog which lay within sight of my way. Never did silly mortal reap such harvest of experience; never had anyone so many bruises to show for it. Thwack, thwack! No sooner had I recovered from one sound drubbing than I put myself in the way of another. "Unpractical" I was called by those who spoke mildly; "idiot"—I am sure—by many a ruder tongue. And idiot I see myself, whenever I glance back over the long, devious road. Something, obviously, I lacked from the beginning, some balancing principle granted to most men in one or another degree. I had brains, but they were no help to me in the common circumstances of life.

It is all true, but even here the Jocasta in his heart is not silent—the self-indulging pleasure principle which is the Jocasta of us all. Gissing is luxuriating in the spectacle of his failure. He told the truth, but it never made him free.

A. B.

DOSTOEVSKY AND THE BROTHERS KARAMAZOV

DOSTOEVSKY, even more than Gissing, is one of those writers whose books send us to their lives to account for persistently recurrent patterns of character, episode, mood, conflict. We suspect that their fiction has been an instrument in integrating their personalities and resolving their problems. The patterns in Dostoevsky's novels hint at this personal conflict and suggest, too, that it was never completely fought through. There are for example violent contradictions in the characters; the soul is in chaos; we have drunkards, says Stefan Zweig, who are such out of the desire for purity; criminals, out of a thirst for repentance; violators of maidens out of respect for innocence; blasphemers out of religious need.[4] These contradictions involve terrific inner conflicts, and the issue often raises more questions than it settles: some characters go insane, others commit suicide or murder. There is no reëstablishment of the violated moral order, as in a Greek tragedy. Murder is another recurrent design; epilepsey still another, with its strange quality of mystic vision in a timeless world. And there are the "doubles," those fantastically paired characters who are perhaps dramatic embodiments of the phenomenon of split personality.

We now have ample material for the study of Dostoevsky's life, in his own letters, the diaries of his wife, and the reminiscences of his contemporaries. We also have volumes of critical speculation and interpretation from every conceivable angle—literary, philosophical, psychological, religious, racial; and if there is not yet an economic Marxian interpretation, I am sure there soon will be. Thus any simple direct approach to the novels is blocked by formidable breastworks:

as if the commentators declared, "There is no open road.
Find some secret way into the castle of the Holy Grail. Come
to the Dark Tower through the Waste Land"—until the enterprise seems so hopeless that we are relieved to hear a man
like Marcel Proust exclaim: "What overwhelms me is the
solemn way in which they speak and write of Dostoevsky."

The Christian interpreters are sweetly solemn. They dwell
upon the beautiful figure of Alexey Karamazov as a symbol
of the Christ; upon the saint-like Zossima, prostrating himself before Dmitri Karamazov as before one dedicated to suffering; upon Raskolnikov, the murderer, at the feet of Sonia,
the prostitute, exclaiming, " 'I do not bow down to you, but
to the suffering of all humanity!' " And almost do they persuade us to regard Dostoevsky as the preacher of a mystical
religion of suffering, as the Christ-like healer of sick souls.
But with their eyes fastened upon the Jesus aspect of Dostoevsky's character, they overlook what D. H. Lawrence
called "the little horror." [5]

Though they leave a good deal of Dostoevsky out of the
picture, these sentimental critics do not seriously distort. It
takes the symbolic and metaphysical interpreters to do that.
Where, without their aid, we were in danger of seeing the
three Karamazov brothers, for instance, as human beings
who lived and thought and suffered, we are invited to see
the Russian Soul. "Oh," says the lion-hunting Guinea Hen
in Rostand's *Chantecler,* as she effusively greets a Russian
Cock, "the Slav Soul we have heard so much about! Charmed
beyond words!" She had little reason to be charmed. The
Russian Soul threatens the downfall of Europe. Hermann
Hesse, tormented like so many Germans by a Russian nightmare, sees all the four Karamazovs merging into the "approaching man of the European crisis." And this Russian
man is "assassin and judge, ruffian and tenderest soul, the
completest egoist and the most self-sacrificing hero . . .

This ideal man of the Karamazovs loves nothing and everything; fears nothing and everything; does nothing and
everything; he is primeval matter, he is monstrous soulstuff." [6]

Abandoning the interpretation of Dostoevsky for the moment, we try to interpret Hesse, and find him, behind the
smoke screen of his vaticination, not so very occult. For he
seems to mean something like this: that in such historical
periods as the present, when an old culture is decaying and
a new one emerging, many individuals appear whom the old
sanctions no longer bind; neglected possibilities of human
nature, suppressed and distorted impulses seek and find expression. The Karamazovs are such people—releasing themselves from old inhibitions, questioning the established,
searching for the new—pronounced criminals or prophets
according to which of the shifting standards of a changing
era they are judged by. We feel some pride in being able
thus to interpret the symbolism. But we are not much nearer
to comprehending the Karamazovs. Such comprehension
might result from regarding the book merely as a work of
art, but this is a procedure scorned by Hesse. "When," he
observes with withering contempt, "the Unconscious of a
whole continent has made of itself poetry in the nightmare
of a single prophetic dreamer, when it has issued in his awful
blood-curdling scream, one can of course consider this
scream from the standpoint of a singing teacher."

That after all may be the best thing to do. But meanwhile
one must pause to admire the phrase, "the Unconscious of
a whole continent." Are not the individual Unconscious and
the collective Unconscious enough to cope with, without this
Continental Unconscious?

Janko Lavrin begins, intelligibly enough, with a division
of Dostoevsky's protagonists into God-seekers and God-strugglers, and we agree with him that Ivan Karamazov belongs

with the God-strugglers. But when, in order to explain Ivan more fully, he starts to map out the Unconscious, we begin to sink. "The subconscious corresponds to the subliminal region of the magical element, while the super-conscious corresponds to the subliminal region of the mystical element in our consciousness. Thus the subconscious and the superconscious may be defined as two opposing factors, forming the duality of the Unconscious." [7] We offered this sentence to a friend on good terms with mediaeval schoolmen as well as with psychoanalysts: "That of course," he said, "is just Manichaeism: the conception of the universe as the battleground of the forces of Good and Evil. Some people resort to magic to propitiate the evil force, and some to mysticism to be absorbed into the good."

Again we return to the brothers Karamazov. Here they are as they appear to Mr. Middleton Murry, when he is going in for a really metaphysical mood: they represent epochs of human consciousness; the father is the blind force of life, containing the germs of many possibilities, but still chaos unresolved, loathsome and strong; this old life must be slain by its successor; the sons—life as it now is in our present epoch of consciousness—know good and evil; but mind and body, spirit and flesh, are at war in them; Dmitri is body conscious of mind; Ivan is mind conscious of body and fearing it; in the man of the future there must be harmony of body and mind—and that is Alexey.[8]

That the Karamazovs, in their peculiar way, may be prophetic of a coming epoch of consciousness where all is harmony, is scarcely within the vision of the critics who regard them all as lunatics. "A strange crew," says Percy Lubbock. "A plague-stricken collection of clinical cases," remarks Dmitri Merezhkovsky—though not of the Karamazovs alone. "A collection of the most repulsive types of mankind—lunatics, half-lunatics, criminals in germ and in reality, in all possible gradations . . . permeated with the atmosphere of the lunatic asylum"—thus Prince Kropotkin.

Perhaps at this point in our survey of the commentators and critics, we are prepared to appreciate one of the most recent books on Dostoevsky, that by Mr. E. A. Carr (1931), thus commended by D. S. Mirsky, who knows whereof he speaks: "There is no nonsense in Mr. Carr's book, and this is probably the first book on the subject (published outside Russia) of which so much can be asserted." Yet, ungratefully enough, one feels at the end that Mr. Carr has been too sensible. He stresses too much what Dostoevsky said his intentions were, in his rationalized explanations of his philosophy, politics, religion; he stresses too little by comparison what Dostoevsky unintentionally reveals in his flashes of insight into the dark recesses of human nature. It is unsafe—as Virginia Woolf has pointed out in an essay on Turgenev [9]—to rely on what novelists say of their purposes: a novelist "lives so much deeper down than a critic that his statements are apt to be contradictory and confusing. They seem to break in process of coming to the surface, and not to hold together in the light of reason." Dostoevsky's philosophy looks rather shabby and secondhand when it is set forth; he was a mediocre philosopher, but a supreme psychologist, and his books are great in spite of his philosophy. Moreover, though it is important to have Mr. Carr's well-documented accounts of those passionate and sentimental interludes with women, which throw light on the genesis of Dostoevsky's love-hate psychology, yet there remains to be accounted for that "secret beauty" in Dostoevsky's women of which Proust speaks in a striking passage:

This novel beauty remains identical in all Dostoevsky's works; the Dostoevsky woman (as distinctive as a Rembrandt woman) with her mysterious face, whose engaging beauty changes abruptly, as though her apparent good nature had been but make-believe, to a terrible insolence . . . is she not always the same? . . . . As in Vermeer there is the creation of a certain soul, of a certain color of fabrics and places, so there is in Dostoevsky creation not only of people but of their homes, and the house of the murder in *Crime and Punishment* . . . is it not almost as marvellous as the masterpiece of the House of Murder . . . in which Rogozhin kills Nastasia Philipovna? That novel and terrible beauty of a house, that novel beauty blended with a woman's face, that is the unique thing which Dostoevsky has given to the world.[10]

Secret beauty, or symbol, or prophecy—no matter what Dostoevsky wittingly or unwittingly wrote into his books— he presented his characters as human beings. Suppose we look at the people in *The Brothers Karamazov* as in essence much like ourselves.

To begin with we find them described with great vividness. If we have read Merezhkovsky's comparison of Tolstoy and Dostoevsky, we are surprised at that; for he tells us that Tolstoy is rich in physical detail about his characters, whereas Dostoevsky relies on speech almost entirely; in Tolstoy, we hear because we see; in Dostoevsky, we see because we hear. But surely we "see" Alexey and his brothers and his father with great vividness.

Alexey was a

well-grown, red-cheeked, clear-eyed lad of nineteen, radiant with health. He was very handsome, too, graceful, moderately tall, with hair of a dark brown, with a regular, rather long, oval-shaped face, and wide-set shining dark grey eyes.

And Dmitri:

a young man of eight and twenty, of medium height and agreeable countenance [who] looked older than his years. He was muscular, and showed signs of considerable strength. Yet there was something not healthy in his face. It was rather thin, his cheeks were hollow, and there was an unhealthy sallowness in their color. His rather large, prominent, dark eyes had an expression of firm determination, and yet there was a vague look in them too . . . He was stylishly and irreproachably dressed in a carefully buttoned frock-coat.

Here is the father, Fyodor Pavlovitch:

Besides the long fleshy bags under his little, always insolent, suspicious, and ironical eyes; besides the multitude of wrinkles in his little fat face, the Adam's apple hung below his sharp chin like a great fleshy goitre, which gave him a peculiar, repulsive, sensual appearance; add to that a long rapacious mouth with full lips, between which could be seen little stumps of black, decayed teeth. He slobbered every time he began to speak . . . "With my goitre I've quite the countenance of an ancient Roman patrician of the decadent period." He seemed quite proud of it.

With such clear visualization, not all the exploits of the critics in comparing old Karamazov to aboriginal chaos or unregenerate Russia can quite make us forget the figure of the drunken old miser.

These three people and the other two sons—Ivan and the bastard Smerdyakov—after years of separation, have gathered together over family matters involving an inheritance. Dmitri, the oldest, believes his father has swindled him. Further complicating this relation, Dmitri and his father, alike in their sensuality, desire the same woman, Grushenka. The two younger sons by a second wife watch this drama, Ivan with scorn, Alexey with pity. And the unacknowledged son finds in it his opportunity for robbery and murder. Such passions and such family tensions are not uncommon; nor is murder an unlikely consequence.

Most of us can think of families with whose history the events in *The Brothers Karamazov* may to a degree be paralleled. If we have observed a large family over a period, say, of a score of years, with its quarrels, its spites, its jealousies, its cruel treatment of member by member; if we disregard the "time out" for recovery of breath and "warming up," and quicken the tempo for the purposes of art, stringing along one distressing performance after another, with occasional flashes of piety, sympathy, affection; if we make the further allowance for the American environment, where reserve is more the trapping of the human animal than in the Russian scene, and imagine the American family letting itself go with the abandonment to emotion and impulse which characterizes the Russian—then there is not such a chasm of difference between the American family and the Karamazovs. Even among the Karamazovs there are moments of poignant spirituality: the love of the old man and of Ivan for Alexey; Dmitri's hatred of his own baser self; his generous treatment of Grushenka. The book is very far from being filled—as some people assert—with nothing but "disease, putridity, and crime."

The Karamazov history is woven into a pattern. Most family histories are not. So the Karamazov happenings actually appear less chaotic, less insane and purposeless, more ordered than such happenings in life. It is, says Proust, "a sculpturesque and simple theme, worthy of the most classical art, a frieze interrupted and resumed on which the tale of vengeance and expiation is unfolded." [11] He cites for illustration the story of the village idiot, Lizaveta, who comes to the old Karamazov's courtyard to give birth to his child. This scene stands at the beginnings of the frieze; and at the end, twenty years after, stands the murder of the old man by this natural son, and the suicide of the instrument of destiny, now that the vengeance is complete. Intricate and complicated as the Karamazov story is, a close survey reveals each design in the pattern as related to the whole. In sheer plot the book is one of the best detective stories in the world. It is amazingly clever in construction—this account of the events leading up to the murder, the murder itself, the entanglement of clues, the trial with its analysis of the circumstantial evidence that convicts the innocent Dmitri—innocent in fact, though not in intention. It is not, however, the events themselves, but the inner drama of character that invites speculations upon good and evil, the degree of human responsibility, the possibilities that lie hidden in our own natures. Especially these possibilities.

It will always remain a mystery how Dostoevsky came to fathom what lies deep down in the human consciousness. The bewildering world that he saw within us, with instinctive and prophetic accuracy, we now find mapped out by the psychologists and psychoanalysts. His anticipations, his intuitions, his discoveries, are all provided with a scientific terminology. We quote it glibly and it gives us, as do all terminologies, a largely delusive sense of mastery over the phenomena that in Dostoevsky's world go about nameless and strange and unclassified.

One of the most revealing of the Karamazovs is Dmitri, who during our entire acquaintance with him is in a state of intense excitement, when the ordinary barriers erected by the conscious mind are down. He is ruled by jealousy and sensual passion—jealousy of his father, desire for Grushenka. Because so much of his behavior is the expression of a very objective nature, with exceedingly strong animal instincts, he is the most easily understood character in the book. There are bewildering intricacies in his conduct, but they are not to be compared with the labyrinthine thoughts of Ivan. Motivation is not complicated in natures whose impulses find immediate expression in action. Even when, crazed with brooding over his sexual desires, blind with jealousy, and turbulent with liquor, Dmitri—believing that Grushenka has given herself to the old Karamazov—rushes in, knocks his cowardly father down and kicks him in the head—even then Dmitri is understandable. Sensuality runs like a flame through the book, smouldering underground, breaking out whenever it can; but in no one, not even in the old man himself, is there a stronger flame of desire than in Dmitri.

He has, however, a redeeming spirituality: specifically in his treatment of Grushenka in the tavern at Mokroe; in his respect for Ivan's mind; in his love for Alexey; and especially in his magnanimous behavior towards Katerina, on that occasion when he sends word to her that if she will yield to his desire, he will give her the money necessary to save her father from disgrace. When she comes to his room, prepared for the sacrifice, Dmitri to his own astonishment refuses to accept it. Swept by the most contradictory emotions, he hands her the money and bows her out. After she has gone, he draws his sword and contemplates stabbing himself, but instead kisses the sword and replaces it in the scabbard. He felt toward Katerina fearful hatred, that hatred, he realizes, "which is only a hair's-breadth from love, from the maddest love." He knows he felt that way, and behaved that way, but further than that he doesn't try to analyze himself. " 'Let that pass,' " he exclaims in telling the story, " 'and to hell with all who pry into the human heart.' "

Biographers have risked Dmitri's curse by prying into Dostoevsky's heart in the search for some experience to explain the fascination that contradictory emotion—ambivalence—had for him. And they have discovered his passionate interlude with Pauline Suslova.

It was she [writes Mr. Carr] who showed him how intimately hate may be interwoven with love. She had revealed to him the appetite for cruelty and the appetite for suffering, the sadistic and the masochistic, as alternating manifestations of the sexual impulse. He had learnt from her that self-humiliation and self-degradation are the opposite facets of imperiousness and truculence, and that diseased pride will assert itself as readily in the former as in the latter. Others besides Dostoevsky have explored the secret places of the human heart where antitheses are resolved and opposites become one. But none has probed deeper than he;

and it was, unless all our evidence misleads us, his experiences with Suslova which first laid bare these dark recesses to his piercing insight.[12]

Ambivalence always characterizes Dmitri. In this he is the true son of his father. Old Karamazov was drunk when he heard of the death of his first wife:

The story is that he ran out into the street, and began shouting with joy, raising his hands to heaven: "Lord, now lettest Thy servant depart in peace." But others say that he wept without restraint, like a little child, so much so that people were sorry for him, in spite of the repulsion he inspired. It is quite possible that both versions were true, that he rejoiced at his release, and at the same time wept for her who released him.

It is the expression of contradictory emotions that to Marcel Proust accounts for the unique beauty of Dostoevsky's women. The Moscow Art Players gave two scenes which dramatized this in Lise and Grushenka, both characters in *The Brothers Karamazov,* and their subtly realistic interpretation made it seem natural that little Lise should express by turns love and hate for Alexey; and that Grushenka should reveal deep tenderness for her rival Katerina, and then suddenly fling away the hand she had asked to kiss. " 'Do you know, angel lady,' she suddenly drawled in an even more soft and sugary voice, 'do you know after all I think I won't kiss your hand . . . so that you may be left to remember that you kissed my hand, but I didn't kiss yours.' " [13]

Into such self-lacerating individuals as Lise, Dostoevsky has deep insight. Janko Lavrin devotes a chapter to them, under the imposing caption of "Cosmic Mutiny, a Contribution to the Psychology of Satanism." The insulted and injured of all ages have retired to their tents to nurse their suffering. Rejected by the world, they take revenge by rejecting the world, and so transform their weakness into an illusion of strength. Each new indignity justifies the defiance. The sense of being a castaway through self-will is, as Lavrin says, an enhancement of the ego. Nastasya in *The Idiot* cherishes her contempt and hatred; she does not want to be happy after all she has undeservedly suffered. Ivan Karamazov prefers to remain with his unavenged suffering and unsatisfied indignation—even if he is wrong. And this, Alexey murmurs, is rebellion.

Ivan's rebellion proceeds from an impulse most of us have had occasion to observe in our friends and to overlook in ourselves. In Ivan, to be sure, it is raised to the nth power. A friend of ours had a grandmother, an estimable old lady, who, when she felt "injured and insulted," made soap. She hated soap-making; it was the dirtiest, smelliest, and most unnecessary job she could think of, to dramatize the fact that she considered herself overworked in the service of an unappreciative family. Soap-making in that family became the humble symbol of what in its highest manifestations Lavrin calls cosmic mutiny.

Behavior like that of Lise, Dmitri, Katerina, and Grushenka looked more like incipient lunacy twenty-five or thirty years ago than it does today. In view of what we now know of psychology, we are less tempted to label it abnormal. Dr. Hart (*The Psychology of Insanity*) says of the symptoms of the lunatic, "even the most bizarre symptoms are not so very different from processes to be discovered in our own minds, and . . . the lunatic appears more and more like ourselves the better we are enabled to penetrate into the tortuous recesses of his spirit." [14]

It is not the capacity for feeling "two opposite feelings at one and the same time" that is exceptional, for that is the universal, if often unconscious experience of mankind . . . "What is exceptional is the clarity with which this is recognized by Dostoevsky's characters and expressed in Dos-

toevsky's art. Dostoevsky wrote of the unconscious as if it
were conscious: that is in reality the reason why his characters seem pathological, while they are only visualized more
clearly than any other figures in imaginative literature." [15]

The characters so far discussed reveal little more than anyone addicted to introspection might discover in himself. But
Ivan Karamazov, the most complex of the brothers, presents
a more difficult problem.

"It is a tradition in our family," writes Dostoevsky's daughter, "that my father portrayed himself in the person of Ivan."
Lavrin speaks of him as the character through whom Dostoevsky "voiced his most intimate secrets." One of his most
intimate secrets is certainly his preoccupation with murder
and his brooding over the question of guilt. There is the
murder of the pawnbroker and her sister in *Crime and
Punishment;* the murder of Nastasya in *The Idiot;* the
assorted murders in *The Possessed;* and, most significant, the
murder of old Karamazov. This preoccupation with the murder theme is usually accounted for by Dostoevsky's enforced
contact with criminals during his imprisonment in the
House of the Dead; or by the theory that, like other creative
artists, he was tempted to express, in art, forms of experience
he had not himself known. Little stress has been placed in
the past upon the murder of his own father by serfs, mad-
dened by cruel treatment; for this tragedy, which happened
when Dostoevsky was eighteen, was considerately overlooked
by friends of the family when they noted down their reminiscences.[16] But forty years after his father's violent death,
Dostoevsky writes a book in which the great event is the
murder of an old miser and drunkard by one of his servants.
He paints the old landowner sufficiently like his own father
to justify his daughter's supposition that her grandfather sat
for the portrait. In avarice and drunkenness, though not in

sensuality and buffoonery, the likeness holds. Ivan Karamazov's conviction that he is *morally* implicated in his
father's murder drives him across the borders of sanity. If
Ivan is Dostoevsky's prototype, must we not conclude that
Dostoevsky himself suffered from some obscure sense of guilt
regarding his father's death? He must at all events have had
the tragedy very much in mind, for (as Mr. Carr notes) in
1877, before writing the *Brothers,* he revisited, after forty
years, the farm, Darovoe, where the murder took place. The
name of the village where Ivan intended to go during the
interval when the crime was committed, Tchermashnya, was
the name of the village Dostoevsky's father was going to
when he was killed.

The Brothers Karamazov is thus more clearly linked with
Dostoevsky's youthful experiences than any of his other
books. The determining influence at that early period was
that of his father. In his own letters and in the reminiscences
of his daughter we have hints enough to throw light on the
relationship between father and son, and to link it with that
between Ivan Karamazov and his father. The household of
the Dostoevskys was a strict one. The father, exacting and
niggardly, "suspicious in his cups," was the pattern of a
stern male parent. The children did not love him. (The submissive mother they apparently adored.) Most of Dostoevsky's letters after he went away to St. Petersburg to
school are concerned with his efforts to get money from
home. One dated May 10, 1838, opens with a paragraph
cringing in tone: "At present I beg of you, dearest Papa, to
reflect that in the literal sense of the word I serve." With
suave flattery he goes on to tell his father that he needs
money to enable him to conform to the demands of the
school environment: "You will readily understand this, dear
Papa. You have mixed enough with men to do that." What
he really thought and felt about his father he writes with

more candor to his brother Mikhail: "But do you know Papa is wholly a stranger in the world. He has lived in it for fifty years, and yet he has the same opinion of mankind that he had thirty years ago. What sublime innocence." And what contempt!

Beneath this servile manner is the feeling of proud superiority. Probably he despised his father, thought of him (as many youths do) as a necessary evil, a fortuitous convenience or inconvenience. It is humiliating to beg money from someone he despises. Restrained by fear (for which he hates himself) from an open display of his real feeling, he hides what is in his heart with the cloak of humility. It is significant that the letters which passed between Dostoevsky and his brother just after the murder of their father were destroyed, and that later in their letters, the brothers never mention their father.[17]

One of Dostoevsky's deepest fears was that he might come to resemble his father, especially in his miserliness. He rushed to the other extreme of prodigality and flung money away as if the rouble notes themselves contained the germs of his father's corruption. The diary of his second wife pictures him as gambling away all the money they had, all the publishers advanced, all the family could send, all that could be secured by pawning all their possessions down to their wedding rings. And when he won money at roulette, he came home followed by a procession of boys bearing baskets of flowers and fruits and candies for the wife whose personal belongings were even then in the pawnshop.[18] The gambling fever eventually burned itself out, and his wife gradually acquired control over the finances. But we feel that it is Dostoevsky himself who is suffering when Ivan Karamazov is horrified by Smerdyakov's accusation: " 'You are fond of money, I know that . . . You are like Fyodor Pavlovitch, you are more like him than any of his children; you've the same soul as he had.'" It is the voicing of Dostoevsky's unacknowledged fear.

Ivan Karamazov is Dostoevsky partly as he was and partly as he would have liked to be. This is often what is meant when a character is said to be its author's prototype. The points of difference are even more suggestive than the points of resemblance. We do not see Ivan physically as clearly as we see his father and his brothers, but we are offered within the first twenty pages some significant direct information about his character. "Of Ivan I will only say that he grew into a somewhat morose and reserved, though far from timid boy." At ten he had realized that he was a charity lad not living in his own home, and that his father was "a man of whom it was disgraceful to speak." Ivan was forthright in his behavior: "he left the family of Yefim Petrovitch when he was hardly thirteen, entering a Moscow gymnasium, and boarding with an experienced and celebrated teacher." He showed a "brilliant and unusual aptitude for learning," and on that gift he concentrated. There was a force of character which one sometimes sees in a child of thirteen, good equipment with which to face the world, an instinctive self-reliance. But it often means a terrible strain upon the will, and in Ivan this strain showed itself later. The boy was forced to keep himself most of the time, though he knew his father was supposed to pay for his education. But he did not even attempt to communicate with him, "perhaps from pride, from contempt for him, or perhaps from his cool common sense, which told him that from such a father he would get no real assistance."

Dostoevsky clearly admires young Ivan very much. Ivan wrote no humiliating letters to his father. Ivan left the house where he was living and went with a spirited independence to Moscow. He made his way with his pen, because "he had practical and intellectual superiority over the masses of needy and unfortunate students." All of this Dostoevsky would like to have accomplished. And perhaps out of self-excuse he makes Ivan pay dearly later for his independence, his contempt, and his pride.

Such a youth, "so learned, so proud, and apparently so cautious," we should expect to be a relentless egotist, intolerant, uncompromising, the severest judge of his weak and dissolute father. But when the story opens they have been living for two months on the best possible terms. No one, least of all the old Karamazov, can understand why Ivan is in Russia when he has money enough to go abroad. Had he cared for dissipation, the old man would have been a boon companion; but for this Ivan has no taste. Ivan has deliberately adapted himself for his own purposes to the environment of his home; the kind of adaptation Dostoevsky had not been able to make with his father. Ivan's quietly contemptuous detachment worries the old man, who—even after he has been kicked by Dmitri—asks: " 'But what does Ivan say? . . . I'm afraid of Ivan. I'm more afraid of Ivan than of the other.' " Of Dmitri's attack Ivan remarks: " 'One reptile will devour the other. And serve them both right, too.' " He enjoys the spectacle of this deadly rivalry; he enjoys his father's fear of him. And through Ivan, Dostoevsky expresses his contempt for his own father. Ivan's way of looking at life, of presenting an unruffled surface, his aloofness, his scorn of humanity with its pettiness, its folly and cruelty—all this is an elaborately evasive compensation for Dostoevsky.

By the end of the third chapter, there stands Ivan, to all appearance master of himself—yet withal "an enigmatic figure." The mask through which he looks at life shows no trace of the turbulence within. But the mask is laid aside in the great scene in the Metropolis Tavern, where—purely on the spiritual and intellectual plane—he is merged in com-

plete identification with Dostoevsky, and he reveals his suffering and his religion of despair in the confession to his
brother Alexey.

At first he had had only amused pity for the quiet, saintly
brother to whom he is later drawn by the triple appeal of
blood, loneliness, and affection. It is therefore unexpected
and touching when Ivan runs downs the steps from the
upper room in the tavern to chaperon Alexey, who is reluc-
tant to enter a public house in his monastic garb. Here, in
the outpouring of his affection, Ivan is most lovable. Not
only had he despised the mental powers of the young novi-
tiate, he had suspected his spirituality as well. And at the
outset he says: " 'But in the end I have learned to respect
you. The little man stands firm, I thought . . . You seem
to love me for some reason, Alyosha?' "

Of course Alyosha loved him. What Ivan really means
here is: "I have grown to love you, Alyosha, for some reason." But he is afraid of his own emotion. Yet it is this love
for his brother, as well as for Katerina, that releases the
coldly intellectual youth. Conscious of his powers, torn by
emotion when he thought himself most securely entrenched
in his aloofness, he purges his mind and soul in the presence
of the brother he has fixed on in his love. The self-conscious
detachment of his earlier attitude is gone, and his intellectual arguments, his keen analysis of good and evil in the
human soul, throb with passion. His thought burns quietly
with the heat of an unearthly intensity, and it lights up all
the obscurest corners of his own experience.

Here, with time seemingly at a standstill, he arraigns God
before the pained and astonished Alexey. In his torture of
his young brother his love is curiously like hate. He flings
at him facts of cruelty and horror that put Alexey's religion
to the severest test: stories of brutality to children, like that
of the serf lad torn to pieces by hounds at the command of

his master. And when Alexey lifts his eyes to Ivan with a pale twisted smile and mutters his agreement that the wretch deserved to be shot, Ivan is genuinely delighted. " 'You're a pretty monk! So there is a little devil sitting in your heart, Alyosha!' "

But if Ivan tortures Alexey he does not spare himself. All his doubts he reveals. If there is a God, it is a strangely inhuman God who will tolerate such cruel sufferings as he has related. After he has argued the pros and cons of good and evil, the problems of sin and suffering and retribution, Heaven and Hell, and faced them in a way worthy of Job, Ivan makes it clear that he will accept no fiat of a voice speaking out of a whirlwind. He hands back his entrance ticket to God: " 'It's not God that I don't accept, Alyosha, only I most respectfully return Him the ticket.' " If Ivan could have entered here into that possible future harmony and found a pillow of peace for his weary head, he would not have been able to accept it. And yet in his doubts there is little of the spirit of Lucifer's contemptuous rebellion; there is the active torture of an essentially ideal nature. The tragedy for Ivan is that he sees no way out. He knows this and dares to face it, even if facing it means death or madness. The revelation of Ivan's mind and soul in this scene has—in spite of the discursiveness of the writing—the unity and concentration of Greek tragedy.

Although Ivan beholds within himself a desperate hopelessness, he discovers also the desire and the will to live. For him suicide is not the way out. He could hand back the ticket he was offered for the future harmony, but he could not hand back his life. At least, as he says naïvely, not until he is thirty: " 'All I want is to live on to thirty, and then . . . dash the cup to the ground!' " And when Alexey cries out that Ivan cannot live with such a hell in his heart, he replies: " 'There is a strength to endure everything . . . the strength of the Karamazovs—the strength of the Karamazov baseness.' " It is this Karamazov love of life that makes cheap, cynical disgust with life not possible for Ivan. He had prefaced his arraignment of God with these remarkable words:

"If I lost faith in the woman I love, lost faith in the order of things, were convinced, in fact, that everything is a disorderly, damnable, and perhaps devil-ridden chaos, if I were struck by every horror of man's disillusionment—still I should want to live, and having once tasted of the cup, I would not turn away from it till I had drained it!"

In this unconquerable zest for living even in torment one is reminded of Dostoevsky himself, who said that he had the vitality of a cat; and we believe it when we find him writing to his brother after he was released from prison that he had severe rheumatism, his digestion had gone to pieces, and he had had several attacks of epilepsy; but aside from that, he felt quite well!

This talk to Alexey is the first confirmation we have of the terrible tension in Ivan's soul, his absorption in the "eternal questions" that tormented Dostoevsky all his life. But it is still life out there, objective life, upon which he is brooding. Unlike Job, he does not need the lash of personal misfortune to make him look upon the facts of pain and evil and question the justice of God. When his personal tragedy begins, he is already at the point where Job ended. When events strike home, the youthful idealist, unable to resist the pressure from all sides, finds himself more than ever flayed by doubts. His physical strength goes with the terrible psychic upheaval, and he crashes through to the margins of madness.

He grows in upon himself to a depth only the mind of Dostoevsky could fathom, and he meditates especially upon the evil which lives within himself. There he sees a microcosm of the whole. Never was a man more quiveringly conscious of his own evil. This realization first comes to him after his talk in the tavern. Vaguely troubled he leaves the place; in this mood he meets Smerdyakov, and at once divines that the trouble in his own soul is somehow connected with this half brother.[19] He approaches Smerdyakov, planning to say something cruel:

"Get away, miserable idiot. What have I to do with you?" was on the tip of his tongue, but to his profound astonishment he heard himself say, "Is my father still asleep, or has he waked?" . . . He asked the question softly and meekly to his own surprise.

We begin to see the possibility of Ivan's breakdown. His growing conviction that the evil within himself is embodied in Smerdyakov becomes for him a horrible obsession; and for us a thrilling dramatization of split personality—or, if one prefers, of the double each man carries within himself, the uncharted elements in each man. (This conception of the "double" fascinated Dostoevsky from the time of one of his earliest stories, where the double is magical rather than pathological, as it later becomes.) To Ivan his evil self stands revealed in Smerdyakov, a mocking presence, intensifying with peculiar cruelty his fundamental question: how can anyone accept happiness in the face of evil? As the pressure of events grows greater, Smerdyakov comes more and more into the foreground, making Ivan increasingly conscious of the conflicts and tensions within his own soul. His complete breakdown is imminent by the time he contends in delirium with the nightmare devil whom he looks upon as his own past sinful self: " 'You are the incarnation of myself, but only one side of me . . . of my thoughts and feelings, but only the nastiest and stupidest of them.' "

He has come to this crisis through the events of his father's murder. He is inexorable in facing his relation to it—even to the extent of looking upon himself as an accomplice in fact. "'*You* murdered him,'" accuses Smerdyakov, "'you are the real murderer, I was only your instrument.'" This is Ivan confronting his other self. It is this terrible certainty that is killing him. But he was one "who did not want millions, but an answer to his questions." And if ever he were to find answers, he must be true to all he found in his own heart. And there he found the desire for his father's death.[20]

We are told (it is now a Freudian commonplace) that each of us desires in the unconscious mind the death of the father. The myths of the race bear testimony to the wish. But it was by no means a commonplace when Dostoevsky had Ivan, speaking out of the clairvoyance of his approaching madness, testify in court at the trial of Dmitri:

"He [Smerdyakov] murdered him, and I incited him to do it. Who doesn't desire his father's death?"

"Are you in your right mind?" broke involuntarily from the President.

"I should think I am in my right mind . . . in the same nasty mind as all of you . . ." He turned suddenly to the audience. "My father has been murdered, and they pretend they are horrified," he snarled with furious contempt. "They keep up the sham with one another. Liars! They all desire the death of their fathers!"

The end comes, and Ivan is irrecoverably insane. A tragically ironical solution, this answer to his questions. He had told Alexey how stupid he thought it was for Russian boys to spend their time talking endlessly of the eternal questions —of God and immortality. But he could not keep off the subjects himself, especially when he had capitulated to friendship; "'I want to be friends with you, Alyosha, for I have no friends and I want to try it.'" Then a flood of overwhelming emotions came upon him, and he was beset by tragic events lit with horror and fear, and his sanity was doomed. Had he been allowed to work out his love for Alyosha and for Katerina, he might have come through. A more cruel experimenter than the God of Job, Dostoevsky piled horror upon horror, and at last Ivan went under. Ivan is one of the tragic people in literature. Those who like him are lacerated in spirit form a rare group, consecrated by their terrible sufferings: Lear, Hamlet, Œdipus the King.

When we stop to reflect upon the fate of Ivan Karamazov, we understand what Mr. Olgin means when he speaks of the vivisection in Dostoevsky's novels, the cruel dipping into the most obscure corners of human souls, the uncanny joy in the pursuit of victims. As Stefan Zweig says, people interest Dostoevsky only as they are at odds with themselves; he likes them to the degree in which they suffer, are disintegrated and tense and chaotic. But it was his own agony that motivated his probing, for he was by his own confession tortured always by the questions of God's existence and God's justice and God's mercy; if he accepted Christ as the supreme value, he had arrived at this belief only through whirlwinds of doubt. For his own salvation he was forced to be an experimental seeker into human nature.

Merezhkovsky compares his experiments to those of the chemist who creates artificial conditions in his laboratory, and, by increasing the pressure of the atmosphere to a degree impossible to nature as we know it, changes air from a gas to a liquid. Dostoevsky himself had been subjected to extraordinary pressure—before the firing squad, in his Siberian prison and exile. In turn he places his characters in conditions extraordinary and artificial, and awaits the result of the experiment.

In order that unforeseen aspects, powers hidden in the depths of man's soul, may be revealed, he needs a degree of pressure of the normal atmosphere rarely met with. He submits his characters either to the icy air of abstract dialectics, or the fire of elemental animal passion, fire at white heat. And in these experiments he sometimes arrives at states of the human mind as novel and seemingly impossible as liquefied air . . . What is called Dostoevsky's psychology is therefore a huge laboratory of the most delicate and exact apparatus for measuring and testing and weighing humanity. It is easy to imagine that to the uninitiated such a laboratory must seem something of a devil's smithy.

It is this devil's smithy effect that is conveyed to us in Percy Lubbock's comparison between the normal daylight that bathes the scenes and characters in Tolstoy's novels with the blackness that hems in "the ominous circle of *The Brothers Karamazov.*"

Dostoevsky needed no lucid prospect around his strange crew; all he sought was a blaze of light on the extraordinary theatre of their consciousness. He intensified it by shutting off the least glimmer of natural day. The illumination that falls upon his page is like the glare of a furnace mouth; it searches the depth of the inner struggles and turmoils in which the drama is enacted, relieving it with sharp and fantastic shadows.[21]

We draw back from the glow of the furnace, deceived by the fantastic shadows in Dostoevsky's world into thinking that it is peopled by strange creatures unlike ourselves. But these strangers stand at the very threshold of our consciousness, waiting, like that enigmatic other self of Raskolnikov, the hero of *Crime and Punishment,* while Raskolnikov, between nightmare and waking, pretends to be asleep. At length he abandons the pretense, and speaks to the stranger at the door who is yet curiously familiar. " 'Come, tell me what you want.' 'I knew you were not asleep, but only pretending,' " the stranger answers oddly. Like Raskolnikov, we had better abandon the pretense of non-recognition of our other selves. It is true that Dostoevsky's exploration is into the night side of human consciousness, the realm of the pre-rational, the dream, the impulse. What he discovered there, Freud's study and practise of psychotherapy has established and placed in a reasoned scheme. Is it better to pretend to be asleep, or, like Raskolnikov, however reluctantly, speak to the stranger at the door? This is a profoundly pertinent question. Thomas Mann offers an answer, in his discussion of the charge, freely made, that the effect of Freud's studies has been to lessen the power of the conscious mind, and to contribute to the strength of anti-intellectualism and of the whole modern movement glorifying impulse and decrying reason. Parenthetically, if we apply this test to *The Brothers Karamazov,* we note how futile Ivan's reason is, how it destroys him; whereas the impulsive, passionate, uninhibited Dmitri comes out alive from the desperate ordeal, with the hope of salvation ahead of him. But, says Mann,

Freud's anti-rationalism consists in seeing the actual superiority of the impulse over the mind, power for power; not at all in lying down and grovelling before that superiority, or in contempt for mind. "We may," writes Freud, "emphasize as often as we like that intellect is powerless compared with impulse in human life—we shall be right. But after all there is something peculiar about this weakness; the voice of the intellect is low, but it rests not till it gets a hearing."

Freud's work, concludes Mann, is "one of the great foundation-stones to a structure of the future which shall be the dwelling-place of a free and conscious humanity." [22] He believes in the ultimate transcendence of disorder by way of ever-increasing consciousness. Let the stranger cross the threshold, then. We shall learn how to deal with him.

IV

CONRAD'S NOSTROMO: THIRTY YEARS AFTER

"Works of art are the only media of complete and unhindered communication between man and man that can occur in a world full of gulfs and walls that limit community of experience." [23] For the artist, in the words of Conrad, speaks to

our capacity for delight and wonder, to the sense of mystery surrounding our lives; to our sense of beauty and pity and pain; to the latent feeling of fellowship with all creation—and to the subtle but invincible conviction of solidarity that knits together the loneliness of innumerable hearts, to the solidarity in dreams, in joy, in sorrow, in aspirations, in illusions, in hope, in fear, which binds together all humanity—the dead to the living and the living to the unborn. [24]

The gulfs and walls that limit community of experience had an almost obsessional interest for Conrad. Sometimes a man is isolated by outer circumstances—like Almayer—among a people and a culture alien to him. Sometimes he is cut off by his own act, like Falk, who had eaten human flesh, or Dr. Monygham, who under torture had betrayed his friends. Or he is alone through some peculiarity of temperament, like Captain McWhirr, with his lack of imagination, or Heyst, who had lost his capacity for illusions, or Lord Jim, with his morbid sense of honor, or those unhappy girls, Flora and Lena (in *Chance* and *Victory*), who had come to feel that no one could possibly care for them. In *The Rover,* the heroine has been set apart by a terrible experience in the French Revolution, when she had been made to share in an orgy of blood that had overpowered her senses and made her for a time a part of the mass madness. [25]

Sometimes, as in *Lord Jim,* these separated souls never break through the barriers. Sometimes the thrilling moment of the story comes when this isolation is pierced, perhaps only at the brink of death—as when the love in which Heyst had refused to believe unites him to Lena. *The Secret Sharer* is exciting enough in outer events, but the inner significance of the experience for the young captain is that he is out of communion with his crew and his ship. His secret has isolated him; he has an agonizing sense of spiritual remoteness, relieved only when the fugitive whom he has hidden in his cabin slips over the side into the darkness.

In the similarity of their predicaments these people in Conrad's world are united, but they are sharply distinct in their personalities. To Conrad each person is unique, and each is something of a mystery to the end. He always gives the impression, as Mr. Mencken once pointed out, that he is as much puzzled by his characters as the reader is:

he too is feeling his way among shadowy evidences. The discoveries that we make about Lord Jim, about Nostromo . . . come as fortuitously and as unexpectedly as the discoveries we make about the real figures of our world. The picture is built up bit by bit; it is never flashed suddenly and completely as by best-seller calciums; it remains a bit dim at the end. But in that very dimness, so tantalizing and yet so revealing, lies two-thirds of Conrad's art. What he shows is blurred at the edges, but so is life blurred at the edges.

His technique—his usual way of telling a story at two or three removes—his devotion (as Henry James put it) to the way of doing a thing "that shall make it undergo the most doing"—grows out of his effort to convey to the reader the quality of his own perplexity. And his feeling about other people was the result perhaps of being puzzled about himself. His friend Richard Curle says, "I do not suppose that he understood himself, and I am quite certain that nobody else understood him." And again, "Unless I have suggested . . . the sense of a recondite riddle in Conrad's personality, I have failed utterly to convey a true impression of the man." [26]

Conrad could hardly escape a strong conviction of the mystery of personality when the two crucial events in his own life were the fruit of impulses that remained inexplicable to himself as well as to those around him: how he, a Polish boy of an inland race, untouched by any knowledge of the sea, should have been irresistibly impelled, against the amazed remonstrances of his relatives, to become a sailor in the English service; and how twenty years later "the soul of a novelist was born into the body of the seaman," and the English master mariner, forced by illness to leave the sea, began the creation of significant and beautiful English fiction.

In his two exclusively sea books—*The Nigger of the Narcissus* and *The Mirror of the Sea*—and in a few short stories like *Youth* and *Typhoon*, Conrad tried

with an almost filial regard to render the vibration of life in the great world of waters, in the hearts of the simple men who have for ages traversed its solitudes, and also that something sentient that seems to dwell in ships—the creatures of their hands and the objects of their care.[27]

Though he has been called a writer of the sea, he is at pains to point out that in the body of his work barely one-tenth is what may be called sea stuff.

I have written of the sea very little if the pages were counted. It has been the scene, but very seldom the aim, of my endeavor. It is too late after all those years to try to keep back the truth; so I will confess here that when I launched my first paper boats in the days of my literary childhood, I aimed at an element as restless, as dangerous, as changeable as the sea, and even more vast; —the unappeasable ocean of human life.[28]

With all the wealth of exciting incident in his fiction—and many of these incidents had happened to himself or come under his observation during his years of active service at sea—his preoccupation is always with the mysteries of human psychology. A critic [29] speaks of the way Conrad drops or flings us the deeds of his characters as "something too obviously irrelevant for concealment." They have an intensity of spiritual experience that makes the physical adventure seem relatively unimportant. Even the characters themselves feel a little that way about it—to that extent Conrad projects his own feeling upon them.

Though they may be successful men of action in the violent life to which fate or inclination has accustomed them, it is never action which really holds their hearts . . . It may come in their day's work to take bloody revenges or to wade through blood to safety, but it is always with an air of detachment greater than Arnold Bennett's heroes could maintain in buying a railway ticket. What preoccupies them is rather some sinister trait in humanity, or some unspeakable fascination in a face or a coastline, which seems to hide a solution for those riddles about life and death that inarticulately possess their souls.

The reader may begin by being fascinated as Conrad himself was by the "surrounding vision of form and color, sunshine and shadow," by the swift pageantry of action; and end by sharing Conrad's absorption in the mystery of the human heart.

No one book better reveals this double fascination than *Nostromo*, that tale of revolutionary turmoil in a South American republic bordering upon a gulf incongruously named Placid. It is incredible that *Nostromo* should have emerged from a "strangely negative mood," wherein it seemed to Conrad that there was nothing more in the world to write about. For it grew into what he called his largest canvas, "the most anxiously meditated of the longer novels."

In his preface to the later editions of the book, he tells the history of its genesis. In 1875 or 1876, when he was very young, "in the West Indies—or rather in the Gulf of Mexico, I heard the story of some man who was supposed to have stolen single-handed a whole lighter-full of silver, somewhere on the Tierra Firme seaboard during the troubles of a revolution." Crime as crime did not interest him, and he forgot the incident until, twenty-six or twenty-seven years afterward, he found a reference to the story in a sailor's auto-biography, picked up outside a secondhand bookshop, where the thief was represented as an "unmitigated rascal, a small cheat, stupidly ferocious, morose, of mean appearance, and altogether unworthy of the greatness this opportunity had thrust upon him."

The significance of this episode covering only a few pages was that it evoked

the memories of that distant time when everything was so fresh, so surprising, so venturesome, so interesting; bits of strange coasts under the stars, shadows of hills in the sunshine, men's passions in the dusk, gossip half-forgotten, faces grown dim . . . Perhaps, perhaps, there still was in the world something to write about. Yet I did not see anything at first in the mere story . . . It was only when it dawned upon me that the purloiner of the treasure need not necessarily be a confirmed rogue, that he could be even a man of character, an actor and possibly a victim in the changing scenes of a revolution, it was only then that I had the first vision of a twilight country which was to become the prov-ince of Sulaco.

It is *Nostromo* that John Galsworthy called a brilliant piece of work, "his most sheer piece of creation." And Arnold Bennett once said that he read it over every year, to remind himself how a story ought to be told. But Mr. J. W. Beach, a brilliant analyst of technique in fiction, de-clares that reading it is like cutting one's way through the dense growth of a tropical forest, though he admits that the

characters are worth an exploring expedition.[30] Conrad notes
(*A Personal Record*) that the tale was sometimes mentioned
in connection with the word "failure" and sometimes in con-
junction with the word "astonishing." He goes on:

I have no opinion on this discrepancy. It's the sort of difference
that can never be settled. All I know is that, for twenty months,
neglecting the common joys of life that fall to the lot of the
humblest on this earth, I had, like the prophet of old, "wrestled
with the Lord" for my creation, for the headlands of the coast,
for the darkness of the Placid Gulf, the light on the snows, the
clouds on the sky, and for the breath of life that had to be blown
into the shapes of men and women, of Latin and Saxon, of Jew
and Gentile. These are, perhaps, strong words, but it is difficult
to characterize otherwise the intimacy and the strain of a creative
effort in which mind and will and conscience are engaged to the
full, hour after hour, day after day, away from the world, and
to the exclusion of all that makes life really lovable and gentle—
something for which a material parallel can only be found in the
everlasting sombre stress of the westward winter passage round
Cape Horn. For that too is the wrestling of men with the might
of their Creator, in a great isolation from the world, without the
amenities and consolations of life, a lonely struggle under a sense
of over-matched littleness, for no reward that could be adequate,
but for the mere winning of a longitude. Yet a certain longitude,
once won, cannot be disputed. The sun and the stars and the
shape of your earth are the witnesses of your gain; whereas a
handful of pages, no matter how much you have made them
your own, are at best but an obscure and questionable spoil.
Here they are. "Failure"—"Astonishing": take your choice; or
perhaps both or neither—a mere rustle and flutter of pieces of
paper settling down in the night, and undistinguishable, like
the snowflakes of a great drift destined to melt away in sunshine.

There is justification for the charge that *Nostromo* is difficult to get into. The narrative works backwards and for-
wards in retrospect and anticipation. If one likes to play
with the alphabet, as some critics do, one can create a bizarre

and topsy-turvy effect by arranging the main incidents in an ABC . . . chronological sequence, and then rearranging the letters to correspond with the actual narrative order: XAML . . . Up to the fifth chapter in "The *Isabels*" the tale threads its way back and forth, characters are casually introduced. We are told of the relations of the Goulds, father and son; we are with the young student of mining engineering when he meets the future Mrs. Charles Gould in Lucca. And we are carried from Don José, the patriot of Costaguana, to Holroyd, the financier in San Francisco, and back to Sulaco to meet the old Garibaldino and his family, Captain John Mitchell and his man Nostromo. One has sympathy for the readers who feel that this oscillation, pointed though it is with moments of acute psychology and descriptive beauty, isn't really getting anywhere; who feels a stage being set for events of great dramatic excitement, with always a letdown at the moment when one might look for something to come off. Excepting the mob circulating in Sulaco, and Nostromo's melodramatic rescue of the Viola family, and the departure of the troops in a whirl of Latin-American excitement, the action falls off each time one's attention is focused for a climax. We look on at Nostromo's masterful rule of the people, we see him rousing the cargadores to work after a night of fiesta, we watch him swagger through a picturesque Carmen-like love scene. Yet each of these pictures seems at the moment an end in itself, unrelated to the others.

But at this Chapter V the sails fill at last. We have been becalmed in the Placid Gulf like the ships that sometimes for thirty hours at a stretch drift there at the mercy of capricious airs. It has been like the nights when the clouds

smother the whole quiet gulf below with an impenetrable darkness, in which the sound of the falling showers can be heard beginning and ceasing abruptly, now here, now there . . . Your ship floats unseen under your feet, her sails flutter invisible above your head. The eye of God Himself . . . could not find out what a man's hand was doing in there.

We feel now a brisker speed, a ground swell of passion. We are conscious that we have at last reached a focus wherein the preceding scenes fall into a pattern.

Reconstruct the scene of this chapter. It is the book in microcosm, showing all the interlocked veins and tissues. Don José, his daughter Antonia, Decoud, and Mrs. Gould have returned to the Casa Gould on this hot late afternoon, from the excitement of seeing troops embark. The emotion of the patriots had been drained off by this event, and a pause—a suppressed intensity—had fallen upon them. But Decoud is no patriot and on him no pause has fallen. He had shown in Paris a superficial interest in internationalism and a contempt for South American revolutions. He begins to talk, and with that intellectual acumen which enables him to look clearly at love and call it his "supreme illusion," he lights up the motives of all the participants in the drama. This "nondescript dilettante" challenges even Charles Gould's disinterestedness, when he suggests to Antonia Avellanos that the test would come if Gould were asked to throw his mine into the melting pot for the Cause; and a spark is struck which kindles emotion. The characters come to life as if something in the air had got into each one, stirring his heart, demanding expression; and this something has emanated from Martin Decoud's mind.

For Don José Avellanos, usually eloquent, speech is for the moment trivial. He has seen the army depart with deadly rifles; he feels an "ecstatic confidence." As they enter the house, Don José tells Decoud—turned journalist for the love of Antonia—that the newspaper " 'must have a long and confident article upon Barrios and the irresistibleness of his army at Cayta. The moral effect should be kept up in the country.' " Don José is being practical.

Decoud walks restlessly up and down the room, eager to make his peace with Antonia. For being caught in the trap of the revolution, he is angry with himself; his being caught in the trap of love for Antonia is a torture of delight he doesn't want to resist. And he has the added intellectual thrill of knowing that he has fallen under "the supreme illusion of a lover."

Then we read: "Mrs. Gould sank low before the little tea-table." The action has begun. Decoud's walking up and down the drawing-room is symbolic of the weaving of the strands in the plot; back and forth in front of Mrs. Gould's tea table, in front of Don José, in front of Antonia. A servant announces: " 'The Señor Administrador is just back from the mountain,' " and with that the spirit of the San Tomé mine enters the drawing-room and from that instant hovers ominously in the air. Yet none of the actors, save Mrs. Gould and to some degree Decoud, realizes that it is the mine which lies at the bottom of this revolution; that the mine's preservation is based on revolution and counter-revolution, *ad infinitum*.

Decoud's mind, inflamed by his passion for Antonia, burns with intense power, lighting up all the sentimentalities of patriotism. His deepening emotion has strangely sharpened his skepticism. He cries out almost hysterically his conception of the truth; and is indignant when he sees all this lost on Antonia, "resolute puritan of patriotism." He hates himself for his calling of names even as he hurls into the scene a dramatic *Gran Bestia* when the traitor Montero is announced. He turns to Antonia with a comment on the absurdity of this name-calling business of journalism. Intellectually he sees that any direction he turns means defeat for him. But his intellectual clarity is of no avail. The hope of his passion lures him on, and identifies him, not without the cynic's gesture, with the Cause.

Here the actors shift. Antonia steps out on the balcony overhanging the street and Decoud follows. The drama, playing up to these two, discloses the conflict going on between Antonia's illusion of patriotism and Decoud's illusion of love. More is said of politics than of love, but profound pauses, filled with a sense of intimacy, "fall upon the rhythm of passion." We listen to Decoud's appeal to Antonia to think of the cruelty of inciting poor ignorant fools to kill and die—which has already destroyed his self-respect. We hear his desperate words: " 'I shall go to the wall.' " Antonia replies: " 'Martin, you will make me cry.' " We feel the triumph of Decoud's love, and at the same moment are conscious of a fateful futility lurking in the drawing-room and in the street below, where suddenly appears the "illustrious Capataz de Cargadores"—Nostromo.

The horseman passed below them with a gleam of dim light on the shining broad quarters of the grey mare, on a bright heavy stirrup, on a long silver spur; but the short flick of the yellowish flame in the dusk was powerless against the muffled-up mysteriousness of the dark figure with an invisible face concealed by a great sombrero.

Decoud, seizing his chance, pleads with her to leave all this miserable turmoil, and attacks her patriotism with the cold facts of the sordid situation: there is no disinterested person anywhere, it is all a maze of bribery and corruption. Her convictions challenged, she faces him and begins to argue. At first he is entirely absorbed in his sensuous pleasure in the tones of her voice, the pulsations of her throat; puzzled a little now and then by the sheer sagacity of a phrase that replaces his fascination "by a sudden unwilling thrill of interest." He would prefer not to believe in her intellect, but in spite of himself he begins to answer her seriously.

Suddenly he introduces the idea of secession, the separation of rich Sulaco from the part of Costaguana east of the mountains. The darkness into which they are gazing seems to blend with the mystery of the birth of Decoud's idea at this moment.

Outside it had grown dark. From the deep trench of shadow between the houses, lit up vaguely by the glimmer of the street lamps, ascended the evening silence of Sulaco; the silence of a town with few carriages, of unshod horses, and a softly sandalled population. The windows of the Casa Gould flung their shining parallelograms upon the house of the Avellanos. Now and then a shuffle of feet passed below with a pulsating red glow of a cigarette at the foot of the walls; and the night air as if cooled by the snows of Higuerota refreshed their faces.

They glance back into the salon. Decoud's keen absorption in the psychology lying back of behavior drives him to attack the new guests who begin to fill the Casa Gould. There is Antonia's uncle, Father Corbelan, of whom he says: " 'But I know him, too. The idea of political honor, justice, consists in the restitution of confiscated Church property.' " The impenetrability of the English Charles Gould somewhat upsets the young boulevardier's poise; but even of Gould he makes the significant guess " 'that he thinks of nothing apart from his mine, of his *imperium in imperio*.' " Then we have a glance at that "sinister" Dr. Monygham, and through Decoud see into his devotion to Mrs. Gould.

Of course it is only when we have finished the book and go back to this chapter that we see how all these characters are being spun into the plot. We are told that the "tide of political speculation was beating high within the four walls of the great sala." The motif of Nostromo's worth is played again and again: linked first with Decoud's idea of secession, and prophetic of a later journey of tragedy which they take together; linked then with the name and exploits of Father Corbelan.

The guests withdraw, leaving Charles Gould with one visitor—Señor Hirsch—and we are introduced to the Jew seeking security for his material interests, who later figures conspicuously in the tale. He mentions a contract with the San Tomé mine for dynamite. At the word Gould's mind springs like a trap set off: " 'I have enough dynamite stored up at the mountain to send it down crashing into the valley —to send half Sulaco into the air.' "

This fanaticism is the last note—and it is prophetic. We hurry on, then, through this relentless story of people involved materially and spiritually; a story with tragedy inherent in Gould's obsession with the mine, Mrs. Gould's unhappiness, Decoud's illusion, Antonia's patriotism, Nostromo's courageous, uneven encounter with the contemptuous gods.

Nostromo is our modern life in miniature, portraying not only the activities of Costaguana and Sulaco and the San Tomé mine, but those of the financial world of London and San Francisco. What could a man like Conrad, a follower of the sea for years, be expected to know of the intricacies of international capitalism? "The true peace of God," he remarks in *The Nigger of the Narcissus,* "begins at any spot a thousand miles from the nearest land." Whenever he boarded his ship he felt relief in leaving behind him the complexities of our economic and social order. But in this book he turned "with anxious meditation" to face them. More than most artists, and as completely as most propagandists, he makes the ideas and compulsions of economic imperialism stand out. Yet he is always more directly interested in fathoming the complex character of a Charles Gould, an exploiter, than in exhibiting the processes of economic exploitation.

Charles Gould is moved by two passions—his love for his

wife, and his loyalty to his father, which involves righting the wrong done his father in connection with the mine. The mine must be made to succeed—only in that way will the wrong be redressed. At the outset this desire works in harmony with his love for his wife; it is her idea as well as his, and had come to them both "at the instant when the woman's instinct of devotion and the man's instinct of activity received from the strongest of illusions, love, their most powerful impulse." But as Gould begins to work the mine, it gradually becomes an idol, displacing slowly, but with cruel inevitability, his affection for his wife. As Decoud says, Gould attaches a strange idea of justice to this mine, and to the seduction of this idea he surrenders his wife's happiness. The more he is obscurely aware of the subtle wrong he is doing her, the more tenaciously he clings to the fixed idea of the mine's success. And Mrs. Gould fails in her effort to save him from the consequences of this cold and overmastering passion.

Gould works the concession with the ideals others of his class have had—of establishing order, peace, good faith, and security; and of postponing the establishment of justice and democracy until the foundations of a true economy have been laid. His weapon is the wealth of the mine, a weapon poisoned with the cupidity and greed of mankind. The concession has to fight for its life with such instruments as can be found in the mire of universal corruption: "There was something inherent in the necessities of successful action which carried with it the moral degradation of the idea."

Eventually the Gould forces are triumphant, and an order is established, dominated by those whose power lies in economic mastery. Then Mrs. Gould is forced to share the ironic perception of Dr. Monygham that the time is coming " 'when all that the Gould concession stands for shall weigh as heavily upon the people as the barbarism, cruelty, mis-

rule' " of the earlier régime. " 'The mine will be more piti-
less and autocratic than the worst government, ready to
crush innumerable lives in the expansion of its greatness.' "
Here, offered as something incidental, is profound analysis
of the processes of modern civilization; offered in its connection with the suffering of Mrs. Gould, defeated in her hope
that the spell of the mine would be broken with the achievement of order.

Of other characters as deeply probed as Charles Gould,
we can mention only two or three. There is Dr. Monygham,
one of the loneliest people in Conrad's world. He had been
the victim of one of the many revolutions, those puerile
bloodthirsty games, "played with terrible earnestness by de-
praved children." Under torture he had betrayed his friends
and he can never entirely recover his self-respect. His short
hopeless laugh expresses immense mistrust of mankind—
"really it was most unreasonable to demand that a man
should think of other people so much better than he is able
to think of himself." One must go to Dostoevsky for a picture more revolting than that of the priest who tortured
Dr. Monygham, the man he dreamed of on the nights when
he rose and walked the floor and waited with a lighted candle
for the daylight. Father Beron, after torturing his prisoner,
had returned to the examination with "that dull surfeited
look which can be seen in the eyes of gluttonous persons
after a heavy meal." Dr. Monygham's only release from complete isolation lies in his devotion to Mrs. Gould. They
understand each other; they can share an unspoken consolation. When waves of loneliness sweep over Mrs. Gould, she
reflects that he is the only man who would ever again ask
her with solicitude of what she was thinking; and he would
find surcease from his own loneliness in asking her, because
he is devoted to her with the utter absorption of a man

"to whom love comes late, not as the most splendid of illusions, but like an enlightening and priceless misfortune."

And there are the two sharply contrasted characters, Nostromo and Decoud, joint actors in the most dramatic episode of the book—the escape with the silver. Here we have a beautiful instance of how the inner drama in Conrad's fiction transcends the outer drama—and there are thrills in plenty in the external episode. Decoud is the intellectual aristocrat, the disbeliever in the value of action; Nostromo is the man of the people, who sees no value in anything but picturesque action. When Decoud, the man of thought, involves himself in action; when Nostromo, the man of action, involves himself in thought—it is the beginning of the end for them both.

One cannot forget the dramatic moment of Nostromo's awakening in the old fort near the beach, when for the first time in his life he is induced by some devil really to think:

Nostromo woke up from a fourteen hours' sleep and arose full length from his lair in the long grass. He stood knee-deep amongst the whispering undulations of the green blades with the lost air of a man just born into the world. Handsome, robust, and supple, he threw back his head, flung his arms open, and stretched himself with a slow twist of the waist and a leisurely growling yawn of white teeth, as natural and free from evil in the moment of waking as a magnificent and unconscious wild beast.

Up to this point he has been completely the man of action, fitting comfortably into his own type, adapting without difficulty to the world about him. "Then in the suddenly steadied glance fixed upon nothing from under a thoughtful frown, appeared the man." From this point on, Conrad traces the paralyzing intrusion of thought into Nostromo's life, leading him to unwonted speculations about other people's motives, increasing his sense of betrayal by the *finos hombres* who have, he feels, exploited him for their own ends. His moral disintegration has begun.

With Decoud, deserted on the *Isabels,* the solitude to which he was temporarily condemned becomes very swiftly a pathological state of the soul. Only the simplest of us, says Conrad, can withstand solitude; and Decoud is not simple. Had he been a man of action he might have coped with the situation. But he had undertaken under the illusion of his love for Antonia a rôle foreign to his nature. The illusion fades for him when he is cut off from the woman he loves. His personality breaks down under the strain imposed by his attempt to overstep his own limitations. For this new demand upon him he has had no warning or preparation; and the shock is so extreme that he loses all belief in the reality of his action past and to come. He grows completely into himself. All exertion seems senseless, except that needed to snap the cord of existence with a pistol shot.

In both men there has been a complete disintegration of personality, leading to suicide in one, to moral chaos in the other. They are victims, one of "the disillusioned weariness which is the retribution meted out to intellectual audacity," the other of "the disenchanted vanity which is the reward of audacious action."

The dice of the gods are loaded against Martin Decoud. The illusion of love itself, by which he is lured to his destruction, represents the greatest ironic malevolence. This cynic who had dismissed the tragi-comedy of revolution with a *quelle farce* is whirled into the most ignominious of revolutionary rôles and cruelly pushed to the wall. Yet there is a nobility about Decoud through which he triumphs—his clear-sighted intellectual honesty which supports a love for Antonia, beautiful in its intensity, simple in reference to his actions. And such qualities in Conrad's world are exalted above malign destiny.

So there is after all a kind of consolation for Decoud's fate. But one searches in vain for any consolation for the neglected love of Mrs. Gould. It requires a heart tranquil as the gods of Lucretius to look with equanimity at the suffering of Mrs. Gould, who from an ethical universe deserved, if ever a human being did, treatment different from what she received. She was guilty only of the "sin" of universal comprehension, of too great good-will, of the observance of all the delicate shades of self-forgetfulness. For exercising these gifts she is left at the end of the story a tragic and lonely figure, "robbed of all the intimate felicities of daily affection."

With a prophetic vision she saw herself surviving alone the degradation of her young ideal of life, of love, of work—all alone in the treasure house of the world.

We emerge from our absorption in *Nostromo* still dazzled by the splendor of scene after scene, still wondering about the secret springs of personality, still questioning the meaning and purpose of a universe that tortures a Dr. Monygham, rewards a Mrs. Gould with the loss of all she holds dearest, and slays a Decoud through the one sincere and beautiful emotion of his life. Is this the more harmonized universe into which we escape through the magic of art? The cry of the reader to the writer of fiction, says Conrad, is "Take me out of myself!" But does one want to be taken out of oneself into an imagined universe that in its disregard of human aspirations, its "immense indifference," its casual cruelties, as well as its unexpected beauties, has all the disconcerting characteristics of our own familiar universe? When we go into Hardy's world, we find there just that ideal cruelty, that certainty of evil chance, which set it a little apart from our own experience; and the lurking sense of defeat which few of us entirely escape is soothed by the feeling that after all no one can win out against an Immanent Will so blindly ruthless. But the world of *Nostromo* has undergone no simplification, either for good or evil.

Nostromo dramatizes a philosophy of life which Conrad rather casually throws out in *A Personal Record*. Forced to dismiss any idea that the universe may be ethical—for that involves us in too many absurd and cruel contradictions—he has come to suspect that the aim of creation is purely spectacular: "a spectacle for awe, love, adoration, or hate . . . but never for despair. These visions, delicious and poignant, are a moral end in themselves." And perhaps our appointed task is simply the unwearied self-forgetful attention to every phase of the living universe reflected in our consciousness, so that we may bear true testimony to "the visible wonder, the haunting terror, the infinite passion, and the illimitable serenity; to the supreme law and the abiding mystery of the sublime spectacle." In this purely spectacular universe, everything—even the prose artist of fiction—has a place among "the kings, demagogues, priests, charlatans, dukes, giraffes, cabinet ministers, Fabians, bricklayers, apostles, ants, scientists, Kafirs, soldiers, sailors, elephants, lawyers, dandies, microbes, and constellations."

To become capable of this self-forgetful attention involves a supremely difficult discipline of heart and mind: for one must acquire what Conrad calls "the detached curiosity of a subtle mind and the high tranquillity of a steeled heart." With this rare equipment, one may succeed in rising above the pain and tragedy and beauty of existence into a realm of disinterested impersonal contemplation. This may be what Conrad means when he explains his phrase, "take me out of myself," by adding, "out of my perishable activity into the light of imperishable consciousness."

For those to whom this detachment and tranquillity are inaccessible, there remain one or several of the illusions by which men veil from their eyes the "terrible, the revolting insignificance of life." This is Conrad's phrase—one of the many unobtrusive comments about life scattered through his writings. "In our activity alone," he says in *Nostromo*, "do we find the sustaining illusion of an independent existence as against the whole scheme of things of which we form a helpless part." "Every age," he writes in *Victory*, "is fed on illusions, lest men should renounce life early and the human race come to an end." And when Decoud disappeared without a trace, he was "swallowed up in the immense indifference of things."

The immense indifference of things, the scheme of which we form a helpless part—this is what Conrad believes to be the truth of the universe. And he faces the truth. But he too has his illusion—the illusion of beauty. Through the devotion with which he has tried to make us feel, hear, and above all, see, he has made it possible for his illusion to become ours. The great artists, according to de Maupassant, are those who make us share their own particular illusion. Conrad has achieved his aim: "To arrest, for the space of a breath, the hands busy about the work of the earth, and compel men entranced by the sight of distant goals to glance for a moment at the surrounding vision of form and color, of sunshine and shadows; to make them pause for a look, for a sigh, for a smile." And when that task is accomplished, "behold! all the truth of life is there: a moment of vision, a sigh, a smile— and the return to an eternal rest." [81]

V

TIME PASSES: MAUGHAM, BENNETT, MANN

CERTAIN novels, we said in discussing Gissing, seem so completely detached from their authors that few traces of the relation between the creator and his work remain to tease our curiosity and make us half-glimpse a psychological drama. If they had their inception in the maladjustments, the unresolved conflicts, the unfulfilled dreams of their author, these have been so effectively projected and dramatized that they live their own rounded and independent life. Such a dramatic novel as *Pride and Prejudice,* or such a serene birth-to-death chronicle as *The Old Wives' Tale,* has this autonomous air. Who stops his reading to wonder uneasily about its author, as one wonders about the author of *Sons and Lovers* or of *Crime and Punishment?* What has been called the chronicle novel is perhaps more likely to present this effect of detachment than the dramatic novel. The author's effort to resist absorption in this or that intense individual experience, to stand apart and watch the stream of life flow past for a long period of years, must tend to create in him a mood impersonal and contemplative. The ability to achieve and sustain this mood is in itself evidence of at least temporary balance, adjustment, and release. It would seem that a chronicle novel could scarcely be written except in this mood, and that one way of evoking the mood is to apprehend time as itself the leading character in the human story. In the chronicle, as Edwin Muir puts it, time is external:

it flows past the beholder; it flows over and through the figures he evokes. Instead of narrowing to a point, the point fixed by passion or fear or fate in the dramatic novel, it stretches away indefinitely, running with a scarcely perceptible check over all the barriers that might have marked its end.

In the case of dramatic novels, the tendency of the reader is to become deeply involved in the conflict; to identify himself with the Paul of *Sons and Lovers,* or with Ivan Karamazov, or Mary Olivier. When the tension is relaxed, the conflict resolved, and the arena vacant, he reassumes his own personality, and comes back into his waking life as from a vivid dream. But the effect of such novels as *War and Peace*, *Buddenbrooks,* and *The Forsyte Saga* is usually quite different. As the years slip by in these books, and as one generation insensibly replaces another, we are gradually detached from individual lives and left in contemplation of life, flowing through and past the generations. "This cosmic progression," to quote Edwin Muir once more, "gives a different value to all the particular happenings, making the tragic pathetic, the inevitable accidental, the final relative." Our mood becomes meditative, elegiac. We are tranquilized by a process quite different from the catharsis of the dramatic experience, and left brooding, not over the significance of this or that individual destiny, but over the meaning of the whole human adventure.

This effect is not, one imagines, easy for the artist to achieve. To chronicle events through the years may result in a meaningless catalogue. The individual must lose some of his significance in the long perspective; but there is danger that life, too, may come to seem trivial. The question of form is a less sharply defined problem than in the dramatic novel, where it grows out of the conflict, and where the novelist's task is to show how the conflict came about, what forces are involved, what complications develop, and how it is at last resolved, in destruction or reconciliation. In contrast with such a strict and logical progression, we have in the chronicle a "loose concatenation of episodes," bound together only by the conception of time. How can we be given the satisfaction that comes from the shaping of events, the tracing of cause and effect relationships, the movement to a climax, and the falling away into a solution? There must be a design if we are to be left tranquil and satisfied, not weary and confused. How Tolstoy deals with the problem in *War and Peace* has been made the subject of illuminating analysis by several critics—notably Percy Lubbock. That is the supreme example of the chronicle novel. But other novels less great give the same kind of pleasure and are worth study.

Somerset Maugham's *Of Human Bondage* is no family chronicle, no slow birth-to-death progression. Its very title suggests an emotional involvement, a struggle for escape, that promises a dramatic development. Fill out the title from Spinoza's *Ethics*—"Of Human Bondage, or the Strength of the Emotions"—and one is prepared for a plunge into some intense form of human experience. And one takes it, too: such a deep plunge that there are probably few characters in modern English fiction with whom readers more readily identify themselves than with Philip Carey.[32] For all that, there are qualities in the novel—to be noted presently—that leave one at the end in a mood very different from that in which, for example, a Dostoevsky novel leaves us, though Philip's emotional entanglements are almost Russian.

The most lasting bondage in which Philip is held is that of his own temperament, and his temperament is determined largely by the accident of his deformity—a club foot. Thinking over his life, towards the end of the book, he realizes how this deformity has warped his character, and yet how it has developed in him a power of introspection that has given him as much delight as misery. One of the pitfalls of his nature is self-pity. A little boy, just after his mother's death, he weeps, yet keenly enjoys the sensation he is causing among some sympathetic ladies by his sorrow, and wishes he could stay longer with them to be made much of. Awakened to acute self-consciousness by the brutality with which he is treated by curious boys in the school dormitory, his school life becomes one of intermittent torment. He soon learns that when anyone becomes angry with him some reference will be made to his foot. He finds himself doing odd bits of playing to the gallery to excite compassion, as when a school-mate accidentally breaks a penholder belonging to Philip, and Philip, with tears, declares it was given to him by his mother before she died—though he knows he had bought it a few weeks before. "He did not know in the least what had made him invent that pathetic story, but he was quite as un-happy as though it had been true." The habit continues even after he has learned to understand it, and he lapses into it whenever he is weakened by suffering. On one oc-casion, when Mildred was irritated by his persistent love,

he hesitated a moment, for he had an instinct that he could say something that would move her. It made him almost sick to utter the words [but he uttered them nevertheless] "You don't know what it is to be a cripple. Of course you don't like me. I can't ex-pect you to." He was beginning to act now, and his voice was husky and low.

And she softened at the pathos.

He developed ways of escape and defense: reading, first, in his uncle's queerly assorted library, where he forgot the life around him and formed

the most delightful habit in the world—reading. He did not know that he was thus providing himself with a refuge from all the distress of life; he did not know either that he was creating for himself an unreal world which would make the real world of every day a source of bitter disappointment.

The wide knowledge gained from his books made him con-temptuous of his companions' stupidity, and he found he had a knack in saying bitter things, "which caught people on the raw." Thus he could defend himself, but he couldn't make himself popular, and he longed for easy intercourse with his schoolmates, and would gladly have changed places with the dullest boy in the school who was whole of limb. He develops a cool ironic manner; he even learns to control his sensitive blushing; he can protect himself, but he is still in bondage. When the physician at the hospital where he is studying asks Philip casually to display his foot, to compare it with that of the patient under examination in the clinic, Philip forced himself to appear indifferent, allowed the students to look at the foot as long as they wished—" 'When you've quite done,' said Philip with an ironical smile . . . And felt how jolly it would be to jab a chisel into their necks." He becomes an adept in self-analysis—"a vice as subtle as drug-taking."

What Philip suffers from his deformed foot is mild compared with the misery he undergoes when he falls in love with Mildred. It is an emotion so different from anything he has ever dreamed or read about—this aching of the soul, this painful yearning—that he is profoundly shocked when he is forced to identify it as love. Mildred, with her insolent pale thin mouth and anaemic skin, has been described somewhere as an implacable pale green worm who crawls through the book. The very fact that Philip is blinded by no illusions about her, that he sees how unhealthy, commonplace, odiously genteel, vulgar and selfish she is, convinces us that the passion is irresistible. Lovers of unworthy objects in fiction are usually clearly deluded; we, the readers, see that, and look for the waning of the passion with the discovery of the truth. But Philip knows the truth from the beginning, and we agonize with him over this divorce between reason and emotion, this split in consciousness where the reason watches, disgusted, repelled, estimating the passion at its true value, but unable to affect the emotions, which go their own lamentable way.

His reason was someone looking on, observing the facts, but powerless to interfere; it was like those gods of Epicurus, who saw the doings of men from their empyrean heights and had no might to alter one smallest particle of what occurred.

There are moments when he loathes Mildred, moments again when he feels noble because of the sacrifices he makes for her, other moments—like the blessed pauses in an illness—when the temperature falls and he thinks he is released. Once when she treats him with an insolence that humiliates him,

he looked at her neck and thought how he would like to jab it with the knife he had for his muffin. He knew enough anatomy to make pretty certain of getting the carotid artery. And at the same time he wanted to cover her thin pale face with kisses.

He tastes the depths of voluptuous self-torture when he gives Mildred and Griffiths—his friend for whom the apparently passionless Mildred has a violent infatuation—money to go off together on a week-end trip. He is sick with anguish when he makes the offer, yet "the torture of it gave him a strange subtle sensation." The devil of self-torture always lurks in him. There is a strange sequel when he later takes Mildred and her baby into his little flat and supports them, though he no longer has any desire for Mildred. This physical indifference so piques Mildred that she throws herself at his head, and, rejected, takes a vicious revenge by utterly destroying all the furnishings of the apartment, even slashing Philip's few paintings, relics of his art studies. But even that is not the end of Mildred; she comes back again and again, with each reappearance more degraded. When she is finally lost, Philip sometimes wanders through the streets haunted by prostitutes, wishing and dreading to see her, catching a glimpse of someone resembling her that gives him a sharp stab of hope or of sickening dismay—he scarcely knows which. Relieved when it is not she, he is yet disappointed and seized with horror of himself.

Would he never be free from that passion? At the bottom of his heart, notwithstanding everything, he felt that a strange desperate thirst for that vile woman would always linger. That love had caused him so much suffering that he knew he would never, never be quite free of it. Only death could finally assuage his desire.

There are times in the course of this strange passion when Philip could step over into Dostoevsky's world and feel at ease with the most accomplished masochist of them all.

Compelling as is the drama of Philip's struggle, it is to other aspects of the novel that the final impression is due. There is the sense of change, of relentless moving on, that marks the chronicle, though the space of years actually covered in *Of Human Bondage* is not great—perhaps twenty-five or thirty. Philip, moving from one group to another in his restless search for adjustment, loses sight of this or that person for a time; then sees him again, changed, older. There are his clergyman uncle and his aunt, middle-aged when they take the orphaned nephew into their home, growing into old age, dying; there is Hayward, fascinating and brilliant in the eyes of twenty-year-old Philip, gradually revealing himself as Philip grows more astute to be a shallow poseur, whose mind grows more and more flabby and his charm more and more tarnished. There is Cronshaw, the poet of the Montparnasse cafés, center of a little circle of the initiated, leading an ever shabbier and more sordid life, coming to die wretchedly in London. Mildred herself runs rapidly through the stages that take her from a curiously attractive waitress in an ABC teashop to a diseased prostitute haunting Piccadilly. It is Philip's reflective attitude towards all these mutations that helps to create the effect of philosophic detachment characteristic of the chronicle novel.

Philip's career is so varied and experimental that he seems to have led several lives. There is such richness of detail in the account of his art studies in Paris, his medical training in London hospitals, his dismal interlude as a shop clerk—there are so many people in each little universe whose lives Philip observes with the same sort of interested detachment with which Maugham himself observes Philip—that we feel we are watching the unrolling of an elaborate panorama. There is not the rigid selection of detail that in the dramatic novel makes everything bear directly on the main conflict. For the interest is not so much in the final resolution of the conflict as in Philip's arrival at a comprehension of its nature and its place in some general scheme of human existence. Quite early he begins seeking consciously to understand the meaning of life, as well as to make his own difficult adjustments to it. Often this intellectual need—stimulated by his emotional difficulties—is more pressing than a decision about his career or an escape from the degrading bondage to the unspeakable Mildred. The reader begins presently to share Philip's philosophic concern with what life is all about.

It is toward the chapter that follows "Of Human Bondage" in Spinoza's *Ethics* that the novel is moving, though one can scarcely say that it arrives—"Of Human Freedom, or the Control of the Understanding." From time to time Philip feels that he understands himself and life and can control both. When he talks with Cronshaw in Paris, he is challenged to say what he really thinks he is in the world for, and he answers vaguely—to do one's duty, to make the best use of one's faculties, and to avoid hurting other people. This he calls abstract morality, and he is indignant with Cronshaw for ridiculing his weak reasoning, and for setting up a thoroughly self-centered philosophy—that men seek but one

thing in life, their pleasure. Philip had always believed conventionally in duty and goodness. As he goes on through his
own difficult experiences, and especially as he watches day
after day the procession of humanity through the clinic of
the hospital, he comes to see only facts. The impression was
neither of tragedy nor of comedy . . . It was manifold and various; there were tears and laughter, happiness and woe; it was
tedious and interesting and indifferent; it was as you saw it;
it was tumultuous and passionate; it was grave; it was sad and
comic; it was trivial; it was simple and complex; joy was there
and despair; the love of mothers for their children, and of men
for women; lust trailed itself through the rooms with leaden feet,
punishing the guilty and the innocent, helpless wives and
wretched children; drink seized men and women and cost its
inevitable price; death sighed in these rooms and the beginning
of life, filling some poor girl with terror and shame, was diagnosed there. There was neither good nor bad there. There were
just facts. It was life.

Philip cultivated a disdain for idealism, which he had
found meant for the most part a cowardly shrinking from
life, but, meeting a man with a passion for Spain and particularly for the painting of El Greco, he began to divine
something new, to feel on the brink of a discovery, a new
kind of realism in which facts "were transformed by the
more vivid light in which they were seen." There was some
mysterious significance in these paintings, but the tongue in
which the message came was unknown to him.

He saw what looked like the truth as by flashes of lightning on a
dark stormy night you might see a mountain range. He seemed
to see that a man need not leave his life to chance, but that his
will was powerful; he seemed to see that self-control might be as
passionate and as active as the surrender to passion; he seemed to
see that the inward life might be as manifold, as varied, as rich
with experience as the life of one who conquered realms and explored unknown lands.

These remain but flashes. He finds most satisfaction in the conviction that life has no meaning. "Life was insignificant and death without consequence." He exults as he had in his boyhood when the weight of a belief in God was lifted from his shoulders. He feels free. "If life was meaningless, the world was robbed of its cruelty." But Cronshaw had once given him a little Persian rug, and told him that the meaning of life was hidden in its pattern; and now he thinks he discerns it.

As the weaver elaborated his pattern for no need but the pleasure of his aesthetic sense, so might a man live his life, or if one was forced to believe that his actions were outside his choosing, so might a man look at his life, that it made a pattern . . . Out of the manifold events of his life, his deeds, his feelings, his thoughts, he might make a design, regular, elaborate, complicated, or beautiful; and though it might be no more than an illusion that he had the power of selection, though it might be no more than a fantastic legerdemain in which appearances were interwoven with moonbeams, that did not matter: it seemed, and so to him it was . . . There was one pattern, the most obvious, perfect, and beautiful, in which a man was born, grew to manhood, married, produced children, toiled for his bread, and died; but there were others, intricate and wonderful, in which happiness did not enter and in which success was not attempted; and in them might be discovered a more troubling grace.

Philip felt he was casting aside the last of his illusions in throwing over the desire for happiness. Measured by that desire, his life was horrible, but it might be measured by something else. Happiness and pain were details in the elaboration of the design. Anything that happened to him henceforth would simply be one more motive to add to the complexity of the pattern. When the end came and it was completed, he would find it none the less beautiful because he alone knew of its existence and "with his death it would cease to be."

Philip's final acceptance of the most obvious pattern is brought about by his meeting with Sally, a girl with a very simple, pagan attitude toward living, as radiantly healthy as Mildred was sickly, as tranquil as Philip is restless, as soothingly maternal as any man could wish his ideal woman to be —yet not as convincing as the dreadful Mildred, who seems the reality, whereas Sally is one of the dreams belonging to the Golden Age. Freedom to Philip suddenly takes on the aspect of lonely voyaging over a waste of waters; a quiet home with Sally is a fair harbor.

He thought of his desire to make a design, intricate and beautiful, out of the myriad, meaningless facts of life: had he not seen also that the simplest pattern, that in which a man was born, worked, married, had children, and died, was likewise the most perfect? It might be that to surrender to happiness was to accept defeat, but it was a defeat better than many victories.

There is nothing more obvious than the fact that all old people were once young. Here is the simplest aspect of the part played by time in our lives. But every now and then a commonplace like this strikes upon a sensitive imagination like a revelation and induces a profound emotion out of which grows a work of art. This happened to Arnold Bennett one evening in 1903, when he was dining in a restaurant in Paris, and an old woman, laden with parcels, came in, looking so fat, clumsy, and grotesque that everyone laughed.

I reflected [Bennett wrote], that this woman was once young, slim, perhaps beautiful—certainly free from these ridiculous mannerisms. Her case is a tragedy. One ought to be able to make a heart-rending novel out of the case of such a woman as she. Every stout aging woman is not grotesque—far from it; but there is an extreme pathos in the mere fact that every stout aging woman was once a young girl with the unique charm of youth in her form and movements and in her mind. And the fact that the change from the young girl to the stout aging woman is made up of an infinite number of infinitesimal changes, each unperceived by her, only adds to the pathos. It was at that instant that I was visited by the idea of writing the book which ultimately became *The Old Wives' Tale*.

De Maupassant's *Une Vie* had recorded the life of a woman from girlhood to old age, with the average experiences of young love, marriage, motherhood, sorrow, loss, and disillusionment; this novel Bennett admired so much that he determined to create its English counterpart, but with characteristic assurance, he wished to go de Maupassant one better, and to write, not of one woman, but of two.

He placed his two heroines, Constance and Sophia Baines, in the midst of the Victorian era and in the heart of the provincial district in England which he knew most intimately. He had grown up in one of the Five Towns in Staffordshire, where is made all the everyday crockery used in the United Kingdom; and had passed his own childhood in the house in St. Luke's Square where the Baines family lived, next to their draper's establishment. The county is in the center of England, the Five Towns in the center of the county, and St. Luke's Square in the center of the oldest of the Five Towns. It is all as English, all as average as possible —a life "unsung by searchers after the extreme." Bennett had withdrawn from it soon enough—he was twenty-one when he went to London—to be enabled to view it in perspective. With a strong sense of its humorous aspects and its limitations, yet deeply in sympathy with it, he gives a convincing representation of its intimate daily life and a moving interpretation of its people. These are the men and women who stay on Main Street; here are Mid-Victorian parlors, Nottingham lace curtains, kitchens, sulky servants, afternoon teas, children's parties, pampered fox terriers, local fairs and local scandals, marketing and churchgoing—the whole world of the commonplace and the everyday.

Sophia and Constance, delightful girls at the outset of the

tale, grow up in this little world of the Five Towns, fundamentally alike in the sterling traits of character belonging to
the Baines stock, but different enough to seek different stages
on which to play their parts. Constance, the more pliable and
conventional, marries the head clerk of her father's shop,
remains in the house in St. Luke's Square, and retraces almost every design in her mother's life, as housekeeper, wife,
and mother. Sophia, more rebellious and spirited, elopes to
Paris with the attractive, irresponsible Gerald Scales, lives
through some ecstasies and many bitter disillusionments, cuts
herself off completely for thirty years from the Five Towns,
adapts herself to Paris life after her worthless husband disappears, and becomes the successful manager of a most exem-
plary pension. First we follow the story of Constance through
the years up to the point where her grown son leaves her to
study art in London. Then we go back and pick up the
thread of Sophia's life, follow it through the same span of
years, until an illness and the accidental renewal of contact
with the Five Towns lead her to rejoin her sister in St.
Luke's Square. The currents of their lives then flow in one
stream to the end.

Sophia's life had more spectacular possibilities. One might
have expected her to develop traits very different from those
of her home-keeping sister. But throughout all her French
experience, there persist in Sophia the characteristic Five
Towns virtues and limitations. Sophia is as impermeable to
Paris as Strether in *The Ambassadors* is vulnerable. She
learns to speak its language, to play the game of making a
living according to its rules, and to manage its people in
the service of her ends. On the common ground of thrift, she
and its tradesmen can meet in understanding and sympathy.
But the beauty of Paris, its art, its atmosphere, its sense of the
value of the passing moment, the many graces of its living, all
these have no voice for her spirit. She is captivated during

the brief days of her happiness with Gerald by the gaiety and glitter of the café life. But she is soon aware of the hollowness of that. And later she sees the underside of the lives of the prostitutes on Montmartre, and condemns such living —not so much for its immorality as for its laxity and its untidiness and its ultimate failure. Not " 'What a sinner!' " but " 'What a fool!' " she thinks of the woman who had nursed her in her illness; " 'If I couldn't have made a better courtesan than this miserable woman, I should have drowned myself.' " It is the Five Towns instinct for good workmanship cropping up.

Once only does Paris almost win out over the Five Towns. This is during Sophia's little holiday dinner with Chirac, the journalist, who in many of her most difficult experiences had come to her assistance with delicate consideration. The atmosphere of the tiny restaurant is agreeable, reassuring, friendly; Chirac's love-making is not unexpected. Curiosity not merely about him but about herself had tempted Sophia tacitly to encourage him. She is close to that experimental attitude toward life that had amazed her some years before in Chirac—when he had gone to see a guillotining as a psychological experience, " 'to observe himself in such circumstances.' " " 'How strange even nice Frenchmen are,' " she had thought. Now she herself is almost on the edge of experimentation. But from some obscure instinct she repulses him. Bennett, with that rather hard, unshaded certainty of his, which is in such great contrast to Conrad's tentativeness in the face of the psychological problem, explains her refusal as the result of a certain haughty moral independence, leading her to despise any open expression of emotion—a Baines trait, a Five Towns trait. Chirac suffers too openly. If ever there was a chance for Sophia to flower into graciousness and become sensitive to other than Five Towns values in life, it was at this moment. The danger was that she would close her doors against enriching experience and grow harder, narrower, more barren. And she does. She becomes the landlady —efficient, stylish, diplomatic, armed against every trickery, who could not be startled and could not be swindled. After thirty years in Paris, all that she brings back to St. Luke's Square—aside from a skill in dressing that no one in the Five Towns possessed—is the French poodle, Fossette.

After the funeral of Constance, who outlives her sister, no one is left in the house but the cook and the infirm French poodle, Fossette—"sole relic of the connection between the Baines family and Paris." The tearful servant prepares the dog's dinner and places it before her in the customary soup-plate in the customary corner. Fossette sniffs at it and then walks away and lies down with a sigh in front of the kitchen fire. She has been deranged in her habits that day and is conscious of neglect owing to events that passed her comprehension.

However after a few minutes she began to reconsider the matter. She glanced at the soup-plate, and, on the chance that it might after all contain something worth inspection, she awkwardly balanced herself on her old legs, and went to it again.

So the curtain falls on *The Old Wives' Tale*. It contains many episodes that, if isolated on their little stage, would furnish the material of a dramatic novel.

There is the murder committed by a relative of the Baines family, a tragedy that might well be the climax of a dramatic novel. But it is important in the story simply because Constance's husband, Samuel, embraced his unfortunate cousin's cause, wore himself out in the effort to save him from the gallows, lost the fight, and died of exhaustion and disappointment. The story flows on past this tragedy. More significant still in creating the final effect of *The Old Wives' Tale* is the handling of the siege of Paris in 1870. Sophia is in Paris during the siege, struggling to draw together the broken threads of her life after her illness and her desertion by Gerald. With the business sense that is her Five Towns inheritance, she has managed to secure lodgers, provide them with food, and find a modest profit in it. "For Sophia the conclusion of the siege meant chiefly that prices went down . . . The signing of the treaty reduced the value of Sophia's two remaining hams from about five pounds apiece to the usual price of hams." Bennett had acquired this sense of what the siege meant to ordinary people by questioning an old French servant about his experiences at the time: "You went through the Siege of Paris, didn't you?" he asked. The old man turned uncertainly to his wife: "The Siege of Paris? Yes, we did, didn't we?" The siege was only one incident among many in their lives and time had reduced it to a faint memory.

"An infinite number of infinitesimal changes" marks the change from young girl to aging woman, and these Bennett traces without any effect of monotony. Both sisters grow steadily slower and less flexible in activities, emotions, sympathies, hopes, interests. Constance, realizing suddenly that Samuel, her husband, was nearly forty and that she had been married six years, reflected that nothing had happened. She had obtained a sure ascendency over her mother—not by seeking it, but just by the passing of time; she had acquired skill in the management of her household and her shop; she had constructed a chart of Samuel's individuality with the submerged rocks and perilous currents all carefully marked, so that she could voyage safely in those seas; and Fan, the puppy, whose entrance into a hitherto dogless home had been one of the revolutionary changes wrought by her marriage, was now a sedate and disillusioned dog, with a son in the house and grandchildren scattered over the town.

It is by giving us vividly the quality of certain moments of realization in the lives of the sisters that Bennett most

effectively conveys the sense of the passing of the years.
These are the moments when life seems to pause and to reveal something of its meaning to them, so that they think they
understand what they have been living through and how
they have changed since the last moment when they were
fully conscious of themselves. Such a moment comes to
Sophia, when, as a young girl full of ambition and energy,
she stands beside the bed of her paralytic father and listens
to his prohibitions and his commands—this wreck, she suddenly realizes—dictating to her youth! And she is saddened
into profound grief by the absurdity of the scene. In a momentary ecstasy of insight, she feels older than her father in
her understanding of life. Pure pride of youth and joy of
living possess Sophia driving with Gerald down the Champs
Élyseés; with intense, throbbing emotion, she longs with
painful ardor for more and more pleasure then and forever.
Compare this simple ecstasy with the curiously complicated
and subtle emotion, colored by reflection and disappointment, of the Sophia of the restaurant scene with Chirac. And
then watch Sophia at fifty, looking out once again on the
Square of her girlhood, remembering its aspect on winter
mornings, remembering her own youth, finding it all beautiful and touching; and suddenly reflecting that not for millions of pounds would she live her life over again. Then the
tragic moment, ten years later, when she is shocked into a
kind of primitive emotion, uncolored by any moral or religious quality, by the sight of the dead old man who had
been Gerald. It made no difference that Gerald had wasted
his life or caused her sorrow. What affected her was that he
had once been young and that he had grown old and was
now dead. Youth and vigor always came to that—everything
came to that. " 'Yet a little while and I shall be lying on a
bed like that. And what shall I have lived for? What is the
meaning of it?' " Constance, who in her more placid way

had embraced more completely such experiences as came to her within the narrow limits of St. Luke's Square, ends not with the tragic question, but with a half-ironic affirmation. Old and alone and sick as she was—just a rheumatic old lady in the eyes of the rising generation—when she surveyed her life and life in general, she would think with a sort of tart but not sour cheerfulness, " 'Well, that is what life is.' "

Although Fossette is alone on the stage when the scene closes, there is no feeling of emptiness, for we have been kept aware of Constance's son and his friends, and Samuel Povey's nephew, and others of the generation that has been gradually coming to look on the two sisters as mere pathetic survivals from an earlier time. Life in the Five Towns moves on. And it moves on too in the old German town of Lübeck after the family of Buddenbrook, prominent in its merchant society for over a century, is exhausted and dying.

The movement of Thomas Mann's *Buddenbrooks* is one of growth and decay through four generations. The curtain rises on a family gathering, about 1830—a hearty feast, with children, grandchildren, poor relations, old friends.

There they all sat, on heavy, high-back chairs, consuming good heavy food from good heavy silver plate, drinking full-bodied wines and expressing their views freely on all subjects. When they began to talk shop, they slipped unconsciously more and more into dialect, and used the clumsy but comfortable idioms that seemed to embody to them the business efficiency and the easy well-being of their community.

At the end, some fifty years later, there are a few aging, grief-stricken women, talking of the death of little Hanno, the delicate boy who should have carried on the family name. Hanno had been born when his father had brought the Buddenbrook fortunes to their highest point; when he was about to build an imposing new house and to be elected Senator. But the decline had already begun; the Senator felt himself losing his firm grip on events; and in a moment of sad clarity, he reminded his sister that

often the outward and visible material signs and symbols of happiness and success only show themselves when the process of decline has already set in; the outer manifestations take time—like the light of that star up there, which may in reality be already quenched, when it looks to us to be shining its brightest.

Little Hanno sees more of death than of birth in the family, more losses than gains. When his old governess says good-by to him, after his father's death,

his face wore the same brooding, introspective look with which he had stood at his father's death-bed, and his grandmother's bier, witnessed the breaking-up of the great household, and shared in so many events of the same kind, though of lesser outward significance. The departure of old Ida belonged to the same category as other events with which he was already familiar; breakings-up, closings, endings, disintegrations—he had seen them all.

And with a characteristic little mannerism, he lifted his head and seemed cautiously to sniff the air, as if he expected to catch "that odour, that strange and yet familiar odour which, at his grandmother's bier, not all the scent of the flowers had been able to disguise." In one of his short stories, Mann speaks of an old merchant family that for generations had lived, worked and died in its fine old gabled house; at the end it produced an artist or two. And he adds: "It often happens that a race with dry, practical, bourgeois traditions, finds itself again towards the end of its days in art." So it happens with the Buddenbrooks, for Hanno is a gifted musician. So it seems to have happened with Mann's own family, for *Buddenbrooks* is—under the usual disguises of fiction—the story of his own family, patrician, conservative merchants of Lübeck.

As we read *Buddenbrooks,* his first novel, and the short
stories collected in the *Death in Venice* volume, we become
aware of Mann's deep concern with the problem of the artist—what he is, whether he is to be trusted or regarded with
suspicion. His studies of artists are sometimes satirical,
sometimes broadly humorous, sometimes deeply sympathetic,
but always questioning. What is the truth of the artist's relation to himself and to society? As one reads these studies, one
finds a certain pattern recurring significantly over and over
again. The hero of *Death in Venice* is an author of distinguished fiction; on his father's side he comes of a family of
officers and magistrates, men who lived severe, steady lives
in the service of the state; but his mother was the daughter
of a Bohemian music-master; "a marriage of sober, pains-
taking, conscientiousness, with the impulses of a darker,
more fiery nature, had had an artist as its result." Tonio
Kröger, artist hero of another story, is the son of a leading
merchant in a North German city, and of a beautiful black-
haired woman from the South, a musician. Tonio's story
arises out of the conflict of impulses in his blood and the
compelling need of reconciliation. Hanno Buddenbrook is a
musician; his father had married a bride from Holland, with
an exotic strain in her inheritance—a woman of musical, artistic gifts, quite different from the practical-minded German women around her.

The reason for Mann's preoccupation with this theme lies,
as one would suspect, in his own heredity and his own deep-
seated inner conflict. His father was such a German merchant of fine old traditions as he pictures in Thomas Buddenbrook; his mother the daughter of a German planter and
a Portuguese-Creole Brazilian. The two strains in his inheritance did not blend readily. The world of art, thought,
music, is his world; but his artists are often troubled with
a sense of their own feebleness in that world of practical,

balanced, sane activity, of easy adjustment to the demands of
society, where the German burghers moved so easily and with
so much dignity. Mann can satirize the dullness, the materialism, the insensitiveness of the practical man; but he can also
dissect the artist's posing, his self-preoccupation, his sickly
introspection, his moral laxity and lack of dignity. Tonio
Kröger confesses to sharing at times all the suspicions against
the typical artist which any of his respectable forefathers
would have felt against a mountebank or strolling player
who might have entered the house. He feels that the artist,
who must stand apart from the human before he can play
with it, present it coolly and impartially, is himself somewhat inhuman. "The gift for style, form, expression, already
presupposes this cool and critical relationship with the human, even a certain human poverty and desolation." He
finds literature more of a curse than a calling—a curse that
begins to show itself early, at a time when one should by
right still be living in peace and accord with God and the
world.

You begin by feeling yourself set apart, in some mysterious antagonism to others, to the usual, the ordinary. The abyss of
irony, disbelief, opposition, knowledge, feeling, which separates
you from people, yawns deeper and deeper . . . What a fate!
Provided that your heart is sufficiently alive, sufficiently loving,
to feel it as frightful.

He concludes by confessing to a stealthy, devouring hanker-
ing after the bliss of mediocrity.

This love of the ordinary life, this yearning for the normal, the respectable, the likable, which Mann makes his
Tonio express, is beautifully wrought into the structure of
Buddenbrooks. It is a record of the common life, of ordinary
people. Only Christian Buddenbrook, who might have been
a comic actor, had there been any place for artists in the
scheme of the family traditions, but who is only a marred

business man and a hopeless hypochondriac, and little Hanno, who was too weak to bring his gift of music to fruition—only these two are markedly different from the other Buddenbrooks and the inhabitants of the North German town. The background of the family chronicle is the staid old Free City, with its granaries on the water front, its ships in the harbor, the gray-bearded craftsmen in the narrow shops built into the arcades of the market square, its fishwives and dairy-women, its burgesses in the senate house, its gray Gothic buildings and gabled houses. On this background is woven the pattern of a closely knit family life—births, celebrations, marriages, deaths, quarrels, scandals, ambitions, anniversaries. The family is the hero, the characters but cells in its organism.

Our perception of the continuous life of the family is sharpened by a device deftly employed by Mann: the family book of records, kept with religious care by the head of the family in each generation. Here is Consul Buddenbrook, early in the novel, recording the birth of his second daughter and piously thanking God for all his mercies. "The pen hurried glibly over the paper, with here and there a commercial flourish, talking with God in every line." Parenthetically he notes, " 'I have taken out an insurance policy for my youngest daughter, of one hundred and fifty thaler current. Lead her, O Lord, in Thy ways, give her a pure heart,' " and so on for several more pages. Sometimes the record has a deciding voice in the fate of some member of the family. Tony, the Consul's daughter, has fallen in love with a poor medical student whom her family will not permit her to marry. They do their best, in ways for the most part kindly, to cure her of this unfortunate fancy. They find for her a suitor of the prosperous merchant type of which they approve. But, loathing the long golden whiskers of the importunate Herr Grünlich, she resists all their arguments and entreaties and thinks longingly of the student, so different from anyone she has ever known. Then, one day, in a mood of weary idleness, she turns over the pages of the family record, becomes absorbed in it, is impressed by the simple but stately chronicle style which mirrors the family attitude, its modest self-respect, its reverence for tradition.

No point in her own tiny past was lacking. Her birth, her childish illnesses, her first school, her confirmation—everything was carefully entered, with an almost reverent observation of facts, in the Consul's small, flowing, business hand . . . What, she mused, would be entered in the future after her name? All that was yet to be written there would be conned by later members of the family, with a piety equal to her own. She leaned back sighing; her heart beat solemnly . . . Like a link in a chain . . . She was important precisely as a link in this chain . . . Such was her significance—to share by deed and word in the history of her family.

And Tony, looking long at the blank space after the last entry under her name, at last picks up the pen, and with feverish decision, writes down the date of her betrothal to Herr Grünlich.

A generation later, little Hanno unconsciously draws the line of his own fate and that of his family. Finding the book open one day, amused by all the names and the odd flourishes of handwriting and the different colored inks, toying with his mother's gold pen, he finds his own name—Justus Johann Kaspar; and mechanically, dreamily, he draws a beautiful double line diagonally across the page, under his name. Questioned somewhat angrily by his father later as to what possessed him to do such a mischievous thing, Hanno stammers, " 'I thought—I thought—there was nothing else coming.' "

Throughout the novel two characters hold our interest without a break, Tony and her brother Thomas, both children at the outset. Tony is charmingly drawn: a person of the type that does not develop but keeps her fundamental characteristics unchanged; she is spontaneous, resilient, emotional, naïve, intensely loyal to the family. Her little stock of general ideas she had acquired during her brief love affair with the student, a young radical. And thereafter she had lovingly cherished them; and whenever she was thoughtful or felt that the occasion demanded some reflections upon life, she produced these old ideas, with a touching faith in their truth and durability. At the death of her favorite brother Thomas, when his wife and son are unable to weep under the sudden shock, Tony surrenders herself utterly to one of the refreshing bursts of feeling which her happy nature always had at its command.

Her face still streamed with tears, but she was soothed and comforted and entirely herself as she rose to her feet and began straightway to occupy her mind with the announcements of the death—an enormous number of elegant cards, which must be ordered at once.

Tony's two marriages are unlucky, her daughter's one attempt even more so; she is growing old with nothing left to console her in the decline of the family. But we leave her talking about life, making observations upon the past and the future—"though of the future there was in truth almost nothing to be said."

Strikingly different is her brother Thomas, a complicated character that steadily develops and subtly alters. In Thomas are impulses in conflict with the ordered, active, practical life of a merchant, which he, as head of the Buddenbrooks, is called upon to lead. He has some turn for introspection and some half-conscious yearnings for philosophy and art. Early in his life, however, he is offended by the eccentricities of his brother Christian, the frustrated artist. He feels something indecent, undignified, in Christian's endless concern with himself, endless self-analysis, and wearisome communicativeness. He tells Tony that he has thought a great deal about this curious and useless self-preoccupation, because he once had an inclination to it himself; but he observed that it made him unsteady, harebrained, incapable, and for him, control, equilibrium were the important things. In one of the quarrels between the brothers, Thomas cries, " 'I have become what I am because I did not want to become what you are. If I have inwardly shrunk from you, it has been because I needed to guard myself.' " He has won for himself the reputation of a good merchant and a successful man of action.

But the impulses that he starves out take their toll; the incessant hidden conflict going on below the surface fatally weakens him. Long before any signs are apparent to the outside observer, the process of disintegration is far advanced in him; and with this inner decay of Thomas himself, the decay of the great house keeps pace. His yearning for a kind of life different from that set before him by the family tradition leads him to make an unusual marriage with the daughter of a musician who is herself absorbed in music. His delicate only son is the very embodiment of all that was repressed in Thomas's nature. The relation between father and son is handled with subtlety and pathos: the disappointment of the father who sees his hope that the son will succeed where he has failed gradually vanish, as the boy turns away with distaste from all the studies and activities that would develop him into a successful merchant. Hanno is happy only when he slips into the music room to listen to his mother and the church organist playing Bach fugues; or when he sits up in the organ loft with Herr Pfühl, high above the pastor in his pulpit, in the midst of a mighty tempest of rolling sound. While the sermon is going on, the two laugh softly at the funny mannerisms of the pastor—for both were of the opinion "that the sermon was silly twaddle, and that the real service consisted in that which the Pastor and his congregation regarded merely as a devotional accessory—the music."

Hoping to stimulate self-confidence in his son, to make him realize the value and the interest of intercourse with his fellows, the father sometimes takes him on a round of visits, where he displays his own tact and skill in dealing with each person according to his character and position.

But the little boy saw more than he should have seen; the shy, gold-brown, blue-shadowy eyes observed too well. He saw not only the unerring charm which his father exercised upon everybody; he saw as well, with strange and anguished penetration, how cruelly hard it was upon him. He saw how his father, paler and more silent after each visit, would lean back in his corner of the carriage with closed eyes and reddened eyelids; he realized with a sort of horror that on the threshold of the next house a mask would glide over his face, a galvanized activity take hold of the weary frame . . . And when he thought that some day he should be expected to perform the same part, under the gaze of the whole community, Hanno shut his eyes and shivered with rebellion and disgust.

Once in a while when the father involuntarily betrays some movement of fear or suffering, Hanno meets his gaze with a comprehension beyond his years:

Hanno might fail his father in all that demanded vitality, energy, and strength. But where fear and suffering were in question, there Thomas Buddenbrook could count on the devotion of his son.

The hopeful, hearty confidence in life and growth that breathes through the earlier fortunes of the Buddenbrooks has been lost in this exquisite but morbid sensibility.

Something of the effect of drama is secured by the steady ascent, the climax, and the decline of this family, as if it were in a struggle with time, like the tragic hero's struggle with destiny. Yet the dominant impression at the end is of the "cycle of birth and growth, death and birth again"—of time flowing on past the beholder, "over all the barriers that might have marked its end."

MAY SINCLAIR: NEW LIGHT ON OLD VIRTUES

BEFORE 1914 or thereabouts—the novels we have been talking about were all written before 1915 [33]—characters in fiction did most of their thinking with a certain dignity, in the well-lighted and well-ordered drawing-rooms of their minds. What went on elsewhere in the house was a domestic secret. But evidence had been piling up of the truth of a theory casually mentioned by Samuel Butler, in his novel *The Way of All Flesh* (completed, though not published, in 1884): "I fancy that there is some truth in the view that is being put forward nowadays that it is our less conscious thoughts and our less conscious actions which mainly mould our lives and the lives of those who spring from us." He himself did little with the theory in his novel, except to contrast the "good" reasons that his people gave for their behavior with the "real" reasons lurking unacknowledged in the background. But presently his successors began to explore the dimly lighted regions beyond the bright focus of consciousness. Characters took to ways of behaving that in the old days would have been called abnormal—ways that were called abnormal when Dostoevsky's Russians pursued them. They were bewilderingly inconsistent; they felt quite opposite emotions at the same moment; what used to be considered virtues revealed themselvs as lurking vices. May Sinclair, in a series of novels and stories, threw this strange new light on such veteran virtues as self-sacrifice. "By the newer psychology we are all potentially abnormal; the normal are those who do not manifest all their innate qualities." [34]

The greatest influence in this new interpretation of the human mind was of course that of Sigmund Freud. A clear and just estimate of Freud's work is to be found in Stefan Zweig's *Mental Healers*. The following passage sums up the rôle of the "unconscious" in our lives:

Far less than was formerly imagined does the upper world of consciousness really belong to the alert will and the positive intelligence, for the lightning flashes which are our real decisions emerge from the dark cloud of the unconscious, and from the depths of the impulsive life come the earthquake thrusts that determine our destiny. In that obscure realm, huddled together pell-mell, lies all that, in the sphere of the conscious, seems delimited in orderly fashion by the transparent walls of the categories of space and time. The buried treasures of a long-forgotten childhood still live greedy lives in the unconscious, accounting for the otherwise unaccountable lusts that drive us like chaff before the wind. Terrors and anxieties that have no meaning for the conscious mind rise from the depths and suddenly take control of our nerves.

Because of our tendency to thrust what is painful and disagreeable out of sight and out of mind—in the old sense of mind—exploration of the unconscious has tumbled a great many skeletons out of closets, and unlocked many unsightly Bluebeard chambers. Yet it is worth remembering that the "unconscious" does contain pleasant things, even charming and amusing things, too, and from it proceed creative impulses out of which beauty is born.

With all this new material to assimilate, writers of fiction have of necessity had to experiment with new forms. The older molds of the novel were able to hold the traditional material of fiction; the new material bursts the mold and the novelist must shape new ones. These questions of form and of technique become especially important in dealing with the work of James Joyce and Virginia Woolf, and others whose innovations have had a far-reaching influence on other writers.

Novels have been written in the past, and are still writ-

ten, to tell a story and to point a moral—to amuse and to
edify. They have been written, also, under the influence of
the "art for art's sake" theory, and under that of the "art for
life's sake" creed that governed the famous Russian realists
of the nineteenth century. With the coming of Lawrence and
Joyce and Proust and other modern writers, we begin to
speak of "art for the artist's sake." Art has always been for
the artist's sake in a fundamental sense; it has been an instrument in his adjustment to life, even when he himself was
unaware of the fact and assigned quite different reasons for
his activity. But of recent years so much emphasis has been
laid on the artist's duty to himself of "expression"—a therapeutic measure that may heal the conflicts in his own personality—that the duty of "communication" to the reader has
sometimes been lost sight of. What has been called a "cult of
unintelligibility" [35] has developed, based on material furnished by novelists and poets and on ingenious justifications provided by conscientious critics. The writings of Gertrude Stein, the later experiments of Joyce, offer difficulties
that most readers who are not literary specialists will not
make the effort to surmount. But the obstacles to understanding and enjoying many of the modern books have been
much exaggerated. The obscurities of one age often become
the truisms of the next. A day may come when Joyce's *Work
in Progress* will be pushed aside as too obvious for the consideration of active minds; a Gertrude Stein libretto is already as clear as Mother Goose to delighted audiences.

That day has not yet arrived, but it is true that readers
today find Proust, Virginia Woolf, and the Joyce of *Ulysses*
far more easy of comprehension than did those of ten years
ago. For minor authors, picking up and using this or that
technical device first tried out by the innovators, have been
training the public. The best attitude, in approaching the
work of transition writers, is not that of a distrustful "What

does this mean?"—but that of a receptive "What am I getting out of this?"

For the appreciation of much ultra-modern work . . . the reader must be willing to coöperate, to insinuate himself into a strange mood . . . to lend his emotional equipment to the appreciation of a series of experiments, tentative gropings, new combinations, delvings into the recesses of painful, fugitive moods.[36]

May Sinclair, like all artists, has worked in collaboration with her deeper self, where lurk certain fears that have found expression through the fates of her characters. In her fiction, over a period of twenty-five years, there are striking indications of a fear of intellectual, emotional, spiritual starvation; of frustration and non-fulfillment, through the malevolence of circumstances, of people, or of ideals. One or all of these malign influences in her novels may encourage acts of self-sacrifice on the part of their victims; and the self-sacrifice rarely appears as a liberating, but more often as a maiming force, a vice rather than a virtue.

Where fear is, there also is hatred. In May Sinclair's world is a hatred, somehow touched with love and pity, of the fathers and mothers who demand sacrifice as their right, and a hatred spiced with malice of the women who, with a cunning born of their sensual desire, take what they want. Any form of self-deceit, so often the companion of self-sacrifice, is cruelly punished. Above all virtues Miss Sinclair prizes intellectual freedom, emotional clarity, lucidity of soul.

Among the earliest of her stories is *Superseded,* in her own opinion the best of her work before *The Divine Fire.* In *Superseded* is Miss Juliana Quincy, aged forty-five, in appearance fifty, a teacher of arithmetic in St. Sidwell's School. There she is cruelly overworked; at home she is cruelly sacrificed to the comforts and caprices of her eighty-year-old aunt Mrs. Moon. Miss Quincy is a repressed, washed-out, little person, altogether atrophied except in that part of her brain which does recurring decimals and cube roots. Her self-effacement had begun when she had stepped aside to make way for the career of her more clever sister Louisa: "It had been considered unnecessary for Juliana to develop an individuality of her own; enough for her that she belonged to Louisa." Mrs. Moon's deceased husband had run through Juliana's money; yet it was the old lady's foible to exact from her niece a belief in the wisdom and rectitude of Tollington Moon. There in Camden Town Mrs. Moon sits among the relics of past gentility and accepts Juliana's devotion as a proper offering to the household god, all the while despising her for this very sacrifice.

Juliana toiling from morning to night for her eighty pounds a year; Juliana painful and persistent, growing into middle age without a hope,—Juliana was an incarnate reproach, a perpetual monument to the folly of Tollington Moon.

So Juliana's youth "withered away in the sour and sordid atmosphere born of perishing gentility and acrid personal remark."

Miss Quincy is always getting in the way of the school procession—both literally and figuratively—and being asked to stand back. One day she collapses, and the young and brilliant Rhoda Vivian, the most vital of all the teachers in the school, happens to be the one to succor her and get her a doctor. The doctor and Miss Vivian are moved to pity by Miss Quincy's condition, and through that common pity fall in love. Miss Quincy begins to bloom a little under the half-humorous, half-pitying attentions of the two. What Miss Quincy interprets as the doctor's interest in herself is really his love for Rhoda. She exhibits a pathetic awakening. She buys a mauve silk blouse. "All her dim and germinal desires burst and blossomed in this sinful passion for her blouse." Mrs. Moon cruelly shatters her little illusion. " 'Whatever possessed you to make such an exhibition of yourself? Much too young for you! Why, bless me, if it doesn't throw up every bit of yellow in your face.' "

As a desperate venture she invites the doctor to tea. Says the old lady: " 'Why invite the doctor to tea? You know perfectly well that I don't enjoy my tea unless we have it by ourselves.' " Oh, yes, Juliana knew; they had been having it that way for five and twenty years. When for a month or two she doesn't see the doctor, she exhausts herself in speculation as to the cause of his indifference; then her heart begins to act strangely. She summons the doctor. His stethoscope finds nothing the matter. And the dreadful Mrs. Moon gives an ironical chuckle: " 'If you had wanted to tell him plainly that you were in love with him, you couldn't have set about it better.' " It is a terrible shock; but poor little Miss Quincy hasn't been all these years a teacher of mathematics for nothing; she acknowledges the truth. She sees it now, the thing they had all seen—"she had sinned the sin of sins, the sin of youth in middle age."

If Mrs. Moon had let her alone

her folly might have put on many quaint disguises, friendship, literary sympathy, intellectual esteem. There were a thousand delicate subterfuges and innocent hypocrisies, and under any one of them it might have crept about unchallenged in the shadows and blind alleys of thought.

But it has been hauled out into a sudden glare of light and exposed to the stethoscope. Humor or subtlety might have saved her, but Miss Quincy was neither humorous nor subtle. A woman of the world could have explained to her that there was nothing remarkable or shameful in her folly. As it was, "she could only creep shivering to bed and lie there, face to face with her own enormity." Her usefulness gone as a teacher of cube roots, Juliana is dismissed from the school. She drags on, finding no place where her self-respect can rest.

And when her heart begins to act up again, she thinks it is hysteria, resolutely ignores it—and dies. With the unthoughtful cruelty of youth, Rhoda and the doctor think that Miss Quincy has justified her existence by bringing them together.

A quarter of a century later, in *The Cure of Souls*, May Sinclair portrayed Miss Lambert, deaconess, forty-five, who loves the self-centered, indolent, sleek Canon Chamberlain, disguising her love as the love of God. She is a woman, as the Canon is not slow to perceive, "devoted to the last extremity, a woman with a sacred vocation, a woman who would lift all burdens from his back." As always, there is some person through whom Miss Sinclair's cruel lucidity finds voice; here it is the Canon's sister Charlotte, who tries to make her brother recognize that Miss Lambert is in love not so much with God as with him. " 'It isn't a crime to be in love with you. I never said she wasn't innocent. But your innocence I'm not so sure about. I can see you exploiting that poor lady's infatuation for all it is worth.' " The Canon refuses to understand his sister's shocking, unorthodox diagnosis; Miss Lambert is too useful to him. To satisfy her spiritual needs, he recommends to her a course of reading in mysticism. "To get the best practical results out of Agnes Lambert, he had to sustain her in her state of exaltation." Eventually she grows so exalted that she has to retire to a sanitarium. Miss Sinclair is kinder to her than she is to Miss Quincy, and leaves the deaconess quietly at peace in her love of God.

These repressed and sacrificed women are in the middle years of their lives. But there are younger women who are on the way to joining their ranks. There are Effie and Phoebe, in *The Fault*, two charming, devoted girls, slaves to the bath chair of their invalid father, their individualities not yet completely submerged, but moving steadily towards the fate of the two daughters of the late Colonel in Katherine

Mansfield's story. And there is Freda, in *The Gift,* a delicate woman whose frail but exquisite gift of literary expression is brought to life by a love unacknowledged even to herself. Her happiness is diabolically destroyed, under the guise of friendship, by one of those viciously nice women that May Sinclair depicts with peculiar zest.

Occasionally in the world of May Sinclair a victim just misses being sacrificed. Freda Tancred, in *The Cosmopolitan,* whose dreadful old bore of a father exacts from her a whole-souled fidelity to his needs and the management of the estate, has sternly suppressed in herself every wayward desire and every hopeful curiosity. But her will to live her own life is at last roused through love for a man who sees nothing whatever in her, but who casually advises her to cut loose from the old man and try it on her own. This is all her latent independence and energy require; Freda actually makes a successful "getaway," in an exit scene of delicate comedy. The father is left to a providential widow.

More complicated are the examples of self-sacrifice in *The Helpmate* and *The Combined Maze,* books in which, for a change, men are the chief victims. Both books are studies of marital experience; and one feels, after reading them, the force of Dr. Johnson's comprehensive dictum: "Marriage has many pains, but celibacy has few pleasures."

Having been intensely interested in writing books which landed her characters in an impasse, Miss Sinclair has then seemed to take an equally intense interest in experimenting with ways out of this dilemma. In *The Life and Death of Harriett Frean,* the whole idea of self-sacrifice is satirized, and is pointedly shown up for the vicious thing it is. The problem is solved in a highly entertaining fashion in *Mr. Waddington of Wyck;* in a less novel, but equally diverting way in *The Cure of Souls;* and in a not wholly convincing but very suggestive way in *Anne Severn and the Fieldings*. Thus she begins with satire and proceeds to tentative solutions.

Harriett Frean is called the story of a life and death. One thinks of *The Old Wives' Tale,* or of de Maupassant's *A Woman's Life.* We get no sense of the slow passage of time; we do not feel Harriett growing old, as we feel Constance and Sophia growing old, in *The Old Wives' Tale.* "Her Harriett is a child, then suddenly a girl, and then an aging elderly woman." One may praise the book by saying that it is stripped of all irrelevancies. "There is a sense in which flesh and blood are irrelevant to a skeleton." We have the skeleton—we have all that is relevant to the "case." We haven't the woman, as we have Constance and Sophia. Flesh and blood are quite relevant to a living human being.

But take it as a satire. Is there any ideal that has been more exploited and admired in fiction than self-sacrifice? Especially for women; it has been their peculiar virtue, their beauty. In Fielding's novel, Amelia's whole existence is a sacrifice to her husband and her children. Even Jane Eyre laid her own happiness and Rochester's on the altar of an outworn, unjust law that chained a man to a loathsome, murderous lunatic. George Eliot, though she approved the act of Jane's renunciation, regretted it had to be made in the interest of that law. And remember Maggie Tulliver: she and Stephen love each other; he is betrothed to her cousin Lucy; he tries to persuade Maggie to let him break that engagement and marry her; Maggie refuses. This refusal is quite consistent with her whole growth and development— it is her own act, dictated by her own ideals, not by those of other people. George Eliot clearly approves of Maggie.

But George Eliot shows us none of the consequences of Maggie's sacrifice, for she kills her off, and Stephen doesn't marry Lucy, until, presumably, his old love is forgotten.

May Sinclair takes the same situation: Harriett and Robin
are in love with each other; Robin is engaged to Prissie, her
friend; Harriett insists on handing Robin over to Prissie.
Judgment on an act can't be entirely dissociated from its
consequences, which in this case are dire. Sacrifice, says
Dewey,[37] if one surrenders some possession or possibility to
the requirements of new growth, may enlarge the self; but
often self-sacrifice means merely self-maiming. And the
maimed self demands compensation in some later possession
or indulgence. Harriett's self, by this act, is not enlarged, it
is crippled by this suppression of her only chance of emotional growth. As for Prissie, her subconsciousness, with its
terrifying acuteness, knows that Robin does not love her. In
the absence of the reality, she craves the external signs, at
least, of affection and devotion. So she develops paralysis, and
thus during a long invalidism exacts everything from Robin.
Harriett is consciously ever so sorry, and somehow appeased
and happy subconsciously, because these people for whom
she sacrificed herself are so miserable. Robin uses up all his
capacity for unselfishness in this enforced devotion, and
when, after Prissie's death, he remarries, he is a selfish monster. Everyone concerned here is stunted and deformed.
And Harriett cannot see anything but the beauty of her own
act.

Harriett is shocked when Robin's niece announces her engagement to Geoffrey.

"But, my dear, you told me he was going to marry your little
friend, Amy. What does Amy say to it?"

"What can she say? I know it's a bit rough on her——"

"You know; and yet you'll take your happiness at the poor
child's expense."

"We've got to. We can't do anything else."

"Oh, my dear—(If she could stop it)—I knew a girl once who
might have done what you're doing, only she wouldn't. She

gave the man up rather than hurt her friend. She couldn't do anything else."

"How much was he in love with her?"

"I don't know how much. He was never in love with any other woman."

"Then she was a fool. A silly fool. Didn't she think of him? . . . She thought of herself. Of her own moral beauty. She was a selfish fool."

"She asked the best and wisest man she knew, and he told her she couldn't do anything else . . . That was my own father, Hilton Frean."

"Then it was you. You and Uncle Robin and Aunt Prissie. How could you?"

"I could because I was brought up not to think of myself before other people."

"Then it wasn't even your own idea. You sacrificed him to somebody else's. You made three people miserable just for that . . ."

"There was Prissie. I did it for her."

"What did you do for her? You insulted Aunt Prissie . . . handing her over to a man who couldn't love her even with his body. Aunt Prissie was the miserablest of the lot. Do you suppose he didn't take it out of her?"

"He never let her know."

"Oh, didn't he! She knew all right. That's how she got her illness. And it's how he got his. And he'll kill Aunt Beatie. He's taking it out of her now. Look at the awful suffering. And you can go on sentimentalizing about it."

One doubts whether this conversation ever could take place; it is too stripped of the unessential, too crystal clear. It is diagnosis rather than dialogue. But what astoundingly accurate diagnosis!

"The book ruthlessly exposes the danger of being beautifully brought up. It carries Harriett, the only child of cultured parents, straight through her blameless life from her black walnut crib to her spinster old age." In all this time Harriett never uses her mind or her emotions except in the

manner in which she was brought up to use them. The moral
maxims of her parents have been indelibly stamped upon
her: Forget ugly things; always behave beautifully.

Mr. Waddington, in *Mr. Waddington of Wyck,* is a monument of conceit and selfishness, and would exact, if he
could, every form of self-sacrifice from the people around
him. One remembers how his earlier prototype, Sir Wil-
loughby, in *The Egoist,* exploited Letitia Dale and his old
aunts and his cousin Vernon. But Mr. Waddington's wife, his
son, his ward, and his secretary escape the burden through
their detached and humorous appreciation of his gorgeous
perfection. They know he cannot be changed; but he can
be enjoyed. If we felt depressed over the intolerable pathos
of little Miss Quincy's mauve silk blouse, we are amply con-
soled by the broad comedy of Mr. Waddington's canary
waistcoat and the magenta forked-lightning pajamas. The
people in his household plot to keep him on his pedestal,
because they all have, as Francis Hackett has remarked, "a
subtle sense that stripped of his conceit, this kind of egoist
would be as indecent and as miserable as a shorn collie." [38]

After a witty and remorseless castigation of the selfish
Canon Chamberlain, in *The Cure of Souls,* Miss Sinclair
lets him down even more easily than she does Mr. Waddington. He is removed by a discerning widow of the same temperament as his own from his cure of souls to an existence
where he can harm no one. The widow, too, is in love with
ease and cushions and sun-warmed peaches and Rolls-Royces;
and she loves the Canon as she would love the beauty of a
sleek cat. True, it is too late to save Miss Lambert. But Miss
Lambert would be safe only in a nursing home anyway, as
long as the church exists to feed her emotions, and to supply
her with curates and vicars and canons to adore.

In all these finely written and cleverly conceived books,
with their extraordinarily competent use of the instrument

of psychoanalysis, one feels a slight dissatisfaction at the end, because the "case" sticks out now and then somewhat prominently. The danger here is that of new labels for old; a danger that lies in the facts and technique of psychoanalysis; and they are only convincing when they are used less consciously and with discretion and finesse, as in *Mary Olivier* and *The Three Sisters*.

Perhaps Miss Sinclair came to the writing of this tragic book, *The Three Sisters,* through speculation upon the lives of the three Brontës, into whose experiences she had lived with vivid intensity.

What would have happened to Charlotte Brontë (she seems to have asked) if she had not been able to express herself, and her father had had no curates to provide her with a husband? What might conceivably have saved Branwell Brontë from ruin? This latter problem is worked out in part through the character of Jim Greatorex, who has many of Branwell's vices, but who is saved by his tender devotion to Ally Cartaret. The closest likeness in the book is in the character of Gwenda Cartaret, who has Emily Brontë's impersonal passion for nature and indestructible yearning for freedom. Gwenda can make no poetry of her mysticism, and so a life of much potential power goes to waste.

Miss Sinclair has built more upon the unfounded traditions of the Brontës than upon the facts—traditions that her own critical study has done much to disprove. The Vicar Cartaret has traits of the eccentric and violent father of the Brontë legend. But the real Mr. Brontë Miss Sinclair calls "a poor and unhappy and innocent old man," a man "with good points as fathers go." He made companions of his small daughters and was later intensely proud of their gifts. This was an unusual reaction indeed for a Mid-Victorian parson. "The average evangelical parson would have been shocked

into apoplexy at the idea of any child of his producing
Wuthering Heights or *Jane Eyre.*" The vicar of *The Three
Sisters* is actually shocked into apoplexy by the disgraceful
love affair of his daughter Ally. The picture that May Sinclair gives of this youngest daughter resembles the gentle
Anne Brontë physically; but spiritually, in her yearning for
a husband, she is like the Charlotte of the legend. The closest
likeness to Mary Cartaret, out of the Brontë drama, is to be
found in Mme. Héger of the Brussels school, who is feline
and unscrupulous and jealous.

The setting of both dramas is the same—the Yorkshire
moors and their tiny villages and their isolated farmhouses.
Here is Haworth:

the black-grey, naked village, bristling like a rampart on the
clean edge of the moor; the street, dark and steep as a gully,
climbing the hill to the parsonage at the top; a small oblong
house, naked and grey, hemmed in on two sides by the grave-
yard, its five windows flushed with the wall, staring at the grave-
yard where the tombstones, grey and naked, are set so close that
the grass hardly grows between.

The village of Garth, in *The Three Sisters,*

crouches bare with a crook of the dale behind and before it . . .
Under the mystery and terror of its solitude it crouches, like a
beaten thing, cowering from its topmost roof to the bowed back
of its stone bridge . . . North, where the high road begins to
rise again, the Vicarage stands all alone . . . The garden slopes
down to the churchyard, and a lane leading to the pasturage runs
between.

In the difference between Haworth, which bristles, and
Garth, which crouches, there may be an intention. Out of
Haworth comes defiance, and achievement and success; out
of Garth comes only defeat.

The themes in this book appear elsewhere in the work
of May Sinclair. Here all these strands of plot and situation
are brought together into a fabric exceedingly simple in

design, very rich in texture. Vicar Cartaret demands the same
sacrifices that Mary Olivier's mother does. He has three
daughters, Mary, Gwenda, and Ally, with whom he has fled
to this grim northern parish to escape the gossip about his
youngest daughter Ally, who has horrified him by a tendency
to love not wisely. He cannot bear the sight of sensuality in
anyone when he is obliged to live a life so enforcedly continent; his third wife has refused to live with him or to give
him a divorce.

The idea of any of his daughters marrying was peculiarly disagreeable to him. He did not know why it was disagreeable and
it would have shocked him unspeakably if you had told him
why. And if you had asked him he would have had half a
dozen noble and righteous reasons ready for you at his fingers'-
ends.

He fears Gwenda, because she has moments of terrifying
frankness in which she holds up this unpleasant truth for
him to look at.

In a great scene, when the assembled family, with the
young doctor Rowcliffe, are in consultation upon the case
of Ally, who has brought disgrace on the Vicarage, Gwenda
confronts them all with a cold utterance of the facts. " 'You're
as bad as she is,' " says her horrified father. " 'How can you
bring yourself to speak of it if you are a modest girl? Are
we to suppose you are defending her?' " At this challenge
Gwenda turns from defence to attack: " 'You ought to be gentle with her, Papa, you drove her to it.' " The Vicar, having
recourse to Scripture, quotes solemnly: " 'Let no man say
he is tempted of God when he is driven by his own lusts.' "
As Gwenda looked at him

it was as if she saw vividly and for the first time the profound
unspirituality of her father's face. She knew from what source
his eyes drew their darkness. She understood the meaning of the
gross red mouth that showed itself in the fierce lifting of the

ascetic grim moustache. And she conceived a horror of his father-hood.

"No man ought to say that of his own daughter. How does he know what's her own and what's his?" she said.

This interview ends in an attack of apoplexy for the Vicar.

As an outcome of Gwenda's impassioned and outspoken defence, Ally is safely married to Jim Greatorex, the yeo-man of the parish, who has all along wished to marry her, but of whom she has been afraid. Jim takes his young bride to his father's house, "a place of sinister and terrible sugges-tions." The spiritual atmosphere of Upthorne is like that of the wind-swept farmhouse of *Wuthering Heights*. It de-presses Ally with many very deep fears:

The sadness of the desolate land, of the naked hillsides, of the moor marshes with their ghostly mists, the brooding of the watchful, solitary house, the horror of haunted twilights, of night-fall and of midnights now and then, when Greatorex was abroad looking after his cattle, and she lay alone under the white ceiling that sagged above her bed and heard the weak wind picking at the pane; . . . her fear of the savage, violent and repulsive ele-ments in the man who was her god; her fear of her own repul-sion . . . the vague melancholy of her secret motherhood.

If Ally had given way to these unacknowledged terrors—of the farmhouse, the moors, her husband—she could never have survived the ordeal of bearing her child. These deeper fears, which she did not dare to face, were masked under one that she could acknowledge—the fear that her stricken father would die as a result of her behavior. And this protective fear she could not only face, but could bring out in the open to Jim. Thus she clung to her husband, knowing instinc-tively it was the only way she could hold him. As soon as the child is safely born, this fear of her father's death van-ishes like mist; "it had served its purpose." Here is a keen presentation of psychoanalysis. But this is no X-ray picture.

Ally's fears are the real terrors of a human heart and not the symptoms of a "case."

The peculiar moral offensiveness of Ally's loving Jim lay in the fact that Jim had seduced the servant maid Essy in the Vicarage. In a later book, Miss Sinclair, with her growing use of economy, sometimes disparaged as parsimony, would probably have omitted this episode as not having a direct bearing on the story. Yet Essy brings out certain traits in the Vicar himself which explain the part he later plays in the lives of his daughters. She also evokes the gentle protectiveness in Gwenda, which prepares us for Gwenda's attitude toward Ally.

Gwenda Cartaret, the most intelligent, most lovable sister, feels the joy of life especially in moments of intense mystical communion with nature. Like Emily Brontë, "her inner life was luminous with intense realization," but, unlike Emily, Gwenda not only has no channel for expression through art, but finds no person to whom she can communicate these deepest realities of her inner life. Rowcliffe, the young doctor, whom she as well as the other two sisters loved, resents Gwenda's passion for nature, which he can neither understand nor share. Again and again in their walks on the moors, when he is on the point of proposing to Gwenda, something—he scarcely knows what—puts him off.

A thousand things distracted Gwenda; the cry of a mountain sheep, the sound and sight of a stream, the whir of dark wings and the sudden "Krenk-er-renk-errenk" of the grouse shooting up from the heather. And on the high roads where they went abreast she was apt to be carried away by the pageant of earth and sky; the solid darkness that came up from the moor; the grey aerial abysses of the dale; the awful, blank withdrawal of Greffington Edge into the night. She was off, Heaven knew where, at the lighting of a star in the thin blue; the movement of a cloud excited her; or she was held enchanted by the pale aura of moonrise along the rampart of Greffington Edge. She shared the earth's silence and the throbbing passion of the earth as the orbed moon swung free. And in her absorption, her estranging ecstasy, Rowcliffe at last found something inimical.

It is in these moments of estranging ecstasy that Gwenda discerns "the hidden soul of the land that had entranced her"; moments such as that in which she sees the thorn trees in flower in the moonlight, enchanted in a great stillness. And a subtle and mysterious joy sweeps her, a passion "as distant and as pure as ecstasy. It swept her, while the white glamour lasted, into the stillness where the flowering thorn-trees stood." The only person who understands Gwenda's emotion is Jim Greatorex: " 'I know what you mean about these thorn-trees. 'Tisn't no earthly beauty what you see in them.' " And it made no difference that Jim understood, and it made every difference that Rowcliffe didn't. Instead of realizing that in her capacity for feeling lay Gwenda's essential beauty, his egotism resented this impersonal love. His innate selfishness with a petulant jealousy stood between him and Gwenda. If she had loved another man, and not the moors and the white hawthorn trees, he would have found that comprehensible. But in Gwenda's great scheme of the universe, where she felt herself absorbed in a mystical union, he could only feel a worm indeed.

The doctor was neither great enough in spirit nor old enough in wisdom to bear the burden of having three women in love with him at the same time. Ally loved him, and when she feared she couldn't have him, she escaped into illness, hoping to hold him that way. The guileless doctor makes it clear to Gwenda that Ally can be saved only by marriage. And although Gwenda knows that she loves the doctor, she feels that if she is out of the way he will marry Ally. So Gwenda leaves the moors she loves for the London she hates. It is a deliberate act of self-sacrifice inspired by her intense affection and pity for Ally. But Gwenda had not counted on the quiet sister Mary who, the moment Ally's inconstant affections turn towards Jim Greatorex, marries the doctor.

Mary wasn't in a sense aware of what she was doing. She worked instinctively—like the cat, for instance. Her enslavement of the doctor is the triumphal act of her life, and she succeeds in holding him by her constant appeal to his biological needs. Mary is a "fount of sensual wisdom." Gwenda stands by and watches the slow dying of everything that was fine and youthful and ambitious in the doctor. His deterioration is the torture of her life. She endures all Mary's unconscious cruelties to herself—Mary's display of the children that she has borne to Rowcliffe, her exhibitionistic performances when she takes Gwenda into their bedroom, hers and the doctor's, her constant suggestion that Gwenda is growing older. " 'Nobody would know you were thirty-three.' " And there is just enough fight left in Gwenda to reply: " 'I shouldn't, Molly, if you didn't remind me every time.' "

She finds herself, at last, completely alone with the half-imbecile invalid father she has never really loved, who holds her merely by the appeal he makes to her pity. The quality of Gwenda's life, the life in which we leave her, is thus marked:

The hours no longer passed in a procession marked by distinguishable days. They rolled round and round in an interminable circle, monotonously renewed, monotonously returning upon itself. The Vicar was the centre of the circle. The hours were sounded and measured by his monotonously recurring needs . . . The Vicar had desired supremacy in his Vicarage and he was at last supreme. He was supreme over his daughter Gwenda . . . She was his to bend or break or utterly destroy. She who was capable of anything was capable of an indestructible devotion.

She had hours now and again when she shook off the slave woman that held her down. In those hours her inner life moved with the large rhythm of the seasons . . . And the visible world passing into her inner life, took on its radiance and intensity.

But these hours become fewer and fewer until at the end we leave Gwenda a completely defeated spirit. We know it is the end when the crushing realization comes upon her that everything she had loved in Rowcliffe is dead, and that the joy that she had received from her communion with nature is becoming less and less frequent. For the first time she is afraid. She looks at the village and feels that she will never get away from it.

It had always waited for her; but she was afraid of it now, afraid of what it might have in store for her. It shared her fears, and it crouched there, like a beaten thing, with its huddled houses, naked and blackened as if fire had passed over them.

May Sinclair has been accused of lacking intensity—of penetrating intellectually without participating emotionally in the lives of her characters. While this charge has some basis in *The Life and Death of Harriett Frean* or *Mr. Waddington of Wyck* or *The Cure of Souls*, there is no basis at all for it in either *Mary Olivier* or *The Three Sisters*. These two books represent May Sinclair at her best.

In *The Three Sisters* her prose lacks the intimacy of that of *Mary Olivier*, but it has instead the richness and distinction of writing that flows with rhythmic ease. Being less throbbingly autobiographical, this book has none of the "broken vibrations" of *Mary Olivier*; it has more of the quiet and restrained power of a work of art that is more objective and therefore greater.

The Three Sisters came out of May Sinclair's deepest literary passion, but *Mary Olivier* came out of her own deep personal experience. Both are studies again of self-sacrifice within the complicated network of the family.

Mary Olivier is autobiographical of a very vivid, sensitive woman whom we feel to be May Sinclair herself. The story reflects, not the outer facts of her life, but her inner growth and experience. This we watch throughout the book in a most fascinating interplay of emotional and intellectual life; Mary is led to the writings of Herbert Spencer, for instance, through an interest in heredity that grows out of a very unhappy emotional experience. Her emotions and her disappointments always lead her out into something that is abundantly compensatory.

The book is exceptional when we remember that it is a life done after many years. Without an unobstructed tapping of the depths and extensions of consciousness such a book seems impossible—especially those sections about infancy and adolescence. Everything comes through the consciousness of Mary, in a long succession of glimpses, momentary exposures of scenes and people and situations.

We are taken through events as the bewildered and impercipient spectator was himself taken through them; and when for example the father gets drunk at a party the change is not heralded as drunkenness, but comes as change itself, repugnant and unmentionable, gradually focussing itself into the concept that we know. So also Mary's intellectual zest is not disclosed. It is an urgency, an ache, a nostalgia that only experiment solves for her; just as she has the ecstasy of beauty long before she knows that such ecstasy has a name.

Francis Hackett has said this, and he goes on to speak of the "falls and rapids and the broken vibrations of the style of *Mary Olivier*." It is a style which arises naturally out of the "broken vibrations" of Mary Olivier's adventures of the spirit.

In this story of the struggle for self-expression, amidst the thick of conflicts and tensions in the family, Mary's deepest trial lies in the unacknowledged jealousy which her mother feels of her development. Although the others of the family— Papa and Dan and Roddy and Mark and the Aunts—are all included in Mary's drama, her chief antagonist is her mother. Every achievement in her emotional and intellectual life is gained only after the bitterest struggle; and many of her best possibilities are, in the struggle, completely annihilated. There are moments when we fear Mary must go under; but she is saved by a passion to be true to her real self. If Mary could only have whole-heartedly hated or despised her mother, the struggle would have been sharp, acute, but final.

One of Mary's first perceptions of this jealousy which accents her struggle is the realization of her mother's preference for her brother Mark. Her mother ignores the tower she is building with her blocks, and cares only for Mark's snow man. The child doesn't name what she feels, but that feeling is a resentment of her mother's neglect, expressed in rage against the tower which she demolishes with a blow.

Something swelled up hot and tight in Mary's body and in her face. She had a big bursting face and a big bursting body. She struck the tower, and it fell down. Her violence made her feel light and small again and happy.

The struggle gets more bitter as she grows older and can no longer resort in her resentment to smashing something; when she must suffer the tortures of applying rational judgments to the spiritual problems which are constantly looming in her life.

She was about three then. Later on the flashes of comprehension come with greater lucidity. She divines the father's jealousy of Mark when she sees her father standing at the door watching Mamma and Mark happily planting the sumac tree that Mark had given her, taking no notice whatever of him. When Papa laughed suddenly and went into the house and slammed the door, "You knew that he disliked the sumac tree and that he was angry with Mark for having given it to Mamma."

Practically all of the tensions of the family come from jealousy of one kind or another. Through years of dimly recognizing this condition, Mary after much meditation is eventually articulate about it. She has watched the father bullying the sons in order to torture the mother who loved them. He never teases Mary. She perceives in one of her flashes of insight that he would have bullied her if her mother had loved her as much as she loved Mark. To her father she says, " 'I wish you had. . . . I shouldn't have cared. I wish you'd hated me. Then I should have known she loved me.' " No wonder he looked at the child in wonder and with round startled eyes.

The mother knows deep in her unexplored consciousness that Mary is the clever one of the family, more intellectual, more resourceful, more curious about life than any of the brothers. She tries to keep Mary from learning Greek, because it was Mark who should have learned Greek; she tries to keep her from playing the piano, because she sees how much better Mary could play than she could herself, and how much Mark admires her playing. Every avenue of self-expression that Mary attempts to follow is blocked by her mother, and always for reasons the most praiseworthy. The real reasons Mrs. Olivier never acknowledges, because she can't; she doesn't really see them. Her jealousy is masked under quaint disguises. It is fear for Mary's chances of marriage, lest she become a bluestocking, when the girl's esthetic enthusiasm is aroused by her studying Greek. When Mary is sent home from school because her intellectual precocity is too much for the frail Mid-Victorian curriculum, her mother, deliberately suppressing the fact that they admire her mind at school, leaves her for many of the years of her life under the impression that she has done something disgraceful.

She throws obstacles in the way of every incipient love affair, holding up Aunt Charlotte as a horrible example. As early in Mary's life as the twelve-year-old infatuation for Jimmy Ponsonby, Mark's friend, Mrs. Olivier begins her diabolical work by telling the child that Ponsonby was only making fun of her when he said he loved her. What her mother really felt was a terrible fear of losing Mary. Much later she admits this fear. " 'I don't want my only daughter to go away and leave me.' "

The book is a convincing dramatization of the behavior of people without real intelligence. The members of Mary's immediate family, herself excepted, are propelled by the generative heat of that world illimitable and strange lying below, above, and around the focus of consciousness. Their behavior they call natural, which is only another way of excusing themselves for not being intelligent. Mary comes to be aware of this. It has been made clear to her because her own intelligence and her suffering have driven her through the layers of her self, and in these revivifying waters she has bathed. To get through may have been the dispensation of the grace of God; but it may not have been that alone. There was also at work a strong will and a powerful and courageous mind and a passion for the truth. This passion flamed at the age of thirteen, after she had sat through a family quarrel about the relative values of orthodoxies, when her father had flown into a rage in defense of the Anglican Church, and her steady Aunt Lavvy had become equally irrational in defense of Unitarianism. "The queer thing was that none of them seemed to think that the truth could possibly matter on its own account."

Both the mother and Mark, when held up to the truth by Mary, show glimmerings of intelligence; and these scenes are in the book among the most revealing. Mary and her mother are at last left entirely alone; a softened mother and an older Mary who, though at a terrible expense of spirit, has saved her soul. After one of their long, monotonous evenings together, of playing checkers, and reading aloud, and waiting for ten o'clock and prayers, Mary finds the letter from the

teacher of the school—the letter that praises Mary for her
gifts and for her lovableness. The sight of it revives all the
shock and misery of that very tragic girlhood experience.
"That was the letter you wouldn't let me read." Taxed with
this deception, Mrs. Olivier says innocently: "Really, Mary,
you accuse me of the most awful things." And then, giving
in suddenly, she admits the fact, but says that Mary would
have become even more conceited than she was if she had
been allowed to see that letter. She will not even admit that
she saved it because she was proud of Mary. Then she implies
—still with the same unconscious dishonesty—that Mary had
never cared for her; that Mary had always thought her
stupid. And as if her hidden self had at last found a voice,
Mrs. Olivier tells the truth:

"You weren't like any of the others. I was afraid of you . . . I
felt as if you knew everything I was thinking . . . I suppose I—I
didn't like your being clever. It was the boys I wanted to do
things. Not you . . . I was jealous of you . . . And I was afraid
for my life you'd find it out."

Earlier, Mary has also forced Mark to admit that he had
escaped from home because he was a man and because that
was the only way he could have saved his individuality from
being absorbed by his mother's love. He knew that if he had
stayed he would have been crushed.

"You had to . . . to get away from her sweetness and gentleness,
so that you could be yourself . . . You haven't got away altogether. Half of you still sticks. It'll never get away . . . You'll
never love anybody. You'll never marry."

Mark, who has been accusing her of lying and calling her a
little devil, gives in. "You're right there," he says. But then
he accuses her of not loving their mother. She retorts that
she loves her mother's real self.

"When she is working in the garden, planting flowers with her
blessed little hands, doing what she likes, and when she's reading

the Bible and thinking about God and Jesus, and when she's with you, Mark, happy. That's her real self. I adore it. Selves are sacred . . . I used to wonder what the sin against the Holy Ghost was . . . It's that, not adoring the self in people. Hating it. Trying to crush it."

It is this self that Mary has been fighting for, as she now realizes:

"Ever since I began to grow up I felt there was something about Mamma that would kill me if I let it . . . It's awful fighting her when she is so sweet and gentle. But it's either that or go under . . . She doesn't know she hates me . . . And of course she loved me when I was little. She'd love me now if I'd stay little, so that she could do what she liked with me . . . It's your real self she hates—the thing she can't see and touch and get at—the thing that makes you different."

Although Mary's life appears outwardly to be a complete capitulation and sacrifice to her mother's stupid fear and selfishness, Mary actually achieves an inner life that is safe finally from any violation. Her mystical experience is an ecstasy, an expansion, an assurance of a spiritual reality behind the veil. One night, looking out into her garden, she bursts into tears, as if all the misery and fear and boredom of her life had gathered together to discharge itself.

If I could get out of it all! . . . Her crying stopped with a start, as if somebody had come in and put a hand on her shoulder. Everything went still. She had a sense of happiness and peace suddenly with her there in the room. Not so much her own as the happiness and peace of an immense, invisible, intangible being, of whose life she was thus aware. She knew, somehow, through It, that there was no need to get away; she was out of it all now, this minute. There was always a point where she could get out of it and into this enduring happiness and peace.

It was this awareness that had come to her as a child in brilliant, clear flashes;

it had come again and again in her adolescence, with more brilliant and clearer flashes; then after leaving her for twenty-three years, it had come like this—streaming in and out of her till its ebb and flow were the rhythm of her life.

This experience of mysticism, in which all life seemed to fold its wings, had come to Mary out of the abyss of her anguish. Had she found reality, or had she merely escaped it? Is her cosmic ecstasy a worship of renunciation? If it is, what does it matter? Whether it come from evasion or domination of reality, it is a consummatory experience—expressed with even greater beauty in *The Dark Night,* where Elizabeth, the heroine, walks in her garden, with its larkspurs and the hot smell of the roses, and the tingling spice of the mignonette:

The green tree and the tall blue flowers stand still.
Then suddenly, suddenly, time stood still with them;
Not the tick of a watch, not the beat of a heart, not the tread of
     a thought in the brain,
No sound of any thing;
But hushed peace and an unearthly ecstasy,
While suddenly, in a flash, my garden changed:
The wall and the hot flagged walks were gold,
The larkspurs became a blue light, burning,
The beech-tree a green fire, shining;
And I knew that the light and the fire were the real, secret life
     of the flowers and the trees,
And that God showed himself in the fire and the light.

VII

D. H. LAWRENCE: SONS AND LOVERS

BUT Paul Morel in *Sons and Lovers* achieved no freedom—
not even after his mother's death.

This book, in theme and in discerning insight like *Mary
Olivier,* is wilder, more turbulent in emotion, written with
greater beauty. John Macy has called the book a masterpiece, and many people agree with him that it is a masterpiece

in which every sentence counts, a book crammed with significant
thought and beautiful, arresting phrases, the work of a singular
genius whose gifts are more richly various than those of any
other young English novelist.

Whereas Mary Olivier is a spirit tortured, but working
towards freedom through the orderly ways of the mind, Paul
Morel is caught fast in the toils of his own experience, and
the book is a record of his groping in his confusion.

The important thing is that Mr. Lawrence has created [John
Macy continues] a new version of the old son-mother story
which is more ancient than Sophocles and which shall be a modern instance as long as there are poets and novelists. In its lowest
form it is the sentimental home-and-mother theme so dear, and
rightly dear, to the hearts of the people. In its highest form it is
tragic poetry. And only a little below that poetry is the tremendous pathos of Paul's last whimper in this book.

The world of painting for which Paul Morel lives stimu-
lates his emotional life. Enmeshed in the feelings of the moment, he can never withdraw from his intense affirmation of
sensuous existence to evaluate his own soul. Though he does
not apprehend it then, it is in this crucible that his soul is
being born. He is pitilessly crucified, spirit to flesh, and finds

himself at the last having achieved no peace, only a bitter conviction of the endless, cruel struggle.

Sons and Lovers presents scenes of childhood, adolescence, early manhood. It is a book essentially from the thick of life —life literally picked up and put in the pages, life just as it is lived, stupidly, instinctively, with a few moments of aspiration in which the mystery of existence flits capriciously into consciousness, only to be beaten back or drowned there.

Here are combined and fused the hardest sort of "realism" and almost lyric imagery and rhythm. The speech of the people is that of daily life and the things that happen to them are normal adventures and accidents; they fall in love, marry, work, fail, succeed, die. But of their deeper emotions and of the relations of these little human beings to the earth and to the stars Mr. Lawrence makes something as near to poetry as prose dare be without violating its proper "other harmony."

We do not get the pictures in this book through the eye of the mind alone. Our senses are caught up and opened to all the sounds and sights and smells. As for the human beings, it is as if we were taking the pulse of the family life of the Morels and listening to their breathings, and being aware of their deepest emotional lives. There is never any standing off to make an intellectual appraisal, as in *Mary Olivier*.

Paul Morel's relation with his mother is the heart of *Sons and Lovers,* and Mrs. Morel is the dominating character. In a letter that D. H. Lawrence wrote to Edward Garnett (14 Nov. 1912):

It follows this idea: a woman of character and refinement goes into the lower class, and has no satisfaction in her own life. She has had a passion for her husband, so the children are born of passion, and have heaps of vitality. But as her sons grow up she selects them as lovers—first the eldest, then the second.

The mother urges the sons into life.

But when they come to manhood, they can't love, because their mother is the strongest power in their lives, and holds them . . .

As soon as the young men come into contact with women, there's a split. William gives his sex to a fribble, and his mother holds his soul. But the split kills him, because he doesn't know where he is. The next son gets a woman who fights for his soul—fights his mother. The son loves the mother—all the sons hate and are jealous of the father. The battle goes on between the mother and the girl, with the son as object. The mother gradually proves stronger, because of the tie of blood. The son decides to leave his soul in his mother's hands, and like his elder brother, go for passion. He gets passion. Then the split begins to tell again. But, almost unconsciously, the mother realizes what is the matter, and begins to die. The son casts off his mistress, attends to his dying mother. He is left in the end naked of everything, with the drift towards death.

Lawrence felt that he had written a great book, a great tragic novel. He thought the theme of his book was the tragedy of a number of young men in England. There is underlying the novel a deep moral purpose, a nobility of intention not unlike that of Euripides.

We see Mrs. Morel first, the earnest Puritan daughter of a satirical Puritan father, bewitched by the gaiety of the miner Morel:

The dusky, golden softness of this man's sensuous flame of life that flowed off his flesh like the flame from a candle, not baffled and gripped into incandescence by thought and spirit as her life was, seemed to her something wonderful, beyond her.

We see her after her marriage, living in the corner cottage in the Bottoms in the coal mining town; in her quiet way antagonizing her neighbors with her "airs"; insisting on keeping some contact with the things of the mind, especially after her realization that her husband is incapable of the finer intimacies. We recall her walking up and down the garden in the evening for a breath of air; locked out by her husband one night before Paul's birth, crouching in the

cold summer moonlight, touching the lily and scattering
the yellow pollen on herself, covering her shoulders with
the old rag rug thrown out on the ash heap the day before.
We follow her in her struggle for supremacy over her husband: beginning with her cruel discovery that the furniture
is not paid for, and the house they live in is not their own;
combating Morel's drunkenness; bearing his children. We
watch that relationship die little by little, Mrs. Morel held
to her husband by a love which has been intense, freeing
herself only through agony, tortured that it should be so.
Finally they grow more tolerant of each other—they love
each other less. Mrs. Morel has conquered; she becomes the
center about which the life of the family moves.

Much in this background is sordid, but much also is not.
The children have a happy life of their own, even after they
are old enough to realize the misery of their home, even
after their mother involves them in her own suffering, at
the time Morel is drinking most heavily. In the evenings
they played out around the lamppost, and there were moments, even indoors, when they felt a peaceful joyousness.
They were then living in a house on the brow of a hill, exposed to the full force of the west wind that made the huge,
old ash tree creak and filled the children with terror. "This
terror came in from the shrieking of the tree and the anguish
of the home discord . . . The children lay and breathed the
darkness." They were unable to sleep until they heard their
father put down his shoes and come up the stairs in his stock-
inged feet.

As time goes on, the father is taken for granted, even enjoyed occasionally—when he whistles at some odd job about
the house, mends the pit trousers which are too dirty and
too hard for Mrs. Morel to sew, and makes up to the youngest child Arthur, who has singled out his father especially
for his affection.

Out of the soil of this family life the child Paul grows. And what we follow is the growth of the relationship between Paul and his mother. From the beginning the tie between them is strong and vital: "she felt as if the navel string that connected his frail little body with hers had not been broken . . . with all her force, with all her soul, she would make up to it for having brought it into the world unloved." For he was born at the time when she was painfully freeing herself from her husband, and when the family discord was at its worst. She felt as if this unhappiness had stunned some point in the baby's soul. "She noticed the peculiar knitting of the baby's brows, and the peculiar heaviness of its eyes, as if it were trying to understand something that was pain."

In a terrible scene one evening, not long after Paul's birth, her drunken husband throws the drawer from the table at her. It cuts her head, and the child is baptized in his mother's blood. As the boy grows older he shares his mother's sufferings; and out of these experiences he evolves a private religion—of hatred for his father. When he prays to God, it is to let his father die, though he modifies his prayer by asking God not to let him die down the pit.

Thus we know Paul when, in adolescence and early manhood, he comes to the most intense experiences of his life. Two real efforts he makes during his mother's lifetime to break through to freedom, to cut the cord binding him to her. There is in his behavior a defiance, indicating how hopelessly he is chained. Yet his mother makes no open opposition, no spoken disapproval.

He is drawn first to Miriam, perhaps because she is so much like his mother—strong and courageous, a Puritan, whose hold is upon his mind and spirit rather than upon his senses. Lawrence is unsurpassed in his treatment of this prolonged relationship, in all its phases of varying intensity, in its emotional intricacies. Miriam has a deep passion for nature, a brooding, personal passion that Paul resents, because he fears that he may be so absorbed into this world of Miriam's that his soul will be lost. "To her, flowers appealed with such strength, she felt she must make them part of herself . . . Paul hated her for it."

Their drama is played out in superb scenes on the farm, in the woods and fields. They have many moments of the communion that Miriam reverences and that stir Paul deeply; and when Lawrence writes of these scenes he does so with unusual poetic power:

It was very still. The tree was tall and straggling. It had thrown its briers over a hawthorn-bush, and its long streamers trailed thick, right down to the grass, splashing the darkness everywhere with great spilt stars, pure white. In bosses of ivory and in large splashed stars the roses gleamed on the darkness of foliage and stems and grass. Paul and Miriam stood close together, silent, and watched. Point after point the steady roses shone out to them, seeming to kindle something in their souls. The dusk came like smoke around, and still did not put out the roses.

Paul is not at all clear about the danger of being absorbed by Miriam; he simply feels intuitively a need to struggle against her. His mother is clearer. Her dislike of Miriam arises from jealousy of the woman who, she feels, has the power to draw her son away from herself. She is enough like Miriam to know that she is right when she says: " 'She is one of those who will want to suck a man's soul out, till he has none of his own left.' "

Clara Dawes is the second woman with whom Paul lives intimately. Toward her Mrs. Morel feels no antagonism; she knows that Clara would never absorb Paul's spirit—that what his mother loved most in him would be saved intact for herself. She does not hate Clara because she does not fear her. Nor does she discountenance Paul's relations with her, although Clara is married, lives apart from her husband, and is much older than Paul. Whereas Mrs. Morel is tense, abrupt, emotional, whenever she speaks of Miriam, she can talk quietly and with detachment to Paul about Clara.

Miriam's freedom from jealousy is more puzzling. She knows of Paul's relations with Clara—but perhaps she has an instinctive assurance that Paul will not wander from her for long. Her feeling is thus strangely like Mrs. Morel's: "She could let him go to Clara, so long as it was something that would satisfy a need in him, and leave him free for herself to possess."

Paul was held off from complete and abiding union with Clara or Miriam, first because his was a soul still childishly guarding his ego from annihilation, and therefore always repelled at the moment of merging; and second because he was bound by the slavery of his mother's passionately jealous love. Though there is much antagonism, expressed and un-uttered, between Paul and his mother, it never destroys the beauty that lives between them—the beauty of their com-radeship, their intellectual sympathy, and their love. Paul knows a gaiety with her that he knows nowhere else. He gives her flowers, he touches her hair, buys her a new dress, jokes with her about her stylish hat. When in one very poignant scene his mother tells him in broken phrases that she has never really had a husband, Paul "stroked his mother's hair, and his mouth was on her throat." It is a torture to him when he suddenly realizes that his mother is getting old. During one of their happiest excursions together to Lincoln Cathedral, "He saw her face, the skin still fresh and pink and downy, but crow's-feet near her eyes, her eye-lids steady, sinking a little, her mouth always closed with disillusion." He breaks out bitterly: " 'Why can't a man have a *young* mother? What is she old for?' "

If only he could have hated or despised her, he might

have gained release. But she was not stupid, like Mary Olivier's mother, nor really selfish and really jealous of his development. She was always his intellectual superior, and she intensely desired his success. "Only let him not be wasted" is the cry from her heart.

But we feel the utter futility of this love in helping Paul to a realization of himself. Until he could cut the cord, until he could be the man his mother so wanted him to be, he could never, ironically, respond whole-heartedly to a love that would help him to his mother's ambitions and the fulfillment of his own dreams. In spite of the wisdom of Mrs. Morel and her love for her son, there is that in their life together which constantly tortures Paul, which draws him to his mother only to encounter an incestuous barrier from which he rebounds. And whenever he draws near another woman he feels hovering between herself and him the shadow of his mother. Even at the end, the death of Mrs. Morel marks in the rhythm of Paul's life merely a pause, one believes, before he will swing back through the same path.

Of the style of *Sons and Lovers* Lawrence wrote at the end of 1913 and the beginning of 1914:

I shan't write in the same manner as *Sons and Lovers* again, I think—in that hard, violent style full of sensation and presentation . . . I have no longer the joy in creating vivid scenes, that I had in *Sons and Lovers*. I don't care much more about accumulating objects in the powerful light of emotion, and making a scene of them.

He must have been weary of creation when he made the latter statement. In the novels and stories that followed *Sons and Lovers* are to be found precisely these qualities that he thought he would not manifest again, except that in no subsequent novel did he ever surpass the power of "sensation and presentation" that he displays in *Sons and Lovers*. There seems to be a falling off of intensity in his realizations of external scenes, but only a slight falling off if you consider *The Plumed Serpent* and *Lady Chatterley's Lover*—and this may be explained by a deepening interest in the problems of human relationships.

This struggle—of human beings adjusting to each other—continued to occupy Lawrence in all of his writing. He had, as we know from his work and from his letters, an aching desire to get some original thought expressed. Perhaps he never stated it with sharp articulation. His books are sometimes more bewildering than clarifying. He is even less articulate in his essays where he attempts to state the ideas that his novels are dramatizing. Whatever else may be said of Lawrence, this is true, that he was endeavoring to express some new evaluation of human relationships based upon a recognition of that part of our lives that lies buried deep below our everyday consciousness. He wrote to Edward Garnett:

All the time, underneath, there is something deep evolving itself out in me. And it is *hard* to express a new thing, in sincerity . . . But primarily I am a passionately religious man, and my novels must be written from the depth of my religious experience.

He knew that account must be taken of the warfare inherent in emotional contacts today, a warfare arising from the very human desire for communion, opposed to the jealous watch the soul keeps over its freedom. Knowing this, and building from it, he imagined another order.

You learn to be quite alone, and possess your soul in isolation, and at the same time to be perfectly with someone else . . . taking one's way alone, happily alone in all the wonders of communion, swept up on the wings, but never swept away from one's very self . . . Two eagles in mid-air, grappling, whirling, coming to their intensification of love oneness there in mid-air . . . but all the time each lifted on its own wings.

Lawrence finds all this and more as he delves deep into his own heart. Ironically, the more he tries to be clear about what he finds, the less he achieves and evidently the less he cares to achieve artistry. In his *Studies in Classic American Literature* he offers his Credo to which he has been guided in his search.

That I am I.

That my soul is a dark forest.

That my known self will never be more than a little clearing in the forest.

That gods, strange gods, come forth from the forest into the clearing of my known self, and then go back.

That I must have the courage to let them come and go.

That I will never let mankind put anything over me, but that I will try always to recognize and submit to the gods in me and the gods in other men and women.

Lawrence was aware that there are beasts in this forest too. It is, really, the forest in which Dostoevsky moved about among the beasts and the gods as familiarly as if he had always lived there. It is likewise the forest into which May Sinclair makes excursions with a high-powered searchlight and a gun and brings down interesting specimens. Not only in this enunciation of his Credo, but in his essays and his stories and novels, Lawrence tried with very deep sincerity to fathom his own self. But there was a conflict in him that he never quite transcended. He must have felt this, with all its painful difficulties. There are moments in which this author exhibits an almost uncontrolled hysteria as he painfully extracts each sentence from the deeps of his own labyrinthine mind.

It is a delicate matter to make assertions about the autobiographical elements in the works of novelists. But Miss Sinclair has herself affirmed the truth to her own inner experience of Mary Olivier's story, and the autobiographical nature of the material in *Sons and Lovers* is an uncontradicted commonplace of all comment on D. H. Lawrence. Regarding these books for the time as expressions of their authors' lives, we see a fascinating contrast in the final pages.

We leave Mary in early middle age; Paul Morel is still under thirty; and these ages nearly correspond to those of the authors at the time they wrote the books. The two mothers, the determining influences in the lives of both characters, are dead. Paul, capable of deep emotional experience, has found but a brief moment or two of fulfillment and happiness in his tumultuous and difficult life. Both have expressed their deeper selves, to some degree, in art. Both have a capacity for mystical experience. And in these pages at the end it is the quality of this experience that gives the key to Paul and to Mary.

After the death of his mother, Paul felt behind him "the gap in life, the tear in the veil, through which his life seemed to drift slowly as if he were drawn towards death." He is lost in the void.

Where was he? One tiny upright speck of flesh, less than an ear of wheat lost in the field . . . On every side the immense dark silence seemed pressing him, so tiny a spark, into extinction, and yet, almost nothing, he could not be extinct. Night, in which everything was lost, went reaching out between stars and sun. Stars and sun, a few bright grains, went spinning around for terror, and holding each other in embrace, there in a darkness that outpassed them all, and left them tiny and daunted. So much, and himself, infinitesimal, at the core a nothingness, and yet not nothing.

His agony is the sense that he is not whole, and that he bravely desires to be at one with life; that he knows only this, but not how to gather together the parts of his personality that lie scattered in the past—in his adolescent boyhood, with Miriam and with Clara, and buried with his mother. If, like Mary Olivier, he had found freedom, there would be none of this sick crying out in despair. We should have an authority that derives from the peace that understands because it has grown out of spiritual tumult. But Paul couldn't let himself be drawn through the gap, even if that might have meant the emergence upon a new plane of consciousness. For him there was to be no peace, rather the beating of the eagles' pinions. He could do nothing but turn back to the struggle, with fists clenched and mouth set, to look for some surcease from this tearing of his soul.

Lawrence never found peace. He found only the artist's satisfaction of stating over and over again the crucifixion of his own soul. His novels are all filled with these problems, with the individual's effort and agony to know and realize his own essential self. All of Lawrence's greatest creations exhibit this fearful and difficult need of self-realization. Sometimes his characters are overwhelmed by conventional society; but it is their own inner conflicts that spin their plot, and they are "betrayed by what is false within."

When for many years we have read novel after novel by Lawrence and have found this theme iterated, and one character, in the name of the author (or the very personal author himself) crying out the agony of his need, and pointing the way to a happier life, we must wonder about D. H. Lawrence himself. What were his own difficulties, that he should have taken so many years and expended so much creative energy to find eventually a kind of solution to his problems? One thing Lawrence clearly rebels against—the Pauline conflict; and he seems to be trying always to bind together this Christian cleavage of body and spirit into an integration of man made whole.

In his letters, published shortly after his death, we find this idea stated over and over again, but we find of course much more: kind and charming letters to acquaintances;

letters filled with extremely interesting ideas and entertaining and penetrating comments on personalities and books. We find one friendship (with Middleton Murry) traced from its beginning through its growth to its extermination. We re-create Lawrence the man through his prejudices, his antipathies, his intolerances, and through his devotions, his generosities, and his love. One deeply religious feeling runs through the volume: the man's crucified love of the God within himself. And all of these bear out what he is trying to articulate in his novels.

It is not unusual to be interested in this man's personal life, because, more than most writers of our time, he has struck impressionable young readers with a strong emotional impact. Why is this? Lawrence decries the evils that beset the personality in modern life, and he makes constant statement of his faith in a way to surmount these evils. His novels breathe the fervidness of a dogmatic religion. Lawrence points specifically to what he believes to be bad, evil, and good. All great novelists, perhaps, have been teachers, some of them have been frankly preachers. One cannot help feeling sometimes that Lawrence falls in this latter group. His manner, though not his subject matter, is evangelical "chapel," so it is not at all surprising to read in many of Lawrence's best critics that he is a very religious man. Now, without being pedantic as to the etymology of the word religion, we may take the explanation of Cicero, who believed the word to mean to read or to relate again, and we may also take the way of Augustine, who believed it meant to bind together. Lawrence seems to fit in with both derivations. What he reads is the vision of his own soul (or self) struggling in this world, and there is no peace for him until he can relate all of this again; no peace for the man until he can express himself as artist. In one letter (to A. D. McLeod, dated 27. 10. 3) Lawrence writes: "But one sheds one's sicknesses in books—repeats and presents again one's emotions, to be master of them."

Then, further, having found a way that leads for him toward truth, his desire is to gather those he has taught, to bind them together in this truth for their own salvations. There is much of the Messianic outlook in D. H. Lawrence. The God of whom he had illuminating glimpses, he seems almost surprised to discover is himself—all of him, his good and evil self, his superficial conscious self, and the deeper self of his unconscious, more specifically designated by Lawrence as the self that is motivated and adjusts to existence through the rhythm of the blood.

It is quite an easy matter to find statements of Lawrence's Credo in his essays and in his novels, but we choose this succinct statement of the core of his own religious conviction from a letter written (17 Jan. 13) to his friend Ernest Collinge:

My great religion is a belief in the blood, the flesh, as being wiser than the intellect. We can go wrong in our minds. But what our blood feels and believes and says, is always true. The intellect is only a bit and a bridle. What do I care about knowledge. All I want is to answer to my blood, direct, without fribbling intervention of mind, or moral, or what-not. I conceive a man's body as a kind of flame, like a candle flame, forever upright and yet flowing: and the intellect is just the light that is shed on the things around. And I am not so concerned with the things around—which is really mind—but with the mystery of the flame forever flowing, coming God knows how from out of practically nowhere, and being *itself*, whatever there is around it, that it lights up. We have got so ridiculously mindful, that we never know that we ourselves are anything—we think there are only objects we shine upon . . . My God, I am myself.

But this was evidently easier for Lawrence to state than to achieve. He was a sensitive man, and he felt the problem deeply; because he was a gifted artist, he expresses it often superbly. But in the man the conflict remains, is constant; and his interpretation of life and of letters is colored by the conflict that is himself. You will observe how he includes himself (and all men) in the following statements instigated by his reading of Hawthorne's *The Scarlet Letter:*

Blood-consciousness overwhelms, obliterates, and annuls mind-consciousness.

Mind-consciousness extinguishes blood-consciousness, and consumes the blood.

We are all of us conscious in both ways. And the two ways are antagonistic in us.

They will always remain so.

That is our cross.

Lawrence, gifted with intellect, was damned by it, and the bitter irony of his life was that he knew this. With his mind he posited a more mindless existence in which he had greater faith, but his very knowing process closed to him the entrance into this unself-conscious life of the blood rhythm. Then he says: "For the human soul must suffer its own disintegration, *consciously,* if ever it is to survive." (The italics are the author's.) I have been taught to believe that this was the reflection of Jesus on the cross.

Lawrence, speaking of Poe, says:

Man does so horribly want to master the secret of life and of individuality *with his mind.* It is like the analysis of protoplasm. You can only analyse *dead* protoplasm, and know its constituents. It is a death process.

For the purpose of clarification this conflict can be very simply stated. Here was Lawrence, with senses so delicately organized as to be almost sick, with brilliant intellectual power of analysis, but all of this supported by a body never very robust. He wants to be the kind of man God did not make him. He admires the Italian peasant, growing as it were in and from the soil, with no disturbing intellectual processes, knowing only the rhythms of his blood, responding straightforwardly to his simple bodily needs.

That he could know the desirability of this and never achieve it was his crucifixion. He felt himself doomed, yet he tried to escape that doom. He thought (or sensed is perhaps the better word) that he could be healed of this disease of knowledge by finding primitive races and participating in their rhythms of unconscious being. We have spoken of the Italian peasants. He sought the natives of Ceylon and Australia; the southwest American Indians; the Mexicans. He sought unintegrated and agonizing white souls like himself; he sought, finally, the Etruscans. In every adventure, he found—himself. And a self, again ironically, more knowing, more conscious, more despairing. As you would expect of such an artist, he found the greatest solace in imaginatively re-creating the Etruscans from shreds of archeological evidence. He wrote his final statement of this inner conflict in his book *Apocalypse,* in which the reader feels that Lawrence has expressed a meaning in which at least one individual is most happily at home. That individual is Lawrence himself. It makes one think of John sitting aloft and serene on Patmos and pleased with the beautiful rhetoric of his own imprecations.

It was a circular treadmill that Lawrence panted around in all his life, but in his act in the ring, he gave some splendid exhibitions of new and exciting moral gymnastics. His almost hysterical desire to bring together his disparate selves drove him literally to the farthest places of the earth, and to the farthest reaches of his consciousness, both in the focus and in those deeper and more extended areas that he calls the dark forest of himself. His value is in his beautiful reporting of what he found there. He knew that he was a soul "ordained to fail." But he never wanted really to believe this. It was too desolating. An ultimate statement of his acknowledgment of a kind of defeat is to be found in his essay *On Human Destiny:* "Let us accept our own destiny. Man *can't* live by instinct, because he's got a mind." But he must have some hope, and he continues:

When the Unknown God whom we ignore turns savagely to rend us, from the darkness of oblivion; and when the Life that we exclude from our living turns to poison and madness in our veins: then there is only one thing left to do. We have to struggle for a new glimpse of God and of Life. We have to struggle down to the heart of things, where the everlasting flame is, and kindle ourselves another beam of light. In short, we have to make another bitter adventure in pulsating thought, far, far to the one central pole of energy. We have to germinate, inside us, between our undaunted mind and our reckless, genuine passions, a new germ. The germ of a new idea. A new germ of God-knowledge. But a new germ . . . To plant seed you've got to kill a great deal of weeds, and break much ground.

It was this belief in the deeper self, in this "one central pole of energy," and this piety before it that Lawrence desired above all things to be true to, to respect, and, in a way that is not to be misunderstood as cheap egoism, to be in love with. He early discovered that one revelation of this mystery and beauty in one's own life is through the tangible and deeply mysterious way of sex. To him this was not mere lip-service. The ideal of the divineness of sex was a profound reality, giving the full force, to one who can follow Lawrence's art, of a very religion of beauty. To read anything else than this in his work is, as Aldous Huxley says, to violate most wantonly this artist's deepest and most pious conviction.

Thus, to Lawrence, sex is the white light containing all the color and beauty of life. It taps the source of life—of man's "divine otherness"—what is not, cannot, and should not be known by the intellect, but is "sensed" as a fusion of and as something beyond all sensation—something again most deeply mystical, and therefore, as with Blake, most truly if most personally religious. It was an ideal that he believed could be achieved, though there is evidence to suggest that he himself did not achieve it, because he voices so constantly in his letters and in his novels a vicious antagonism in love. His most unholy fear is to lose himself, to be absorbed. It would seem that he had no understanding and therefore no patience with the idea of losing one's soul to find it.

From the evidence it seems that the very crux of Lawrence's problem is a Puritan tortured by sex maladjustment. I say this because this is precisely what is dramatized in half a dozen or more of his long novels—dramatized often with great tenderness and insight and beauty. But he is not merely the usual Puritan. He was the kind of man who looked deep into himself and found what he would like to be by the sharp contrast with what he was. As artist, he created for himself and for other men an ideal of what sex might become; he resymbolized his own deficiencies and his needs in fictional works of moral value and beauty.

A. B.

VIII

JAMES JOYCE AND ULYSSES

No book in our time has created such a furor as James Joyce's *Ulysses*. It has been suppressed in the United Kingdom and in the United States, and has kindled the fires of the Inquisition. James Joyce says in his letter to Mr. Bennett A. Cerf, April 2, 1932: "Shipments of copies of *Ulysses* were made to America and to Great Britain with the result that all copies were seized and burnt by the Custom authorities of New York and Folkstone."

Intemperate as the official censorship has been, the personal censorships have if possible been even more violent. Repeatedly one hears individual readers denounce the book as immoral, filthy, and obscene. Equally extravagant have been those who indiscriminately lavish upon the book all the praises that can be given to a work of art. They speak glowingly of its multiple wonders—and especially of its architecture, its creation of character, its verbal brilliance, and its initiation of a new genre. And to find a sound critical evaluation in the midst of this confusion is bewilderingly difficult.

The official censorship has now been removed. Within this year *Ulysses* has come at last to be available to any who care to buy or borrow a copy of the Random House edition. Perhaps one of the most reflective critics the book has had is Judge John M. Woolsey, United States District Judge, who wrote the decision establishing the legality for publication of the novel in the United States. He says:

In writing *Ulysses*, Joyce sought to make a serious experiment in a new, if not wholly novel, literary genre . . . Furthermore *Ulysses* is an amazing *tour de force* when one considers the success which has been in the main achieved with such a difficult objective as Joyce set for himself.

Judge Woolsey's considered opinion is that *Ulysses* is a "sincere and honest book."

The case was carried up to the United States Circuit Court of Appeals for the Second Circuit, in order, if possible, to reverse Judge Woolsey's decision. Early in August, 1934, the court handed down its decision: Judges L. and Augustus N. Hand affirmed the lower court's decision; Judge Manton dissented. The dissenting opinion states:

Who can doubt the obscenity of this book after a reading of the pages referred to, which are too indecent to add as a footnote to this opinion? Its characterization as obscene should be quite unanimous by all who read it.

The opinion continues:

The people do not exist for the sake of literature; to give the author fame, the publisher wealth and the book a market. On the contrary, literature exists for the sake of the people; to refresh the weary, to console the sad, to hearten the dull and downcast, to increase man's interest in the world, his joy of living and his sympathy in all sorts and conditions of men.

And Judge Manton adds: "Masterpieces have never been produced by men given to obscenity or lustful thoughts— men who have no Master."

The affirming judges speak of *Ulysses* as a pioneer book in the

stream of consciousness method of presentation . . . It attempts to depict the thoughts and lay bare the souls of a number of people, some of them intellectuals, and some social outcasts, and nothing more, with a literalism that leaves nothing unsaid. Certain of its passages are of a beauty and undoubted distinction, while others are of a vulgarity that is extreme and the book as a whole has a realism characteristic of the present age . . . But it is fair to say that it is a sincere portrayal with skilful artistry of the "stream of consciousness" of its characters . . . The net effect even of portions most open to attack, such as the closing monologue of the wife of Leopold Bloom, is pitiful and tragic rather than lustful. The book depicts the souls of men and women that are by turns bewildered and keenly apprehensive, sordid and aspiring, ugly and beautiful, hateful and loving. In the end one feels, more than anything else, pity and sorrow for the confusion, misery and degradation of mankind.

But all the affirming judges are in full agreement with many readers and critics that *Ulysses* is a very difficult book.

That is true. The novel is sometimes brilliant, sometimes dull, often unintelligible, occasionally a "strong draught" for even the most seasoned of adult readers. It is because of this difficulty that I have attempted to give in the following pages a very brief résumé of the book. Such a résumé may have but little interest for those who are familiar firsthand with *Ulysses,* unless it be to match their insight against mine; but for those readers who have encountered the difficulties and been momentarily subdued by them, this résumé may spare them the discipline of ever reading the book.

Ulysses opens with Stephen Dedalus, and in a sense it closes with him. The last pages of Mrs. Bloom's reverie bring him very vividly into the picture. Though Stephen appears a great deal throughout the novel, and is a very important character, he is not the focusing character. Leopold Bloom is the hero, and we have very little difficulty in coming to know Bloom well. But there is more difficulty in understanding Stephen, unless we are familiar with Joyce's earlier book, *A Portrait of the Artist as a Young Man,* in which the life of Stephen Dedalus is presented fully up to that moment when he leaves Dublin for Paris. *Ulysses* begins shortly after Stephen has been called back to Dublin by the illness of his mother. So far as the delineation of Stephen is concerned, then, *Ulysses* is a continuation of the *Portrait.* But whereas the *Portrait* covers a period of about twenty years, *Ulysses* covers, in action, one day: Thursday, June 14, 1904, in the City of Dublin. The greatest space of *Ulysses* deals with Bloom and there is a constant reaching back into

earlier years in order to complete the character. All of
Bloom's background is built up in *Ulysses* itself. In the de-
lineation of Stephen, Joyce presumes a familiarity with the
Portrait. That is why it is necessary for an understanding of
Ulysses that the *Portrait* should be read first.

In the *Portrait* we first meet Stephen as quite a little boy,
a student at Clongowes Wood College, and a very homesick
boy he is. "He longed to be at home and lay his head on his
mother's lap . . . He thought that he was sick in his heart
if you could be sick in that place." Later he is ill and he
writes: "Dear Mother, I am sick. I want to go home. Please
come and take me home. I am in the infirmary. Your fond
son, Stephen." He thinks he may die, even on a bright and
sunny day, and he imagines his funeral, the tolling of the
bell, the Mass; and he says over a song that his nurse had
taught him.

> Dingdong! The castle bell!
> Farewell, my mother!
> Bury me in the old churchyard
> Beside my eldest brother . . .

The words of his own dirge were so beautiful to him that in
their beauty he forgot his own mortality and a "tremor
passed over his body." "He wanted to cry quietly, but not
for himself: for the words, so beautiful and sad, like music."

These passages are premonitory of the Stephen we are to
see on a Thursday in 1904. In the artist's love for words he
never changes; as Joyce has never changed. In his love for
his mother, there are to be accidental changes, none that are
essential; his love for her comes to be complicated with
religion, with the collapse of the Dedalus family fortunes,
and with the restrictions that both place upon the young
man's free development as an artist.

The boy comes home from college for the Christmas holi-
days, and the Christmas Day dinner is broken up by the in-

trusion into the conversation of Parnell, the priests of the
Church, and Irish politics. This rather famous dinner scene
in the *Portrait* is the epitome of a crisis in Stephen's life: in
the maelstrom of such seething Irish political passions, where
at all is the place for the artist? What the boy then felt deep
within him, he will have to bring to the clear light of consciousness later in his life.

Stephen does not return to Clongowes, and "he understood in a vague way that his father was in trouble," and
that was the reason for his not returning. At home, he "did
not want to play. He wanted to meet in the real world the
unsubstantial image which his soul so constantly beheld."
All of the complacent middle-class snobbishness that his
father dins into Stephen—and he accents this as his own
fortunes ebb—means nothing to the boy. He is interested in
other things. "Nothing moved him or spoke to him from the
real world unless he heard it in an echo of the infuriated
cries within him." In Cork with his father and his father's
cronies, with their drinking and singing and gossip and his
father's showing off before the boy—in all of this confusion
around him, Stephen felt only that an "abyss of fortune or
of temperament sundered him from them." Only, at the
moment, in poetry is he able to "forget his own human and
ineffectual grieving." It is the voice of the artist crying
through his heart, exorcising his alienation by a potent magic
in words.

Then he goes with a prostitute, and the overwhelming
consequence of that adolescent act is at first a sense of blessed
release. At this time he is at Belvedere under the Jesuits,
and their insistence upon doctrine sinks into Stephen's mind
only to call forth a long and agonizing questioning of faith.
With the other little brothers in Christ Stephen attends a
retreat, and there the eloquently rhetorical priest admon-
ishes the children to put away worldly thought, to serve only

God's will and save their immortal souls. He takes them cinematographically through death and judgment; Adam and Eve and the Fall, to the coming of Christ, and thence to a sermon on Hell which, for fire and brimstone and the unholy machinations imposed upon an innocent Deity by the morbid imaginings of men exulting in the fall from grace, is probably not elsewhere to be matched either in sacred or profane letters. There is the calling forth of conscience, the implacable focusing upon guilt and the sense of sin. For the young Stephen, this does the trick. He returns to his room, drags himself to bed, cannot sleep, experiences a ghastly nightmare. "He flung the blankets from him madly to free his face and neck . . . He stumbled towards the window, groaning and almost fainting with sickness. At the washstand a convulsion seized him within; and, clasping his cold forehead wildly, he vomited profusely in agony." A step in Stephen's purification. He prays, he feels better, he will confess his sins. And he does confess, to a kindly and understanding priest, is given absolution, and receives the sacrament. But before that: "He knelt to say his penance, praying in a corner of the dark nave: and his prayers ascended to heaven from his purified heart like perfume streaming upwards from a heart of white rose."

For a short time the idea of becoming a priest engages him, but stronger than that impulse is his love for words. At this time he is sixteen, a confused boy, yet with all his confusions working together in that mysterious way that they do work for the bringing to birth of the artist. What is it about words, he reflects, that so entrances him? Their colors? Poise and balance, rhythmic rise and fall?

Or was it that, being as weak of sight as he was shy of mind, he drew less pleasure from the reflection of the glowing sensible world through the prism of a language manycoloured and richly storied than from the contemplation of an inner world of individual emotions mirrored perfectly in a lucid supple periodic prose.

The moment that he had always known would come, when he would encounter in the real world the image that his soul so constantly beholds, comes at last and unexpectedly. He meets some of his friends bathing, and the knowledge is born. It is precipitated by his friends calling the magic of his name. " 'Stephanos Dedalos! Bous Stephanoumenos! Bous Stephaneforos!' "

Now, at the name of the fabulous artificer, he seemed to hear the noise of dim waves and to see a winged form flying above the waves and slowly climbing the air . . . His heart trembled in an ecstasy of fear and his soul was in flight . . . He would create proudly out of the freedom and power of his soul . . .

This whole scene is as fine as anything Joyce has ever written. The vision is the world of the artist and the flight is his joyful meeting of the challenge. He will in the years be dragged back to the bewildering and soul-sickening realities, but never for long.

In the midst of increasing poverty and squalor, Stephen goes on with his studies at the University. He comes to hate his father, and to feel increasing pity for his mother and for the other children. Through all of this he is trying to save himself; not to be lost in the domestic upheaval; not to be engulfed with the rest of them. His one refuge is his own mind and his own creative reverie; the poet within him that he must be true to, even though he is accused by all the world outside. The accusations of his own conscience in not giving up his life and his gifts to aid his father's family he can bury deep in his own heart.

His thinking was a dusk of doubt and self-mistrust, lit up at moments by the lightnings of intuition . . . [and at these moments] he felt that the spirit of beauty had folded him round like a mantle and that in reverie at least he had been acquainted with nobility.

During his university years Stephen's mind grows more and more in relentless clarity; he distrusts the theology of the orthodox; he sees through the politics, particularly the politics of Ireland, and he will have nothing to do with them. There is a dedication within him that he cannot very easily share with others. His friends bring pressure to bear that he take some interest in the cause of Irish liberty; that he use his reason less logically against theological questions of faith. Davin says to him: " 'You're a born sneerer, Stevie.' " Davin wonders, what with the strange name of Dedalus, and Stephen's ideas, his unashamed personal revelations, his apathy about politics, whether he is Irish at all. " 'This race and this country and this life produced me. I shall express myself as I am,' " Stephen replies. Davin argues and pleads for patriotism (nationalism) until he finally produces this retort from Stephen:

"No honourable and sincere man has given up to you his life and his youth and his affections from the days of Tone to those of Parnell but you sold him to the enemy or failed him in need or reviled him and left him for another. And you invite me to be one of you. I'd see you damned first."

Davin reminds him that these patriots died for their ideals. And Stephen says:

"The soul . . . has a slow and dark birth, more mysterious than the birth of the body. When the soul of a man is born in this country there are nets flung at it to hold it back from flight. You talk to me of nationality, language, religion. I shall try to fly by those nets . . . Do you know what Ireland is? Ireland is the old sow that eats her farrow."

In a calmer moment with his friend Lynch, Stephen says:

"To speak of those things and to try to understand their nature and, having understood it, to try slowly and humbly to express, to press out again, from the gross earth or what it brings forth, from sound and shape and colour which are the prison gates of our soul, an image of the beauty we have come to understand —that is art."

The mood in which the young Stephen leaves Dublin is described in two places toward the very end of the *Portrait.* First, he tells his friend Cranly:

"I will not serve that in which I no longer believe, whether it call itself my home, my fatherland or my church: and I will try to express myself in some mode of life or art as freely as I can and as wholly as I can, using for my defence the only arms I allow myself to use, silence, exile and cunning."

The book ends on a note of audacious prophecy:

"April 26. I go to encounter for the millionth time the reality of experience and to forge in the smithy of my soul the uncreated conscience of my race."

All of this lies behind Stephen when we open the first page of *Ulysses,* and are told that "Stately plump Buck Mulligan" calls from the stairhead to Stephen Dedalus to come up and be talked to whilst Mulligan shaves. Stephen is twenty-two. He is sharing summer quarters with Mulligan and Haines, an Englishman, in an abandoned fortress tower near the bay. He has been called back to Dublin because of his mother's illness. And those last days before her death are in his mind. He remembers the Fergus's song he had sung for her.

"I sang it alone in the house, holding down the long dark chords. Her door was open: she wanted to hear my music. Silent with awe and pity I went to her bedside. She was crying in her wretched bed. For those words, Stephen: love's bitter mystery."

He remembers too the vision of his mother in a dream— though this is somewhat later—and he cries out: " 'No, mother. Let me be and let me live.' "

Before she died his mother had asked him to pray for her

soul, and out of his hardly won intellectual pride of a resolved apostasy from the Roman Catholic Church, he had
refused. His refusal haunts and tortures him throughout this
day, and it must be kept in mind if one is to grasp the
motivation of much of Stephen's thought and behavior. The
spiritual wound is kept open by Mulligan, a blaspheming,
mocking, shallow medical student, who tells Stephen that
his aunt says that Stephen, when he refused to pray, killed
his mother. Stephen admits that someone killed her. But
after a day of brooding in agony over this accusation and
all that it implies of social opprobrium, Stephen in the house
of prostitution in the nighttown scene, cries out that he did
not kill his mother; that cancer killed her.

It is not only because of his mother's death that he feels
pain and conscience-stricken remorse. His being called back
from the Continent has for the time being broken his career,
and he is weary and hopeless and discouraged. He had refused to pray when his dying mother had asked him to
because he feels that her religion is one of the nets settling
upon him that he had said he would try to fly by. But there
is not peace in his heart because his refusal, he knows, if it
did not kill his mother, broke her heart.

Pain, that was not yet the pain of love, fretted his heart. Silently,
in a dream she had come to him after her death, her wasted body
within its loose brown graveclothes giving off an odour of wax
and rosewood, her breath, that had bent upon him, mute, re-
proachful, a faint odour of wetted ashes.

Before this day and night have passed, Stephen must find
some resolution of this fretting pain.

Though he keep his career and his ambitions safe and
inviolable in his heart, yet he has the practical problem of
earning his living. He has a job at this time, teaching in a
boys' school—work that he particularly detests. There is no
place for him in his father's house. But he would not have

gone there anyway; it is too utterly painful to him to see his sisters struggling in the midst of a heartbreakingly squalid poverty; for another reason—he hates his father. Stephen had loved his mother, and he must be able in time to live at peace with her memory. His father he has really never loved. Near the end of the *Portrait* Stephen had traced satirically his father's downward career:

"A medical student, an oarsman, a tenor, an amateur actor, a shouting politician, a small landlord, a small investor, a drinker, a good fellow, a storyteller, somebody's secretary, something in a distillery, a taxgatherer, a bankrupt and at present a praiser of his own past."

And we shall see Mr. Simon Dedalus in the course of *Ulysses,* and know with his son that there are sometimes more important values in life than filial piety. Some kind of father Stephen is nevertheless seeking. He will find only a stopgap approximation to his ideal late this night in his encounter with Leopold Bloom.

The book proceeds with the wanderings of Leopold Bloom and Stephen Dedalus as the chief characters throughout the day and night: a day and night momentous because of the crises it marks in the lives of each of these men. The second scene of the day's progress is one of the finest in the book for its truth and illumination; it is in the schoolroom with Stephen teaching the little boys. He helps young Sargent do his sums, and in Sargent he sees his own unhappy boyhood days at school; he thinks of Sargent's mother, and of his own mother. Mr. Deasy, the headmaster, pays Stephen his wages, and gives him the usual conventional advice about always paying your way, never owing anything. Mr. Deasy also gives Stephen a letter he has written about the foot-and-mouth disease and asks him to use his influence among his literary friends to have it printed. Stephen will do him the favor;

but Mr. Deasy and his letter and the subject matter represent to Stephen the futility and the stupidity of many of his own people.

A difficult section follows, in which Stephen wanders along the shore, alone with his reveries. It is important, because here is the first opportunity we have to begin to look into the most secret places of the young man's heart. With much distaste he recalls visiting his aunt and uncle, and he knows with greater certainty than ever that for a man like himself, desiring to create, beauty will not come to birth in the atmosphere of his family. He turns his irony upon himself, remembering all the things he had planned to write, and behind the irony lies a profound discouragement. " 'Who ever anywhere will read these written words?' " Yet one must stand, and one must stand alone. His father's telegram comes to mind: " 'Mother dying come home father.' " And instantly Paris is in his thought, and his present unhappy, trapped existence, and his interrupted work.

Here the hero is introduced: "Mr. Leopold Bloom ate with relish the inner organs of beasts and fowls." Mr. Leopold Bloom is a resident of Dublin, half Jew, half Irish. He is the husband of Marion Bloom, a concert singer, and what you might call a well-known "woman about town." In the course of his life (Bloom is now in his late thirties) he has had all sorts of jobs. He had begun as a traveling salesman for his father's firm, selling little toys and knickknacks. The business had failed, and the father had taken poison in an Ennis hotel. At the present moment, Bloom is soliciting advertisements, a difficult life for his unassertive temperament. What he would like to achieve is the management of his wife's concerts. But that has been taken over by a flashy individual named Blazes Boylan, who is Molly Bloom's cur-

rent lover. All of this Bloom knows. He knows perfectly well
that on this day he will be cuckolded. Molly's whole life
with Bloom has been made up of such affairs. Bloom resents
this, but not having the vitality or the courage to act, his
resentment dams up within him as a form of brooding, hurt
jealousy—with a futile desire to find revenge in sporadic and
cheap and sentimental affairs. Underlying all of Bloom's behavior are his consciousness of personal failure and his sense
of persecution. One wonders whether or not he really loves
Molly; in any event, he is constantly remembering his wife
in nearly every contact he has throughout these twenty-four
hours, and it is chiefly through this constant recollection that
the character of Molly is presented to us so that we are more
or less prepared for the staggering forty pages of reverie with
which *Ulysses* closes. It is of course the ego of Bloom that is
repeatedly hurt by his wife's attitude toward him. He thinks
that he might well give Molly a divorce and be rid of her;
but he is rather a canny person, shrewd in a petty way, and
he thinks that if he could manage a concert tour for her, she
would be a good "property."

They have had two children. Millicent, the daughter,
about sixteen, has been sent away from home to work; really
she has been got out of the house by her father so as not to
be in the atmosphere of a home regularly sullied by adultery.
They had had a son, Rudy, who had lived only a few weeks.
This loss had been a terrible blow to Molly, and we suspect
from her reverie that it in some way accounts for her pro-
miscuous life. As for Bloom, he has never recovered from
the loss. In every crisis of his life the vision of Rudy appears. His lack of confidence in himself, his vacillation, his
ineffectualness and his futility all take something of their
complexion from little Rudy's death. He has lived his life
dominated by this regret, and has gone around in circles.
Bloom has a kind of intelligence, but it helps him very little

in his practical life. He has been seeking always for the symbolical equivalent of a son; someone who will give purpose and direction to his life, someone to love. He will have a glimpse of this ideal when he rescues Stephen from the gutter of nighttown and takes him home.

Bloom is much less aware of what is happening to him than Stephen is, for Stephen is a most intelligent and intellectual young man—one who has formed the habit in early life of reflecting, of examining his conscience, of weighing the qualities and the motives and the conduct of other people as well as of himself, and who has to a marked degree what André Gide says is so important for a writer— the capacity for "depersonalization." Bloom has nevertheless come in his own way to a place in his life where he feels he cannot go on as before. The morning begins for him as hundreds of mornings have begun. He gets up, feeds the cat, quietly goes in to his wife, asks her if there is anything she wants, says he is going round to the corner, will be right back; goes to the butcher's, buys a kidney, and comes home. But this takes about four pages, because what Bloom actively does is unimportant. What his reveries are in the little journey to the corner are of significance. He sees a young girl, hurries out of the shop to follow her and to be titillated by his own lascivious thoughts; he recalls Marion Bloom as a young girl in Gibraltar; he dreams for a vivid moment of a little place in the sun for himself—a recurring, atavistic reverie—perhaps an orange grove or an immense melon field some place north of Jaffa. The sunny Mediterranean! It was there he had met Molly, and there she had consented to marry him because she thought him strangely foreign. These wistful Levantine longings have been induced by a company circular extolling the advantages of settling in Palestine or Syria. Anything, he feels, to get himself and Molly out of this Dublin life, where he is constantly made to feel an alien.

He cooks breakfast for himself and for Molly, and carries her breakfast upstairs to her on a tray. This is an established rite. Then he reads a letter that has arrived from Milly. Rudy, he thinks, would now be eleven if he had lived.

Perhaps no writer has so perfectly realized the importance of man's bodily functions as Joyce. It has been a convention in fiction that calls of nature can very well be taken for granted, that they are not a part of life that should be introduced into art. As a result any comment on this aspect of life rarely gets into criticism. Yet when one stops to think of it, how very important these natural processes are: how dependent is man's mental outlook upon the regularity and health of these functions! A man's food, digestion, elimination make a man what he is. In any event Joyce has included this part of life—not, as some people contend, merely to be nasty, but because he is aware of its significance. He has described fully the sensations and the reverie that Bloom experiences during this part of his morning rituals. I have heard it said that such a character as Tom Jones would be more credible and vivid to us if once in that long book we had been told that his great good health, his lustiness, his virtues of character were closely attributable to his perfect digestion and the rest.

His morning rituals performed, Bloom goes for a walk to the post office where he receives a letter addressed to himself as Mr. Henry Flower. It is from a cheap little girl named Martha. This is the pathetic and furtive liaison he is carrying on in revenge, as he hopes, for Molly's abundantly adulterous life. Bloom carries the letter about with him and often thinks about Martha, and the whole thing makes one feel rather sad and ashamed, for that is the way Bloom feels about it himself. Yet if he thinks about Martha once, he thinks about Molly a hundred times . . . He drops into a church. His thoughts are hardly those of a devout believer,

but they are the thoughts of a man who has at least one passion—for music. He names over some of his favorite works of sacred music; he remembers how some of the old popes were great lovers and patrons of that art; is struck with the remembrance that they had eunuchs in their choirs. And this leads him to thoughts of sexuality—his chief obsession. " 'Eunuch. One way out of it.' " Then he goes to a public bath, and bathes, because he is going to the funeral of Paddy Dignam at eleven o'clock.

Bloom rides in the same carriage with Mr. Simon Dedalus to the funeral, and at one point in the progress Bloom sees Stephen and mentions him to Simon, who has failed to see his son but asks Bloom, "Was that Mulligan cad with him? His *fidus Achates?* No, Mr. Bloom said, he was alone." Bloom hasn't seen Stephen for many years, not since the boy was about five or six, but of course Bloom has heard about him, Stephen having already gained somewhat of a reputation as a poet. Again Bloom remembers: "If little Rudy had lived. See him grow up. Hear his voice in the house. Walking beside Molly in an Eton suit. My son. Me in his eyes. Strange feeling it would be." This is significant, because it reminds us that there are really two kinds of impulsions to reverie that are this day in conflict in Bloom. One set is the sexual, that he as a morbid, lonely man knows. These impulsions are thoughts that send him ever deeper within himself; they are uncreative, barren, really self-destroying. The other set revolves around little Rudy, the idea, the hope of a son; these are thoughts that lead him out of himself, that make him desire to lose himself in an outside interest in order to find his own soul.

A very fine piece of writing, as Joe Hynes might say, is this account of the funeral. It is amazingly well realized in the easier method of Joyce's *Dubliners;* and it has humor both in dialogue and in comment. It helps much in the characterization of Bloom, in that it shows us his contacts with a few of his Dublin acquaintances. We have, up to this place, seen Bloom at home, with Molly. Now we find out what he thinks of some of his friends and what they think of him. Mr. Power asks how the concert tour is getting on, and Bloom knows then that the other three men in the hack know about Molly and Blazes Boylan. But he must not let them know that he knows they know. He carries it off, but the hurt has been done. It is bad enough for a man to know that he is being cuckolded; it is even more humiliating to know that outsiders share the knowledge. And it is even harder for a man like Bloom—sensitive, weak, and feeling persecuted—to undergo the social effort of concealment. It is not surprising that Bloom suffers the unfocused anxieties and apprehensions of a man too hopelessly turned in upon himself. Yet there is evidence that Bloom rather loves to suffer, for he knows that if a man hurts him, that man will later be sorry; and so Bloom will "get the pull over him that way." At the same time Bloom has sense enough to realize the sterility of such an attitude. But he has not sufficient intelligence and vitality to combat it within himself. The courage must be injected from without; or rather something from without will have to stimulate within him more self-respecting impulses that may lead to courageous action. At this point in the book, one feels that perhaps in his love for Stephen he may find his stimulation.

The press may reflect a people accurately and it may not. Here in *Ulysses* is a series of mock editorials, news stories, letters, comments. They are funny, they are irresponsible, they are satirical, they are profound. There is a gusto in this part of the book. It is broken up, each subject pointed, and easy to read. There is no doubt that Joyce exposes and dissects the press; and there isn't much in Irish life that he misses. Bloom has come to the newspaper office in his line of duty—soliciting advertisements. He doesn't stay long, but in this brief glimpse, we see how essentially jealous his nature is. It is a mild, not a monstrous jealousy, true to his weak character, sick indeed with a pale and confused thought. Shortly after Bloom leaves, Stephen comes in, and blushingly gives Mr. Deasy's letter to Myles Crawford, the editor. Professor MacHugh is there, and Ned Lambert. Lambert had a little earlier indicated the intelligent Irishman's disgust with Irish political and sentimental oratory and bombast. Stephen would see eye to eye with him about that. Then the Professor: " 'We were always loyal to lost causes. Success for us is the death of the intellect and of the imagination.' " That also Stephen would subscribe to. But while all of this active and practical Dublin life of commonplace affairs is whirling about Stephen, he lives in his own thoughts. The editor will print the letter, he tells Stephen.

Then comes an important moment.

The editor laid a nervous hand on Stephen's shoulder.—I want you to write something for me, he said. Something with a bite in it. You can do it. I see it in your face . . . Give them something with a bite in it. Put us all into it, damn its soul.

This brings forth from those present recollections of the past: Mr. J. J. O'Molloy, who has not accomplished all that his gifts had promised, excuses himself by recalling an old murder case and the brilliant defense of a great lawyer named Seymour Bushe. Why had O'Molloy himself not had that kind of success? He had the gifts. The feeling is, will young Stephen here, whom they like, and who has real gifts, be able to work out his potentialities; or will he grow up to become like themselves? In their own lights they outline careers for him. O'Molloy quotes a bit of the rhetorical oratory of the past, and asks Stephen if he likes it. "Stephen, his blood wooed by grace of language, blushed." That is Stephen's only reply, except to take one of Mr. O'Molloy's cigarettes.

No doubt Myles Crawford was very sincere in what he said to Stephen, but he didn't know the young man. His bite and Stephen's bite are not the same, but the editor's words made an impression. Put them all—these Dubliners—in it; and write something with a bite in it. Damn their souls. Yes, Stephen would do that. But had any one of them any realization of what that meant to him? To write of them truly, from the deeps of his own temperament, he would have first to face the certainty of giving up Ireland, and doing to them what they could only feel to be calumniation, full of hatred, bitterness, despair. The very depth of his hatred indicates the measure of his desire to love a regenerated and enlightened Irish people. But he is not ready yet to write of them. To the professor he says: " 'Dublin. I have much, much to learn.' " He adds: " 'I have a vision, too.' "

Bloom enters with his futile soliciting, revealing how completely out of date his ideas are, and making one realize how his forced interest, born out of the necessity to live, is yet a violation of his temperament. Bloom is royally rebuked by Myles Crawford, and as Bloom watches Stephen move along with the editor, he reflects: "Wonder is that young Dedalus the moving spirit." If Dedalus stands with them, Bloom is obliged to feel, he must of necessity be against me. But Bloom doesn't know young Dedalus very well as yet. Nor does Stephen suspect that it will be Bloom who will be the only one to understand something of what the young writer hopes to do and whose understanding will help him.

Proceeding through DEAR DIRTY DUBLIN Stephen encounters LIFE ON THE RAW. His observations are keen; he will use this material some time.

Bloom walks along the streets, and from his thoughts we
gain more knowledge of him and of Molly. An evangelical
pamphlet attracts his attention. "Are you saved?" This is a
question that in its larger significance concerns Bloom, and
it concerns young Dedalus as well. In this they have common cause. Orthodoxically Bloom is saved. He has been
thrice baptized; the third time in the Roman Catholic
Church, in the hope probably that that would make him
more Irish, less alien. He remembers Spain. "Before Rudy
was born." He sees one of Simon Dedalus's daughters outside Dillon's auction rooms, and he thinks she must be selling off some furniture. "Home always breaks up when the
mother goes." The richness of this part, the ingenious manipulation of the reverie you will have to accept on my statement until you read it. To choose salient bits that will fit
into the scheme of such a brief paraphrase of the novel as
this is difficult. But this it is important to know, that when
Bloom meets his old friend Mrs. Breen, he learns from her
that Mina Purefoy is at the lying-in hospital enduring the
third day of an agonizingly long childbirth. Bloom is moved,
and he vows to call at the hospital and inquire for Mrs.
Purefoy. From a mood as deeply human as this, Bloom's
thought jumps to the sight of a young woman whose stock-
ings are loose over her ankles. A thing he detests . . . He
dislikes the dreamy, cloudy Esthetes. He thinks a certain
kind of food may produce their thin and decadent work.
"For example one of those policemen sweating Irish stew
into their shirts; you couldn't squeeze a line of poetry out
of him." His thought shifts again to Molly: he had been
happier in the past, when he was twenty-eight and Molly was
twenty-three. But you can't bring back the old time. His
little Martha calls him her poor naughty little boy who is
not happy in his home, and she wants to sew on buttons for
him. He must write her an answer in the library. "With

hungered flesh obscurely, he mutely craved to adore." Not Martha, but Molly—or maybe, Stephen.

The first place he stops in for lunch is such a filthy eating house that Bloom can't endure it and leaves. At another place he gets a cheese sandwich and meets Nosey Flynn who brings the talk around to Blazes Boylan. "A warm shock of air heat of mustard haunched on Mr. Bloom's heart." He looks at the clock; only two. It is not yet time for Boylan and Molly to be together. And this arouses a reverie in Bloom that circles poignantly around sex. In this mood on his way to the library he catches a glimpse of Blazes Boylan. A comic and pathetic scene follows wherein Bloom manages to escape being seen by his wife's lover.

The place is the National Library where Stephen goes to read. He meets there some friends, and some of the literary men of Dublin, with whom he finds it exciting to match his wits. In the discussion that follows, Stephen in effect composes an essay of impressionistic criticism on Shakespeare. His interest hovers chiefly around the father-son relationship in *Hamlet,* and, as he develops his ideas, he makes clear certain analogies with his own son-father problem. Stephen tries to reconstruct the early life of Shakespeare, using material from the plays themselves. One of the men present, Russell, says there is little value critically in probing the gossip of the poet's life; that we have the plays— *Lear* for example, and that is immortal. Stephen does not agree, and where he has not sufficient evidence to work with, he will supplement with the internal evidence from the plays, and with his own imagination. He will create. For Stephen believes that there is one strong idea, perhaps obsession, that directed the work of Shakespeare's mind.

But before he states his ideas, those present reflect generally and specifically about the problems of the artist, about esthetics. The Quaker librarian speaks, and John Eglinton, Mr. Best, Russell—and later Buck Mulligan appears. Russell says that all these questions about the historicity of Shakespeare are purely academic. " 'Art has to reveal to us ideas, formless spiritual essences. The supreme question about a work of art is out of how deep a life does it spring.' " But Stephen believes it is necessary to remember that Shakespeare—or any poet—was boy and young man first, and that in some experience of deep intensity in early manhood may be discovered the reasons or explanations for his unique creations. He would work back to this through a consideration of *Hamlet*. He reconstructs the time, the place, the performance of *Hamlet,* and Shakespeare himself one of the players.

"Elizabethan London lay as far from Stratford as corrupt Paris lies from virgin Dublin . . . The flag is up on the playhouse by the bankside . . . Canvasclimbers who sailed with Drake chew their sausages among the groundlings . . . Shakespeare has left the huguenot's house in Silver street and walks by the swanmews along the riverbank . . . The play begins. A player comes on under the shadow, made up in the castoff mail of a court buck, a wellset man with a bass voice. It is the ghost, the king, a king and no king, and the player is Shakespeare who has studied *Hamlet* all the years of his life which were not vanity in order to play the part of the spectre. He speaks the words to Burbage, the young player who stands before him beyond the rack of cerecloth, calling him by a name: *Hamlet, I am thy father's spirit* bidding him list. To a son he speaks, young Hamlet and to the son of his body, Hamnet Shakespeare, who has died in Stratford that his namesake may live forever."

What does this signify? That Shakespeare feels himself to be the murdered father, Hamlet the dispossessed son, and the mother the guilty queen—Ann Hathaway. Eglinton protests that there is nothing to be gained in disinterring the laid ghost of Ann. But Stephen believes that Shakespeare's secret is closely related to Ann. He thinks of her as wife and mother, and this leads him with a circling repetition of pain to think of his own mother and the deathbed scene he has recently been through.

"Mother's deathbed. Candle. The sheeted mirror. Who brought me into this world lies there, bronzelidded, under few cheap flowers. *Liliata rutilantium.* I wept alone."

He proceeds with his argument. Why should Shakespeare, who created some of the most beautiful women, have chosen " 'the ugliest doxy in all Warwickshire to lie withal.' " It is true he left her and gained the world of men. The answer is that Shakespeare did not choose; he was chosen; he was seduced by Ann Hathaway, who was older than he. " 'If others have their will Ann hath a way.' " This must have been followed by Shakespeare's withdrawal, for the later plays show a reconciliation with Ann, and that would be impossible, Stephen insists, unless there had first been a sundering. This early experience with Ann has maimed Shakespeare. " 'Belief in himself has been untimely killed. He was overborne in a cornfield first (ryefield, I should say) and he will never be a victor in his own eyes after nor play victoriously the game of laugh and lie down.' " Shakespeare's creations are in part determined by this belief in himself untimely killed. " 'He goes back, weary of the creation he has piled up to hide him from himself, an old dog licking an old sore.' " But Stephen feels that it may be the very loss of belief in himself that drove Shakespeare to build it up again through his work. Of the poet Stephen says: " 'He passes on towards eternity in undiminished personality, untaught by the wisdom he has written or by the laws he has revealed.' " When at this moment Buck Mulligan enters with a mockery on his lips, Stephen asks: " 'Hast thou found me, O mine enemy?' "

All of Shakespeare's life in London was a crucifixion. "Twenty years he dallied there between conjugal love and its chaste delights and scortatory love and its foul pleasures . . . But all those twenty years what do you suppose poor Penelope in Stratford was doing behind the diamond panes?"

Shakespeare had three brothers, says Stephen: Gilbert, Edmund, Richard. There is no Gilbert in the plays; but there is an Edmund and a Richard.

"Of all the kings Richard is the only king unshielded by Shakespeare's reverence, the angel of the world . . . Richard, a whoreson crookback, misbegotten, makes love to a widowed Ann (what's in a name?), woos and wins her, a whoreson merry widow."

So his brother Richard had lain adulterously with his wife Ann Hathaway, and this, Stephen believes, was in Shakespeare's life a wound from which he never recovered. Just why, Stephen does not here make clear. But in the plays Shakespeare uses constantly the theme of the " 'false or the usurping or the adulterous brother or all three in one . . .' " His good name had been filched from him, or the attempt had been made; and whereas he desired a decorous domestic life in Stratford, he is obliged to slave in London—for money and for fame and the reëstablishment of his good name.

So the recurring note throughout Shakespeare is the " 'note of banishment, banishment from the heart, banishment from home . . .' " and Stephen is convinced of the autobiographical basis of the plays. " 'We walk through ourselves meeting robbers, ghosts, giants, old men, wives, widows, brothers-in-love. But always meeting ourselves.' " This note of banishment

"repeats itself again when he is near the grave, when his married daughter Susan, chip of the old block, is accused of adultery. But it was the original sin that darkened his understanding, weakened his will and left in him a strong inclination to evil . . .

[This banishment, Stephen continues] is between the lines of his last written words, it is petrified on his tombstone under which her [Ann Hathaway's] four bones are not to be laid. Age has not withered it. Beauty and peace have not done it away. It is in infinite variety everywhere in the world he has created, in *Much Ado About Nothing,* twice in *As You Like It,* in *The Tempest,* in *Hamlet,* in *Measure for Measure,* and in all the other plays which I have not read."

Stephen "laughed to free his mind from his mind's bondage."

Whether this be valid literary criticism is beside the point. It is brilliant. And we read it not so much for what it says of Shakespeare as for what it tells us about Stephen. It is not at all surprising that this thesis should appeal strongly to him. His own family life has tumbled about his ears. Very clearly the thought of banishment, even though it is a self-imposed banishment, accords with Stephen's reflections about the work he desires to accomplish; with his stern realization that, to write about Ireland as he must, banishment from his native land is the personal forfeit.

Weary, unhappy, more than ever absorbed in his own thoughts, Stephen goes out with his enemy Buck Mulligan; and "a man passed out between them, bowing, greeting." It was Leopold Bloom, whom Mulligan calls the Wandering Jew, and says: " 'Did you see his eye? He looked upon you to lust after you. I fear thee, ancient mariner. O, Kinch, thou art in peril.' " But Dedalus does not reply; only in his mind he thinks, "Offend me still. Speak on." He is so weary now, he would cease to strive; he desires only the peace of the druid priests of *Cymbeline.*

Here we find searchlights playing into the lives of several Dubliners, and the word searchlight is advisedly used. The chapter begins with the very reverend John Conmee going for a walk at five minutes to three. He represents the complacent man of God; he sees only what he wants to see in this city of doleful misery. From present evils he diverts his eyes and the eyes of his flock, and points to the joys that await them in Heaven. He is a very practical man, conscious of power; sentimental, and, withal, kind in the way of the stereotyped charity of the patronizing Christian. John Conmee walks out of the focus and the light reveals the home of Simon Dedalus, where we see Katey and Boody Dedalus in their poverty, trying to sell whatever they can to buy food; brought at last to try to sell what are left of Stephen's books . . . Blazes Boylan sends Molly a basket of fruits and wine that he buys from the blonde girl in Thornton's . . . A short scene between Stephen and the Italian Almidano Artifoni . . . Miss Dunne sits in the office and has her own thoughts about clothes and a good time, and waits for a telephone call from her employer, Blazes Boylan . . . Ned Lambert, showing the historic council chamber of Saint Mary's abbey to a young clergyman antiquarian, Mr. Love, then meets Mr. J. J. O'Molloy . . . Tom Rochford shows his invention to Nosey Flynn. M'Coy and Lenehan exchange gossip with an emphasis on Bloom and Molly. M'Coy's opinion is that Bloom is a cultured all-round man . . . " 'There's a touch of the artist about old Bloom.' " But only a touch, we feel; for knowing Bloom much better than M'Coy knows him, we cannot accept his statement.

We have a glimpse of Bloom in a dingy shop selecting a book for Molly. He chooses *Sweets of Sin* . . . In a very striking short scene Dilly Dedalus with persistence duns her father and extracts from him a shilling, and two pennies. Effectively, in social contrast, "The viceregal cavalcade passed, greeted by obsequious policemen, out of Parkgate . . ." This cavalcade now takes on a good deal of importance, because as it passes along the Dublin streets, it attaches to itself, figuratively or imaginatively, nearly all the characters involved in the book. It is the pomp and circumstance and the symbol of the power that rules them. There isn't a life that is not in one way or another affected by the spectacle, as there is not a life that is not affected by the fact of English rule. It awakens memories, it stirs resentment. It is merely colorful pageantry, for example, to the two barmaids at the Ormond bar, as we discover later on . . . Mr. Bloom is nearly run over by it—a narrow escape . . . Stephen walks the streets reflecting about death and self-destruction, but only for a short moment. He passes a bookshop, and thinks he might find one of his pawned school prizes. Here he encounters his sister Dilly with her "high shoulders and shabby dress." He remembers that he had told her of Paris. Dilly tries to hide a book from Stephen, but he discovers it and finds it is a French primer. " 'To learn French?' " he asks. "She nodded, reddening and closing tight her lips." A deep poignancy strikes him for this child trying pathetically to improve herself; and he cautions his own emotions. He must show no surprise, make it seem natural. But his heart is deeply moved, and his conscience, too. Is it his duty to save her from drowning? The voice of conscience says yes; but there is in him the deeper voice, the conviction of the unsentimental artist, that if he tries to save her he will drown with her. There is nothing to do; there is only more misery to contemplate.

Father Cowley and Simon Dedalus meet and walk together jauntily . . . Martin Cunningham goes about soliciting a fund for the family of Paddy Dignam, buried this morning . . . Buck Mulligan and Haines have tea together and talk for the most part about Stephen. Haines believes that Stephen has some sort of fixed idea, but just what it is Haines cannot fathom. Mulligan has an easy explanation:

They drove his wits astray by visions of hell. He will never capture the Attic note. The note of Swinburne, of all poets, the white death and the ruddy birth. That is his tragedy. He can never be a poet. The joy of creation . . .

Mulligan adds that Stephen has said that he would write something in ten years, and Haines, though it seems a long way off, thinks that perhaps Stephen will . . . Almidano Artifoni in a hurry brushes his coat against the cane of the blind young man who roundly curses the Italian . . . Master Dignam, in mourning, is sent an errand . . . And at the end the viceregal cavalcade's progression through the streets of Dublin is more fully described.

"Bronze by gold heard the hoofirons, steelyringing." At first this opening has very little meaning; we are enchanted by the sounds. But it has its meaning. In the previous section appears: "Bronze by gold, Miss Kennedy's head by Miss Douce's head, appeared above the crossblind of the Ormond hotel." They are the barmaids and they too have been watching the cavalcade. For a page and a half at the outset Joyce tries to reproduce the sounds of the procession, the sounds in the street, and the sounds within the bar—the throbbing content of Bloom's sensory life. This whole picture, though it deals at considerable length with the barmaids and others, is really focused upon Bloom. Everything that takes place in the bar has a reference to the hero; he sits here and brings together, as it were, the characters of the narrative, and in his reverie the action of the story advances. It is impossible to telescope this part in any detail. We discover what these young barmaids think of Bloom. For example, Miss Kennedy, giggling, " 'O greasy eyes! Imagine being married to a man like that.' " Bloom senses what they feel. Yet they are young and for Bloom they incite lascivious thoughts. Mr. Simon Dedalus comes in and banteringly flirts with Miss Douce. There is between them a kind of camaraderie in badinage that the subjective Bloom would never be able to have. Miss Douce polishes a tumbler and gaily trills: " 'O, Idolores, queen of the eastern seas!' " And that first line of the then current musical comedy *Floradora* creates a mood very true to the time and place. That tune, to anyone who remembers it as sung then, will evoke memories as few other details could. Joyce remembers and he has used it with splendid effect. Lenehan brings to Simon a mock greeting " 'from the famous son of a famous father.' " The father drinks. "With faraway mourning mountain eye." Blazes Boylan comes in for a drink, and he is greeted as the conquering hero. Bloom watches and wonders what he's doing at the Ormond bar: does he have a cab waiting? People come in and go out. Then Simon Dedalus is urged to sing, and Father Cowley will accompany him. He sings, and Bloom listens. "Through the hush of air a voice sang to them, low, not rain, not leaves in murmur, like no voice of strings of reeds or whatdoyoucallthem dulcimers . . ." He loves the music, he feels both happy and sad. The song makes him think of tenors and how successful tenors are with women—and he's off again in reverie about little Martha and sex. And it's only a step once more to thought of Blazes Boylan and his wife; and he wishes Dedalus would sing more so that he could keep his mind off his domestic unhappiness. Yet he bore no hate. "Hate. Love. Those are words." And this, after all, is Mr. Bloom's tragedy—this lethargic indifference, this regret, this death-in-life of his existence.

The next part is easy reading. It moves along in the spirit and the manner of Joyce's earlier work, especially *Dubliners*. The narrator is a breezy, gusty, drinking Irishman, and he meets Joe Hynes who is a very good listener and a good foil for the running line of stories and gossip of the speaker. The language is vigorous, colorful, and bawdy. They begin to drink, and at the bar they meet the citizen—a synthesis of all that Joyce must loathe as representative of a fairly typical Dubliner. One of the stories has to do with a certain humorous attitude these men have toward injustice perpetrated against a small Jewish merchant. There is writing here with a bite in it, but the bite is not the kind that the editor, Myles Crawford, had expected when he spoke to Stephen. "Who comes through Michan's land, bedight in sable armour? O'Bloom, the son of Rory: it is he. Impervious to fear is Rory's son: he of the prudent soul." Impervious to fear is to be read satirically. The talk is high of gossip and of politics and of that woeful Irish discontent that a few pints can easily tap, sometimes known as Celtic melancholy.

Bloom is waiting outside the bar and the citizen is sinisterly keeping watch on him. The dog growls at Bloom, and the citizen tells Bloom to come on in, he won't eat you. They invite Bloom to have a drink, but he excuses himself and says he'll have a cigar, and nothing could sow more distrust in the Dubliners' minds (he will not drink with them). In Bloom it is in part also a prudence because of the cost of drinking; but apart from that he is temperamentally not the kind of Irishman who can drown his sorrow easily in liquor. Bloom listens to the talk and tries to be at least clear and conciliatory, but the liquor in the citizen is turning him in the mean direction, and the atmosphere is getting tense. Then the citizen begins speaking of the Irish language and the unpatriotic Irishmen who don't know it, and Bloom, the Irish in him aroused for once, discusses "the Gaelic league and the antitreating league and drink the curse of Ireland." For Bloom is a man who likes to talk. His is a speculative mind; he prefers something pseudo-scientific to the mere gossip and stale politics of the publicans. The storyteller comments on Bloom's talking abilities.

"I declare to my antimacassar if you took up a straw from the bloody floor and if you said to Bloom: *Look at, Bloom. Do you see that straw? That's a straw.* Declare to my aunt he'd talk about it for an hour or so he would and talk steady."

The comments pass to sport and prize-fighting, and once more Blazes Boylan's name comes up as having won a large sum on a prize-fight bet. Joe Hynes questions Bloom about the concert tour and the management by Boylan, and Bloom attempts to carry it off casually. The citizen's irrational drunken resentment is circling closer around Bloom. He says it is the Irishman's fault that the strangers were let come in; the English brought them; and then, as you might know, he calls up the name of the dishonored wife, Kitty O'Shea, the traducer of Parnell, and, through him, of Ireland and her hopes. England comes in for its scourging; and Bloom attempts to defend England, or at least to be honestly impersonal about the necessity for discipline, and explains how it's the same everywhere. Probably the moment of most raucous low comedy is the narrator's gossipy maladversions upon Queen Victoria and Edward VII. All of this disturbs the serious Bloom, and he says how bad is all the persecution of the world. " 'Perpetuating national hatred among nations.' " He tells them he knows, even if not completely as an Irishman, because he belongs to a race that is hated and persecuted, now, this very moment. They want to know if he has in mind the New Jerusalem. He says he is talking about injustice; that insult and hatred are no ways for men and women to live. There is the opposite virtue for which men should live, and when they ask him what that is, he says, very simply, it is love, the opposite of hatred. And then he explains that he has to go now, leaving the pub in the hands of his enemies, and chiefly in the hands of the citizen.

The drunker they get the more they revile Bloom. A religious procession passes; and the two pages describing this, if read aloud, will produce the musical effect of chanting as it rolls and piles up in a high vaulted church. Bloom returns and this meeting reaches a climax when Bloom reminds these men that Christ was a Jew, for it is here that the citizen dashes back into the shop to get a weapon with which to brain the " 'bloody jewman for using the holy name.' " He grabs the biscuit box, and rushes out, some of them trying to restrain him. Bloom is getting into a carriage; the citizen, the sun in his eyes, throws the biscuit box, misses Bloom, but frightens the nag into action and Bloom escapes uninjured.

Now we meet Gerty MacDowell—and she is indeed a perfectly realized character. Joyce places her in a splendid parody of the sentimental novel, and through this medium reveals her. Form never more perfectly fitted the subject matter. The section begins, at least, as a parody until the characters are established, and then, as in Fielding's *Joseph Andrews,* the characters dominate the parody and are real. Joyce begins: "The summer evening had begun to fold the world in its mysterious embrace." There are three girls, Cissy Caffrey, and Edy Boardman, and, sitting a little apart from them, Gerty herself. Then there are the children, the baby in the pushcart, and the little Caffrey four-year-old twins, Tommy and Jacky.

It is Gerty that holds our interest, for we are let into her reveries, only after she has been fully described in the most high-sounding and conventional way. She is in love with Reggy Wylie, a boy much above her class; but class distinctions are no barriers to daydreams. She dreams of marriage with him, but Gerty yearns in vain.

No prince charming is her beau ideal to lay a rare and wondrous love at her feet but rather a manly man with a strong quiet face who had not found his ideal, perhaps his hair slightly flecked with gray, and who would understand, take her in his sheltering arms, strain her to him in all the strength of his deep passionate nature and comfort her with a long long kiss. It would be like heaven.

They hear an organ and voices, and they know it is the temperance retreat going on in the near-by chapel. Gerty wishes they would take the squalling brats home, so that she can be alone with her thoughts. For she has seen a man on the beach, and her heart has gone pitapat the moment she knows that he is looking at her. "Yes, it was her he was looking at and there was meaning in his look. His eyes burned into her as though they would search her through and through, read her very soul." And now there is a mounting excitement in her reverie. She doesn't want the other girls to know that she's flirting with the man; she doesn't want them to go, because she would have to go with them, or find some excuse for staying behind. The prayers and the music are going on in the church and these are merged with Gerty's more profane reflections. Here is an example:

Queen of angels, queen of patriarchs, queen of prophets, of all saints, they prayed, queen of the most holy rosary and then Father Conroy handed the thurible to Canon O'Hanlon and he put in the incense and censed the Blessed Sacrament and Cissy Caffrey caught the two twins and she was itching to give them a ringing good clip on the ear but she didn't because she thought he might be watching but she never made a bigger mistake in all her life because Gerty could see without looking that he never took his eyes off of her and then Canon O'Hanlon handed the thurible back to Father Conroy and knelt down looking up at the Blessed Sacrament and the choir began to sing *Tantum ergo* and she just swung her foot in and out in time as the music rose and fell to the *Tantumer gosa cramen tum*.

When the tomboy Cissy twits Gerty about her flirting, Gerty, knowing that she has caught the strange man, has an assurance that heretofore has been lacking. And now with this elderly gentleman in the hand, as it were, a proud defiance rings in Gerty's reverie.

As for Mr. Reggy with his swank and his bit of money she could just chuck him aside as if he was so much filth and never again would she cast as much as a second thought on him and tear his silly postcard into a dozen pieces.

In this delineation there is not a false note, not a moment when the illusion is broken.

The other girls rush away toward the fireworks of the bazaar, whilst Gerty stays behind through "one of love's little ruses." The man meanwhile is leaning back against the rock a little beyond where Gerty is sitting. "Leopold Bloom (for it is he) stands silent, with bowed head before those young guileless eyes." Gerty awakens in Bloom a flow of sexual consciousness in which there is very little of carnality that is overlooked. In thought there has been a seduction; but in thought alone. This, as with everything else in Bloom's life, ends in frustration and futility. So that, as a means to restore his self-respect, he dwells, not on the barren and hopelessly frustrated sexuality of his life, but he seizes upon the one outstanding event so far in this day that he can at least have a little pride in. He remembers the drunken ranters at the Ormond bar, and the citizen trying his best to injure him. Those men, he thinks, ought to go home and laugh at themselves. He can feel himself superior to them. But they are afraid to be alone; they must always be swilling in company. If the citizen had hit him, that would have been "three cheers for Israel." He had had the courage to stand up and say to them that their God was a Jew. He walks toward the town. "Far in the grey a bell chimed." The cuckoo clock on the mantelpiece in the priest's house strikes. It is, in short, nine o'clock; the cuckoo clock has struck it; and Bloom is a cuckold.

The scene is in a lying-in hospital, and the writing is as involved and difficult—and on occasion as beautiful—as any in the book. There are passages which at first seem reminiscent of St. Anselm, say, discussing the nature of being, or prophetic of Gertrude Stein, talking about nothing at all. Take for example this paragraph:

Before born babe bliss had. Within womb won he worship. Whatever in that one case done commodiously done was. A couch by midwives attended with wholesome food reposeful cleanest swaddles as though forthbringing were now done and by wise foresight set: but to this no less of what drugs there is need and surgical implements which are pertaining to her case not omitting aspect of all very distracting spectacles in various latitudes by our terrestrial orb offered together with images, divine and human, the cogitation of which by sejunct females is to tumescence conducive or eases issue in the high sunbright wellbuilt fair home of mothers when, ostensibly far gone and reproductitive, it is come by her thereto to lie in, her term up.

I construe this to say, among other things: Long before the baby was born there had been a moment of bliss. Within the womb the child had won the worship of the mother. Now Mrs. Mina Purefoy will have all the comforts and advantages, spiritual and scientific, that a modern hospital can offer: wholesome food, clean swaddles, and intelligent people to aid her—as opposed to the primitive deliveries that the majority of women undergo. She will have drugs and the necessary surgical instruments; there will be no distracting spectacles to distress her mind. More than that, she will be surrounded with images human and divine to look at, and such images are conducive to peace of mind, to reassurance, and finally to an easier childbirth.

There are many readers, I am sure, who if cornered to a choice would here prefer me to Joyce; but for myself I am convinced that so to abstract Joyce into mere grammatical clarity is to evaporate all the rich essences of his eloquence and music and poetry: to reduce Sir Thomas Browne, as it were, to a diagram, or *Antony and Cleopatra* to a syllogism.

Withal, this digression must not be allowed to stand in the way of Mr. Bloom's arrival at the hospital to inquire for Mrs. Purefoy. As Joyce puts it:

Some man that wayfaring was stood by housedoor at night's oncoming. Of Israel's folk was that man that on earth wandering far had fared.

The next sentence would say that straightforward compassion had led Bloom to come alone to the hospital. Childbirth recalls Molly and their children, and something as nearly approaching love for his wife as Bloom exhibits at any time now springs up in his heart: "her to forgive now he craved."

The narrative takes on the flavor of tales of long ago and of mediaeval romance. The hospital is the castle, the doctors and interns are the goodly knights; Leopold Bloom is the weary traveler who is welcomed to their company; and the evening will be passed in exchanging stories of their adventures and their experiences and their high and low, moral and immoral reflections. This section deals with some of the most profound of human and moral and ethical problems. Much of it is couched in allegory, but the matter is that which confronts the modern world. It deals with breeding, with birth control, with childbirth. These subjects are not treated very sacredly; in fact they are, by the interns and doctors, discussed with that desperate, swaggering, bawdy tone that seems to be a part of the ritual of young doctors' initiations.

Most of those present are medical students: Dixon, a learning knight; Lynch and Madden, scholars of medicine; Lenehan; an Englishman, Crotthers; Punch Costello; and Stephen "with mien of a frere"—looking like a monk. And of course Bloom. Malachi Mulligan has promised to come; he arrives later. They are all "right witty scholars." The wassail bowl passes round. Costello is quite drunk and Stephen rather so. In Bloom's reverie through this part there is a deeper and finer quality of soul. It is as if he had sloughed off much in his sojourn on the beach and is climbing towards a more comforting and happy outlook through awakening love. We are told that he sits there—"Woman's woe with wonder pondering." The tongues are loosened. In childbirth crises, the mother should live and the baby should die; and this conflict between Church and medicine is argued. All laugh at the profane discussion save Stephen and Bloom, and Bloom cannot laugh, out of pity for any woman who bears a child. Stephen quotes classical authors against the Church "that would cast him out of her bosom." Bloom remembers Molly and her wild sorrow when little Rudy died, and as he listens to Stephen and watches him, he thinks of his "forepassed happiness." He would not be so sad if he had a son like Stephen, "of such gentle courage (for all accounted him of real parts)." And he grieves that Stephen lived riotously with those wastrels.

A terrible storm crashes, and the assembly is for a while awed. Lynch, who had been talking big, grows pale and says that the Godself is angered with their hellprate and blasphemy. This mood does not last for very long, and, the drink passing and repassing, their talk grows wilder and more abandoned and more lewd and bawdy. Bloom, certainly not a squeamish man, has yet his own standards of taste and decorum; and this ungoverned talk moves him at last to reflect that this mocking is a part of the life of people so young they know no pity; they are like overgrown children, and often not nice. His mind recoils from some of their outrageous words. Mr. Costello's language he finds a bit on the nauseous side. He breaks silence, and says how remarkable it is that these very boisterous and rowdy young men will most likely grow up to be adornments of that noblest of all professions. That he should be at all a censor of morals strikes even Bloom himself as amusing.

After the ghostly visitation to Mulligan of Haines the Englishman, the chapter continues with the thoughts of Bloom; and he remembers himself as a little boy, as a young boy and a young man. Then the story turns again to Stephen whom the drink is beginning to release—release, that is, to speak of himself and his work. The talk is large and high, but there is sincerity in it and there is truth. Why think of the past now, Stephen says: when I the befriending bard call them to life and give them life, they will come trooping back. The past is all lying in his memory waiting to be given form. "He encircled his gadding hair with a coronal of vineleaves, smiling at Vincent." All of that, those vineleaves and that answer, Vincent tells him,   .

"will adorn you more fitly when something more, and greatly more, than a capful of light odes can call your genius father. All who wish you well hope this for you. All desire to see you bring forth the work you meditate."

They all wish he may not fail, that he would not "leave his mother an orphan." Stephen's face grows dark and they all see how hard it is for him to be "reminded of his promise and of his recent loss." He would have left the feast but for the voices all around him quieting his unhappiness.

Meanwhile the safe delivery of Mrs. Purefoy's child is announced in the very midst of this riotous haranguing. There is a lull, a cessation, a quiet interlude, with a new and sudden outburst by Stephen of the word " 'Burke's!' "—and then follow several pages describing the crowd rushing out to the public house; the sights and sounds of the street as the young men rush on; past the evangelical "johnny in the black duds" and the conclusion is a mocking parody of an evangelical sermon.

We arrive at the "Mabbot street entrance of nighttown" and here we stay for one hundred and seventy pages. They are pages in which we experience with Bloom a most dreadful nightmare. It is Bloom's abyss, and Stephen's as well; with them (but consistently from Bloom's point of view) we walk through their dark night of the soul; and with them at the end we emerge.

This section is in dramatic form, with many elaborate stage directions, and the form helps (though not always a great deal) to an understanding of what is going on. It is sometimes spoken of as the Walpurgis Night part; nothing could be more terrible, more unspeakable than some of the things that are spoken here, and some of the things that are done. But there is something mysteriously awful in witnessing any soul being assayed in the fires of hell.

Bloom arrives, after the students, out of breath, and the play really begins. He sees his father and his mother and they both speak to him. And Marion his wife appears, as usual lording it over him, and he responds doubtfully. There is not quite the old vacillation, as if Bloom has somewhat changed, and we are aware of the beginning of a new relationship between him and Molly. A bawd appears, also Mrs. Breen who walks along with Bloom, but Bloom is soon diverted from this silly encounter by his thought of Stephen. " 'What am I following him for? Still, he's the best of that lot. If I hadn't heard about Mrs. Beaufoy Purefoy I wouldn't have gone and wouldn't have met. Kismet. He'll lose that cash.' " Most of the encounters of the day he meets again as ghostly presences. He hears the words of J. J. O'Molloy: " 'When in doubt persecute Bloom.' " Women with fashionable names appear. The timepiece speaks cuckoo thrice, and the stage direction tells us that "the brass quoits of a bed are heard to jingle." As always in waking consciousness with Bloom, the rhythm of his reflection is from an abject self-abasement and lack of any confidence to a more self-respecting and happier viewing of himself. This affirmation in consciousness swings to grotesque exaggeration. He believes himself a Grand Vizier, explaining to his subjects that he is repudiating his lawful spouse and will bestow " 'our royal hand upon the princess Selene, the splendour of the night.' " His new country, described as a place of Oriental magnificence, is to be the " 'new Bloomusalem in the Nova Hibernia of the future.' "

Bloom embraces Mrs. Thornton and bears (yes, Bloom bears) eight "male yellow and white children." He is conscious of Stephen who is surrounded by several of the girls of this bawdy house, as Stephen sits at the pianola playing with two fingers a series of empty fifths. And he listens to the few remarks that Stephen makes. The gramophone raucously sings, "The Holy City," and there is again introduced the idea of souls and the cry for saving them. So that Bloom, now in the guise of himself before his name was changed from Virag, regrets those things that he had intended to do and has not done. There are at least three Blooms in this part of the play: Bloom, Virag, and Henry Flower, the name, you will recall, he had used in his letter to little Martha. Bloom sees Henry Flower dressed as the conventional stage tenor, with an "amorous song on his lips."

Stephen, still at the pianola, thinks of himself and of the way his father plays; he is filling his belly with the husks of the swine—and though partially drunk, he will arise and go: "His Eminence, Simon Stephen Cardinal Dedalus, Primate of all Ireland," all recounted in a fantastic and bitter parody of the symbolic pageantry of the Church.

The most important meeting in this nightmare is between Bloom and Bella. At once she taunts him about his married life and the petticoat government. She is a virago, the most potent and salutary experience in this phantasmagoria. She will break Bloom's spirit completely, or she will force him to an assertion of himself that will, in the end, make all the difference between a man who has dismally failed in life or one who will bring the scattered pieces of his character together and find an affirmation of himself and of life. But before this happens, he must deal with and be dealt with by Bella, who has now turned fantastically masculine, and is Bello, who says to Bloom:

"No more blow hot and cold. What you longed for has come to pass. Henceforth you are unmanned and mine in earnest, a thing under the yoke. Now for your punishment frock. You will shed your male garments, you understand, Ruby Cohen? and don the shot silk luxuriously rustling over head and shoulders and quickly too."

At first Bloom does not seem surprised and does not protest too much; but gradually there creeps upon him a sense of foul debasement. The voice of his sins of the past speaks, and the words they speak in are not pretty words for him (or for us) to hear. The excrementitious is hard for us to fit in with our preconceived and conventional ideas of art. Bello makes Bloom face the worst thing he has done in his life. When he begins to tell, she says merely that he's disgusting. Bello prescribes his domestic duties. " 'What else are you good for, an impotent thing like you?' " She sarcastically taunts him about his wife and Blazes Boylan: and it is the facing of this that forces a reaction from Bloom—first his usual one of feeling sorry for himself, and then a realization that this is driving him mad and that he desires Molly and desires to forgive her; that he loves her. But Bello is relentless: You have made your bed, she tells him, and you are down and out and done for; die and be damned to you. Bloom sees into the deep sewers of himself, and he weeps. He is further tempted by a nymph; the halcyon days have voice and speak. The nymph turns out to be Bella.

Now Stephen comes more prominently into the scene and he and Bloom are brought more closely together. Stephen cries out that his father will never be able to break his spirit; he is Dedalus, he flew, his foes beneath him, and they ever shall be. As a final challenge, Stephen's father asks him to remember his mother's people, whereupon the ghost of Stephen's mother materializes, the choir sings, Buck Mulligan in clown's cap with curling bell appears. This is a very fine scene. The mother reminds Stephen that she was once the beautiful May Goulding. Stephen tries to control with his mind his tortured imagination. Buck Mulligan cries again that Kinch killed his mother. Then his mother comes nearer and speaks kindly, and Stephen says: "(*Choking with fright, remorse and horror.*) They said I killed you, mother. He offended your memory. Cancer did it, not I. Destiny." His mother reminds him that he sang that song to her: *Love's bitter mystery.* "Stephen (*eagerly*). Tell me the word, mother, if you know now. The word known to all men." And his mother tells him of her care for him, her pity for him when he was sad among the strangers, and asks him to repent and pray.

But this is not the word that Stephen has asked for. One cannot help remembering at this moment Ivan Karamazov, whose deepest desire was an answer to his questions. Perhaps the word that Stephen wanted does not exist; perhaps those doubts and misgivings and aspirations and confusions of the young artist cannot be answered by a word. It is possible they can only be answered by the living of life itself, and, for the artist, living the life of creation.

There is a vigorous uprushing of energy as Stephen exclaims that he will not serve; he defies all of them to break his spirit; he will live for the intellectual imagination. Stephen smashes the chandelier and the fight is on. Bella will prosecute. But now Bloom intervenes, gets around Bella, and will be the young man's protector. Out in the street Stephen meets two soldiers with Cissy Caffrey. The soldiers represent the armed force of England, and between them and Stephen is a profound and unpassable gulf—stupid brute force against intellect and imagination. Stephen knows how helpless he is with these bullies, but he will stand up to them if he must, treasuring for his inner satisfaction the thought as he taps his brow: " 'But in here it is I must kill the priest and king.' " Then a little later he remembers that he has said that Ireland is the old sow that eats her farrow. Bloom tries to rescue him from the fight, but Stephen in a supremely satirical moment urges Bloom to stay; this controversy with the soldier who thinks Stephen insulted his girl is called by Dedalus the " 'feast of pure reason.' " Private Carr rushes Stephen and strikes him and knocks him into the gutter. Bloom meets Corny Kelleher, who speaks to the soldiers, and to the police who have arrived, and quiets the mob, leaving Bloom to drag Stephen away with him. But before Bloom can get Stephen up, he calls to him his name, and Stephen, semi-conscious, is speaking the words of the Fergus's song he had sung for his mother. As Bloom listens to the words there is a vision of Rudy, a boy of eleven, in an Eton suit, reading and smiling. Bloom is "wonderstruck, calls inaudibly." Rudy does not answer, but that ghost has been laid in Bloom's heart, for here at his feet is a son coming to life.

Immediately after the nighttown phantasmagoria, the scene changes to a cabman's shelter, the only place open at that time of the night, whither Bloom has conveyed Stephen to get him a cup of coffee and a bun, for Stephen has been drinking this day, but he has eaten practically nothing. There are only a few characters here: a landlogged sailor who regales them with tall stories and his own exploits and comes around to the inevitable Irish politics; the keeper of the shelter, "the once famous Skin-the-Goat, Fitzharris, the invincible," and one or two others. Bloom and Stephen sit apart, and Bloom speaks of Stephen's father as a gifted man, and one who quite naturally takes great pride in his son. Bloom suggests that perhaps Stephen might go back to his father's house, but shortly realizes that this is not possible. Yet something has to be done with Stephen, and Bloom will face that responsibility. But responsibility in his new rôle of father carries with it some prerogatives, and Bloom will take advantage of them; it is a necessary exercise of a somewhat changed Bloom. He would not, he tells the young man, put very much trust in the boon companion who furnishes the comedy element, Mr. Buck Mulligan. Perhaps Stephen has already come to think of Buck as Judas Iscariot. The sailor opens conversation by asking what might Stephen's name be. The sailor has heard of the father, and though the name be foreign, Dedalus he knows is all Irish. "All too Irish, Stephen rejoined." Mr. Bloom has meanwhile ordered coffee for Stephen, and he thinks once more of Molly, and this time in his reflection comes to the homely conclusion that if your wife loves you, she'll wash your clothes for you. Evidently Bloom has made up his mind on this point. " 'Love me, love my dirty shirt.' "

Then the talk drifts to politics. The advice is given that it is well for every Irishman to stay in his own country, work for Ireland and live for Ireland, who, as Parnell had said, could not spare a single one of her sons. Bloom and Stephen pick up the talk and continue it between them, and the ego of the artist asserts itself when Stephen says: "But I suspect that Ireland must be important because it belongs to me." Bloom tries mildly to rebuke him; Stephen asks that since they can't change the country, let them change the subject. They do. But not before Bloom has with some satisfaction recounted to Stephen his run-in with the citizen at the Ormond hotel in the afternoon, and his statement to them that their God was a Jew. Bloom expresses his views on war, on intolerance of any kind which he cannot endure.

Out of his pocket he takes a faded photograph of Molly and asks Stephen would he consider that a Spanish type? He has begun to play with the idea of bringing Stephen home to his own house. But there is the question of Molly, and what she would think, and more important, what she would do. He bolsters up his own desire:

The vicinity of the young man he certainly relished, educated, *distingué,* and impulsive into the bargain, far and away the pick of the bunch, though you wouldn't think he had it in him . . . yet you would. Besides, he said the picture was handsome . . .

It is a shame that a young man so gifted should waste his life; he should find the right woman and marry. "To think of him house and homeless, rooked by some landlady worse than any stepmother, was really too bad at his age." And so it goes on. Certainly, he thinks, Stephen ought to eat something. He asks him when did he dine. Sometime the day before yesterday. Bloom is astounded. That largely settles the matter. He will take him home. It is getting late and something must be done. They can't stay there; it is out of the question at this hour of the morning and in his condition for Stephen to get back to the tower at Sandymount.

Having made this decision in his own mind, Bloom takes on a very paternal outlook. A new life has flowed into him. He thinks of education, the genuine thing, of literature, of journalism, concert tours, and all the rest. Because Bloom has realized that Stephen inherits from his father, or has in his own right, "a phenomenally beautiful tenor voice," he recalls Molly's beautiful singing and Simon Dedalus's in the Ormond earlier. And here is Stephen who could be used

He knows Italian. He could coach Molly in that language, and she and Bloom could coach Stephen in singing, and the three of them could have a very useful and profitable and happy life together. By these affirmative reflections Bloom's jealousy and hurt ego are for the time being displaced. And he takes Stephen home—at least for the night.

There follow seventy pages of questions and answers, a parody of the Longer Catechism. It is a most detailed questionnaire, with the answers all most carefully worked out. Of what did they talk on the way home?

Music, literature, Ireland, Dublin, Paris, friendship, woman, prostitution, diet, the influence of gaslight or the light of arc and glowlamps on the growth of adjoining paraheliotropic trees, exposed corporation emergency dustbuckets, the Roman catholic church, ecclesiastical celibacy, the Irish nation, jesuit education, careers, the study of medicine, the past day, the maleficent influence of the presabbath, Stephen's collapse.

Did they meet happily, seeing eye to eye on many of these topics? They did. In the arts in particular. "Both were sensitive to artistic impressions musical in preference to plastic or pictorial." Each has found someone he can talk to, for neither one is the insular Dubliner. They have both traveled; they have absorbed those cultivating influences of the Continent of Europe that more than anything else transcend nationalism. And what are the arts if not the creation and the perceptions of beauty in one manifestation or other? Along this line lies the only way out of the tremendous conflicts potential in nationalistic European politics. It is a conviction that each one of them shares—the conviction, incidentally, that John Galsworthy preached all his life.

From international policies we turn to very personal matters. We learn that Bloom likes to bathe. Stephen does not and he has not had a complete bath for a very long time:

to be specific, his last bath was in October, 1903—just eight
months back. And they comment on the relation between
genius and dislike of bathing. There seems to be a correla-
tion. Bloom feels that the predominant qualities of Stephen
are "confidence in himself, an equal and opposite power of
abandonment and recuperation."

Bloom starts the fire in the kitchen and puts the kettle on
to boil. He makes Stephen some cocoa and uses Molly's special cream that has heretofore always been saved for her
breakfast. As they drink their cocoa Bloom reflects upon the
pleasure derived from literature of instruction rather than
of amusement. He had often gone to Shakespeare for answers
to perplexities in real or imaginary life; but he had not
always found the answers.

We are told exactly what other meetings had taken place
between the two men; that once Bloom had been invited to
dinner at Stephen's home. Did he accept? "Very gratefully,
with grateful appreciation, with sincere appreciative grati-
tude, in appreciatively grateful sincerity of regret, he declined." But now Bloom reflects his happiness in being with
Stephen; he would like to be young with him, to exercise, to
be fit. He feels shy in Stephen's presence; neither openly al-
ludes to their racial difference. But one feels a slight restraint. Bloom represents (we are told, though it is difficult
to take this too seriously) the scientific temperament; Stephen
the artistic.

To Stephen, Bloom represents the accumulation of the
past, all the centuries of Jewish life and culture; Stephen
embodies for Bloom "the predestination of a future." And
the more Bloom contemplates his guest, the more he desires
some permanent arrangement. He feels there would be many
advantages for both of them and for Molly to have Stephen
living in the house. For Stephen "security of domicile and
seclusion of study." For himself "rejuvenation of intelli-

gence, vicarious satisfaction." And for Molly "disintegration
of obsession, acquisition of correct Italian pronunciation."
Was the invitation given to Stephen accepted? "Promptly,
inexplicably, with amicability, gratefully it was declined."
And when they went out in the back yard for a few moments
the spectacle of the night confronted them, and as "the
heaventree of stars hung with humid nightblue fruit," they
discussed the constellations and astronomy and astrology,
and the old affinity between woman and the moon.

As they take leave of each other, they listen to the "sound
of the peal of the hour of the night by the chime of the bells
in the church of Saint George." And the echo of this in
Stephen's mind is the choir singing the *Liliata rutilantium*
at his mother's funeral.

When Stephen has gone, Bloom roams about the house.
He bumps against the furniture that Molly has changed
around in the room. He opens a box on the "majolicatopped
table," takes out a little cone of incense, lights it, and sits
down to enjoy it; at the same time he looks at himself in the
mirror. There follows a catalogue of the books in his house,
from which we learn the variety of his interests; the super-
ficiality of his sporadic reading is shown by markers in the
first few pages of many of the volumes.

With the departure of Stephen and Bloom's inducing a
kind of trance with the incense, our feeling towards him undergoes a further change. It is as if Stephen's refusal to come
to live in his house had been a real blow to Bloom. His
character has been forming towards affirmation. There seems
to be a setback. It may be only a temporary one, we cannot
be sure. Some of his faith in himself and much of his vitality
departs with Stephen. His reverie takes him into a world of
fantasy in which he builds his ideal house along the most
conventional and approved lines of the well-to-do British
upper middle class. The reverie is not an awakening, but a

succumbing, or a going back away from the real world in which he must live. Having thus built his mansion, he thinks of improvements that would be added, he gives the place a name. With such leisure and comfort, he would indulge in his intellectual pursuits: "Snapshot photography, comparative study of religions, folklore relative to various amatory and superstitious practices, contemplation of the celestial constellations." And he arranges in his mind a list of lighter recreations and dwells upon what his civic functions would be. He proves to himself that he has always loved rectitude, that he would be a good dispenser of justice. He dreams of the most impractical and impossible and naïve means to gain sufficient wealth to make all of this a reality; and he has projects of even wider scope. We are told what they are. The question is asked, why did he contemplate schemes that were so difficult of realization? The answer is that from his experience he has found such meditation to have a therapeutic value. This sort of thing before going to bed has alleviated fatigue, and as a result his sleep has been sound, and his awakening a renewal of vitality. But what he holds in mind in the last moments of meditation is an original advertisement that would be a "knock out" to the buying public.

He unlocks some drawers and goes through the contents. We are told precisely what each drawer contains, and what is Bloom's response to the contents. What he dwells over is the insurance he holds against poverty, in its descending scale of possibilities dreadful to contemplate, the deepest point of misery being to think of himself, without these supports, as ending his life "the aged impotent disfranchised ratesupported moribund lunatic pauper." He imagines himself going away, just walking out of the house and disappearing and turning up in some far-off romantic place, a romantic utopia. The outcome of all this reverie is that he

recalls the day he has just been through, with all the causes
for fatigue; he thinks of the advantages of an occupied bed
as opposed to an unoccupied one. So he goes quietly upstairs
and, after performing his rituals, crawls very quietly into
bed with Molly. His pillow is at Molly's feet; his feet, of
course, must be somewhere in Molly's face. His thoughts just
before sleep are of Boylan and Molly, and what he ought
to deal out to each in the way of retribution; but there is an
apathy in Bloom that makes us feel that these too are just a
part of his own secret life of fantasy. Life will go on and
Bloom will go on as in the past.

The final section is the reverie of Molly Bloom. The reverie begins by establishing a mood of resentment against her
husband because he has told her (waking her to do it) about
himself and Stephen, and has told her that he will lie abed
late in the morning, and that she is to cook his breakfast,
two eggs, and bring it up to him on a tray. He has never done
such a thing before, except when pretending to be laid up
with an illness. Molly doesn't know just what to think of
it, but she manages to think a great deal. A part of her resentment is stimulated by a guilt she feels about her life
with other men, with Blazes Boylan, who has been with her
at nine o'clock that night, though, for the most part, there
is in her attitude toward that aspect of her life something
fundamentally healthy, as compared with the furtive and se-
cretive and pornographical attitude of Bloom.

It is clear that Molly is tiring of Boylan. But someone she
must have, and she thinks of paying some nice-looking boy,
or, as we understand it now, engaging a gigolo. She thinks of
having a child, but not by Boylan—and yet, she thinks, he
ought to have good-looking and healthy offspring. Then her
thoughts dwell for some time on Bloom. He knows a lot of
mixed-up things, especially about the body. Into her mind,

and with the flavor of a rather strong resentment, come memories of her husband's excrementitious obsessions, and it is
disgusting to Molly. As one means of rationalizing her adulterous conduct, she protests against the double standard in
marriage. She recalls that Bloom had given her Rabelais to
read, and she hadn't made much of it. He had given her
Moll Flanders as well, and Molly seems to have been shocked
by the shameless life of Moll. She remembers shops and
clothes, and herself as a girl in Gibraltar; and she recalls
minutely and with uncensored biological precision her first
love affair with Jack Mulvey. She thinks well of herself as
a Spanish type, with somewhat the look of a Jewess, which
she probably gets from her mother, but she has no idea who
her mother was, except that she was from the Mediterranean.
The words of songs play through her mind, as, "Once in the
dear dead days beyond recall." She thinks of her daughter
Milly and is proud of her, and she takes great satisfaction in
the fact that she understands Milly in a way that Bloom
never could. And she thinks what a fool Bloom is to be led
astray trying to be young with those medical students. And
what a sneaking person he is: the way he plots and plans,
and is pettily revengeful, not really a man. About what is
called real love Molly is cynical. She remembers what a criti-
ciser Stephen's father is (probably about music and singing)
and then she wonders what sort of person the son is. And
she hates the dirty pictures that Bloom keeps, the pictures
that are sold on the Paris streets. Bloom won't ever let you
enjoy anything naturally. Bloom had shown Stephen her
photograph. " 'I wonder he didn't make him a present of
it, and me too. After all, why not?' " (I apologize for the
punctuation in the quotation. There isn't any in the original, except two periods, one that may have got in by accident
on page 761 and one at the end of the book.) She recalls
Stephen the boy, whom she had seen eleven years before. He

was an innocent boy then, and she figures his present age almost correctly.

She will turn out the deck of cards in the morning and read her fortune. She did it this morning, and, sure enough, she recalls there would be "union with a young stranger neither dark nor fair you met before." When she remembers that Stephen is a learned young man, she regrets her ignorance, and she supposes that her husband put on a lot of dog and pretended to Stephen that he too was a university man. She is sick and tired of men you can't talk to. And it is very amusing to listen to Molly as she begins to contrast Boylan with Stephen, Boylan, "the ignoramus that doesn't know poetry from a cabbage." Then her exclamation " 'O move over you big carcass.' " That ladylike remark, as you can imagine, is addressed to her husband sound asleep beside her. She regrets that Stephen is running wild; a family with as fine a son as that ought to be proud and satisfied. And she has no son. And why didn't Bloom make him stay the night, he could have slept in there on the sofa? He must have been tired, and needed a good sleep, and Molly could have brought him in his breakfast. If he lived with them and wanted to spend the morning scribbling in bed, that would be all right.

Molly recalls how close Bloom is with money. She has a desire for money, for clothes, to get the house cleaned up "in case he brings him home tomorrow." She is thinking of Stephen. Molly would like to have the house filled with flowers. When she thinks of flowers she thinks how stupid are those people who say there is no God. She wouldn't give a snap of her fingers for those atheists; let them go and create something—say, like a flower. But the one true thing that Bloom ever said in his life was when he said she was a "flower of the mountain." And this takes her back again to her girlhood with Bloom in Gibraltar:

yes and those handsome Moors all in white and turbans like kings asking you to sit down in their little bit of a shop and Ronda with the old windows of the posadas glancing eyes a lattice hid for her lover . . . and the wineshops half open at night and the castanets and the night we missed the boat at Algeciras . . . O and the sea crimson sometimes like fire and the glorious sunsets and the figtrees in the Alameda gardens yes and all the queer little streets and pink and blue and yellow houses and the rosegardens and the jessamine and geraniums and cactuses . . . yes when I put the rose in my hair like the Andalusian girls used . . . yes and how he kissed me under the Moorish wall . . . and first I put my arms around him yes and drew him down to me . . . and his heart was going like mad and yes I said yes I will yes.

So, on a soaring note of lyric affirmation, amidst flowers and youth and love, ends what is at once the most original, bewildering, vital, and fructifying book of this century.

Boswell once questioned Dr. Johnson as to the "decency" of a book. Dr. Johnson choked the discussion by the comment: "That, Sir, is an indecent question." Had Johnson lived to see *Ulysses* banned, burned and reprobated, I think he would have been jolted out of the neat complacency of his retort to Boswell, and would have written a defense as tempered and as rightly reasoned as that of United States District Judge John M. Woolsey whose decision appears as a foreword to the Random House edition of Joyce's masterpiece.

After this decision it might appear that Joyce would on moral grounds need no further absolution. But the fact remains that *Ulysses* is still, to many, a bolus that makes them gag—to some, I know, a drastic and authoritative emetic. We tend to forget how recurrent and how hysterical has been the charge of immorality against books in the past, and that the more original the book is the greater the chance that such a charge will be made. To select one attack that

has always amused me, but that was indeed a serious matter
for the moralists of the day, there is the case of *Wuthering
Heights* by Emily Brontë, and the later statements of defense
and denunciation of carping critics by her sister, Charlotte
Brontë. In her editorial preface to the 1850 (or new) edition
of Emily's wild and original novel, Charlotte says first that
she can understand how, to those readers unfamiliar with
the West Riding of Yorkshire and its people, the book must
be either unintelligible or even repulsive. Yet the places
and the people, she affirms, are true. They are all right. She
goes on:

A large class of readers, likewise, will suffer greatly from the introduction into the pages of this work of words printed with all
their letters, which it has become the custom to represent by the
initial and final letter only—a blank line filling the interval. I
may as well say at once that, for this circumstance, it is out of
my power to apologize, deeming it, myself, a rational plan to
write words at full length. The practice of hinting by single letters those expletives with which profane and violent persons are
wont to garnish their discourse, strikes me as a proceeding which,
however well meant, is weak and futile. I cannot tell what good
it does—what feeling it spares—what horror it conceals.

Not for one moment do I believe that Charlotte Brontë
would approve of many words used by Joyce's characters.
Many of them she would not even know. Her experience was
not James Joyce's. But *Ulysses* (if you can grant the subject
matter at all) is the logical exposition and extension of Miss
Brontë's artistic pronouncement.

The scenes dealing with scenery in *Wuthering Heights*
are all right—"What they should be." Miss Brontë is not so
sure of the rightness (in a moral sense here) of her sister's delineation of the wild, ungovernable, and passionate Heathcliff—that strange man of evil genius. But Charlotte was herself an artist; she knew the strange and inexplicable throes
of creation. She says of Emily:

Her imagination was a spirit more sombre than sunny, more powerful than sportive . . . Having formed these beings (Heathcliff and Catherine) she did not know what she had done . . . if it was complained that the mere hearing of certain vivid and fearful scenes banished sleep by night, and disturbed mental peace by day, Ellis Bell [Emily Brontë] would wonder what was meant, and suspect the complainant of affectation.

And finally:

Whether it is right or advisable to create beings like Heathcliff, I do not know: I scarcely think it is. But this I know: the writer who possesses the creative gift owns something of which he is not always master—something that, at times, strangely wills and works for itself . . . Be the work grim or glorious, dread or divine, you have little choice left but quiescent adoption . . . If the result be attractive, the World will praise you, who little deserve praise; if it be repulsive, the same World will blame you, who almost as little deserve blame.

The application of moral judgments (except perhaps in the very widest and deepest meaning of the word moral) to any work of fictional art can of course breed only befuddlement and bad blood. This has been stated over and over again, and exemplified as repeatedly, but it cannot be stated too often; happily we have Professor John Dewey, in his latest book, *Art as Experience,* warning against the confusion of applying moral judgments in the field of art. If good critics did not insist upon this distinction we should have the moralists telling the artists what they should and should not do. Such a situation would be intolerable, because it would strangle the artist; and the artist of all men must not be strangled for he it is who brings to us our deepest knowledge of life; and in so doing brings release to the human spirit.

Writing of *Ulysses* specifically, Judge Learned Hand and Judge Augustus N. Hand would seem to give the sanction of law to the contention of the philosopher:

Art certainly cannot advance under compulsion to traditional forms and nothing in such a field is more stifling to progress than limitation of the right to experiment with a new technique. The foolish judgments of Lord Eldon about one hundred years ago, proscribing the works of Byron, Shelley and Southey, are a warning to all who have to determine the limits of the field within which authors may exercise themselves.

The artist, to paraphrase Professor Dewey, is a man who is impelled by something inherent in the nature of his work (which he himself does not always understand) to do what he must, no matter what external limits may be set by the stupidly conventional or the moralistic. The creative mind, reaching out and using whatever material stirs it, must press out that material until it becomes the matter of new experience. If the artist refuses to submit to the boundaries set by convention, he and his work are frequently denounced as immoral. But Professor Dewey further states:

one of the functions of art is precisely to sap the moralistic timidity that causes the mind to shy away from some materials and refuse to admit them into the clear and purifying light of perceptive consciousness.

Further, no one can restrict the author except the author himself, and he can and must respond only to his deepest interests. But there is one demand the critic and the reader should make and are quite justified in making, and that is to demand of the artist sincerity—"the necessity that he shall not fake and compromise." Is the artist trying with all the truth and honesty of which he is capable, and "unembarrassed by fixed and antecedent rule" to express his own vision of life? Of Joyce that can indubitably be said. And of him further:

Interest becomes one-sided and morbid only when it ceases to be frank, and becomes sly and furtive—as it doubtless does in much contemporary exploitation of sex.

The "contemporary exploitation of sex" is, of course, and in every age and place, in the hands of the self-appointed custodians of public morals, whether they be Catos or Comstocks or any of the others. Surely in Joyce is nothing furtive, or sly, or one-sided, or morbid, though the genteel tradition can and readily does discount him as being "vulgar."

The book has been accused of great vulgarity. This need not necessarily be an adverse comment. Healthy, lustful, fructifying vulgarity can be a very acceptable quality in life and in literature. It can serve as a fertilizer of much beauty that blossoms from it. One feels this in Rabelais, in Fielding, in Smollett perhaps, and in A. E. Coppard. It is refreshing to meet or to read about people who have a direct, unambiguous contact with life—who in their own activities are life itself. Such writers have gusto and vitality, ingenuity and humor. I feel these qualities in the vigorous and coarse stories that the narrator tells to Joe Hynes and the others in the Ormond bar section. But I do not feel this at all when Bloom plays the peeper with Gerty MacDowell, or in Molly's reverie, for the most part. There is a distinction between a Don Juan, a Casanova, a Tom Jones, a Pantagruel, a Gargantua, let us say, and that breed of unadult emotional malingerers that read and write in lavatories. And Bloom belongs much of the time with this latter breed. But there he is—with all his imperfections; and we have always to come back to acknowledge him, if not a great man, a very great creation. So it is, in lesser degree, with the other people in the book.

There is then another perfectly fair question that lies within the province of an esthetic judgment, and that is whether the characters portrayed are true or real. I have no doubt that many inferior writers are "sincere," and yet they are inferior often because they have not succeeded in creat-

ing living and vital characters; they have not the insight
to see beneath the surfaces of human life into their own
souls or to objectify the blind drives from their dark depths,
so that we never believe in their characters, as we believe
in those in such books as *War and Peace,* and, let us say,
Ulysses. Now, apart from whether we like or dislike the people in Joyce's book, let us apply the question as to whether
they exist in their own validity. Do they live for us? For me
they do. Even after one reading, and more after further reading, these people emerge from the pages vividly, and the further one gets away from them, the more clearly do they return to one's imagination, with a life all their own. I realize
that this is not true by any means for all readers; I can only
state my own experience. But this I do know: that some readers are too quickly and too easily repelled by both the manner
and the subject matter ever to remain long enough with
Ulysses to get to know the people; their argument being that
they would avoid such people in life. And surely that is
their privilege. One student read only seventy pages and lost
her dinner; and the only thing that I could think of to say
was that it seemed to me *Ulysses* was worth one dinner.

And this brings me, parenthetically, to remind those subject to seasickness that their squeamishness is more for words
than for the facts that they denote. It is the words that gag
in the windpipe—words that from childhood have had for us
guilty and forbidden connotations, that are heavily charged
with evil, or wicked, or sordid, or disgusting associations; and
by the words we are repelled. Most people are not afraid
of the facts of human life that those words describe.

The words which are criticized as dirty [Judge Woolsey states],
are old Saxon words known to almost all men and, I venture, to
many women, and are such words as would be naturally and
habitually used, I believe, by the type of folk whose life, physical
and mental, Joyce is seeking to describe.

With many readers—maybe most—the attitude toward any piece of imaginative writing is determined by the personal reactions to the characters presented—do we like these people or not—can we make happy intimate identifications with them? If we respond to this book as we have to other great novels we shall probably find some of those qualities that cater to the wish fulfillments in ourselves only in Stephen Dedalus.

With the possible exception of Stephen, practically all of the characters in this book are not pleasant people. They were not intended to be liked. But though we may hate them, they interest us. I am inclined to agree with one critic who wrote that "Joyce was sent to put the fear of God in our hearts." In Leopold Bloom I find no trace of distinction of mind or of personality. He is a wounded, persecuted, pushed-aside weak man, rather whiningly jealous, and obsessed with unfruitful sexuality. He is weak, and he is not vital. But he has kindly impulses (he helped the blind young man across the street, he called to inquire for Mrs. Purefoy), and although he has not sufficient intensity to love anyone or anything straightforwardly or wholeheartedly, he has yet some recognition of these defects in himself and he is in his way trying to make of himself something better than he has been. One begins to feel sorry for him; but it can be very irritating to have to live a long time with someone for whom one's deepest emotion is compassion or pity. It is only when this attitude of pity becomes Bloom's, and he feels thus towards his Dublin associates, and this pity turns to disgust, that we begin to have some respect for Bloom. And he does, in this day, reach an abyss of self-loathing, a state in which no man can live. Then it is, when he has been forced to see and face and accept the worst, that he glimpses signs of hope wherewith to build and perhaps to forge a character for himself that he need not despise. But it is only a hope.

Stephen is a very different sort of man. He is first of all young, and has great gifts, and on both these counts we have faith in him; largely, I suspect, because it is almost impossible not to make a strong identification of Stephen with Joyce himself. And then of course it is easy to sympathize with Stephen's troubles: a disintegrated family, poverty, the death of his mother—which is so closely tied up with Stephen's efforts to escape the paralyzing dominations of the pieties of family and Church. The two outstanding qualities in this young man's character are his desire to love and his desire to fulfill his artistic gifts: and these are both affirmations of life. With his learning and with his intellect, too, we are in sympathy. All in all, there is an integrity in the young man which is made all the more shiningly splendid in contrast with the lack of it in all the people around him. And surely if Joyce intended anything in the novel, it was to make this very clear. For Joyce is a supreme satirist.

Why did Joyce choose to write about these people? Most likely to ease the pain of his own heart, and to fulfill his gifts; to show the stupidity, the futility, the ignorance, the coarseness, the brutality of these people he has known. If he was the Stephen Dedalus of *Ulysses,* we have seen how the people in Dublin seared the young man's heart. Being what they were, they could have no knowledge of a young man like Stephen, and without that, they could have no sympathetic understanding. He could find no place to live among them; they would have killed him. One wonders sometimes if the writing of *Ulysses* was not fraught as well with a spirited and unholy revenge against these complacent boors. But behind this writing lies a deeper and a holier purpose surely. To show them themselves, those Irishmen of the first quarter of a century, just how bad and how hopeless they were, and to show them this (and to show the world, for all of this could probably be matched in other lands) in writing that has a "bite" in it, might be to point the way to something better. In reflecting about this possible purpose, one must be reminded again of that significant statement of Stephen's at the end of the *Portrait*—that he would go to forge in his soul the uncreated conscience of his race.

Understanding the purpose of the novel is only one of the many difficulties we experience before we begin to feel that we are finding our way in this original and perplexing book. We look in vain in *Ulysses* for the kind of hero and heroine about whom we have very definite preconceptions— first, for example, that they should be presented so as to appeal to the reader's sympathy and love. The classical hero was a man of nobility of soul and character shown in conflict with other people, or unevenly pitted against the stronger forces of the gods and goddesses; even though the hero failed, he had in his failure exhibited those higher qualities of courage and nobility that make their appeal. Again, classical heroes are shown in devotion and sacrifice, usually to love. And we are not really prepared by tradition to lay aside our customary emotions and respond to charac ters merely as to whether they are truly or falsely drawn. We therefore find ourselves unequipped and disturbed by such a man as Leopold Bloom because we do not know in just what category of heroes to place him.

There has been moreover a more or less clear-cut traditional form, particularly for the novel, formless though many may seem to be, that we have become accustomed to. Chapter followed chapter in the chronological sequence; the characters changed through a longer or shorter period of years, and we could watch them grow up. They were described easily, their gestures recorded, and the greatest emphasis given to their speech. Their environments, too, were carefully described. But here in *Ulysses* much of this conventionality has been abandoned. No one in the book is noble,

very few of them know anything about the sacrifice of self
for the ideal of love, no one falls in love in the conventional
romantic sense with anyone else. Settings are briefly sketched
in, as if incidentally. Time is reduced to twenty-four hours
of one day, so far, that is, as the immediate action is concerned. (We are taken as far back in time as twenty or more
years before through the reveries of various characters.) The
people are, to be sure, described from the outside, and much
space is given to dialogue. But the device most heavily depended upon for the realization of the people is reverie.
And it is to this device that we have to make the most difficult of all our adjustments. The book, further, is filled with
allusions of every conceivable sort, and, while the story can
be gained with very little knowledge of these allusions, there
is no doubt that the book becomes a richer experience the
more we are familiar with them.

Has James Joyce as novelist no defects? It seems to me he
has. He is so deeply interested in character that he pays little
attention to what we ordinarily understand as plot. He has
very little of that power of inventiveness that characterizes
such other great fiction writers as Balzac and Dickens and
Scott. Occasionally his creation seems overborne by intellect,
as if too much of his creative flow came from the mind and
not enough from those deeper creative levels that we feel
have been tapped by such writers as Dostoevsky and Tolstoy
and Fielding and Richardson. Finally, the difficulties of his
involved manipulations and experimentations with language
repel so many people that it would seem to have been his
desire often to obscure rather than make clear his meaning.
But to the reader once absorbed in the novel these very
difficulties add interest.

About half way through the "Longer Catechism" part
of the book, Bloom, feeling deeply "the painful character of
the ultimate functions of separate existence" expresses

an idealistic desire that such social conditions might be amended. But he also expresses his belief that speculations as to means constitute the task of an intelligence superior to his own. The question is asked:

Did Stephen participate in his dejection?

And the answer is:

He affirmed his significance as a conscious rational animal proceeding syllogistically from the known to the unknown and a conscious rational reagent between a micro- and a macrocosm ineluctably constructed upon the incertitude of the void.

Was this affirmation apprehended by Bloom?

Not verbally. Substantially.

Whether understood "verbally" or "substantially," *Ulysses* is a novel, or purports to be. It deals with people, their problems, their ideas, their relationships, their environments; and as novel it should be judged, and not merely as an architectural masterpiece, a verbal *tour de force,* or a parody of Homer. And to judge it as a novel is what I have tried to do.[39]

A. B.

IX

VIRGINIA WOOLF

FEW novelists have exercised a fine critical intelligence on the art of fiction to the same degree as Virginia Woolf. *Mr. Bennett and Mrs. Brown,* a provocative address delivered at Cambridge University in 1924; *Phases of Fiction,* three articles published in *The Bookman* in 1929; *The Common Reader,* First and Second Series (1925 and 1932), collected critical essays; and *A Room of One's Own* (1929), concerned especially with the problems of the woman writer—all make it possible to examine her own fiction in the light of her opinions about fiction. But if we expect to find convenient critical formulas to assist us, we are disappointed. Writing an acute review of the stories of Ernest Hemingway, and moving forward to conclusions with assurance, she yet disconcerts us somewhat at the end by making a reservation, both candid and ironic: "So we sum him up. So we reveal some of the prejudices, the instincts, and the fallacies out of which what it pleases us to call criticism is made." In *Phases of Fiction* she professes to be doing nothing more than to show a mind—her own—at work upon a shelfful of novels, and to let us watch it as it chooses and rejects, making itself a dwelling place in accordance with its own appetite. On the mind of every reader of fiction, some design has been traced which reading brings to light. "Desires, appetites, however we may come by them, fill it in, scoring now in this direction, now in that." The world we create in this way is always in process of creation, and it is, she admits, a personal world, possibly not habitable by other people, created in obedience to tastes which may be peculiar to one temperament and distasteful to another.

Now it may as well be said at the outset that unless some designs have been traced upon our minds by what is loosely called culture, Virginia Woolf's fiction will touch them in vain. Her own mind is a finely educated one. Miss Winifred Holtby, in a biographical and critical essay on Mrs. Woolf, notes that at the beginning of her second novel, *Night and Day,* is a "description of what it feels like to be born the daughter of a distinguished literary family." The description of her heroine's childhood must in this respect be substantially that of her own, as the daughter of Leslie Stephen, editor of the *Cornhill Magazine* and of the *Dictionary of National Biography,* author of critical, biographical, and philosophical essays, and friend of most of the scholars and men of letters of a distinguished period in English literature. She had the run of her father's splendid library, and could and did read whatever she liked, and read enormously. "If her experience of life was limited"—for she was not strong enough for the usual school education—"her intellectual contacts were entirely untrammelled." [40] Her intellectual freedom and her respect for truth and reason were strongly fortified by early and long familiarity with Greek thought and literature. In an essay, "Not Knowing Greek," she speaks of the excitement of following the argument in a Platonic dialogue, where

what matters is not so much the end we reach as our manner of reaching it. That all can feel—the indomitable honesty, the courage, the love of truth which draws Socrates and us in his wake to the summit where, if we too may stand for a moment, it is to enjoy the greatest felicity of which we are capable.

An unusual conviction, Miss Holtby well says, for a woman of the period still marked by the standards of Ibsen's *Doll's House.* "But Virginia Stephen, rambling about her father's library, reading the classics, reading Plato, had become convinced that for one woman, at least, truth was important." [41]

Fortunately no economic pressure forced her to consider other things more important. She had a "room of her own." She could follow her inclination to write—first criticism, then fiction. She continued, after her marriage to Leonard Woolf, to be more familiar "with people who use their minds rather than their bodies as their equipment for life." And she continued to move among books and to write about them, even after she began to write of the people of her imagination. Miss Holtby pictures the study which Mrs. Woolf uses in the Bloomsbury house where the Hogarth Press is installed—an immense half-subterranean room,

piled with books, packets of unbound volumes, and manuscripts from the press . . . There one seems to move among books and papers as among the rocks and ledges of that submarine cave of which the characters in her books are always dreaming. The light penetrates wanly down between the high buildings overhead, as through deep waters, and noises from the outside world enter only in a subdued murmur, as from very far away.

Mrs. Woolf has been accused by people who, as Clive Bell has said, "are not particularly well off for either culture or intellect," of possessing a "cultivated and intellectual" style.[42] An intelligent person whose mind is not particularly cultivated may come to enjoy a cultivated and intellectual style like that of Henry James. He is deliberate, he provides all the necessary transitions, his references are explicit enough to make us at least aware that he is referring to something a cultivated mind ought to know, and it is always possible to hold fast to the thread of a carefully plotted story. His novels, however elaborate the psychology, are in the traditional form. But the movements of Mrs. Woolf's mind are swift and unpredictable. One must leap with it from one point to the next, without seeking a bridge. She herself says of T. S. Eliot's poetry that its obscurity comes from intolerance of the old usages and politenesses of society—"respect for the weak, consideration for the dull." After flying precariously like an acrobat from bar to bar, she begins to envy the indolence of her ancestors, who, instead of spinning madly through mid-air, dreamed quietly in the shade with a book. Her feeling about T. S. Eliot is precisely that of many readers about her.

Fundamentally dull people will not like Virginia Woolf, says Clive Bell, who admits that he likes her very much. Nor will people whose minds are neat and orderly and practical. Nor very emotional people who seek in fiction chiefly emotional release through identification. But many others, who find an initial difficulty, can overcome it simply by paying a little attention to their own undirected reveries—by exploring the stream of their own consciousness, and becoming aware of its movement:

Miscellaneous, vague, chaotic, composed of memories, moods, sensations, and desires mingled helter-skelter with things tragic and comic, trivial and important treading upon the heels of one another, the stream goes continuously on from the moment we wake until it trails off fainter and fainter into slumber or death.[48]

The need to make practical decisions of all sorts halts our daydreaming and controls our thinking for periods long or short; the need of justifying our actions and opinions to ourselves and others compels the process called rationalizing; and once in a blue moon our thinking may become impersonal and creative. Outside the circle of awareness altogether lie those regions explored by a Dostoevsky or a D. H. Lawrence, where lurk the origins of moods and desires, the strange world outside the focus of consciousness. This world Mrs. Woolf seldom enters. It is our reveries, which psychologists have called the fundamental index of character, that fascinate her and that she chooses to record. Miss Holtby points out in this connection that Mrs. Woolf's approach, in the re-creation of subconscious experience, is an intellectual one; and that this

is the secret of much that has been found puzzling in her studies of psychological processes. She observes "the stream of consciousness"; but she examines it with an intellectual instrument in which she, unlike many contemporary writers, has not lost her faith.[44]

In 1919, Mrs. Woolf, who had been critical reviewer for the *London Times Literary Supplement*, but had also been experimenting with imaginative sketches and stories, published in the Hogarth Press *The Mark on the Wall*—a daydream, a bit of the stream of consciousness. The daydreamer looks at a mark on the wall. Too indolent to get up and examine it, she allows her mind to drift without a rudder, to follow up any association; only now and then, when it drifts into a dull backwater, she brings it back to the mark and starts afresh. Let anyone who has not played the eavesdropper upon his own consciousness in these off moments try this device of intermittently focused reverie. He will probably not find floating on his own stream objects as delightful and fantastic as Mrs. Woolf fishes up from hers. But he will begin to comprehend the value of reverie as an instrument of character portrayal; he will find things out about himself, amusing, disconcerting, and very instructive . . . Even if she examined that mark, thinks the daydreamer, she might not be sure what it was . . . living is such an accidental affair . . . just think of the things we lose in a lifetime—and a dozen incongruous objects, bird cages, jewels, coal scuttles, that have disappeared at different times, recur to memory; and make her wonder that she has any clothes on her back. And that calls up a comparison of living to being blown through the tube at fifty miles an hour and landing at the other end without even a hairpin left— "shot out at the feet of God entirely naked—tumbling head over heels in the asphodel meadows like brown paper parcels pitched down a shoot in the post-office" . . . and then after life . . . a poetic image or two drifting off into vagueness, and then she looks again at the mark. Perhaps it is a bit of dust—"the dust which, so they say, buried Troy three times over, only fragments of pots refusing annihilation." Then feeling herself sinking into drowsiness, she catches at the first idea that passes—Shakespeare, sitting in an armchair looking at the fire—and she sketches a scene in a historical novel, which presently bores her. (But it is interesting that just this scene reappears after ten years as a part of Mrs. Woolf's *Orlando*.) And looking again at the mark, she thinks it projects from the wall and may be a tiny mound—a smooth tumulus like those barrows on the South Downs that are either tombs or camps . . . and she wonders about antiquaries who investigate such matters. What sort of man is an antiquary?

Retired Colonels for the most part, I daresay, leading parties of aged labourers to the top here, examining clods of earth and stone, and getting into correspondence with the neighboring clergy, which, being opened at breakfast time, gives them a feeling of importance, and the comparison of arrowheads necessitates cross-country journeys to the county towns, an agreeable necessity both to them and to their elderly wives, who wish to make plum jam or to clean out the study, and have every reason for keeping that great question of the camp or the tomb in perpetual suspension, while the Colonel himself feels agreeably philosophic in accumulating evidence on both sides of the question. It is true that he does finally incline to believe in the camp; and, being opposed, indites a pamphlet which he is about to read at the quarterly meeting of the local society when a stroke lays him low, and his last conscious thoughts are not of wife or child, but of the camp and that arrowhead there, which is now in the case at the local museum, together with the foot of a Chinese murderess, a handful of Elizabethan nails, a great many Tudor clay pipes, a piece of Roman pottery, and the wine-glass that Nelson drank out of—proving I really don't know what . . .[45]

Proving at least the fertility of Mrs. Woolf's own mind in whimsical speculation, and preparing us for the sort of thing that happens in her novels, though it happens there under control and for a purpose. In *Jacob's Room,* for instance, Jacob is absorbed in certain studies he is carrying on at the British Museum, and we must be steeped in that atmosphere. So we see not only Jacob, but the odd people who sit near him, and we feel the queer minds clicking away near his: Miss Marchmont in her old plush dress and her claret-colored wig, with her gems and her chilblains and her philosophy, which she sometimes puts into pamphlets and gives away . . . and thinking of how Queen Alexandra once acknowledged a pamphlet of hers, she shifts in her seat and knocks over some books into Jacob's lap—which he is too absorbed to notice.

But Fraser, the atheist, on the other side, detesting plush, more than once accosted with leaflets, shifted irritably. He abhorred vagueness—the Christian religion, for example, and old Dean Parker's pronouncements. Dean Parker wrote books and Fraser utterly destroyed them by force of logic and left his children unbaptized—his wife did it secretly in the washing-basin—but Frazer ignored her, and went on supporting blasphemers, distributing leaflets, getting up his facts in the British Museum, always in the same check suit and fiery tie, but pale, spotted, irritable. Indeed, what a work—to destroy religion!

And meanwhile Jacob transcribed a passage from Marlowe. We have never met Frazer before, we never meet him again. He impinged upon Jacob's life for a few minutes, and Mrs. Woolf pursued him for a paragraph, and achieved her usual effect—of making us feel excited about life, with all its queer juxtapositions and contrasts and incongruities.

This paragraph about Frazer suggests what Mrs. Woolf means when she talks about the novelist's interest in people.

All of us have to be interested in people and in character for practical purposes, but novelists continue to be interested long after all practical needs have been served. "The study of character becomes to them an absorbing pursuit; to impart character an obsession." A little old lady sits in the corner of a railway carriage—some Mrs. Brown—saying in effect, "Come and catch me if you can." The novelist pursues this will-o'-the-wisp, and perhaps in the end has to be content with a scrap of her dress or a strand of her hair. But success in the pursuit is the test of a novelist's achievement. The one way not to catch Mrs. Brown, according to Mrs. Woolf, is the way that became enormously popular with novelists of the early twentieth century—excellent novelists, too, in their way —the Wellses, Bennetts, Galsworthys. They laid heavy stress upon details of environment to explain character: on the wages people received, what they could buy with them and where, what sorts of houses they lived in and whether they owned them or paid rent, what amusements were open to them, what diseases they died of or recovered from, what servants they had and how they treated them. If Mr. Bennett saw Mrs. Brown in the railway carriage, he would note every detail:

He would notice the advertisements . . . the way in which the cushions bulged between the buttons; how Mrs. Brown wore a brooch which had cost three-and-ten-three at Whitworth's bazaar; and had mended both gloves—indeed the thumb of the left-hand glove had been replaced. And he would observe at length how this was the non-stop train from Windsor which calls at Richmond for the convenience of middle-class residents, who can afford to go to the theatre, but have not reached the social rank which can afford motor-cars, though it is true there are occasions (he would tell us what), when they hire them from a company (he would tell us which).[46]

And the public has been so thoroughly trained to expect that this is the way to learn about characters in novels, that unless you tell them firmly all about the houses and parents and servants and hot-water bottles and gloves of old women, they won't know that they are old women. But that particular tool for fashioning character is unsatisfactory to Mrs. Woolf, and she thinks it is beginning to be unsatisfactory to many readers. With all this insistence on the fabric of things, there is Mrs. Brown, still in her corner, not imaginatively realized at all, though we know all the facts about her. A way of telling the truth about people must be found—a new way, because there are new truths we have become aware of. Mrs. Woolf is gaily dogmatic and a little unfair to her elders in these comments, but she is right in insisting that those younger novelists who are not merely following well-worn traditions have been trying to express their sense of life and character in new terms. From some of their experiments, she admits, Mrs. Brown emerges disheveled and pale. But somehow or other she must be rescued and set before us.

So we have seen Mrs. Woolf as critic insisting upon success in characterization as the prime essential of the novelist's art. We have seen that she is dissatisfied with certain well-worn tools of the craft and disposed to experiment, and we have noted her peculiar aptitude in handling reverie. No wonder the reverie process fascinates her—it would anyone whose mind worked like hers. What she says of Laurence Sterne is often true of herself: "It is his own mind that fascinates him, its oddities and its whims, its fancies and its sensibilities; and it is his own mind that colors the book and gives it walls and shape." Of her novels, *Mrs. Dalloway* has seemed to critics the outcome of deliberate experiment with a new method. In her preface to the Modern Library edition, she denies that. It is true, she says, that she was dissatisfied with the form of fiction in vogue; or, rather, dissatisfied with nature for "giving an idea, without providing a house for it to live in." The novel was the obvious lodging, but was, it seemed, built on the wrong plan. So her idea

started as the oyster starts or the snail to secrete a house for it-self. And this it did without any conscious direction. The little note-book in which an attempt was made to forecast a plan was soon abandoned, and the book grew day by day, week by week, without any plan at all, except that which was dictated each morning in the act of writing.

Let us regard Mrs. Dalloway of the novel as the Mrs. Brown of the moment, whom Mrs. Woolf is trying to capture, and see how she is put into a book.

Clarissa Dalloway is one of the nice people she writes about; her characters are almost as civilized and as free from eccentricities and obsessions as those of Jane Austen; almost as correct in their behavior as those of Henry James. Mrs. Dalloway is fifty, moves in good society, likes to entertain, is gracious and something of a snob. We share with her one day, which ends with a party, and catch glimpses of that same day in the lives of people casually or intimately connected with her. She goes out in the morning—in the West End of London—to buy flowers for her party; she waits for a royal carriage to pass. Septimus Smith, a shell-shocked soldier, is standing near her. She returns, talks with her maid; an old lover, Peter Walsh, unexpectedly calls. He is just back from India to make arrangements to marry a young grass widow he thinks he loves. Richard, her husband, comes in after a lunch with Lady Bruton, bringing her flowers; her daughter Elizabeth goes out with her grim history tutor, whom Mrs. Dalloway dislikes intensely because of her curious fascination for Elizabeth. All of these little events stir thoughts, memories, associations, that light up her character, her present, her past. She successfully carries off her party, and at midnight it is over. Peter is almost as fully portrayed. After seeing Clarissa, he walks in Regent Park, his mind and

emotions stirred to unusual activity. He looks up at an air-
plane, tracing an advertisement of toffee across the sky; and
Septimus, the soldier, also looks up, and later sits near him
in the park, with his young Italian wife. A few hours afterward Peter passes by the house where an ambulance has just
stopped to pick up the body of Septimus, who has thrown
himself out of the window to escape the psychiatrist who is
planning to send him to a sanatorium. Peter has dinner at
his hotel, goes to the party, sees Sally Seton, who used to
visit Clarissa years ago, when Peter was in love with her. At
last he has a chance to speak with Clarissa, and he knows that
he still loves her and will never marry the young woman in
India. Septimus's fate has been decided in that twelve hours,
and Peter's too. The psychiatrist who frightened Septimus
into suicide comes to Clarissa's party, and mentions the sad
case. Clarissa feels a chill—death at her party. In an earlier
version, Mrs. Woolf tells us, Septimus didn't exist; it was
Clarissa who was to kill herself, or merely die at the end of
the party. But somehow Septimus grew into the pattern, and
in some strange way is Clarissa's double. He has slipped beneath the surface where she still keeps her footing. "She felt
somehow very like him—the young man who had killed himself. She felt glad he had done it—thrown it away." She sees
how the meaning of her own life has been defaced by corruption, lies, chatter; how she had schemed, valued success.
Septimus in his recklessness has preserved something she has
lost. His death was a defiance of the obscure evil represented
by men like Sir William Bradshaw, the psychiatrist—men
who exert an intolerable force upon the soul. Somehow it
was her disaster that the young man had killed himself, and
she forced to stand there in evening dress, receiving guests.
Going to the window, she draws back the curtains and
watches the old lady in the house across the way preparing
for bed. With all the noise and chatter of the drawing-room

behind her, it is fascinating to have this glimpse of a life quietly going its way. Somehow the shock of death has made Clarissa feel the beauty and strangeness and excitement of life more intensely, and she turns back to her party with a certain zest.

The book is a composition of reverie and dialogue, with brief snapshots of the outer aspect of people and things. We have the stream of consciousness and the stream of events. There are long reveries of Clarissa and of Peter, shifting as they notice things about them, or as a chance stimulus brings up a memory, or as they make some contact with people. When the characters are in groups, there is a symphony of reverie and dialogue—what they say aloud and what is drifting through their minds at the same moment. Sometimes Mrs. Woolf draws completely away from her characters, as in the passage inspired by the grey nurse who sits knitting beside the dozing Peter in Regent Park. While Peter sleeps, why shouldn't his creator play with her own mind?

What is the result? Has the character of Mrs. Dalloway been successfully projected? At the end Peter feels a curious stir at the sight of Clarissa coming towards him: "What is it that fills me with extraordinary excitement? It is Clarissa, he said. For there she was." Clarissa *is* emphatically. But there is nothing about which readers differ more than the so-called reality of characters, and perhaps for some readers she *isn't*. She may come to life for some of us, because we want her to. She satisfies a desire. Here is a woman over fifty for whom life is still exciting. She isn't dying of cancer or threatened with a stroke or suffering strange distortions of character from repressions; she is not an object of contempt or ridicule; her husband still loves her, her old lover still feels the attraction of her personality; she isn't consciously or unconsciously sacrificing her daughter, nor is she being sacrificed by her. In short, she offers an extension of experience that makes the prospect of fifty years old less desolating than it is usually made to appear in fiction; and we may want to have the illusion of a pleasant life at fifty just as much as at other times we may want to relive it at twenty. Then, Clarissa is a person we like to believe in because Mrs. Woolf endows her with her own sense of life, as a fascinating pattern of the significant and irrelevant, odd, confused, incoherent, with sudden flashes of meaning. Clarissa always had had the feeling that "it was very dangerous to live, even one day." In one of her moments of self-justification she thinks, "Peter believes me to be a snob, for liking people around me, and Richard regards it as foolish to like excitement when it is bad for my heart . . . but both are wrong." "What she liked was simply life. 'That's what I do it for,' she said, speaking aloud to life." And Clarissa has the revelatory glimpses: "Then for that moment she had seen an illumination; a match burning in a crocus; an inner meaning almost expressed."

The impression Mrs. Woolf gives of the trivial, tragic, confused, lovely, queer mix-up we call life is in one way disappointing, because it leaves us more at a loss than ever for a principle of order. And one of the satisfactions of art is that it simplifies confusion by selecting only certain forms and colors for its design. If by wearing blinkers and seeing only a few aspects of things, we have been able to persuade ourselves that we perceive an order and a meaning, Mrs. Woolf comes along and makes us face the infinite complications of the material. She exposes her reader to "constellations of stimuli," which form patterns of many motifs, the shape and color of each depending largely upon its relationship to each part of the whole design. The result—sometimes, at any rate —is that we become excited at the thought of living in so bewildering a world; and this too is pleasurable, though not quite so soothing as the illusion of simplicity and order.

Every now and then, we are enough shaken out of our habitual routine to catch a glimpse of life as Mrs. Woolf characteristically sees it. Here is a day, for instance, on which a young newspaper reporter, a girl, was faced with the problem of what to do with a desperately sick friend. The problem was complicated by lack of money, by an estrangement between the friend and her family, and by the obligation of the reporter to carry out, no matter what happened, certain assignments for her paper. Part of the day was taken up with telephone calls, long waits for the doctor—who, as it was Sunday and he was getting old, didn't want to come unless he could be sure it was a real crisis—and killing time, between preparing ice packs and broths and taking temperatures, by reading the Yiddish comic strip of the newspaper. Then the sudden irruption of ambulance men, who were rough and hurried because it was late and they hadn't had their supper; the impotent rage of the reporter at the irrelevant intrusion of the ambulance men's supper into her tragic situation; attempts of a friend to reason with her—"But even ambulance men must eat!" Then waiting at the hospital, with a vista of two long wards during visiting hour, certain groups, gestures, sounds, stamping themselves on the mind: a woman incessantly trying to lift her hands, and three men, one a policeman, mechanically pushing them down. A talkative woman, also waiting, explains everything: "Her husband the policeman wants to be alone with her, but her brothers say, 'Ain't we a right to be here too?' " Shrieks of laughter from convalescent patients; a homely girl in a hideous grey dressing gown, walking about, grinning, and sucking a thermometer. A sense of the comedies and tragedies of a score of lives, suddenly broken off and lost forever by the need to dash to Brooklyn and "cover" a church meeting. Subway confusion, suburban streets dimly lighted, a half-empty

church, decorous people, seeming lifeless after the movement and suffering of the hospital, a plump minister droning out a moth-eaten psychology of prayer, a correct usher in
frock coat pointing out the hymn to the harassed young
reporter—something about throwing all your cares on Jesus—
her expression of dangerous irritation, for if it was exasperating that ambulance men have to eat suppers, it was unbearable that people should sing hymns in the outskirts of
Brooklyn. Another dash through subways to the newspaper
office to write up copy. Ten-thirty at night. Elevator man
asleep in the elevator, the cat playing with scraps of paper.
Upstairs a glaringly lighted littered room, a few tired reporters in shirt sleeves, feet on tables, the spasmodic weary
clicking of two or three typewriters. All these universes—the
hospital, the church, the newspaper office; all these lives
brushing against one another, glimpsed for an instant; all
the movement and the incoherent scraps of conversation.
And one's own stream of consciousness flowing steadily on.
Only such a method as Mrs. Woolf's can render the intimate
"feel" of such a day's experience. And it must create the
impression of irrelevance and incoherence without being
either irrelevant or incoherent.

This method is perfectly exemplified in *Mrs. Dalloway,*
which seems to be the successful outcome of experiments
carried on in *The Mark on the Wall, The Voyage Out,* and
Jacob's Room. (Night and Day, Mrs. Woolf's second novel,
is entirely traditional in form.) Yet if one is seeking interesting people to read about, Rachel and some of the other
characters in *The Voyage Out,* and Jacob in *Jacob's Room,*
might be preferred to Mrs. Dalloway, who, with all her insight and grace, is rather limited—lacking in force and originality, deficient in passion, accepting too easily the standards of her own set—whereas Jacob and Rachel, both of

whom die young, seem full of latent possibilities. The theme
of *The Voyage Out* is the awakening of Rachel, who is undeveloped and immature at twenty-four, feeling nothing
deeply except her music. She is quite willing to accept the
people around her as symbols merely, of age, of motherhood,
of learning; she cares little about getting into communication with them. "To feel anything strongly was to create an
abyss between oneself and others, who feel strongly perhaps, but differently . . . It was far better to play the piano
and forget the rest." She takes a voyage on a cargo ship with
her father, a shipowner, and a few other passengers—her
aunt, her uncle, a Greek scholar, and the Dalloways (who
bear little resemblance to their namesakes in the later novel).
Mr. Dalloway, yielding to a casual impulse, kisses Rachel.
That experience, and the subsequent discussion of it with
her aunt, mark the beginning of her coming alive. People,
she realizes, can cease to be symbols, could become exciting.
Presently her aunt, who has not found much to attract her
in Rachel, notices a change and begins to draw her out, in
her humorous detached way, and to suggest to her that she
might become a person on her own account. "The vision of
her own personality, of herself as a real everlasting thing,
different from anything else, unmergeable, like the sea or the
wind, flashed into Rachel's mind, and she became profoundly excited at the thought of living." (The Dalloways,
by the way, debark at the next port, and figure no more in
the story.) Rachel stays for many weeks with her aunt at a
seacoast resort somewhere in South America, while her father
pursues his business in the interior. Near the villa is a hotel,
with a miscellaneous crowd of shifting guests, mostly English, there on business or for a holiday. Rachel is drawn into
a dance at the hotel, then into a picnic on the mountain.
She unfolds more and more. Young Hewet falls in love with
her. They go with a party on a week's excursion up the

river into the jungle, and the relationship with Hewet develops. Then—with the incoherence of life—Rachel contracts typhoid fever and dies. The voyage out takes on tragic significance: a literal voyage out to South America, then the voyaging out of Rachel's adventuring personality, finally a voyage out of life altogether.

Then there is Jacob Flanders: a little boy playing on the beach, a young boy collecting butterflies and beetles, a youth going to Cambridge in October, 1906, taking a cruise to the Scilly Isles on his vacation, spending a week-end at a country house with his college friends, living in rooms in London, going to a Bohemian party, having a casual love affair with the brainless pretty little Florinda, who deceives him, studying in the British Museum, making fashionable calls, riding on buses in Holborn, going to Greece and falling in love with Greek art—and also with an experienced married lady— doing in short what almost any young Englishman of good social position and not much money, and a little more than average intelligence but no extraordinary gifts, might do. Then the War and a swift end. Is Mrs. Woolf really trying to portray the character of Jacob? Perhaps the title is meant to suggest something different—not Jacob, but his room: the place where he lives, all his surroundings, animate and inanimate, upon which he acts and which act on him; all the atmospheres he breathes. An elderly lady sits opposite him in the train, and he lifts her dressing case down from the rack for her; she wonders who he is, but never knows. While he stands at his window, he sees a little girl stand on tiptoe to post a letter in the pillar box. When he is riding on the top of a bus, he watches an errand boy swing down the bus steps and, dodging between the cars, disappear forever in the crowd. We see him hurrying across a court at Cambridge, late at night, the only person passing at that moment, his footsteps echoing back from Chapel, from Hall, from ibrary—"The old stone echoing, 'the young man, the young man, back to his rooms.' " We see his room at Cambridge when he is absent, though his personality pervades it: "Listless is the air in an empty room; just swelling the curtain; the flowers in the jar shift. One fibre in the wicker arm-chair creaks, though no one sits there." Several things happen at the same moment about sunset on a spring day just before the War. They are flashed swiftly before us: Jacob rises from a chair in Hyde Park where he has been idling and, tearing up his ticket, walks away; the windows of Kensington Palace flush fiery rose; "Jacob," writes Mrs. Flanders, with the red light on her page, "is hard at work after his delightful journey"; "The Kaiser," the faraway voice remarks in Whitehall, "received me in audience." And that last, of course, suggests the coming War and the end of Jacob. But before he passes out of sight, his old tutor catches a glimpse of him walking down Piccadilly, remembers the set of Byron he gave the lad, thinks what a fine young man he has become; and Clara Durant, who loves him and knows he does not love her, starts at a glimpse of him in the crowd going in to a concert. When his mother and his friend are going through his possessions after his death, and his mother stands helplessly wondering what to do with an old pair of shoes, the sentence quoted above recurs: "Listless is the air in an empty room . . ." Now Jacob's room is really empty.

Less unified in effect than *Mrs. Dalloway, Jacob's Room* is like a succession of reveries, focused on Jacob. It is as if someone said—Jacob Flanders? Oh, yes, that young man who was killed at the beginning of the War. I remember when he was a little boy and picked up that old sheep's skull on the beach . . . and so on, one association calling up another —people, places, pictures, rumors—discursive, loosely chronological, speculative about the meaning of it all. Isn't Virginia Woolf using Jacob—as in a miniature way she used the mark on the wall—to convey her sense of the queerness and the fascination of life? "The strange thing about life is that though the nature of it must have been apparent to everyone for hundreds of years, no one has left any adequate account of it." [47] One begins to suspect that the Mrs. Brown she is pursuing is not any Jacob or Rachel or Mrs. Dalloway, but life itself. In these books, in *To the Lighthouse* and *The Waves,* Mrs. Woolf "sets life against death as though thus to discern more clearly what it means." [48]

What about *To the Lighthouse,* the novel which followed *Mrs. Dalloway?* One personality emerges triumphantly—Mrs. Ramsay, the organizing and presiding spirit of the house in the Hebrides that her family of husband and eight children and their numerous guests filled to overflowing in the summers before the War. Mrs. Ramsay (to quote Miss Holtby)

gathers and concentrates all thought, all feeling, all action into herself. Her light reveals them . . . She *is* the lighthouse, in some subtle way. The action, which in the first half of the book passes through her, is, in the second part, illuminated by her.[49]

In the first part, "The Window," Mrs. Ramsay is seated at a window amusing her youngest boy James with stories, while Lily Briscoe, an artist guest, is outside painting the scene, and Mr. Ramsay stalks up and down past the window, reciting scraps of poetry when he reaches rough places in his philosophic speculations. Other guests and members of the family drift past on their own business. Through glimpses of Mrs. Ramsay's stream of consciousness we build up the picture of her character, her life, her feeling about everyone connected with her. We also share Lily's reveries and dip briefly into those of other characters. The method is that of *Mrs. Dalloway,* but even more expert and more beautiful in style. James hopes they will be able to sail to the lighthouse tomorrow; his whole being is concentrated on that desire; he hates his father for announcing that the weather will be bad, and for distracting his mother's attention from himself.

He hated him for interrupting them; he hated him for the exaltation and sublimity of his gestures; for the magnificence of his head; for his exactness and egotism (for there he stood, commanding them to attend to him); but most of all he hated the twang and twitter of his father's emotion, which, vibrating around them, disturbed the perfect simplicity and good sense of his relations with his mother.

Not that James understood all that—he simply felt it would be a pleasure to kill his father with the scissors he was cutting out pictures with. They all dine that evening in the candle-lighted room, Mrs. Ramsay bringing the whole group of separate and constrained individualities together by her tact; "the whole effort of merging and flowing and creating rested on her." In the evening she has a quiet hour or two with her husband, who relies upon her absolutely for the sympathy his ego demands. All of these people lean to some degree on Mrs. Ramsay, and that gives her at times a pleasant sense of power. She has the social charm of Mrs. Dalloway, with a deeper and richer nature.

They don't go to the lighthouse. Years pass, and the house remains empty except for the occasional visits of the old caretaker. Nothing happens as Mrs. Ramsay had thought it would. The engagement of two young guests—which she had engineered a bit—ends in an unhappy marriage. Her favorite daughter Prue dies in childbirth; her gifted son Andrew is destroyed in a moment by a shell in the War; Mrs. Ramsay herself dies rather suddenly one night. Ten years later some of the same guests, those of the children who are left, and Mr. Ramsay gather again in the house, rescued from decay by the heroic efforts of the old cleaning women;

and James at last goes to the lighthouse—against his will, hating his father for making them go just as he had hated him before for standing in the way. But against his will, too, he is pleased when his father praises him for his skill in steering the boat. In the effort James makes in the boat to fix a fugitive impression, connected somehow with the lighthouse and with the actual and vaguely remembered hatred of his father—this effort to fish something up from the deeps of memory—we see how his father's attitude that evening years before toward the trip and toward his mother had fixed James's relation to his father.

The handling of reverie is even more deft than in *Mrs. Dalloway*. Take the pages where Mrs. Ramsay is reading from Grimm the story of the fisherman and his wife, allowing her thoughts to drift, now and again taking a turn suggested by the story: "The story of the Fisherman and his Wife was like the bass gently accompanying a tune, which now and then ran up unexpectedly into the melody." There is a typical example of how fantastically several strands of thought are twisted together in reverie when Mrs. Ramsay is walking in the garden with her husband, thinking about him and his work and his problems, and about her own duties as housekeeper and gardener:

She must stop for a moment to see whether those were fresh mole-hills on the bank; then, she thought, stooping down to look, a great mind like his must be different in every way from ours. All the great men she had ever known, she thought, deciding that a rabbit must have got in, were like that, and it was good for young men (though the atmosphere of lecture-rooms was stuffy and depressing to her beyond endurance almost) simply to hear him, simply to look at him. But without shooting rabbits, how was one to keep them down? . . .

In estimating Mrs. Woolf's accomplishment in characterizing people by this special technique of hers, it is important to notice with what skill she conveys marked differences in temperament. The reveries of her characters are as distinct and individual as the gestures, mannerisms of speech, tones of voice, that other novelists rely upon for identification. Marcel Proust, or Dorothy Richardson, experts in the recording of reveries, make us feel that we are constantly in personal and intimate contact with the consciousness of the author; so that the use of this method has sometimes seemed to imply a highly subjective type of writing. But open *To the Lighthouse* upon any passage of reverie, and there will be no mistaking Tansley's for Lily's, or Mrs. Ramsay's for her husband's, or James's for his sister Cam's. We see their minds as objectively as with a Dickens we might see their facial expression or the movement of their hands. Lily the artist, for instance, thinks in sharp visual images; the abstract must receive a concrete embodiment before she can deal with it. Told by Mrs. Ramsay's son that his father was always speculating about subject, object, and the nature of reality, she asked what he meant precisely, and he said, "Oh, think of a kitchen table when you're not there." So Lily usually sees a scrubbed deal table when the thought of Mr. Ramsay's books drifts into her mind, and this phantom table has a way of lodging itself in the fork of a pear tree, its four legs in air, if she happens to be in the orchard; or in some other ridiculous place. All of us are intermittently engaged in self-justification, but we all have our individual ways of satisfying this universal need; and Mrs. Wolf gives to the reveries of all her characters both this universal and this individual stamp. She has created only one character who seems to be the vehicle of her own reveries—Orlando, who lives through three centuries and two sexes and many adventures and pursuits, and whose consciousness is ample enough to contain Mrs. Woolf's.

If one wonders whether the aim of these novels is really

to create character, the wonder is not lessened by *To the Lighthouse,* in spite of the vividness of Mrs. Ramsay. The first movement of the book brings out the interrelationships of the various people in the old house and stresses the integrating quality of Mrs. Ramsay's personality, which draws the whole group together. But then follows the next movement, "Time Passes." There is only an empty house, visited by the winds and storms of many winters, stroked at regular intervals by the beams from the lighthouse, falling into decay from damp and dust, until it is touch and go with it whether the process of decay will be completed and the house will pitch down into darkness. A pair of shoes, a shooting cap, some faded skirts in wardrobes—things people had shed and left—these alone keep the human shape. Memories of Mrs. Ramsay lingering about the house come to life only when the old cleaning women recall this or that trivial detail about her, and then "faint and flickering, like a yellow beam or the circle at the end of a telescope, a lady in a grey cloak, stooping over her flowers, went wandering over the bedroom wall, up the dressing-table, across the washstand, as Mrs. McNab hobbled and ambled, dusting and straightening." The procession of nights and days and seasons passes before us in imagery so beautiful that it would be hard to find in twentieth-century English prose anything to surpass it. And what happens to the human beings who had peopled the house is lightly touched on in a parenthesis here and there, like a poetic or ironic mark of punctuation in the long record of time. For example, there are nights full of wind and destruction when the sea tosses and the restless sleeper wakes and is tempted to ask questions as to the what and why and wherefore of things. "[Mr. Ramsay, stumbling along a passage one dark night, stretched his arms out, but Mrs. Ramsay, having died rather suddenly the night before, his arms, though stretched out, remained empty.]" Lovely summer days drift by; sunsets on the sea, fishing boats against the moon, serenity. Then the apparition of an ashen-colored ship, come, gone; a purplish stain upon the bland surface of the sea, as if something had boiled and bled invisibly beneath. "[Mr. Carmichael brought out a volume of poems that spring which had an unexpected success. The war, people said, had revived their interest in poetry.]"

And so one day the house, rescued, is reopened. It is chiefly through Lily that we get the last, somewhat puzzling, minor movement. She thinks much of Mrs. Ramsay, and she is distressed by Mr. Ramsay's unconscious demand upon her for the sympathy his wife had always had ready for him. To Lily it seemed that "his immense self-pity, his demand for sympathy, poured and spread itself in pools at her feet, and all she did, miserable sinner that she was, was to draw her skirts a little closer around her ankles, lest she should get wet." She begins to work again upon the unfinished painting begun ten years before, and tries to recapture the glimpse of truth that was to be made clear through the relation of masses, lights, and shadows. She reflects that Mrs. Ramsay's gift had been to make of the moment something memorable; she had made life stand still for an instant and take a shape. Lily in her way was trying to do the same thing. There was this truth, this reality, which suddenly laid hands upon her, "emerged stark at the back of appearances and commanded her attention." Wondering about the meaning of life, Lily thinks: "The great revelation had never come. The great revelation perhaps never did come. Instead there were little daily miracles, illuminations, matches struck unexpectedly in the dark." She regains her feeling of completeness about the house and the people, the feeling that ten years ago had made her say she was in love with it.

Love had a thousand shapes. There might be lovers whose gift it was to choose out the elements of things and place them

together, and so, giving them a wholeness not theirs in life, make
of some scene or meeting of people (now all gone and separate)
one of those globed, compacted things over which thought lingers
and love plays.

This is at all events what Mrs. Woolf has made out of the
scene and the people of *To the Lighthouse;* our thought
lingers over this globed, compacted thing rather than over
any individual characters.

One felt more and more dubious about the Mrs. Brown
of the railway carriage, when she appeared as a hero-heroine
in *Orlando,* spanning the centuries from Queen Elizabeth to
Thursday, October 11, 1928—at that moment aged thirty-six
and a lady, though she had started out three centuries before
as a young boy. It began to be clear that Mrs. Woolf was
seeking to capture not characters, but life; and that perhaps
the most significant sentence in her essay on "Mrs. Brown"
was that one slipped in casually at the end—"for Mrs. Brown
is the spirit we live by, Life itself." In capturing that spirit,
characters often serve her very well, but when they don't, an
empty house in the Hebrides or a mark on the wall will do.
Orlando at any moment of his surprising career is no more
alive than his historic house, where "the light airs which
forever moved about the galleries stirred the blue and green
arras, so that it looked as if the huntsmen were riding and
Daphne were flying." Yet life escapes after all. When
Orlando's lover swoops down in his plane on the last page,
there springs up over his head a wild bird. " 'The wild
goose,' " cries Orlando. It had haunted her ever since she
was a child.

"There flies the wild goose. It flies past the window out to
sea. . . . I've seen it here, there, England, Persia, Italy . . .
always it flies out to sea, and always I fling after it words like
nets, which shrivel as I have seen nets shrivel, drawn on deck

with only seaweed in them. And sometimes there is an inch of silver—six words—in the bottom of the net."

There are six lives in the net of *The Waves,* and their story is told in a prelude and nine reveries, in a pattern of monologues, uttered with no pretense of realism by six persons: Susan, Jinny, and Rhoda, Neville, Louis, and Bernard. There are eight interludes, during which the day which breaks in the prelude grows to midday and declines toward sunset, as the lives of the friends move on from childhood to middle age. The waves break on the shore at dawn, fall with muffled thud as the wind rises, mass themselves, curve their backs and crash at flood tide, spread their white fans out over the beach—behave in short as waves would behave throughout a long day—and continue to break at the end of the day and the end of the book, in "the eternal renewal, the incessant rise and fall and fall and rise again." And in these same interludes the birds in the garden of the house near the sea behave in the manner appropriate to birds: a few chirps before the sun rises, a chorus shrill and emulous and ecstatic in the height of the morning, a twittering at evening and a fall downward like a net descending on the tree tops—in all their movements suggesting the lives of the six who utter the monologues, who begin as children and become certain kinds of men and women, scoring a path across life as one treads a path across the fields.

Here, as in *To the Lighthouse,* what the six people do in the way of marrying and dying and achieving a career and bearing children, they do parenthetically. What they voice in their monologues is their essential being. They are like the flames that speak in one of Dante's visions, flames struggling in the wind or quietly burning in a tranquil air. And each flame we come to know, as Dante knew his friends and enemies in those points of fire.

Realizing the nature of Mrs. Woolf's aim, we begin to
understand certain effects of her books upon us. We feel
ourselves becoming detached and contemplative, rather than
involved and emotional. Her own detachment impresses all
her critics, who account for it in various ways. Miss Holtby,
who notes how the thought of the sea haunts her writing,
points out how often the action takes place out at sea, on
an island, on the shore, "because it is there, away from the
land, on a ship, out at sea, on an island, that Mrs. Woolf
sees humanity with detachment. From that vantage point
she can look back on life, look back on death, and write her
parable." [50] R. D. Charques, who thinks (along with a growing number of critics of the "proletarian" school) that imaginative writers must inevitably throw in their lot for or
against the existing order of society, calls Mrs. Woolf "aloofness itself"—"no other contemporary novelist is so far removed from trivial or worldly things, so delicately poised
above the common earth of fiction." [51] According to Clive
Bell, she looks at her people through a cool sheet of glass;
if she is watching a pair of lovers, she knows and puts down
what they are feeling and saying. She herself feels the
romance of the situation, but does not share the emotions of
the actors. She is detached, and we too are detached. She can
give the vision of someone feeling intensely; perhaps she
shared the emotion when her imagination first projected the
person and situation. But she has withdrawn from it and
held it off for contemplation. Compare the experience of
frustration in love that Mary, in *Night and Day,* goes
through, with that of Gwenda in *The Three Sisters* or Philip
in *Of Human Bondage.* One is prepared in Mary's case, as
in the others, to make the usual emotional identification;
the experience of emotional frustration is so common that
most readers possess that key into the realm of vicarious
living. But Mary's struggle and suffering move us as specta-

tors, rather than as participants. We draw away even from our own similar experience, and are contemplative instead of warmly reminiscent.

This effect of looking through glass at a picture may be one result of a constant quality of Mrs. Woolf's style—the concreteness of its visual imagery. Mary in the midst of her sense of defeat realizes that she will presently be able to find a certain solace in work:

Now when all was tempest and high running waves, she knew of a land where the sun shone clear upon Italian grammars and files of docketed papers. Nevertheless from the skeleton pallor of that land, and the rocks that broke its surface, she knew that her life there would be harsh and lonely beyond endurance.

The example is inconclusive; the whole book is needed to test the effect; but it does illustrate the constant touch upon the visual sense. Then the ease with which Mrs. Woolf slips in and out of people's minds keeps us from ever taking up a position permanently in any one character's mind. We live in Strether's mind throughout *The Ambassadors*. We are all but drowned in Ivan Karamazov's. We never desert Mary Olivier; if we wax philosophic, it is with her. But if we become philosophical for a moment with Mrs. Dalloway, the next instant we are outside Mrs. Dalloway, seeing her and her philosophy with the critical eye of Peter, or the slightly amused and ironic glance of Virginia Woolf. There is a constant shift of focus—from one person to another, and from individuals to life in general.

In writing of Laurence Sterne, she has perfectly expressed, as a quality of his style, what is her own as well. There are passages in her work, as in Sterne's, which bring

by the curious rhythm of their phrasing, by a touch on the visual sense, an alteration in the movement of the mind, which makes it pause and widen its gaze and slightly change its attention. We are looking out at life in general.

It is because they bring these alterations in the movement of the mind that her books both keep one excited at the thought of living, and at the same time detached from living any special form of life that, if it comes to disaster, darkens the world. Here for instance is Jacob, reading Plato late one night in his room near the British Museum sitting at his table with his pipe and his book:

Stone lies solid over the British Museum, as bone lies cool over the visions and heat of the brain. Only here the brain is Plato's brain and Shakespeare's; the brain has made pots and statutes, great bulls and little jewels; and crossed the river of death this way and that incessantly, seeking some landing, now wrapping the body well for its long sleep; now laying a penny piece on the eyes; now turning the toes scrupulously to the East. Meanwhile Plato continues his dialogue; in spite of the rain; in spite of the cab whistles; in spite of the woman in the mews behind Great Ormond Street who has come home drunk and cries all night long—"Let me in!"

Life in general: Plato and the drunken woman in Bloomsbury; Jacob's brain, and the brain of mankind through ages seeking a way out of death into life. It is this life in general with which Mrs. Woolf seeks a mode of communication. And this effort gives to her fiction the quality she finds very rare in English fiction—more often present in French fiction—intelligence. By intelligence she means neither brilliance nor intellectual power, but "the sense that the interest of life does not lie in what people do, nor even in their relations to each other, but largely in the power to communicate with a third party, antagonistic, enigmatic, yet perhaps persuadable, which one may call life in general."

And "life in general"? Bernard, in *The Waves,* who has always made stories, attempts to draw together the strands of the six lives and to come to terms with Life. Now he sees a certain order in things, and again another order, and each seems at the moment the true order—but "this is our perpetual illusion." Pretend that life is a globe which we turn about in our fingers:

the crystal, the globe of life as one calls it, far from being hard and cold to the touch, has walls of the thinnest air. If I press them, all will burst . . . Whatever sentence I extract whole and entire from this cauldron is only a string of six little fish that let themselves be caught, while a million others leap and sizzle, making the cauldron bubble like boiling silver, and slip through my fingers.

What is reality?

It would seem to be [she says at the end of *A Room of One's Own*] something very erratic, very undependable—now to be found in a dusty road, now in a scrap of newspaper in the street, now a daffodil in the sun . . . But whatever it touches, it fixes and makes permanent. That is what remains over when the skin of the day has been cast into the hedge; that is what is left of the past time and of our loves and hates. Now the writer, as I think, has the chance to live more than other people in the presence of this reality. It is his business to find it and collect it and communicate it to the rest of us.

To start out with Virginia Woolf in the pursuit of Mrs. Brown, the spirit we live by, life itself, reality, is to share the excited anticipation of Peter, on his way to Clarissa Dalloway's party—watching all the people leaving their houses in evening dress, watching the footmen opening doors:

Everybody was going out. What with these doors being opened, and the descent and the start, it seemed as if the whole of London were embarking in little boats moored to the bank, tossing on the waters, as if the whole place were floating off in carnival . . .

D. B.

X

ALDOUS HUXLEY'S POINT COUNTER POINT AND ANDRÉ GIDE'S THE COUNTERFEITERS

VIRGINIA WOOLF is criticized by those who look in fiction for a reflection of contemporary social and economic conflicts because she is detached and aloof, and finds no place

for the crude strife of material desires, for the harshness and bitterness of the class struggle . . . There clings to her work something of the decadence, the refinement of decay, like a fragrance that is too long prolonged, of the culture of her period.[52]

To detect this particular whiff of decay is the privilege of those who believe the culture of the period is dying; and such believers find this whiff becoming a very bad odor in the work of Aldous Huxley. Mr. Huxley himself is aware of it; and it is appropriate enough to refer, as Mr. John Strachey does, to Mr. Huxley's "now almost automatic gesture of holding his nose." [53] Yet he would rather resort to this gesture when he has to, than risk a new order.

He appears caught in a social groove [writes Mr. Charques]. And no matter how vigorously he lays about him, it is difficult to resist the conclusion that the groove represents for him an oasis in the desert, that he knows of nothing better and much that is worse . . . For all its imperfections, English middle-class society is in a sense his spiritual home. In that environment alone resides culture, erotic sensation, intellectual adventure, art, the spirit and most of the other things to which Mr. Huxley would seem to be attached.

Aldous Huxley writes the sophisticated novel of ideas, a characteristic product of a period when the thinking class in a civilized community is disillusioned and skeptical in temper. One generation gives itself up enthusiastically to the promotion of certain causes, in which it believes and for which it fights. Such a generation grew up under the tutelage of Wells, Shaw, Galsworthy, in England; of Zola, Rolland, in France; of Tolstoy, in Russia. It was nourished on the novels and plays that attacked the evils of society in the confidence that exposure would lead to far-reaching reform. Some Kingdom of God or other was just ahead, if people could be made to see it and work for it. The War—it was possible to regard even that, after the first shock, as a crusade for a new order. Then followed swift disillusionment, the collapse of causes, the undermining of creeds, and the Kingdom of God receded completely out of sight or took on a drab and uninspiring look. Maybe it was possible to bring it about, but was it worth it? It is with a jaundiced eye that Aldous Huxley, in *Brave New World,* inspects the possible Utopia. He was twenty-four when the War ended and he began to express in one brilliantly written book after another a mood typical of the skeptical generation that follows the believing one, which had fought for social causes before the War and then fought the War and tried to make it mean things it did not mean at all. The young skeptics regarded these defeated fighters with a mixture of resentment, contempt, and amused tolerance. They had no faith left in ideas, but illogically enough they still liked to talk about them, and no one could do this better than Huxley. His novels were loose frames for intellectual fantasies, for the play of mind, for witty conversation about anything and everything. The talkers were mouthpieces for the author's ideas, but if the talk was good, what difference did it make?

In the novel of ideas—Mr. Huxley has his novelist reflect in *Point Counter Point—*

"The character of each personage must be implied, as far as possible, in the ideas of which he is the mouthpiece. In so far as theories are rationalizations of sentiments, instincts, dispositions of soul, this is feasible . . . The great defect of the novel of ideas is that it's a made-up affair. Necessarily; for people who can reel off neatly formulated notions aren't quite real; they're slightly monstrous."

And the other defect which he points out is this:

"you must write about people who have ideas to express—which excludes all but about .01 percent. of the human race. Hence the real, the congenital novelists don't write such books. But then I never pretended to be a congenital novelist." [54]

This is Philip Quarles speaking about himself, but it might just as well be Huxley. It is true of him. And another bit of self-analysis by Philip sounds like the critical judgment passed on Huxley: if he didn't write straightforward love stories or detective fiction, said Philip to himself,

"perhaps it was because he couldn't. In art there are simplicities more difficult than the most serried complications. He could manage the complications as well as anyone. But when it came to the simplicities, he lacked the talent—that talent which is of the heart, no less than of the head; of the feelings, the sympathies, the intuitions, no less than of the analytical understanding."

It is this lack that leads Edwin Muir to call Huxley's art, in the portrayal of character, one of exposure rather than of comprehension; and that leads Mr. Charques to refer to the absence of kindness or sympathy or deep emotion as his principal failing as a novelist.

Deep emotion about his characters is absent, but not emotion about the predicament of the class to which most of them belong. He himself is caught in that predicament, involved in the unhappy confusion he describes and satirizes. His mood—in *Antic Hay,* for example—swings between hilarity and disgust, as he watches his menagerie perform. He is both allured and repelled by their lunatic relationships, their excesses of intellectualism or of sensuality. He has—

except in *Crome Yellow* and to a less degree in *These Barren Leaves*—none of the urbane detachment that belongs in the tradition of the kind of novel he writes and that characterizes Norman Douglas's *South Wind* or Thomas Love Peacock's *Nightmare Abbey*. His surface manner is sometimes ironic and aloof, but there are distress and anger underneath. Peacock would probably have put him in *Nightmare Abbey* along with Byron and Shelley. Huxley tries to look at the contemporary scene as a reasonable being, without sentimental preoccupations; as a skeptic, aware of the relativity of all things; as an artist, to whom everything is good for contemplation. But he is also—and this would forever exclude him from Norman Douglas's island of Nepenthe—a moralist, to whom (as Raymond Weaver has put it) "this best of all possible worlds is good, because it is a good world to strangle, and the more it deserves strangling, the better world it is." "A mortal coil of moralist, sceptic, artist—that is Mr. Huxley's baffling pattern." [55]

What is *Point Counter Point* about? Personal relationships, oddities and deformations of character, different ways in which people love and die and grow old, the ludicrous and tragic difficulties they get into and how they get out of them—or talk them out. Walter Bidlake does a little desultory literary work, but his real business is love: he involves himself with Marjorie, grows to dislike her, becomes mad about Lucy Tantamount, is accepted and then tossed away, and drifts back, with a little pushing from his relatives, to Marjorie. Philip Quarles and his wife Elinor are too self-conscious and skeptical to keep their love alive; Elinor is on the verge of an affair with the Fascist, Webley, but the death of her child stops her; there is no solution. Webley, a fascist with a gang of Green Shirts, makes love and orations, and is murdered rather horribly by the degenerate Spandrell, who commits the crime chiefly to drag in the Communist, Illidge, and make him translate his vague talk about killing off the oppressors into a concrete murder. Old Lord Tantamount plays with his laboratory specimens; old Bidlake the painter finds his philosophy of hedonism failing him when cancer takes hold of his pylorus; old Quarles the philanderer is blackmailed by his cheap little stenographer. Burlap—as malicious a portrait as exists in modern fiction of the man of letters—mourns his dead wife and delicately seduces his secretary. Rampion, who suggests a D. H. Lawrence released from his crucifixion, talks about healthy sex and the ills of society. And everybody talks, including Huxley himself, about biology and Bach and painting and love and lust and other people and the peculiar sex habits of certain fish and Shelley and marriage and religion and politics. Much of this talk goes on at those gatherings of the intellectuals that Huxley likes to assemble—at musicales, at taverns in Soho, at London clubs.

Rampion, who has much to say about the "central norm" of humanity, declares the world to be "an asylum of perverts" from that norm, "perverted towards goodness or badness, towards spirit or flesh," perverted by the imagination, the intellect; perverted in morals, politics, science, business, love, always trying to be something other than human. This is the theme of *Point Counter Point;* and the counterpoint is made up of departures from the norm; various forms of rottenness are set against one another and against human soundness—which is postulated rather than portrayed. The deviations from the norm of sex are the most numerous: Lucy Tantamount's sadism; the adolescent perversities of the "reversed ascetic" Spandrell; the sliminess of Burlap, whose ardors were those of an "incestuous child"; the bleating lecheries of old Quarles, and so on. Philip the novelist reflects that probably the acquisitive instinct has more perverts in a social order based on property and profit than the sex instinct; people are odder about their money than about their amours. But he finds himself "less interested in money than the average." Illidge, who comes from the working class, would say this lack of interest in possessions could not flourish except in an atmosphere of easy money; but Philip—who has never had to face the daily bread problem—is quite sure that he is temperamentally indifferent to money. So he does not depict acquisitive characters in his novels. Aldous Huxley, who is clearly using Philip here and elsewhere as his mouthpiece for literary speculation, is less candid on this point than Virginia Woolf. Mrs. Woolf has the same intellectual and upper-class background, but she wrote *A Room of One's Own* to demonstrate that "intellectual freedom depends upon material things," such as an income of five hundred pounds a year. The characters in this little world of *Point Counter Point*—as the critics of communist sympathies do not fail to point out—are drawn from a decadent leisure class and its intellectual parasites. And the miseries in this world, aside from the unavoidable ills of childhood and old age and those emotional frustrations inseparable from living in any period, may be mostly written off as due to the decline of bourgeois culture.

There is an interest in *Point Counter Point* that may outlast for some readers the interest in those "slightly monstrous" characters who "reel off neatly formulated notions." This interest is in its structure. From time to time, Philip Quarles the novelist, who enters about the middle of the book in person, though he has been mentioned before, jots down in his notebook thoughts about the art of fiction. And Huxley puts Philip's theories into practise. Philip talks about the " 'musicalization of fiction. Not in the symbolist way, by subordinating sense to sound . . . But on a large scale, in the construction.' " He meditates on Beethoven, the changes of mood, the abrupt transitions.

"More interesting still, the modulations, not merely from one key to another, but from mood to mood. A theme is stated, then developed, pushed out of shape, imperceptibly deformed, until, though still recognizably the same, it has become different . . . Get this into a novel. How? The abrupt transitions are easy enough. All you need is a sufficiency of characters and parallel, contrapuntal plots. While Jones is murdering a wife, Smith is wheeling the perambulator in the park. You alternate the themes. More interesting, the modulations and variations are also more difficult. A novelist modulates by reduplicating situations and characters. He shows several people falling in love, or dying, or praying in different ways—dissimilars solving the same problem. Or, vice versa, similar people confronted with dissimilar problems . . . Another way: the novelist can . . . elect to consider the events of the story in their various aspects—emotional, scientific, economic, religious, metaphysical, etc. He will modulate from one to the other—as, from the aesthetic to the physico-chemical aspect of things . . ." [56]

Thus, in *Point Counter Point,* there are half a dozen different ways of dying fully set forth—the death of little Phil from spinal meningitis is the most harrowing; and more than a dozen different ways of loving—among which we should give first place to Burlap's as most nauseating. As for the modulations, emotional-scientific-physico-chemical, we watch Everard Webley die, and then consider how from the air "the invisible hosts of saprophytics" begin their invasion:

they would live among the dead cells, they would grow and prodigiously multiply, and in their growing and procreation all the chemical building of the body would be undone, all the intricacies and complications of its matter would be resolved, till by the time their work was finished a few pounds of carbon, a few quarts of water, some lime, a little phosphorus and sulphur, a pinch of iron and silicon, a handful of mixed salts . . . would be all that remained of Everard Webley's ambition to rule and his love for Elinor, of his thoughts about politics and his recollections of childhood, of his fencing and good horsemanship, of that soft strong voice and that suddenly illuminating smile, of his admiration for Mantegna, his dislike of whiskey . . ."

And so forth. Or we listen with Lord Edward to Bach. The air in his laboratory had been set shaking by the playing in the hall below:

The shaking air rattled Lord Edward's *membrana tympani;* the interlocked *malleus, incus,* and stirrup bones were set in motion so as to agitate the membrane of the oval window and raise an infinitesimal storm in the fluid of the labyrinth. The hairy endings of the auditory nerve shuddered like weeds in a rough sea; a vast number of obscure miracles were performed in the brain, and Lord Edward ecstatically whispered "Bach!"

All this is immensely instructive. The effect on the reader's emotions is more obscure. The effect on our grasp of a character in fiction is nothing at all. One is reminded of how Thomas Mann, in *Buddenbrooks,* suddenly breaks off his intimate and warm narrative of little Hanno's life at the point where he falls ill of typhoid fever, and continues in a new manner, impersonal and scientific, to explain the course usually taken by the most virulent form of the disease. Science must somehow be given its place in fiction. Experiments like those of Mann and Huxley are, if nothing else, technically exciting.

As for that aspect of the "musicalization of fiction" that depends on showing different people loving, dying, and so on, in their different ways, there is nothing new in that. These variations on the major themes of life have been played by all great novelists, even though they have not resorted to musical analogies to explain their method. Think of *War and Peace:* the deaths of the little princess in childbirth, of Andrey on the battle-field, of little Petya in the raid, of the old prince in his bed, of the captives before the firing squad. And Pierre, Nicholas, Natasha, Marya, all had their very different ways of loving. Huxley is playing with technique; Tolstoy was creating life and character. But then, he was a "congenital novelist."

It is interesting to compare *Point Counter Point* with André Gide's *The Counterfeiters*. Both novels offer examples of the more intricate narrative patterns that have appeared to challenge the relatively simple biographical and chronological progression we are familiar with. They present striking similarities of method: musical analogies in structure, the novelist Edouard trying for effects like those of a fugue, and Philip for the transitions and modulations of a symphony; novelists in leading rôles, who take notes on the other characters, plan a novel about them, and thus introduce a pleasing confusion in our minds between the actual novelist who wrote the book we are reading and the fictitious novelist who is represented as engaged upon that book. The author must get a good deal of amusement out of this juggling. As one reader has expressed it:

As Gide approaches certain difficulties in characterization or in shifts of viewpoint, Edouard's Journal begins to discuss them as difficulties which arise in the novel Edouard is writing; so that we come to regard Edouard's projected novel as the fiction and Gide's novel as reality. In this way Gide induces our belief. You see Gide is not writing a novel; it is Edouard who is doing that. Keep your eyes on Edouard, while Gide plays tricks on you.

The similarities between Gide and Huxley are so striking that the question whether Gide (whose book came out four years before Huxley's) influenced Huxley enters the mind; and there it had better rest quietly, while we recall something Gide wrote in answer to a correspondent who accused him of unacknowledged borrowing from Saint-Simon.

This modern mania to see influences in each resemblance that one discovers [he says] transforms the criticism of some university graduates into police work and throws many artists into absurdities through their fear of being suspected of resembling someone.[57]

Aside from likenesses in structure, there are likenesses among the characters. And this probably means nothing more than that the intellectual classes of twentieth-century London and Paris can furnish similar animals for the menagerie. Huxley's Lucy Tantamount used a gardenia perfume and Gide's Lady Lillian, sandalwood: that is the chief difference between two predatory ladies who claimed for themselves all the privileges of men. Both were experimental and ruthless. Lucy had inherited her father's interest in seeing how specimens behaved when you grafted a tail where a leg should have been, for example. Lillian, who had seen in a terrible shipwreck what was meant by the survival of the fit, had had a lot of delicate feelings hacked off like the fingers of those who had tried to climb into the overloaded boat. In each book is the more than middle-aged husband playing the fool with his mistress; in each book, a good but tiresome lady expecting an illegitimate baby; in each, a counterfeit literary gentleman—Passavant is the more sinister, Burlap the more slimy; and in each, a distinguished artist grown very old and miserable.

For differences, there is much more of the novel of manners left in *Point Counter Point* than Gide would approve of. For he defines the "pure novel" he is writing as a long prose narrative involving a conflict of characters and of ideas, and specifically excluding elements that do not belong to the novel, like details of local color, sociological background, things seen rather than felt. In Gide's novel details of this sort are few and casually noted; in Huxley's they are numerous and prominent—the country houses, the London club, the Tantamount mansion, the history of the Tantamount fortune, and so on. Huxley's story is more securely anchored in time than Gide's: it has its fascist movement and its characters may be called on to explain why they didn't fight in the War, whereas Gide wanted to get away from the moment. He considered whether to lay his scene before or after the War; decided to have part of the action before and part after; then realized that the passing of counterfeit gold coins (an important incident in the story) could have taken place only before the War, gold coins having been withdrawn after the War; and ended by totally ignoring the War.

The most interesting difference lies in the treatment of the novelist character. Huxley's Philip is away in India until the book is half finished. Not till then does he begin to jot down his notes on the art of fiction and his comments on the fictional possibilities of the people around him. These passages come in solid blocks, and it is very hard to think of Philip as anyone but a thinly disguised Huxley. It would have been just as effective, one sometimes thinks, if Huxley had followed the Fielding tradition and prefaced sections of the novel by little essays. This device, by the way, actually intrigued Gide for a while, when he had been dipping into a translation of *Tom Jones,* and he wondered whether he ought not to intervene with his own comments, but decided instead to involve his Edouard more vitally in the action. Now Philip is not seriously involved in the action of *Point Counter Point.* The situation with his wife is uncomfortable, but it remains unresolved and unresolvable, given their temperaments. He directs the conversation of others, and meditates. Edouard, however, is all tangled up emotionally with Laura and Olivier and Bernard; and he acts to straighten things out. He rescues Laura from her predicament; he gives Bernard the breathing space and economic security he needs; he draws Olivier away from Passavant and suicide just in time. He is also unwittingly responsible for the suicide of little Boris, whom he has placed in the school where the lad's grandfather teaches. In this suicide his nephew George is involved; and Edouard is well aware of the corruption of this little reprobate; but he is too naïve— and in this respect we certainly can't mistake Edouard the novelist for Gide the novelist—to realize just what is going on. He is so shocked by the suicide that he says at the end that he will have to leave it out of his novel, for he doesn't know how to handle it. For another difference, Edouard's Journal is quoted for the events of a year before the story opens; and passages from it are rather evenly distributed throughout the book—filling thirteen of the forty-five chapters. It is taken up with his projected use of the material life is offering him, and with records of the events that crowd in upon him and must somehow be subdued to the demands of the novel. His ideas about the general art of the novel are in a conversation—not in the Journal. To sum up: Huxley's use of Philip is incidental; Gide's use of Edouard is integral. It is controlled throughout by the theme of the book: the struggle between what life offers to the novelist and what he finds it possible to make of it. On that problem Edouard's sister Pauline makes a penetrating comment towards the end of the book. They have been speaking of her relations with her husband, and Edouard expresses surprise that his brother-in-law has not tried to explain about certain compromising letters and clear up a false situation.

"But, my dear friend [replies Pauline], you know well enough that nothing lasts more eternally than a false situation. It's the business of you novelists to try to solve them. In real life nothing is solved; everything continues. We remain in our uncertainty; and we shall remain to the very end without knowing what to make of things. In the mean time life goes on and on, the same as ever."

André Gide, says Arnold Bennett in his preface to Gide's *Dostoevsky,*

is equally interested in the esthetic and in the moral aspect of
literature . . . He writes in the very midst of morals. They are
not only his background, but frequently his foreground . . .
[And] no novelist can achieve anything permanent without a
moral basis or background.

And André Gide, discussing in his own preface Dostoevsky's
moral problems, which are his own problems as well, explains, that in his consideration of the Russian novelist:
"I . . . have sought consciously or unconsciously, what had
most intimate connections with my own ideas." He says, further, that there is no question too transcendent for Dostoevsky to treat, yet "he never approaches a question from
the abstract, ideas never exist for him but as functions of
his characters, wherein lies their perpetual relativity and
source of power." Gide distinguishes Dostoevsky from other
novelists in this respect, that

the novel, with but rare exceptions, concerns itself solely with
relations between man and man, passion and intellect, with
family, social, and class relations, but never, practically never
with the relations between the individual and his self or his God,
which are to Dostoevsky all important.

And to Gide. These problems that Dostoevsky deals with
had been taken over, or belonged more properly, it was
thought, in the field of morals and theology, so that one of
the great services of Dostoevsky was to extend the field and
the range of the novel. In his own work and in his own way
André Gide has attempted somewhat the same thing that
is done with such splendor by Dostoevsky.

In his own way, and this means through the honest vision
of his own temperament. His belief about morals is not the
usual conventional and accepted belief; he has definite con-
ceptions of sex relationships which he has been at pains to
make perfectly clear in his autobiography and in *Corydon*.
His own solution of the antagonisms between the orthodox

and the heterodox moral codes Gide would seem, from his books, to have resolved for himself by the individualistic method. He has written that "Pour chacun la route est unique et chaque route mène à Dieu." If this be true, what are the various "morals" that must be accepted to permit the variety of human souls each to find its way to God?

The autobiography, *Si le grain ne meurt* (as Raymond Weaver says in his "Preface" to the Modern Library edition of *The Counterfeiters*) "either in its earlier or its expurgated state, is certainly one of the most amazing confessions ever published by a man clothed and in his right mind." Of this book, Gide wrote: "I would exhibit to my kind a man in all the truth of nature, and this man—he will be myself." But the autobiography did not satisfy Gide (again according to Mr. Weaver) because the direct narrative in the first person "was less adequate as a means of self-expression than communication by indirection, as if all 'truth' must be 'overheard.' " Many people feel that this 'truth' was achieved for Gide in *The Counterfeiters*, where he seemed to overhear an essential truth about most of his characters.

The chief person is the novelist, Edouard, who is concerned passionately with understanding the people involved in his life, and who has many of the attributes and gifts of Gide himself. It is possible that we are not being too indiscreet when we say that the prototype for Edouard is André Gide himself. Gide would throw us off, stepping into *The Counterfeiters* from time to time in his own person as author and commenting on all the characters, and particularly on Edouard himself. But the subterfuge is self-conscious and obvious; the likeness remains. Of making this identification of author and character, Gide himself writes:

Imprudent, dishonest even, I admit, to impute to the author himself the thoughts expressed by the characters in his novels or tales. But we know this was Dostoevsky's medium of expression, often utilizing a colourless individual to formulate one of his cherished truths.

Gide, one feels, utilizes both his "author" and his Edouard for self-confession in *The Counterfeiters*.

Gide tells us that, according to Dostoevsky, "we have each our reason for living, superior, hidden—hidden often from ourselves—certainly far different from the ostensible goal assigned by most of us to our existence." It is to find this hidden reason for living, and to determine as well each individual's relations to God, as well as to trace the route to that achievement, that Edouard in *The Counterfeiters* exists. But Gide is also striving in his art to discover these things for himself. One recalls Lawrence's statement: "One sheds one's sicknesses in books—repeats and presents again one's emotions to be master of them."

Into *The Counterfeiters* he desires to pour everything, he says; to discover the essences of all his characters, to learn the route that each one is taking on his way to God. Edouard, the novelist, holds the book together, because all of the characters enter either directly or indirectly into his life. He has toward most of the people an aloof reserve, but beneath that is an insatiable curiosity. The book opens with Bernard Profitendieu who has just made the discovery that he is illegitimate; that Profitendieu is not his real father. Something strikes him as a reality which strikes many young boys and girls merely as fantasy; and the revelation so disturbs him that he decides to leave home. In Bernard the humiliation strengthens his pride. But it does more than that. The young boy will leave home in order to revenge this humiliation. Gide says: "The man who has suffered humiliation seeks to inflict humiliation in his turn."

Bernard finds his best friend, Olivier Molinier, in the Luxembourg Gardens and begs to be taken in to his home for the night; after that he will strike out on his own. From

Olivier Bernard learns of Olivier's Uncle Edouard, the novelist, who has been away in England, but who is presently to return to Paris. We learn through the conversation of the boys that night about Vincent Molinier, the older brother, who has a mistress, but not until later does Bernard learn who the young woman is.

Vincent has been sojourning with the Comte de Passavant, the villain—the very suave villain—of the book. De Passavant brings Vincent and his friend Lillian Griffiths together, and that relationship ends in tragedy. He is involved with Strouvilhou, the leader of the gang of counterfeiters. Both de Passavant and Strouvilhou have a passion to bring ruin and destruction upon young boys. They induce the sons of prominent families to pass the counterfeit coins, knowing that these conventional families will do all in their power to avoid scandal, and that the fears of these families will also provide material for blackmail. The Comte de Passavant gets young Olivier into his power by playing on the lad's vanity and offering him the editorship of a review he is backing. He is an altogether vicious man; even Edouard, who makes no easy moral denunciations, believes this.

It is Laura Vedel, now Mme. Douviers, who is going to have a child by Vincent Molinier, and whom he has jilted for Lady Griffiths.

It is at this same hour that Laura, his yesterday's mistress, is at last dropping off to sleep in her gloomy little hotel room, after having long wept, long bemoaned herself. On the decks of the ship which is bringing him back to France, Edouard, in the first light of the dawn, is re-reading her letter—the plaintive letter in which she appeals for help.

We learn that Laura has been in love with Edouard, and that Edouard has urged her to marry Douviers.

Olivier meets his Uncle Edouard at the station. Edouard checks his suitcase in the cloakroom while he and Olivier drop in at a café for a glass of wine. Each loves the other, and yet neither can show it. Olivier is silent, though

he would have liked to fling himself into Edouard's arms and cry. Edouard misunderstood this silence of Olivier's and the look of sternness on his face; he loved him far too much to be able to behave with any ease.

In Edouard's agitation at meeting Olivier he had crumpled up the ticket for his suitcase and thrown it away. But Bernard had been watching the two from a concealed position; and Bernard gets the ticket. He gets the suitcase, too, and discovers five hundred francs inside. He goes to a hotel and what interests him almost more than the money is Edouard's Journal which he reads through carefully. He learns about the novel, *The Counterfeiters,* that Edouard is writing; he learns much about young George Molinier, whose steps are already, at his tender age, turned in the direction of villainy; he learns of Laura's wedding; of Edouard's love for Olivier; of La Pérouse, Edouard's old teacher, for whom Edouard feels a deep affection; and of Madame La Pérouse.

Bernard reads Edouard's reflections:

"There is a kind of tragedy, it seems to me, which has hitherto almost entirely eluded literature. The novel has dealt with the contrariness of fate, good or evil fortune, social relationships, the conflicts of passions and of characters—but not with the very essence of man's being . . . I have suddenly made up my mind to go away . . . To go away because one is too anxious to stay! . . . A certain love of the arduous—a horror of indulgence (towards oneself, I mean) is perhaps the part of my Puritan upbringing which I find it hardest to free myself from."

From Laura's letter and from the Journal Bernard gains information that he hopes he may turn to good use. He decides to call on Laura. When he has dramatized himself to her astonished eyes, they are interrupted by a call from Edouard himself. This is just what Bernard had hoped for;

and he tells the story of his theft and begs to be engaged as Edouard's secretary, and is accepted.

The novel is continued in the Journal. Edouard tells of losing his suitcase and of its recovery, of Bernard, and of Laura, and of his second visit to La Pérouse and the domestic troubles of that family.

Edouard takes Laura and Bernard with him to Switzerland, where they meet little Boris, La Pérouse's grandson. The old man has asked Edouard to do something about Boris, and the outcome of this meeting is that the child is sent to the Vedel-Azais pension school in Paris where George Molinier and the rest of the little counterfeiters are. The story is continued by Edouard's explanation of his theory for his novel.

"Day by day in a note-book, I note the state of the novel in my mind . . . instead of contenting myself with resolving each difficulty as it presents itself . . . I set forth each of these difficulties and study it. My note-book contains, as it were, a running criticism of my novel—or rather of the novel in general. Just think how interesting such a note-book kept by Dickens or Balzac would be . . . more interesting than the work itself . . ."

Discussing Edouard's theory later, Bernard tells Laura that he is very skeptical about it; that he fears Edouard is a mere dreamer.

"That method of work he described to us seemed to me absurd. A good novel gets itself written more naïvely than that . . . I thought at one time I might help him. If he had wanted a detective, I might perhaps have done the job. He could have worked on the facts that my police work would have furnished him . . ."

We learn now that Bernard has fallen in love with Laura, and this love has made him more aware of his own realistic temperament. He knows more about the conflict between reality and ideality than Edouard does. His criticism of

Edouard and the theory is a first step in Bernard's self-confidence and in his desire to be true. And this desire finds its clearest expression in his avowal to Laura of his love:

"Oh, Laura! I should like all my life long, at the very smallest shock, to ring true, with a pure, authentic sound. Nearly all the people I have known ring false. To be worth exactly what one seems to be worth . . . One wants to deceive people, and one is so much occupied with seeming, that one ends by not knowing what one really is."

Laura asks for the counterfeit coin he had shown her, and he gives it to her. She says, " 'Stay with Edouard; you'll help him; and let him help you. He is very good.' "

In the Journal Edouard writes:

"I am beginning to catch sight of what I might call the 'deeply-lying subject' of my book. It is—it will be—no doubt, the rivalry between the real world and the representation of it which we make to ourselves. The manner in which the world of appearances imposes itself upon us, and the manner in which we try to impose on the outside world our own interpretation—this is the drama of our lives. The resistance of facts invites us to transport our ideal construction into the realm of dreams, of hope, of belief, in a future life, which is fed by all the disappointments and disillusions of our present one."

This dichotomy in personality leads to counterfeiting.

Edouard and Bernard learn of Olivier's being in the clutches of Robert de Passavant. Bernard cannot sleep because of the letter he has received from Olivier—a letter so jaunty, so pretentious, so artificial that Bernard is sickened by its falseness. It was written by an Olivier trying to counterfeit himself. What neither of them understands is that the letter was written out of the pride that Olivier employs to cover his jealousy and his humiliation; for the thing that would have given Olivier the deepest happiness would have been to be his uncle's secretary.

Edouard and his entourage return to Paris; and the first

encounter Edouard has is with M. Molinier, who tells him of how his wife has discovered his unfaithfulness. But more important, he tells of M. Profitendieu's investigation and warning of the counterfeiting ring. Edouard pays a third visit to La Pérouse and discovers that Mme. La Pérouse has been sent away to a home, and that the old man is playing dead. He keeps with him a loaded pistol; and what has so distressed him is that he had made up his mind to shoot himself, had tried, and failed, and knows now that he will never be able to do it.

We are introduced then to the little gang of counterfeiters, and a more vicious lot it would be difficult to find. The ringleader is one Ghéridanisol, Strouvilhou's cousin. This group eventually torture little Boris and by their wicked ingenuity force him to shoot himself.

When Bernard and Olivier meet and have lunch they meet in their falsities, and the result is deep unhappiness for both of them. Their love is deflected by the image of Passavant that stands between them. It is only when Bernard begins to talk of Laura and his love for her that some of the falsity of the meeting disappears. Of Laura Bernard tells Olivier,

"what I feel for her is veneration; when I am with her every carnal thought seems an impiety . . . Thanks to Laura, my instincts have been sublimated . . . the turbulence I feel within me oppresses me and my aspiration is to discipline it. It's like steam inside me; it may whistle as it escapes (that's poetry), put in motion wheels and pistons; or even burst the engine. Do you know the act which I sometimes think would express me best? It's . . . Oh! I know well enough I shan't kill myself; but I understand Dmitri Karamazof perfectly when he asks his brother if he understands a person killing himself out of enthusiasm, out of sheer excess of life . . . just *bursting.*"

Olivier says that he too understands. And very ironically it is this conversation that Olivier remembers late that night, after the Argonauts' dinner, where he has got very drunk. From the midst of this brawl, Edouard rescues Olivier.

"Come and bathe your face a little. You look like a lunatic . . ." Of all that Edouard had said to him, he only understood that he had called him "thou." As a stormcloud bursts into rain, he felt his heart suddenly dissolve in tears . . . Then, quivering with distress and tenderness, he flung himself towards Edouard, pressed up against him and sobbed out: "Take me away!"

That night, at Edouard's, after what Olivier feels to be perfect happiness, he tries to commit suicide.

The scene between Edouard and his half-sister Pauline Molinier brings out a quality in Gide that one misses in Huxley—sympathy and comprehension. Pauline has come to Edouard's house to see Olivier, who is convalescing. But she has also come to give her sanction to the relationship that has at last been established between him and her son Olivier. " 'I am reassured by knowing Olivier is with you.' " She shows her perfect awareness of the pederastic nature of this relationship, and this awareness and this approbation somewhat shock Edouard, as Mme. Molinier sees. She says: " 'There are certain liberties of thought of which men would like to keep the monopoly. And yet I can't pretend to have more reprobation for you than I feel.' " Underneath her calm manner there is pleading when she adds, " 'I think you will be able to do him good.' " Edouard had not hoped that Pauline "would push comprehension so far."

He remembers what she had said once in another connection: " 'I prefer granting with a good grace what I know I shall not be able to prevent.' " Edouard is confused and uncomfortable, and he asks, to put a little air between them, about her husband and her younger son, and Pauline suddenly exclaims:

"Do you realize what my life is? I have restricted my happiness; year by year, I have been obliged to narrow it down; one by one

I have curtailed my hopes. I have given in; I have tolerated; I have pretended not to understand, not to see . . ."

Edouard tries to calm her by congratulating her on her reasonableness. " 'It is always when a woman appears most resigned that she seems the most reasonable' "—a reflection that irritated him—"by reason of its very justice." But this bitterness about life itself, Edouard wisely understands, is an indirect outlet for her jealousy and for her anxiety in leaving Olivier in his hands.

This "route" of Edouard and Olivier and their final uniting gives Gide as much satisfaction as any Victorian novelist ever had in marrying off the hero and heroine in the last chapter. But the author, through Edouard, comprehends nevertheless this mother's distress and disapproval; he has entered with his mind and his heart into her emotions. Wherever the reader's own sympathies lie, they can scarcely fail to be evoked in this scene.

Gide was led to reflect about the value of using children in fiction by his interest in Russian and English novels. He says:

Throughout French literature we find a horror of the formless, a certain impatience with what is not formed. This is how I account for the very small place taken by the child in French novels as compared with English or Russian. Scarcely a child is to be met with in our novels, and such authors as do introduce children—all too infrequently at that—are conventional, dull, and awkward.

In Dostoevsky's works children are numerous, and it is worth noting that the majority of his characters—and of these the most important—are still young, hardly set. It seems to be the genesis of feelings that interests him chiefly, for he depicts them as indistinct, in their larval state, so to speak.

It may be that Dostoevsky was wise to portray the indistinctness of many of his children. There is a tendency in

Gide's delineation to make his children a bit too distinct. Gide uses his children to present many of his own ideas; how, for example, parents live in the most deplorable ignorance of what their children do and think; how we tend in our reflections about children to sentimentalize them; and how this evil needs to be corrected. One feels at moments that these unformed or forming children are just a bit too sure, too intellectual, too endowed with some of Gide's own gifts of insight and deduction. This for me is particularly true of Bernard. Olivier is much more credibly drawn.

Referring specifically to Strouvilhou and his cousin Ghéridanisol, and even to young George Molinier—are we to take them as reality or symbol—epitomes of evil in a bad society, especially the first two? Both of these young men suggest a character in Dostoevsky's *The Possessed*—Stavrogin, who has fascinated Gide. Gide feels that Stavrogin is explained by Dostoevsky; but many people do not agree. But much less does Gide explain Strouvilhou or Ghéridanisol for me; and even less does Huxley explain his "Stavrogin" character in *Point Counter Point*—Spandrell. But Gide deliberately avoids any real explanation of these wicked young men: he merely tells us what they did. *Why* they behaved as they did is a fair question to ask of a novelist like André Gide.

For Gide is interested in such analyses and explanations. He has written whole books to present and make clear a "gratuitous act." It is Gide speaking through the novelist Edouard when the latter says in the Journal that ideas interest him much more than people. "Ideas . . . ideas, I must confess, interest me more than men—interest me more than anything. They live; they fight; they perish like men." And men are used to dramatize ideas.

It seems to me dangerous for a novelist to have such a mind. One thing it cannot help leading to, and that is deep self-awareness on the part of the author. Gide himself feels this danger. He was surprised to read a statement made by a colleague: "Seek first to know yourself." Gide's answer is:

The literary creator who seeks himself runs a great risk—the risk of finding himself. From then onwards he writes coldly, deliberately, in keeping with the self he has found. He imitates himself. If he knows his path and his limitations, it is only to keep strictly to them. His great dread is no longer insincerity, but inconsistency. The true artist is never but half-conscious of himself when creating. He does not know exactly who he is. He learns to know himself only through his creation, in it, and after it.

At one time or another all the characters in *The Counterfeiters* do seem to be spokesmen for Gide's own ideas—the same thing we feel in Huxley's novels. But there is in Gide's novel much clearer differentiation of character, more truth. Gide has the creative quality that he attributes to Edouard, when Edouard, commenting on having been with Olivier at Laura's wedding in the Protestant chapel, says:

"The singular faculty of *depersonalization* which I possess and which enables me to feel other people's emotions as if they were my own, compelled me, as it were, to enter into Olivier's feelings —those that I imagined him to be experiencing; and though he kept his eyes shut, or perhaps for that very reason, I felt as if, like him, I were seeing for the first time the bare walls, the abstract and chilly light which fell upon the congregation, the relentless outline of the pulpit on the background of the white wall, the straightness of the lines . . . the whole spirit of this angular and colourless architecture and its repellent want of grace . . . And I fell to regretting that Olivier had never known this early starvation of the senses which drives the soul so perilously far beyond appearances—that his memories were not like mine; but to feel him so distant from the whole thing, helped me to escape from it myself."

Edouard's interest then, as novelist, is to report character —to show misery and villainy and unhappiness where it exists; but his mission is really moral—to understand and to

act towards bringing happiness to several people. He rescues
Bernard and eventually makes the boy desire to go back
to his foster father, who really loves him; he sustains Laura
through the crises of her life, and helps her to meet her
reality; he relieves the emotions of M. Molinier by listening
to him tell about his domestic problems; he is the only comfort that Pauline Molinier has, and through his clear-sighted
sympathy gives her the courage at least of her resignation;
he warns George Molinier of his dangerous and wicked
ways and sends the lad home to burst into tears in his
mother's arms; he pacifies Douviers who was out to kill the
man who seduced his wife; he humiliates the Comte de Passavant! In fact, Edouard is a very saintly person—the embodiment of deep insight and the instrument of affirmation.
The miracle is that he is not a prig. He lives to do good.
Sometimes he makes mistakes; but Gide does not underline
these mistakes with irony. He is further active in his moral
life by showing up and repudiating evil. Edouard has a deep,
though unstated, conviction that it is through love that life
is conquered and God is won. The wicked too have their
routes, and their routes lead, at least for the time we see
them in their evil, to the Devil.

Vice and wickedness, then, are punished in this novel,
and virtue is rewarded. And all of this comes about through
a morality that society reprehends. It is this that gives the
book its unique "savor." Gide is trying to find the "savor"
of each individual in his novel. If in seeking for the essences
he finds the "hidden reason for living," and learns how different that reason may be from "the ostensible goal assigned
by most of us to our existence," it is for him to record that
discovery honestly, to set it forth, as he believes, in its naked
truth—for is that not the "unique route" he speaks of, and
does not "each route lead to God"?

XI

PROLETARIAN FICTION

WITH this title we invite disaster, which we can hope to escape only by establishing an arbitrary definition and remaining within its limits. A few years ago in the field of literary criticism in the United States, a conflict raged over an issue labelled Humanism, a conflict mainly—so it looks in retrospect—of terminologies and personalities. Today the battle, not confined to the United States nor to literature, since painting is in the front line,[58] is over propaganda versus art, with special reference to the proletarian and revolutionary cause. It is a more hotly contested battle than the other, involving many more people; it makes the front page of the daily press when a skirmish takes place over Lenin's portrait in a Rockefeller Center frèsco. It is marked by a hot fire of abusive epithets, and by a confusion of terms that would have made even Socrates glad of the hemlock. Mr. Max Eastman writes a book about artists in uniform in Soviet Russia —artists twisted and tormented in the service of Communist propaganda. Mr. Lincoln Steffens, reviewing the book, retorts that there are artists in uniform in Hollywood and everywhere else, that artists in all ages have worn the uniforms of their class compulsions. The literary past changes its face bewilderingly as critics of opposing viewpoints turn to it for supporting evidence. Mr. William Troy (in *The Nation*) classes Joyce with almost every writer of the last few centuries "whose name comes to mind"—a saving clause— in his refusal to participate in the social and economic struggles of his age; and he refers to the nineteenth-century tradition by which the artist was immune from moral and social responsibility. Mr. Kenneth Burke (also in *The Nation*) states that much of the so-called "pure" art of the nineteenth century was of a pronouncedly propagandist or corrective coloring, and from the text it is clear that this means it concerned itself with social and economic conflict.

Literary criticism: a profession in which impreciseness of idea is a virtue, and a generalized sentiment is better than a fact: thus, contemptuously, writes Mr. Bernard de Voto (in *Harper's Magazine*), with reference to the critics who since 1914 have theorized about such matters as the American Mind and the Frontier. He could draw even more glaring examples from the theorizing over pure art and proletarian art and propaganda.

In the effort to be precise, let us offer this working definition of proletarian fiction: fiction that deals with the working class, the proletariat—and this excludes the "white-collar" class, to which, for example, the hero of Fallada's *Little Man, What Now?* belongs; that deals with the proletariat either as individuals or as the "mass"; that represents these workers as conscious of their class interests as opposed to those of other classes in society, or shows them in the process of becoming class-conscious and of turning to the militant or revolutionary way out of their predicaments. The perspective of the authors of this fiction, whether they are or have been proletarians themselves or whether they are those sympathetic intellectuals whom the Russians call "fellow-travelers," is this: the class struggle occupies the foreground, either in its confused beginnings, or in its conscious and organized activity, or in that later stage—found only in Russia—of "mopping-up" and consolidating the gains after victory. The sympathy of the authors is with the new order—variously conceived, but definitely not the capitalist order—and with the fighters for the new order.

This limitation of theme and spirit separates the novels to be discussed here from those—in a social-service tradition—

that merely expose conditions affecting the working class and point toward reform. Let us be very specific about "working class"; we mean miners, workers in automobile factories and furniture factories and all other kinds of factories, in steel mills and textile mills; we mean coolies in China, shoemakers in Copenhagen, stokers and sailors and longshoremen on all the coasts and seas, builders of cement plants and concrete mixers and dams and construction plants in Russia and Siberia. We do not mean just "bottom dogs"— the wreckage of Gorki's *Night Lodging* or Céline's *Journey to the End of the Night* or Erskine Caldwell's *Tobacco Road* —but people still capable of being roused to a sense of their own dignity as men, still capable of a fight, if only of a last fight with their backs against a wall. Whether these proletarian novels are propaganda or art can be left aside for the moment. We should not discuss them here, if they did not measure up with the best of novels about other aspects of life and other classes of society.

"The nature of art is to encroach continually on parts of life not yet subdued to its treatment. Until art reveals them and renders them permanent, they are in life, indeed, but do not really exist." Fiction has been encroaching on proletarian life long enough to have established a respectable tradition. Let us go back to the nineteenth century—to one of the major novelists who did not decline to participate in the social and economic struggles of his age, Émile Zola, and to his novel about the miners of northern France—*Germinal*.

The scene of *Germinal* is the coal district of northern France, and the center of action is the Voreux Pit, significantly named so as to suggest *vorace*—voracious. Young Étienne Lantier, a worker out of the slums of Paris portrayed in Zola's *Dram Shop,* comes into this region one bitter March night looking for work. Men are still laboring around the mouth of the pit, carting away shale. He falls into talk with an old carter whom they call Jolly Corpse. Why? Oh, because three times he has been taken out of the pit nearly dead—" 'the first time with every hair of my body singed; the second time with my carcase chock-full of earth; the third time with my stomach full of water like a frog's. Then as they saw that I wouldn't kick the bucket, they named me Jolly Corpse, just for fun.' " Others of his family—the Maheus —have not been so fortunate, in the course of the hundred years their race has worked in the pit; his father and three brothers have all perished. From the time he was eight years old he has worked there—as trammer, hewer, quarryman, and now wagoner—and people are urging him to stop, for he is old, weak and rheumatic.

"I'm not such a fool as they think [he remarks cheerfully]. I'm right enough for another two years till I'm sixty, and then I shall have my pension of 180 francs. If I were to say good-bye now, they'd ship me off with one of 150. They're sharp as needles, the masters are."

He speaks of the manager, who is only paid like the rest. But to whom does all this belong? "All that? We don't know. To somebody or other," and he points to some distant undefined spot, peopled by the folk for whom the Maheus had been working for over a century.

His voice had assumed a tone of religious awe; it was as if he alluded to some inaccessible tabernacle, where crouched the insatiable power to which they sacrificed their flesh and blood, without ever beholding it face to face.

Étienne, on this bitter March night, feels a nameless fear of the Pit.

Not a gleam of dawn whitened the lifeless heavens. Only the coke ovens and smelting furnaces threw up a lurid glow . . . And the Voreux Pit, down in the hollow, where it crouched like some evil beast, panted yet more noisily, as if it experienced growing difficulty and pain in its digestion of human flesh and blood.

This sense of the Pit as a monster pervades the book.

Through Zola's vivid and detailed description we come to realize the toll of health and strength which the Pit takes every day from the miners in the village—men and girls and children. We follow them down to the bottom of the eighteen-hundred-foot shaft and through the galleries to the most remote corners of the mine. We feel the oppression of lack of air, the cramped muscles, the heat, the damp. Now and then the monster gives a warning: a leak, a threat of fire-damp or of the collapse of an inadequately propped roof. We understand why the miners gamble with their lives in neglecting the propping: this work is not paid for, and their earnings are so little that they grudge every minute spent away from the coal. " 'Pay us a little more and we'll prop more carefully.' " The monster grows more threatening; a fall of rock kills a man and cripples a little boy—old Maheu's grandson.

At first the spirit of the miners is that of patient slaves, grateful for mere bread. They are sorry for Étienne, looking for a job. " 'After all, we might lose that. We mustn't grumble.' " But times grow harder; there is a financial slump following upon overproduction; the company needs to cut expenses to save dividends. One of the small owners, a decent man, is threatened with ruin and the big company is waiting to swallow him up. Zola treats him with sympathy, and even when he is satirical at the expense of the dull and extravagant stockholders in the big company, he recognizes that the trouble lies in the whole organization of industry. Ugly little subterfuges are adopted by the company to cheat the workmen without their catching on. But they are waking up.

It is Étienne, better read and more widely traveled, who falls naturally into the rôle of agitator and leader. He associates with an educated Russian, an anarchist, Souvarine—a terrorist rather than an anarchist, who nurses schemes of destruction; and they talk of the Socialist International, just beginning to assume importance. Socialist and anarchist theories, notions about provident funds and coöperative societies, ill-digested scraps of evolutionary theory, are all mixed up in Étienne's mind. The revolution comes to mean to him a swift and easy change to a better world. He sees the vision, but as to methods of attaining it, he is vague. He has a gift of eloquence and the prestige of a reader among the illiterate. In the evenings he talks with the Maheus, with whom he is living. Old Jolly Corpse stares in wonder. In his time people had not worried themselves about such things; folk were born among the coal and plied their picks. " 'You shouldn't turn up your noses at anything; a good mug of beer is a good mug of beer. The masters are often scoundrels but there will always be masters . . . It's no use worrying one's head about such things.' " What, Étienne says, haven't the workmen a right to think? " 'In the old man's time, the miner had lived in the mine like a brute, like a machine to provide coal . . . Nowadays the miner was waking up below, germinating in the soil like grain; and one fine morning the world would suddenly see what would sprout up amidst the fields.' " Maheu, the old man's son, has his doubts. " 'The moment a man attempts to stir, he gets his discharge,' " he observes, and they wake up from their dream.

Winter approaches, the need grows, attempts to lower wages irritate, and finally the inevitable strike begins. Zola's narrative is stirring, leaving us with an ineffaceable impression of that black winter of want in the coal regions. The strikers are at first buoyed up by their vision. The climax of this mood comes in a great gathering at night in the forest—a scene displaying Zola's power over mass effects. We see the swaying crowd in the moon-lighted clearing, roused to a dangerous pitch of excitement, ready to rush forth to pillage the wealth of which they have been dispossessed. But gray mornings of hunger follow. They feel the strike failing. Crowds of famished women besiege the stores. To gloom and apathy succeeds desperation, expressing itself in sporadic deeds of violence—such as the cutting of mine cables. And in the end the soldiers come, and events lead up to the inevitable finish —a riot, a volley from the soldiery, the killing of women and children. This stirs Paris, a commission—or whatever the Second Empire called the body that holds post-mortems after a labor outbreak—comes into the district, the mine-owners are now willing to open up and take back the workmen. Étienne is discredited and hated by those who have suffered. He pays the price of their disillusionment.

From this point on, the novel betrays Zola's weakness for melodrama. Souvarine, the Russian terrorist, resolved to bring about a little of the needed destruction, damages the already weak tubbing of the shaft which keeps back the water always threatening to inundate the mine from underground lakes. As if the mine disaster could not have been brought about more plausibly by less startling means, more in keeping with mine history of neglect due to false economy! The disaster itself is a thrilling scene. We get it from above ground, at the pit mouth, where we hear the roar of the water bursting through and the noise of underground cave-ins, and watch the buildings and machinery give way under the subsiding earth. And we get it from below, in the terrible flight of Étienne and Catherine and Chaval before the rushing waters to remote galleries, where, after nine days of suffering and the death of Chaval, they are found.

Étienne, after he recovers from his experience, leaves the region, a probable labor agitator for the rest of his life. The miners go back. Jolly Corpse's daughter-in-law has lost her husband in the riot, her daughter in the disaster, a son in the attempt at rescue, a child by starvation. The company gives her a job, at thirty sous a day, working in a temperature of 104 degrees; she has three other children to support till they too can go down into the Pit. As Étienne goes off through the fields, he thinks he hears the blows of his comrades working in the earth beneath. He has learned the futility of mere violence. He sees all the work of education and organization that must precede the revolution. It is spring; his comrades seem to be knocking nearer and nearer the surface.

Men were sprouting and rising like the seed, a black avenging army of men who were slowly germinating beneath the furrows, growing up for the harvests of the coming century, and soon that germination would rend the earth.

Zola was no proletarian. He got up his material by months of reading and investigation. His aim was to show the dangerous weaknesses of the social structure, which he believed could be strengthened by legislation. When he fought out in the open arena for Dreyfus, it was for "bourgeois" justice. There were, from the standpoint of the modern revolutionist, all sorts of things wrong with his social philosophy. But in *Germinal* he wrote a stirring, memorable story of class struggle in the mines. And the spirit of that final prophecy is revolutionary.

Another novel of class struggle in an early and undeveloped stage is Maxim Gorki's *Mother*, a novel which suffers from long explanatory speeches on socialism of the 1904 brand, and which lacks that power in the handling of mass effects so striking in *Germinal*. It is an imperfect novel, but a recent Soviet version for the screen revealed a vitality in its scenes and characters that led critics even in the bourgeois press to call it art, not propaganda.

Here is an industrial suburb in some Russian city about

1904. The workers in the factory have been drawn from the peasantry, but they have been long enough in the city to give up the dream of land. Conditions of living are wretched. A few only of the younger generation know how to read and write. Mere boys come together secretly to read papers and books about history and the governments of Western Europe and the labor movements abroad. They meet often in the rooms of a widow whose son is a leader in the movement for education. She is an all-but-inarticulate drudge, accustomed to being beaten, as peasant women were by their husbands, and as submissive as was Gorki's own grandmother, who said, when little Gorki suggested that she fight back, since she was the stronger, " 'Is not my husband answerable for me to God?' " When the widow's son asks her what her earlier life was like, what joys she had known, she is perplexed. Neither she nor anyone else has ever thought to examine her life. It is a sign of her awakening when she begins to be able to talk of her life to others and to ponder over its meaning. As she listens to the talk of the lads who come to her house to read, she asks her son, " 'Are these the ones they call illegal people?' " They are mere children, and illegal people are to be feared. These mere children seem to her to be groping with powerful but blind hands in the dark.

The knowledge the young workers seek is not for themselves; they must kindle the flame of reason so that those in the dark may see it. " 'It is not only the stomach that we wish to fill. No, we wish to be men!' " They cannot yet start to fight, but when they read of working-class victories abroad, they are full of joy and feel their spiritual kinship with all workers. Presently they begin to print secretly little leaflets criticizing conditions in the factory, telling of strikes elsewhere in Russia. These leaflets are distributed by all sorts of ingenious ruses. The older people are suspicious and standoffish, but the youngsters are excited, and connections are established between the mass of workers and the secret club. Personalities with capacity for leadership begin to emerge. The ruling class sends its police to search houses and has the bolder workers arrested; but these workers no longer cringe before the police. Then comes a cut in wages under the pretext of draining a near-by swamp in the interests of the workers' health. The workers are not taken in, and Pavel, the son of the widow, becomes the leader in the strike that breaks out, and is sent to jail. An old woman comforts his mother: " 'There's nothing wrong about it. In former years people went to jail for stealing; now they take them for telling the truth.' "

The prison becomes one of the schools of the revolutionary workers, who move from the suburb to the prison, back again to the suburb, or on to some other factory. The first of May is the signal for raising the red flag for the first time in that town. Pavel, out of jail, is to unfurl it in the face of the police—an honor for him and a moment of almost religious exaltation for the crowd. It is a brief moment.

At the end of the street, closing the exit to the square, the mother saw a low gray wall of men, one just like the other, without faces. On the shoulder of each a bayonet was smiling its thin chill smile; and from this entire immobile wall a cold gust blew down on the workmen, striking the breast of the mother.

The leaders were arrested, the banner trampled. But factory workers who had refused to strike that morning now came out to join the "holiday of free men."

Pavel is sent to Siberia. He could have escaped before his trial, but he wants the platform of the courtroom for a speech that he knows will be distributed through the secret press. His mother finds friends among his comrades, and they give her revolutionary work in circulating leaflets. She has found her tongue and her soul—and she finds her death at the hands of the police in a riot. She has grown from dumb submission into revolutionary idealism. Gorki is at his best in this theme that is characteristic of his work: the theme of a mute soul striving to become articulate; the struggle—as M. J. Olgin has put it—of innately sound human material thrown into a primitive environment and groping its way upward to the light. It is Gorki's own story, and he tells it with power, whether he is writing of himself in his reminiscences, or of some creature of his imagination, like his "mother."

In the pattern of proletarian fiction, the strike begins to appear as the central design. In *Germinal* and *Mother,* the strikes are lost. In Nexö's *Pelle the Conqueror,* the great general strike, the climax of the book, is won, but the leader is sacrificed: he is "framed" and goes to prison.

The story of Pelle has four parts: his boyhood on the farm on the island of Bornholm; his apprenticeship in the little island city; the struggle which he leads against the employers of Copenhagen; and his final success after his imprisonment in starting a plan of coöperation among the workers in a garden city. His progress is from peasant to proletarian leader; in his career we see the industrial revolution from the worker's standpoint, and we see it dramatically, unclouded by exposition or theory. From start to finish, the book is the story of the poor, the inarticulate, the exploited, who grope toward a realization of the fact that they are exploited and begin to stir uneasily, half-blindly reaching out after a new order of things, seeking a more abundant life. Nexö—himself born among the Copenhagen poor and successively farm boy, shoemaker's apprentice, bricklayer, and teacher and writer—reveals a deep understanding of every phase of the life of poverty—its pleasures, dreams, consolations, and hopes, as well as its filth, misery, blundering, and sensuality.

Pelle attracts us from the moment we meet him coming

off the little steamer that has brought him with his father over from Sweden to the Danish island in search of work. He has a touching confidence in Father Lasse, which bolsters up old Lasse's pathetic confidence in himself. One of Pelle's earliest lessons on the farm is that his father is unable to protect him from rough treatment and that he must learn to rely upon himself. They find work at one of the big farms, Lasse as herdsman, the lowest of jobs, and Pelle as his helper. Out in the fields near the sea, he can dream during long summer days and learn a kind of wisdom from the earth and the cattle. He sets himself, with his keen perceptions and his thirst for life, to understand the world about him. Sent after a time to a village school, he is despised by the fishermen's sons as a country greenhorn, until on a dare he leaps off the breakwater into the icy winter ocean—a mad act, for he cannot swim, but of the sort to win respect. One of the qualities that wins him leadership is this: he never turns away from a challenge.

Still a boy, Pelle goes to the largest town on the island to look for work, becomes a shoemaker's apprentice, loses his way in a new world full of unfamiliar temptations, drifts into a little stealing, but is set straight again by his master's son, a kindly dreamer with a little book-learning, who takes a liking to the apprentice. Poverty is increasing in the town as a result of the displacement of the handicrafts by machinery, and Pelle becomes a journeyman in his trade just when that trade is being driven to the wall. He turns to one casual job after another, loses self-respect and ambition, becomes one of the lowest-paid workmen on a construction job in the harbor. There one day he sees the dramatic death of an eccentric laborer known as the Great Power, a man with a genius for mechanics but with no education, who has had his ideas stolen from him in one way or another by clever employers and has brooded over his wrongs till he is half insane. His fellow workers dislike him because his bitter talk constantly reminds them of their own slavery; they are chained, but would have been contented with their chains. His death, however, affects them deeply, and they talk over his ideas. Pelle listens: " 'I don't understand why all the poor folk don't make a stand together against the others. If we all acted together and had nothing to do with them that mean us harm, then it would soon be seen that collective poverty is what makes the wealth of the others . . .' " It is the first stirring of class consciousness, but is very faint: " 'But we shall never be unanimous about anything. If one of the gentlemen only scratches our neck a bit, then we all grovel at his feet.' " Pelle, however, is awakened to a new fighting spirit, and determines to go to the capital.

There he takes up his quarters in a crazy tenement called the Ark, and this building becomes a kind of symbol of the workers whom it houses. It is endowed with a life of its own, and Nexö, as Randolph Bourne wrote, makes "its endless chambers and rotting timbers ooze out of them all the tragedy and beastliness and friendliness of the poor." When, after the great strike, the Ark burns and we watch the rats escaping from the horrible cellars that were the last refuge of the wretched, we feel the old filthy servile life collapsing with the burning timbers. Pelle begins to organize his own craft; he loses out in his first tussles with the big shoemakers, but he learns from defeat and becomes a skilful strategist. The respect he wins from his opponents turns into a subtle and persistent temptation to desert his class. The employers want him on their side; he could rise easily out of the poverty of the less gifted and intelligent; and his wife —he marries the daughter of a fairly well-to-do old Socialist— is less loyal to the Movement than to her hope of comfort and security for her children. " 'You have pulled yourself out of the mire,' " Morten, the passionately revolutionary son of the Great Power, tells Pelle; all those who are of use slink away; and he forces Pelle to look again at the depths of suffering in the city which he discovers during his night prowlings. It isn't to be wondered at, he continues, that you and others get weary; " 'even God loses patience with those who always let themselves be trampled upon.' " He tells of a dream he had of God—dressed like a Cossack officer with a knout, to whom he appealed for help: " 'I am of Thy chosen, the poor—I am starving.' " " 'You are starving,' " answered God, " 'and complain of your brothers, who have set forth food for you in abundance?' " and pointed to the fine shops. " 'You do not belong to my Chosen people—away with you.' " And he lashed him over the back with the knout.

So Pelle, against the wishes of his wife, is drawn back into the struggle, and becomes the leader of a long and bitter strike that drags on through a winter of starvation, and triumphs at last. A great procession sweeps through the streets: "We come from the darkness and we go towards the light, and no one can hold us back."

Pelle is sent to prison on a trumped-up charge, and when he comes out some years later, he has his estranged wife to win back, and his dreams of a coöperative community to realize. But most readers are likely to feel with Randolph Bourne [59] that with the burning of the Ark, and the death of old Father Lasse, and the close of the strike, the book becomes dead. Instead of the later Pelle—a little smug—with his coöperative dairies and slaughterhouses, one remembers old Lasse with his unconquered friendliness to the world and an innate dignity that even survives life on an ashheap with a hideous old woman for companion. One remembers how Lasse, the patient and submissive, becomes class-conscious at the very end before he dies.

"I can't find my old views of the world again [he whispers to his son]. On the night when the big employers declared the lock-out, I was standing out there among the many thousands of other poor people, listening. They were toasting the resolution with champagne and cheering, and there my opinions were changed."

And almost his last words to his son were: "Whatever you do, never believe the clergy!"

Proletarian fiction of the period before the Great War and the Russian Revolution is carefully documented. The authors—even Gorki—one feels, think of their readers as members of the relatively comfortable classes, profoundly un-instructed in the actualities of working-class life. So they are prodigal of economic facts and theories—often, but not al-ways, dramatically realized in scene and episode; and all this information is rather courteously offered. The form of the novel is still fairly traditional, with the strike (in which the pressure of mass emotion blows off the lid) taking the place of those climactic scenes in other novels in which the pres-sure of private emotions blows off the lid. In the large dis-orders of the strike, private emotional conflicts may be in-volved, but they are usually subordinated; and if they do usurp the foreground—as in Zola's scenes of love and jealousy in the flooded mine—they wear a melodramatic or anti-quated air. Events follow one another in a time sequence which is usually a cause-and-effect sequence as well; and the familiar biographical pattern is common. Pelle grows from the little boy to the strike leader through one experience after another; Pavel and Étienne develop from a given moment of new impulse through many stages, easy to follow.

In all this fiction, the fact and the nature of the class struggle are made clear. But the hope of a reform within the structure of capitalism is not excluded, though the be-havior of the ruling class, its resort to violence and chican-ery, makes the prospect look rather remote. And whether a

particular strike is lost or won, a particular leader killed or "framed" or driven out of the movement, the awakened spirit of resistance in the workers is in itself a victory. The seed is germinating.

When proletarian fiction comes to the surface again after the wars and revolutions of the second decade of the century, there are significant changes. Explanations and apologies have gone by the board. The reader is no longer courteously entreated—he finds his way as best he can and is forced to put up with many a slap in his bourgeois or intellectual or liberal face. There is an accelerated tempo in many a Russian novel that leaves him gasping. And—just as in the other fields of fiction—traditional patterns are lost in all sorts of experiments to find a way of saying what has never been said before.

What accounts for the truculent tone of much proletarian fiction? Probably more than anything else—Russia: the existence of what the Communist press habitually refers to as the Workers' Fatherland. There lies that huge sprawling fact across the map of two continents; there it has persisted in remaining year after year, incredibly: this workers' republic or workers' dictatorship or Communist tyranny, this anything you like, except, emphatically, *not* the Capitalists' Fatherland. Russia looms in the background of every proletarian novel, whether its scene is laid in Magnitogorsk or Detroit or Shanghai, and all strikes become incipient revolutions. The strike in fiction has an emotional impact now that it never had before October, 1917.

In Germany ten months before the Armistice, Berlin workers struck for more bread—and also for the ending of the War and in protest against the Brest-Litovsk peace. They lost and were sent back to the front lines, but they kept alive the spirit of revolt, and in October, 1918, there broke out a revolutionary uprising of the workers, which is one of the least known of modern mass movements. The war machinery of censorship kept from the outside world anything but the most fragmentary information; the betrayal of the movement was swift; and the rush of events at the Armistice and after, overwhelming. The Germans themselves were taught under the compromise Socialist régime to forget it, and under the Nazis to believe in the legend that, but for the "stab in the back" dealt by Socialists and Marxists, the army would have won the war.

This proletarian revolt is the theme of Theodor Plivier's novel, *The Kaiser Goes, the Generals Remain* (1933). He vouches for the strict historic truth of his narrative: "in so far as exact material was available I have used it for the basis of my work . . . Occasional statements which the sources preserve only in indirect speech are here given direct form. But in no instance has the sense been altered." Truth or fiction, the novel sent its author into exile—over the frontier on foot "with nothing except the clothes on his back and the manuscript of his half-written next novel in his pack."

There is no hero but the revolutionary mass. But there are villains, Social Democratic villains: Noske, Ebert. First we see the Rulers: General Ludendorff and various ministers in conference, discussing the position on the Western Front; Prince Max of Baden, the Chancellor, who hopes to save the dynasty, but becomes incapacitated at the most critical moment by influenza; the leaders of the various parties debating in the Reichstag. The technique is that of cinema close-ups, brief impressionistic glimpses; and the general effect is one of confused purposes and bewilderment among the rulers.

Then we shift to the Ruled: people in a Berlin tenement, especially a mother who takes her dying child to a hospital, then stands for hours in a food queue. Unrest, confusion, suffering. The most completely developed scene is that of the hundreds waiting in line at the slaughter yard for the meat issue, meat from cattle which the inspector has condemned. Even that gives out with seven hundred people still awaiting their turn. "There is a disturbance among the crowd by the street lamp. A few young communists are pushing their way through; they have a pot of paste and a bundle of posters, one of which they stick on the wall," diagonally across an exhortation in beautiful Gothic letters to subscribe to the ninth war loan: " 'It is no sacrifice to invest money at 5 per cent where it is as safe as a ward in chancery.' " The crude letters of the communist propaganda strip read: " 'The war is for the rich! The poor pay for it in corpses!' " The mob of disappointed waiters surges past the police into the sheds, to see with their own eyes that nothing more is left, and to break out in angry cries: " 'Dirty swindlers! Profiteers! Hoarders! Smash up the whole gang!' " The police drive the mob back. We follow the mother of the sick child to the telephone booth; the child has died; then to the hospital, where she is allowed to see the body before it is taken off to the pauper's cemetery; then back to her room, where she sets to work again on soldiers' greatcoats. "It is well that the machine hums, that the needle moves up and down unceasingly, that the grey track appears endless beneath her fingers."

Then we go to the rooms of the training school of the Independent Socialist Party, and a full session of the Revolutionaries, who had led the strike the winter before, and a speech by Karl Liebknecht, Tribune of the Revolution, fired with his dream of the people marching, the people breaking its chains. But there are other leaders, silently disagreeing, nursing other plans. One gains the impression that there is little hope in the leaders and their divided counsels.

The scene shifts to Kiel. The stokers on one battleship refuse to fire up for a sally against the English fleet. Spontaneous, undirected uprisings follow on other ships. Three or four sailors are singled out to focus our attention as the uprising spreads from the fleet to the shore, rolling up like a snowball. There is little bloodshed, for officers are conciliating or at least readily disarmed. Military prisoners are set free. Deputies from the Independents and the Social Democrats arrive in the coast cities and begin political maneuvering for position; they want to be on both sides—to lead the revolters and keep in with the government. Noske gets himself elected governor of Kiel by the Workers' and Soldiers' Council—and has the appointment formally confirmed by the Secretary of State for the Navy; "now he is covered on both flanks. Supreme Commissar of the Revolution—but always with the approval and formal sanction of the Imperial Government." Sailors take over the offices of the Hamburg-Amerika Line in Hamburg, and Albert Ballin—

contracting party to so many trade-union agreements, co-founder of the North Atlantic Pool, despotic ruler of the world's greatest shipping combine, intimate adviser of the Emperor and of the Imperial Government—now sits back wearily in his chair and hears the people in revolt moving noisily about in the rooms below.

After twenty-eight triumphal years . . .

emigrants—a whole exodus of peoples at five dollars a head—steerage passengers, stateroom passengers, tourists, bankrupt merchants, cargoes, transports, wars—he had made something out of them all.

The mutineers go inland, and the wave of revolution reaches Brunswick, where the Duke is forced to abdicate, and finally Berlin begins to march. It is the ninth of November. Liebknecht proclaims the Soviet Republic from the balcony

of the Palace to a vast throng below. Inside the Palace a
crowd has penetrated to the kitchens, unused since 1914, and
is gazing incredulously at the piles of provisions, but their
bewilderment does not last long:

With all the greed of starving men they fall upon the imperial
hoard: 800 sacks of snow-white Ukrainian flour, countless bags
of coffee, boxes of tea, preserves, thousands of eggs, pots of lard,
bottles of sauce, rows of sugar loaf, quantities of pulse foods,
chocolate, cigars, cigarettes . . . the smell of the good things of
which they have so long been deprived intoxicates the senses of
these famished creatures—munition workers, soldiers, wounded
men—even more than the food which they so greedily stuff into
their mouths.

From the balcony Liebknecht is invoking the ghosts of millions of women and children who have perished in want and
misery, and millions of victims of the World War, and calling for an oath of dedication to the cause of world revolution. Soldiers fraternize with the people—but behind their
backs the bargaining goes on.

In the last scene Ebert is alone in the Chancellor's room.
What Noske has done for Kiel must now be done for Berlin.

What concerns Ebert is not socialism, but the Social Democratic
Party. And if the Workers' and Soldiers' Councils get the upper
hand, this great instrument will surely come under the wheels
and be ground to powder—unless . . . Can he call the officers
of the old imperial army to his aid?

A telephone conversation. At a price the Generals offer to the
new government the protection of their bayonets and guns;
the Officers' Corps invites the Government of the Reich to
fight Bolshevism.

Ebert hesitates before giving his answer. He looks up at the
thickly padded door; he turns towards the window and listens
for any sound from the street, where he fancies he already hears
the enraged shouts of the workers. Then in a confident voice he

replies: "Convey to the General Field-Marshal the thanks of the Government."

The Kaiser has gone, but the generals remain.

The revolution in Austria was lost in the depression. Rudolf Brunngraber in his *Karl and the Twentieth Century* (1933) tells the story of Karl Lakner, one of the hundreds of thousands of unemployed in Vienna; his story is also an economic history of the last forty years, "a history which explains the fate not only of this Karl, but of millions of other Karls, whether they were born in Vienna, or Berlin, or New York, or London, or San Francisco." It is the individual destiny against the world background. Instead of the dramatic close-ups, the swift march of events during a brief period of crisis, and the passionate proletarian sympathies of Plivier's novel, there is the surface objectivity of the economic report and the case history. Underneath the surface one feels emotion tempered with irony. We follow Karl step by step from babyhood to suicide, when he is thirty-five or forty. After a paragraph or two about Karl comes a passage recounting developments in industry and politics. To illustrate the method: Karl, a boy, trying to help his mother by carrying bags for travelers near a railroad station, finds one day a gang in possession of the stand. He thereupon enlists the support of a little gang of his own.

Next day, when at Tshshima, the Japanese fleet was blowing the Russians out of the water, Karl's gang took possession by force of the disputed trolley stop . . . The place was unique in Vienna and therefore the combat that raged for its mastery resembled that for the coalfields of Manchuria.

Or this example: Karl takes an examination for the training college for teachers, and writes an essay on the text

"Though life be cruel and though the powers of this world be to a great extent malicious, in the last resort a pure heart, a

pious intent, a lofty ideal, will win through to victory . . ." At
the moment Karl was writing these words, the United States was
in the throes of a financial panic, one of the periodic crises of
the capitalist system . . .

Karl of course goes into the War; he is as brave as any
other soldier—even something of a hero, so that later on he
can starve with decorations on his chest. On his furloughs in
the last year, he hunts food and coal for his mother in a
starving city—"a huge conglomeration of chilly dwellings
filled with pestilence," its miseries underlined by the "luxury of the automobiles and furs sported by the mistresses of
the war profiteers." The war went on,

if only for the reason that the armament industries were earning money hand over fist . . . The armament industries constituted the only Internationale that the war had not dismem-
bered . . . At a time when the German army command was
unable, through the most urgent representations, to secure a
monthly increase of fifteen thousand tons in the output of steel,
Stinnes and some of the lesser steel magnates were exporting on
the average 150,000 tons. Unceasingly German iron made its way
to France and Italy; without pause German rails were delivered
to the Russians. Special works were erected in Switzerland to
obliterate German trade-marks from German rolled steel. . . .
The British were bombarded with British-made artillery.

After the war, Karl's educational contract is no longer
good: the government is changed. He is thrown out of work
again and again: by the winding-up of the American relief
association, by the reorganization of a factory, by the collapse of two swindling currency speculators, by the bank-
ruptcy of a sound firm through competition among the
banks. He is caught in the machinery of unemployment relief and tossed out again. Once the Vienna county council
finds it possible to send a flock of swallows to Italy in air-
planes, when the winter comes on too suddenly, but it can't
feed Karl. There is no escape over the borders. Of the Rus-

sian famine of 1921, partly the result of the Allied blockade, Brunngraber writes:

In those days the view of individualist economists, that life can only be successfully carried on when there is at least a moderate shortage of the prime necessaries, celebrated its most signal triumph . . . Policemen at Buenos Ayres, set to keep watch over the fruit thrown away by those who wished to keep up prices, could while away the time by studying in their illustrated papers photographs of Russian mothers who were lying naked in the street and had eaten their dead nurslings. These Russian mothers had drafted an appeal in which they declared themselves willing to renounce all rights over their children (whom the world wished to save from the plague of bolshevism), if only this same Western world would take pity upon the starving little ones. Certain Scandinavian philanthropists wanted to make the appeal widely known, but the governments of the states that had declared the boycott had forbidden its publication in their respective countries. For . . . the Russian mothers had not offered to hand over either Lenin's head or the oil wells of Baku; and in the second place the Western world had to be logical. It could not mitigate the blockade just because of a famine, even though this blockade was disastrous to its own business interests. England, where unemployment was steadily increasing, had been compelled for lack of the Russian market, to throttle its fishing industry—for though a slump in the price of fish would have supplied the unemployed with cheap herrings, it was essential to the fish companies to maintain prices by restricting the output.

Karl, at his wit's end, cold, hungry, homeless, can listen to the radio outside a shop.

"I should like you to realize [says the announcer] that you will hear this concert from Java sooner than those actually present in the concert hall between seven and eight thousand miles away . . ."

These are the luxuries of the homeless.

This book seems to illustrate nothing but economic fatality, until one reflects that Karl is kept isolated all through the story from any working-class group. If he had joined any group at all, he might have at least died in comradeship with others in the street fighting early in 1934—not as a lonely suicide. I think there is implied—though never stated —in Karl's intensely individualistic outlook and his lack of social vision of even the most elementary sort, the necessity of group action for the proletariat. Karl belongs with the group pictured in Ilya Ehrenburg's account of the 1934 Vienna uprising on its second day:

In front of the municipal relief stations the usual lines of un-employed were forming. Exhausted, demoralized, humiliated by long privations, they preferred to beg rather than to fight. All of them, both the jobless waiting for a handout and the laborers hurrying to work, sympathized with the insurgents. But on that damp morning, wet through with rain, the insurgents felt them-selves abandoned, if not betrayed. They felt that nothing sep-arated them from the other workers; they belonged to the same unions, the same sprawling and formless party. But on that morning an unprecedented something had come between the vanguard of the working-class which was fighting to its last drop of blood and that dispersed, weaponless and uninspired mass which wished to live at any price.[60]

So it is only in a somewhat ambiguous and indirect way that *Karl and the Twentieth Century* can be included in our definition; only as it forces the reader to face the issue: the destruction of the individual worker, or the revolt of the mass.

In the United States the proletarian novel is in its first crude beginnings. At least, that is the view of Michael Gold, who can speak with some authority on this subject, for he wrote one of the earliest and best of such novels—*Jews With-out Money*—and he reviews them in the *New Masses* and else-where. "We shall have to understand," he says, "the inevi-table crudity of our first rough-hewn shelters and their rela-

tion to the shining cities of tomorrow." Such a young proletarian writer as Jack Conroy, author of *The Disinherited,*
who belongs to the class he writes about, is making a first
report of "a strange life; there are too many unprecedented
facts, and he is so involved in each one, that sometimes he
cannot piece them together in any satisfactory pattern." [61]
The sketch form of *The Disinherited* is the result, and that
form, continues Mr. Gold, is a dominant proletarian form
today. But even in *The Disinherited* the old biographical
pattern is present. We begin with the boyhood of the leading character (who is in large part the author himself) and
follow his growth to manhood and his gradual absorption in
the labor movement. The same pattern is followed in Grace
Lumpkin's *To Make My Bread* even more carefully and
more closely in accord with the familiar tradition. There is
a straightforward narrative movement in both books, and the
life line of the leading character creates the effect of unity.
Other novels experiment more freely. Robert Cantwell's
Land of Plenty and William Rollins's *The Shadow Before*
choose a brief period (months or weeks) of tension in a mill,
ending in an outbreak of strikes and violence; the character
emphasis is almost equally distributed over a dozen or more
people—owners, superintendents, foremen, organizers, scabs,
workers, policemen, wives and sweethearts in both camps;
and in technique there is a resort to devices such as the
"stream of consciousness" (especially in its Joycean form),
the flash-backs and close-ups that recall the moving picture,
the quotation (with ribald and ironic effect) of typical newspaper headlines and editorials, and the more mechanical
tricks of changes of type, grotesquely run-together words,
and disregard of punctuation and capitals. The mill machinery in *The Shadow Before* clickety-clacks and clickety-clacks
until the reader is hypnotized into the daze of the exhausted
workers—if he is not merely bored by being reminded of the

choo-choos of children's stories. In both novels there is plenty of rough hard-boiled speech and emetic words, which may reflect the Elizabethan vigor of proletarian language— or merely the influence of Joyce and Hemingway.

The proletarian writer is often warned by his friendly critics among the intellectuals to guard against the temptation to borrow stylistic devices from the bourgeois novelists— Joyce, Hemingway, Faulkner, Proust, and the rest. For, they say, these styles are ingrained in their contents; such writers, refusing to face the misery and degradation imposed upon the majority of men and women by the capitalist system, were forced to develop styles marked by polished discrepancies, subtle capers, brooding contortions, erratic syntax—all of it evidence of pretense, futility, and decay.[62] Yet it cannot be denied, writes Mr. Bodenheim, "that their minds and hearts, secluded and inverted in a false vision of scope, are nevertheless capable of plausible and often accurate details pertaining to minor psychology, and to sexual contention, confusion." And Mr. Gold regrets that young authors like Jack Conroy, "in avoiding the sickly introspection of the bourgeois autobiographers of youth" often miss psychological reality; their characters are not completed; "they neglect the major problem of all fiction, which is the creation of full-blooded character." It is comforting to see that Virginia Woolf and Michael Gold could shake hands on this point.

The characters in *The Disinherited* are interesting, even if it is true, as Mr. Gold says, that they are not quite typical enough, that too many of them are social sports and eccentrics. He excepts the hero's mother from this criticism. With husband and older sons killed in mine accidents, Mrs. Donovan keeps the younger children alive by her drudgery over the washtub at the spring in the ravine, where the miners' wives have to do the washing for themselves and the well-to-do people in the town. Once the little boy drops a molten image of Horatius which he has modeled out of a lump of gumbo (someone had given him Macaulay's *Lays of Ancient Rome*) into the boiler full of clothes, and they are stained a hideous saffron. The boy quakes at the thought of having to face the wrath of the rich storekeeper's wife when he delivers the clothes. "Mother divined my thoughts. 'I'll take them back myself. You're only a lad, and I don't want to see your spirit crushed too soon. There's little enough fun for a lad in a coal camp.'" One night a huge negro staggers into the lonely house; he has been badly beaten up, and the children are frightened at his looks. He has been thrown into a coal car somewhere down the line, and has tumbled out at a crossing. He doesn't know why he has been beaten—they had called him a scab. "'Oh, you were scabbing!' Mother said accusingly. 'You were taking another man's job. You should expect to get beaten up for that.'" This is news to the negro; a white boss had offered him a job and shipped him up from Mobile to Missouri; he doesn't "aim to do nobody no dirt." Mrs. Donovan feeds him and treats him kindly; and the boy—who has always regarded a scab as a sub-human beast—catches his first glimpse of the scab as a puppet manipulated by those who never braved the wrath of the strikers in their own persons. He can't hate this negro.

Young Donovan clings for some time to his father's ambition for him—to be a white-collar man. While working on any job he can get, he takes correspondence courses and believes the prospectus of the school and dreams of a cozy bungalow, a baby on his knee, a wife leaning over his shoulder looking proudly at a bankbook. "'Just think, dear,' I would say, 'two years ago we didn't know where the next meal was coming from. But like Lincoln, I prepared myself with home study. Today the superintendent called me into his office . . .'" and offered him the management of an important branch . . . and so on. He goes from one job to another, in automobile factories, rubber-heel plants, canning factories, steel mills; he is one of the floating millions of migratory workers. And the power of the book lies in the amazingly vivid realization of what all these different jobs feel like. Handling a rivet hammer on a bridge-building job, for example, when you are a new hand:

Wind plays a high bridge like a harp; the structure sways to a weird rhythm. To nervous feet a hundred feet in the air, steel is like the glass mountain in the fairy tale. From a platform far below, a bored rivet heater tossed fiery rivets to Ed, who was supposed to catch them in a large cone with handle attached, but more often he missed and they fell hissing in the river, followed by a shower of sparks like the tail of a comet . . .

And what does it feel like to have been out of a job for months?

Nothing impairs morale like the dissolution of a last pair of shoes. Maybe it starts with a little hole in the sole; and then the slush of pavements oozes in, gumming sox and balling between your toes. Concrete whets Woolworth sox like a file, and if you turn the heel on top and tear a pasteboard innersole, it won't help much . . . I worried about pants. Every icy blast off the lake found the thin spots unerringly. I brooded about the disastrous consequences of a sudden breaking asunder . . . You walk and stare in shop windows. A pink and white ham simmers in the Bandbox Lunch. You suck up your guts as the sergeant used to tell you to do . . . Ye Cosy Radio Shoppe flings harmony for five blocks and a thunderous optimist yammers . . . "We are now in the dining-room of the Commodore Perry Hotel. Lights! Good food! Music! Youth! Is everybody happy! The orchestra enters into the spirit of the occasion with that tuneful selection: Happy Days are Here Again."

And how does it feel to get some miserable job and to have to truckle to a stupid wise-cracking foreman?

The snitch and the yes-man always find the foreman's most trivial pun howlingly funny. This job had gathered the disinherited from many a closed and crippled factory; and the cruel competition for bare existence made rats of them. They pecked eagerly for small favors like expectant sparrows following a well-fed horse.

From a German Spartacist in a rubber factory—a man temporarily broken, but wise with his class wisdom, Donovan learns to see ways out of all this chaos, and he no longer feels any shame at work in ditches and on roads:

I knew that the only way for me to rise to something approximating the grandiose ambitions of my youth would be to rise with my class, with the disinherited: the bricksetters, the flivver tramps, boomers, and outcasts pounding their ears in flophouses. Every jibe at any of the paving gang, every covert and open sneer by prosperous looking bystanders infuriated me but did not abash me. The fat on my bones melted away under the glare of the burnished sun, and the fat in my mind dissolved, too. It dripped in sweat off the end of my nose on to the bricks.

Hans the German teaches Donovan to get along without the "fifty-cent words" he has been shooting at the workers—ideology, agrarian crisis, rationalization. Hans, like Pelle, has a gift for illuminating theories with anecdotes. Arguing with a man who thinks the workers will never wake up, Hans tells how he and other boys, back in Germany, used to steal into the orchard of a neighboring estate and stuff themselves full of fruit.

"We liked the pears best. They were huge and sweet as sugar. Sometimes we'd start to grasp one in a hurry and it would crumble between our fingers. Wasps had entered it through a tiny hole near the stem . . . and eaten all away but the rind and seeds. Things that seem as solid as a rock may be fragile enough to collapse at a pinch. But you've got to pinch first."

We leave Hans, Donovan, and the rest out in the discontented farm belt, developing their skill at "pinching."

Grace Lumpkin, author of *To Make My Bread,* lived for a while with a family of workers in the steel mills near Pittsburgh. The man worked in the mills all night and came home and wrote for an hour. Then he spent six hours sleeping and wrote again for an hour or so, when he had to go to work again. "It is a tragedy when a writer is divided half and half into worker and writer. But how can one write if one is not mixed up in the struggle?" [63] She herself wrote about workers in the Southern cotton mills because she was born among them and lived among them.

I took a group of mountain people in the Great Smokies in North Carolina. I have lived there and know the types of people who are my characters, although I did not take any character straight from life . . . but made composite pictures from people I knew. John, Bonnie, and the others were there in the mountains, living a life that was hard, but had a certain amount of independence in it. A sawmill came along and drove them out and they had to enter the factory, and I tried to describe their experiences and the loss of independence, and the gradual coming of a realization that there was only one way out for them.

To Make My Bread is a simply told and rather slow-moving book. The strike in the cotton mill is the climax, and the incidents recall the famous Gastonia strike. But though actual strikes may be brilliantly and sympathetically reported, the fighters and victims are strangers to us; whereas Miss Lumpkin's cotton-mill workers are people we have grown to know from the time they were children in the mountains. Half the book is over before they are drawn down to the mill town, and they are solidly established in our sympathies before they become "proletarians." That is where a proletarian novel using the old-fashioned method of beginning at the beginning and letting the characters grow up slowly with much homely detail has an advantage with readers whose class prejudices may be all against strikes and labor agitators. The impatient revolutionary reader, on the other hand, may feel that the strike is a long time coming.

But it is a good strike when it comes. And the way out is one that John McClure is prepared to take, after the bitter experience of seeing his sister killed. It is John Stevens, the "outside agitator," who puts it clearly for him. Referring to the clergy (in a way that reminds one of old Lasse's deathbed admonition), he says

"And, so we won't do anything about our misery, they keep us in the darkness of ignorance and talk about death, to keep our eyes on death and heaven, so we won't think too much about life. We are taught that to struggle is a sin.

"But it ain't a sin, John . . . We must join with all others like us and take what is ours. For it is our hands that have built, and our hands that run the machines and ours that dig the coal and keep the furnaces going, and our hands that bring in the wheat for flour. And because we have worked and suffered, we will understand that all should work and all should enjoy the good things of life. It is for us who know to make a world in which there will not be masters, and no slaves except the machines."

Robert Cantwell, we are told by his publishers, has a lumber-mill background, "and learned to write novels by reading the prefaces of Henry James, a bourgeois writer, whenever he was out of a job." Perhaps some time Mr. Cantwell will explain just how the prefaces helped him in dealing with material that would have made Henry James shudder.

Here is a sash and door factory on the West Coast. Here is the night shift, with a distinctly neurotic foreman, unpredictable in his sudden dislikes, capricious in wielding an authority that he is inwardly not sure of. This is Carl, with the power of the job over a number of human beings. The men are working overtime to complete a rush order on the eve of the Fourth of July holiday. Suddenly the lights go out. The place is transformed into a strange hostile terrain, full of machinery and things you stumble over and trap doors that drop you down into a still more sinister region under the factory, which is built upon a sort of marsh. In successive chapters, each devoted to one person, people stumble around and whisper and shout. And Carl feels a growing panic and a growing resentment against a man he already hates and chooses to blame for the accident, which he insists was premeditated. Hagen, the electrician, is this man. Other workers are Hagen's young son Johnny, Winters, a half-breed Indian with a sick wife much on his mind, a couple of girls rather involved in dubious love affairs, Walt Connor, a boy from a well-to-do home, and so on. There is great tension in these opening scenes; by feeling around like the bewildered workers, one pieces together the facts of the depression and a ten per cent wage cut and the fear of losing their jobs that worries the men. This is Part I—"Power and Light." Part II is "The Education of a Worker," and the worker is Johnny Hagen, whose education begins with the discharge of his father. This injustice to Hagen—who is quite innocent of blame—precipitates a strike, in which the workers seize the factory. But at last they are defeated, and we see Johnny walking off at the end—his father has been killed—like Étienne in *Germinal,* off to new fields of labor activity. (" 'I was feeling,' " says John in *To Make My Bread,* at the end, " 'as if everything was finished.' " " 'No,' " John Stevens says. " 'This is just the beginning.' " This conclusion is typical of the spirit of proletarian novels.)

The book has one particularly admirable feature: it shows how the clear issues of a labor conflict are complicated by all sorts of little irrelevant antagonisms and irritations and personal problems. Mr. Cantwell calls his book "quite simply, a work of propaganda." Of one problem in it he wanted critical discussion from the reviewers of the book—discussion he didn't get. This problem concerned the seizure of the factory.

I tried to imagine what would actually happen, in the sort of community I pictured, when the workers entered the factory, what new factors entered a strike situation, what advantages were gained, what hazards encountered . . . I couldn't imagine clearly what would happen, and the novel suffers as a result. But I wanted at least to state the problem, in the hope that it might be discussed, critically, that the imaginations of others might be directed to envisioning it more clearly than I could . . . That seems to me to be a great part of our task as novelists and critics: we can work out in our own imaginations some of the problems the working-class must face in actuality; we can fight out on paper some of the real battles that are coming, and so be a little better prepared for them. If we can visualize them concretely, in detail, the terrible costs of progress may be a little reduced.[64]

That, apparently, is what he means by propaganda.

Let us leave our American proletarian fiction to its future, convinced that it has one, and that here art is encroaching upon parts of life not yet subdued to its treatment; and pause in China on the way to the Workers' Fatherland. A Frenchman, André Malraux, writes about the Chinese revolution, himself a participant in its events. How simple Vienna seems, or Berlin, or Copenhagen, or one of our mill towns, in comparison with Shanghai! One difficulty for many of us in reading Malraux's book is that of sheer ignorance of Chinese complications. And Malraux makes no effort to explain things. We have to pick up our facts as we go along and try to match them with confused memories of newspaper dispatches.

On March 21, 1927, the Communists in Shanghai declared a general strike and with the aid of General Chiang Kaishek, leading the forces of the Kuomintang, secured control of the city. They already dominated Hankow. They were acting with the Kuomintang, trying to use it for their own purposes, although well aware that it was devoted to the interests of the petty bourgeoisie and had no intention of giving the land to the peasants. Three weeks later, on April 11, General Chiang betrayed his Communist allies, dissolved the labor unions, seized the local headquarters, secured the weapons, and tortured the leaders to death, throwing them into boiling oil or into the fireboxes of locomotives.

Here is the revolutionary drama: the eve of the general strike; the shortage of weapons; the necessary murder of the man who has the authorization to get guns from a ship in the harbor; the seizure of the weapons; the proclaiming of the strike; the capture of police, telephone, and telegraph stations in a series of bloody contests; then an interlude, during which the betrayal of the Communists is secretly maneuvered by foreign capitalists working with General Chiang's representative and the chief of the foreign police and Chinese financial interests. During this pause, the Communists make an unsuccessful effort to get assistance from Hankow and to persuade the representatives from Moscow to change a policy that is smoothing the way to betrayal by their supposed allies. Acting on his own initiative, a Communist terrorist throws a bomb at the General's car—but the General doesn't happen to be in it. This is the signal for the drastic measures that are now prepared for: the seizure of Communist posts and the executions of the leaders.

Here also are the private dramas played out within the larger movement. Gisors, French philosopher, once professor at the University of Peking, loses his dearly loved son by a Japanese wife, and has only his opium left for consolation and escape. Tchen, young Chinese Communist, told off to commit the murder that opens the story, becomes obsessed, like a character out of Dostoevsky, with an agonizing loneliness, and is driven relentlessly on to more terrorism; when he throws the bomb at the General's car, it is really his own death that he is seeking. Hemmelrich, the Belgian Communist, is torn in a conflict between his loyalty to his Chinese wife and sick child and his desire to participate actively in the uprising; he is released in a horrible manner when he finds his phonograph shop (a Communist meetingplace) cleaned out with grenades and his wife and child torn to pieces. Kyo, Gisors's son, disciplined for death and dedicated to his cause, is yet tortured at the moment of supreme crisis by jealousy of his wife. And Katov, the old Russian revolutionist who has grown up in the civil wars, is familiar with firing squads, and has no personal ties—Katov hands over the precious poison that would save him from burning alive to two young Chinese prisoners who face the same fate.

That scene of sacrifice in the prison yard will remain in memory along with certain scenes in Dostoevsky marked by the same kind of horror, tension, and exaltation. In the prison yard night was rising from the ground, "where the groans seemed to run into one another like rats, mingled with a frightful stench." When Katov is ordered to that section of the wall where are gathered those destined to death by torture, "all those of the wounded who were not in the throes of death followed him with their eyes. His shadow grew upon the wall of those who were to be tortured." Near him on the ground are the Chinese boys. When he has given them his cyanide, and has heard their last suffocated cries, he has nothing to do but wait. His answers to the officers who come to take him and find the dead bodies make known to the other prisoners what he has done. As he is led to the prison gate, they silence their moans and watch.

The lantern threw Katov's shadow, now very black, across the great windows framing the night; he walked heavily, with uneven steps, hindered by his wounds; when the swinging of his body brought him closer to the lantern, the silhouette of his head vanished into the ceiling. The whole darkness of the vast hall was alive and followed him with its eyes, step by step . . . All the heads, with a slight movement, followed the rhythm of his walk, with love, with dread, with resignation. All kept their heads raised: the door was being closed. A sound of deep breathing, the same as that of sleep, began to rise from the ground: breathing through their noses, their jaws clenched with anguish, motionless now, all those who were not yet dead were waiting for the whistle.

Each time a victim was thrown into the firebox, the locomotive whistled.

It has been stated in reviews of this book that the revolution is not the principal theme, but the "setting and the pretext for a novel that is, in reality, a drama of individual lives"; [65] that the single emotion binding together these lives is not the desire to revolt or to achieve justice, but the feeling of personal solitude, of inadequacy in the face of life and helplessness against death. If this were true, *Man's Fate* could scarcely be included among proletarian novels in our definition. And another reviewer [66] declares that among the things missing in this book is the revolution itself. Where are the underfed coolies, the peasants taxed to the breaking point, the workers of the trade unions, the picket lines, the demonstrations?

The answer might be that the coolies, peasants and the rest are overwhelmingly implied in the spirit, the purposes, the activities, and the sacrifices of the leaders. Must the coolies actually pant across the stage? Malraux's literary gift—in this novel, at least—is not for the broad mass effects of which Zola is master. But consider Kyo Gisors, who had left his father and had lived in Canton and Tientsin the life of day-laborers in order to organize the syndicates.

His life had a meaning, and he knew what it was: to give to each of these men whom famine at this very moment was killing off like a slow plague, the sense of his own dignity. He belonged with them . . . "There is no possible dignity, no real life for a man who works twelve hours a day without knowing why he works." That work would have to take on a meaning, become a faith.

Kyo had chosen action, in a grave and premeditated way, in the revolutionary cause; "his Japanese training had imposed the conviction that ideas were not to be thought, but lived." When there was no longer any possibility of action, and no dignified death possible but that of his own inflicting, he took his cyanide in the prison yard. Malraux tells the story of the end, not of the beginning, of his career. But the impulse at the beginning, to throw in his lot with that of the day laborers, makes the end much more than a private drama.

The defeat of Ferral, the French banker who has been intriguing in Shanghai in the interests of his Consortium, has little meaning or interest as an individual drama; it is an incident in the triumph of the ruthless internationalism of capital. The scene of Ferral's appeal for financial support to the Minister of Finance and the bankers in Paris follows the nightmare agonies and exaltations of the prison yard. " 'Thanks to the bonds that unite the Consortium,' " says Ferral, " 'to a great part of Chinese commerce, I have participated in the most effective way in the seizure of power by General Chiang Kai-shek.' " We have just lived through the full horror of that seizure; we know what lies behind these conferences of bankers, this bargaining in a conventional and ornate language that reminds Ferral of the ritual languages of Asia.

"The maintenance of the Consortium [concludes the minister, sealing Ferral's defeat] does not in any way interest us. A share in the building of the railways is assured to France by the treaties. If the Consortium fails, another enterprise will be formed . . ." "And this new corporation [says Ferral, turning to the bankers], instead of having industrialized Indo-China, will distribute dividends. But, as it will have done nothing for

Chiang-Kai-shek, it will find itself in the situation in which you would be here, if you had never done anything for the State; and the treaties will be manipulated by some American or British society with a French screen . . . to whom you will lend the money which you refuse me."

Do the closing pages of the book justify the complaints of the critics that the revolution is missing, or is merely a pretext for a drama of individual lives? Kyo's widow has gone to see his father in Japan, to accompany him to Moscow, but he refuses to go. It was Kyo who had attached him to men, and Kyo's death has released him into a profound indifference. She quotes his own words to persuade him, the words of the lectures he had once given, and he replies that he still thinks these things, but for him life is over.

"You used to say [she reminds him], 'They have awakened with a start from a sleep of thirty centuries, to which they will never return.' You also used to say that those who have given a consciousness of their revolt to three hundred million wretches were not shadows like men who pass—even beaten, even tortured, even dead . . .'"

He is too absorbed in freeing himself from his life. But while you are freeing yourself from your life, she was thinking, other Katovs are burning in boilers, other Kyos . . . And she recalls the letter she has just received from one of the revolutionists who had escaped to Moscow: "it was in work pursued with warlike energy, released over the whole Russian land, in the will of a multitude for whom this work had become life, that her dead had found refuge." The letter told her that Hemmelrich had said, " 'Before, I began to live when I left the factory; now, I begin to live when I enter it. It's the first time in my life that I work and know why I work, not merely waiting patiently to die.' " And the letter quotes from Gisors's lectures:

" 'A civilization becomes transformed when its most oppressed element—the humiliation of the slave, the work of the modern worker—suddenly becomes a *value,* when the oppressed ceases to attempt to escape this humiliation, and seeks his salvation in it, when the worker ceases to attempt to escape this work, and seeks in it his reason for being. The factory, which is still only a kind of church of the catacombs, must become what the cathedral was, and men must see in it, instead of gods, human power struggling against the Earth.' " "Yes [she reflects] no doubt the value of men lay only in what they had transformed. The Revolution had just passed through a terrible malady, but it was not dead. And it was Kyo and his men, living or not, vanquished or not, who had brought it into the world."

Clandestine groups were forming again in all the provinces.

And, one may add as postscript, seven years after this uprising, General Chiang Kai-shek is still buying arms from the great international armament merchants to fight a Sovietized section of China embracing, it is said, eighty millions of inhabitants.

We are going to deal very briefly with the Russian novels of the new proletarian life, selecting from those available in translation a few that are typical of popular themes. What has fiction done to reflect that process of transforming the factory into a cathedral, in which men see "human power struggling against the earth"?

Published some years ago, when the process was in a very early stage, was F. V. Gladkov's *Cement.* Its hero is Gleb Chumalov who had been a factory worker in a Black Sea port before the Revolution. After years in the Red Army, he returns to find the factory dropping to ruins, his wife changed and unapproachable, absorbed in her Soviet work, and his child in the local Children's Home. It is about 1920. The new social machinery creaks and stalls, there are still Green bandits lurking in the hills, and the threat of White attacks. Animal-like famine victims creep in from stricken

districts. A discouraging prospect; but Gleb has stores of unexhausted energy. The factory must be started up and his wife won back. He succeeds in the first enterprise, but it isn't easy to say where the book leaves him so far as the second is concerned. The most powerful official whom Gleb has to work with loves Gleb's wife, and there is an undercurrent of strong antagonism between them. But the interests of the community win out every time over personal jealousy, which is as it should be under Communism. Gleb's wife refuses to "belong" to anything but her work. Even her child must share the lot of the other children in the Home, and that finally means the child's death. But the wife, Dasha, has faced too many terrible experiences not to face this, too. " 'The old life has perished and will not return,' " she tells Gleb. " 'Everything will come through and attain new forms, and then we shall know how to forge new links.' "

The book is written in a vigorous dramatic style, with a rapid tempo. It is permeated by the conviction that the times require energetic optimism and activity, and to the devil with psychology. It celebrates the Machine.

Like a dead planet the factory slept in these idle days. The northwest winds had splintered the icy windows; the mountain torrents had laid bare the iron ribs of the concrete foundations . . . There were no doors . . . Cobwebs, heavy with cement dust, fluttered like ashen rags.

But the engine room had survived the decay, for a man had lived on there, doggedly tending the machines.

The Diesel engines stand like black marble idols, bedecked with gold and silver. Firmly and solidly they stood in long regular rows, ready for work. Just a touch and their polished metal limbs would start dancing . . . The engines stood in rows, like altars demanding their sacrifice.

When Gleb penetrates to this austere temple of the engines, the engineer-priest greets him:

"Look at these devils! How clean they are! It needs only one word, 'Start her off, Brynza!' and all this jolly machinery would start turning and trumpeting out an iron march . . . When I'm with the engines, I'm an engine myself, and you can all go to the devil with your politics, yelling, and brawling."

This Brynza is not, however, the high priest of the dynamo. That is the technologist, the master who knows all the intricate life of the factory, an old German who has existed hidden away in a corner as in a tomb. He belongs to the past and expects nothing but death from the violent forces of the present. But Gleb routs him out—this man who had once ordered Gleb the striker to be shot—and Comrade Technologist is put in harness again: " 'Get your brains in hand, and we'll get to work. We'll build bigger things even than these—a new world, Comrade Technologist!' " Gleb has to carry on his fight in the midst of the yelling and brawling of politics, but at last he gets the great human machine under way. "Thousands of hands raised in thousands of efforts; the clamor of spades and picks; thousands of bodies in unanimous action moved mightily as one body. A living human machine that shook the stones to their depths." Gleb had no life apart from this tumultuous mass.

The book closes with a noisy triumph, a celebration of the reopening of the factory, of this victory on the economic front. Sirens shriek, the crowd thunders, the banners flash like wings of fire.

Ilya Ehrenburg, a "fellow-traveller" who has evolved (so states Joshua Kunitz in the *New Masses*)[67] from the extreme right to "his present position of unqualified acceptance of the Revolution," gives in his novel *Out of Chaos* an amusing picture of the predicament of many a Soviet writer called upon to promote the success of Five-Year Plans.

The author **Gribin had to write a new** novel. The critics harried him. They declared that Gribin eschewed contemporary themes. Gribin got from a magazine editor an advance on a novel about a construction works and reserved a sleeper in an International car. He now stood outside the administration office and watched the passers-by. Beside him a riveter was wrapping his feet in cotton cloth. With a wry face Gribin remembered that his wife had forgotten to put eau-de-cologne in his bag. He thought of his wife, of his study with a picture of Pushkin on the wall, of his snug home now so far away, and he was depressed. But work had to be done. He drew a note-book from his pocket and wrote down, "A large structure. Called Cowpers. Gives an impression of striking grandeur. To put in the chapter where a shock-worker falls in love." Wearily he yawned and trudged off to the canteen for foreigners.

Novels written in this spirit do not glow. And many of the novels about the front line of industrial construction must have been written in this spirit during the dictatorship of RAPP, the Association of Russian Proletarian Authors, which was disbanded in April, 1932. Art was forced to co-operate in an obvious and crude way with politics; "psychology," "eternal and universal problems," were taboo; there were only class problems, and these were narrowly conceived. A few months after the dissolution of RAPP, Gorki's play *Yegor Bulichev and Others* was produced. Gorki played an important rôle in the dissolution of the dictatorship; under its control, his play would have been frowned upon, for reasons that probably seem rather odd to people outside Russia: because Gorki allows the audience to sympathize with Bulichev, a capitalist exploiter; because he shows Bulichev as anti-religious, and it is a tenet of Soviet doctrine that capitalism and the Church are allies; because Bulichev's daughter becomes a revolutionist—and can a bourgeois girl become a real revolutionist?—and because the "worker" in the play plays a very minor rôle. Under RAPP, Ilya Ehrenburg could scarcely have painted so complete and sympathetic a portrait as that of his Volodia in *Out of Chaos*. Volodia really belongs in Turgenev's *Smoke* or Goncharov's *Oblomov* or a short story by Chekhov. Since it is particularly difficult for the foreign reader to follow Virginia Woolf's counsel in mastering the perspective of the recent Russian novels, he can well be grateful when waifs and strays from the old world of the Russian novel turn up in a Soviet construction camp. Here is something familiar; here is an introspective intellectual meditating suicide once more; and the familiar figure throws into relief some young shock trooper who rushes with shouts of joy to beat Kharkhov's world record at pouring concrete.

It would be interesting, reflects Volodia towards the end of *Out of Chaos*, " 'to trace how the heroes of Dostoevsky's works had adjusted themselves to dialectical materialism.' " And this is really what Ehrenburg has done. Volodia, Kolia the shock trooper, and Irina, the girl schoolteacher who is loved by both the young men, work out their problems of love and work in Tomsk, the half-dead Siberian city where the old university has taken on a new lease of life, and at Kuznetsk, where the Giant, a huge steel plant, is under construction. In the camp

men lived as in a war. They blasted stones, felled trees, and stood up to their waist in icy water, fortifying the dam. Every morning the newspaper published a digest of victories, of breaks in the program, of the starting of a blast furnace, of new deposits of ore, of an underground tunnel, of the power of the Morgan crane.

Workers came from all over Russia: fly-by-nights, to snap up government coats, peasants from collective farms to "earn something for a cow," Young Communist Leaguers to build a Giant—some led by hunger, others by faith; and some were brought—dispossessed kulaks and criminals, absent-minded bookkeepers, Turkestan bandits, "incorrigible churchmen." And from other countries came technicians, who lived here "as if at the Pole or in the Sahara" and expressed surprise at everything: "the enthusiasm, the lice, the frosts." "In what had been a wasteland, an industrial plant was rising, and around the plant a town was blossoming as in other days towns had risen around the cathedrals."

Volodia and Irina are both students before they become workers; but Kolia has been a worker first, and it is an awakened eagerness for knowledge that sends him to Tomsk for some special instruction. Volodia is one among a few dozen odd fellows who were labelled *izgoys*—"struck off the list"— by the professors; class enemies or the doomed, by others. He writes in his diary:

"My heart takes no part in the life that surrounds me . . . If I had lived a hundred years ago I should have been perfectly adjusted . . . Whether because of class instinct, or because of my blood, or, finally, because of my frame of mind, I have become attached to a dying culture. It follows that I am not fit for constructive work. In mining, I believe, this is called waste rock . . . In other epochs a man could admire mountain tops without thinking whether one could get good iron out of the landscape. Lermontov discovered in the Caucasus, not ores, but the Demon."

Irina, though she loves him and thinks him superior to others in intelligence, says that he notices only evil and scoffs at it; she too sees much that is disgusting; "our constructive work is taking place not in a beautiful and spotless laboratory, but . . . in a cattle yard." But this realization only spurs her on to renewed effort.

One night Volodia and a young ne'er-do-well get drunk and wander into Dostoevsky Street in Kuznetsk. Only a little old man remembers who Dostoevsky was and where he once lived during his exile and at what window he used to sit and write of his "poor unfortunates." Volodia had never been there before. When he saw the name of the street,

suddenly everything was different. This drunken night among the snowdrifts turned out to be the continuation of many other nights, equally dark and wild. Whenever he read Dostoevsky he felt ill. Those were not books, but letters from a man intimately related to him . . . He was convinced that only one man had told the whole truth about men. It was a truth that was incontestable and lethal. It could not be lived with. It could be held out to the dying, as the Holy Sacrament had once been. But to sit down at a table and have a meal, one must forget it.

He rambles on in a fantastic monologue:

"Dostoevsky Street and beside it a Giant of Steel . . . On the one hand, a man, just an ordinary man—a beard, roulette, patriotic verses, love difficulties, illnesses, quarrels with publishers. On the other hand, everything grand—the biggest blooming-mills in the world, not card-games, but 'diamat' [i.e., dialectical materialism], not the search for lice, but mutual cleansing, a record in brick-laying . . . You were wrong, Fedor Mikhailovitch, in despising warm water-closets. We have learned to appreciate them. We want to have the best water-closets in the whole world. Like those in Chicago. You mustn't smile into your beard. It smells of moth-balls. It can be shaved off—shaving brushes are disinfected today. And so are thoughts. No microbes allowed . . ."

Before the scene ends, Volodia and his half-crazy companion begin to seem like degenerate ghosts of Ivan Karamazov and Smerdyakov.

Nobody can help Volodia. The future belongs with his successful rival Kolia. At the May Day celebration that closes the book, an old "Red irregular," who had fought the civil war in Siberia, makes a speech, pays his tribute to the old fighters made of iron who won against the Whites, and then turns to Kolia and the other boys who are building the Giant: Lenin said iron is the chief foundation; " 'with such men we shall get iron, too, because they are stronger than iron. As an old Red irregular, I say to you that now I can die in peace, because, comrades, we have real men.' "

"Write the history of factories and plants. Write the history of the Red Army . . . May not the smallest detail of our inimitable, heroic days of the first Five-Year Plan be forgotten." Valentine Kataev is quoting Maxim Gorki, and in *Time, Forward* he tells of the success of one detail of the Plan—the attempt of Ishchenko's brigade at Magnitogorsk to beat the world's record for pouring concrete. All the energies of the people in the book are concentrated on this drive, though not all the people are working for its success; there are slackers and skeptics. The engineer Nalbandov himself is skeptical: " 'This is construction, not a stunt . . . We are not interested in making records. It is risky, speeding up expensive imported machines like that.' " But the other engineer, Margulies, checks his figures and raises the tempo—and goes without food—he seems to have had nothing but gumdrops for twenty-four hours; for Russia cannot wait. Let the machines wear out ahead of time; she needs her factories now. He is not disturbed by the thought that eats into the enthusiasm of Nalbandov, who tells the visiting capitalist author, " 'Here will be a socialist city for a hundred and fifty thousand workers and service men.' " But when the visitor retorts, " 'Yes, but will humanity be any happier because of that?' " Nalbandov thinks, " 'He is right,' " though out loud he says stubbornly, " 'You lack imagination . . .' "

Kataev, whimsically, places Chapter I at the end, in the form of a letter to a special correspondent at Magnitogorsk, who taught him "to see a garden in a drop of rain." It is a dedication, and it contains the dénouement—which came seven days after the brief twenty-four hours of the struggle to break the record; for the dénouement depended on the quality of the concrete, and that could not be determined for seven days. He describes the jubilation of workers when the concrete is proved to be up to the standard. Kataev is writing this dedication from Paris, where he found a sense of history that Russians had not yet acquired. But they would acquire it. They must create the history of the great Russian proletarian revolution.

And is not the Jaeger concrete-mixer with which the shock-brigades of proletarian youth set world records, more deserving of being preserved in the memory of future generations than the rusty blade of the guillotine, which I have seen in one of the gloomy cells of the Conciergerie?

In a stirring passage towards the end of the book—a kind of "song of the train" which is taking one of the characters back to European Russia—the spirit of the new Russia speaks.

We move like a shadow from the west to the east. We return from the east to the west like the sun. We cross the Urals . . . To lower tempos means to fall back, and those who fall back are beaten. But we do not want to be beaten . . . This was the history of old Russia: it was continually beaten because of backwardness. It was beaten by Mongol khans. It was beaten by Turkish beks. It was beaten by Swedish feudal lords. It was beaten by Polish and Lithuanian gentry. It was beaten by English and French capitalists. It was beaten by Japanese barons. It was beaten because of military backwardness, cultural backwardness, governmental backwardness, industrial backwardness, agricultural backwardness . . . That is why we cannot be backward any more . . . Dawn. The train crossed the Urals. Flickering across the windows from right to left swirled the obelisk: Asia-Europe. A senseless post . . . Never again shall we be Asia! . . . Clouds, elevators, fences, Mordovian sarafans, water pumps, caterpillars, echelons, churches, minarets, collective farms, village soviets. And everywhere . . . the transmission poles of high tension wires marched on diagonals in open formation. Six-armed and four-legged, they marched monstrously, like Martians, flinging checkered shadows over woods and mountains, over groves and rivers, over the straw roofs of villages . . . Never again shall we be Asia! Never!

D. B.

XII

A NOTE ON PROUST'S REMEMBRANCE OF THINGS PAST

PROLETARIAN fiction looks to the future. Beyond present struggles, defeats and temporary triumphs, it reaches after the shape of things to come. What forms of society, what kind of leaders, what individual sufferings and satisfactions, what mass emotions, will come out of the confusions of these decades we are passing through? Prophecy, in fiction, presents a more difficult problem in form than retrospect; it is struggling with new and intractable material. Compare Nexö's *Pelle the Conqueror* with Hamsun's *Growth of the Soil*. Hamsun looks back to the traditional and idealized figure of the sower of grain and to the old agricultural life, the root life of the centuries. He pictures a long-established way of living, with rooted customs and traditions, with constant relationships between men and between man and his environment. He has at his command forms of beauty already molded; he can appeal to emotions and attitudes to which his readers have been long habituated. But Nexö looks forward to the new leader rising out of the mass in a machine civilization. That leader is down on a battle-field "swept with confused alarms of struggle and flight"; and the emotions with which readers regard him are as confused and violent and contradictory as the struggle itself. Hamsun can give the clear beauty of sculpture to the immemorial figure of the sower. No wonder we turn from Pelle, whom we have to strive with Nexö to bring to life, and look wistfully back at Isak.

Yet really to recapture the past is, for the imagination of the novelist, a stupendous task that makes glimpses into the future seem relatively easy and irresponsible. Marcel Proust has taught us in some fourteen volumes what it means to go in search of the "lost time" of our own little personal life. Thomas Mann has begun to show us what it means to plunge into history, tradition, legend, archeology, comparative religion, and mythology, to recover a fragment of the "lost time" of the race. And to some consideration of these two efforts this and the next chapter will be devoted.

Proust retired after years of a social life active in spite of his semi-invalidism, to remember things past and to make of them a work of art. How he came to see that all the material of a literary work was in his past life is the subject of a long passage in the middle of the last volume, *Time Regained*. He acquired this material

in the midst of frivolous amusements, in idleness, in tenderness and in pain, stored up by me without my divining its destination or even its survival, as the seed has in reserve all the ingredients which will nourish the plant. Like the seed I might die when the plant had developed and I might find I had lived for it without knowing it.

Remembrance of Things Past is written throughout in the first person, mingling autobiography with the memories of an observer. It attempts the resurrection of life in art by means of memory. The past—that is Proust's field, "the present being merely an instant of the past, upon which he focusses the light of other moments of the past, more or less distant." Proust is convinced that we recapture the past with its emotions, not by any conscious effort of the intelligence, but through the accidental stimulus of an odor, a musical phrase, a movement of the body, a flavor upon the tongue. When we try to direct and control its operations, memory can give us only information about the past—facts, emptied of all the emotional content that some chance association, working below the threshold of consciousness, will revive. The incident at the beginning of *Swann's Way*—the resurgence of his childhood memories of Combray with the taste of the little cake soaked in tea—is only one of many fascinating examples of the working of association. We have all had the experience of elusive moods and fugitive memories, revived suddenly through the touch on some sensory spring; they are gone before we can track them to their source, though we often tease ourselves with the question— "Now why, just then, did that feeling come over me or that forgotten picture flash into my mind?" Sometimes there seems a curious significance about these resurrected moments that we try in vain to grasp. Now Proust, with long practice, became amazingly expert in bringing the submerged past into the present. Clive Bell (in a little essay, *Proust*) calls him the most resolute deep-sea fisherman that ever cast a net. While we are passing through an experience or a particular phase of our lives, we are too much involved, too much under the compulsion to play an active part, to be able to contemplate it and extract its meaning. And when it is over and we can look back upon it with some detachment, it has already begun to fade; the details have become blurred or obliterated, and the intensities of feeling dimmed. But suppose we could bring this lost experience up out of the buried mind, vivid as a dream is vivid and warm with the intimate emotions that once belonged to it—could we not then make it deliver up the secret of its meaning in our lives?

So with Proust, pursuing the paths of memory association is not just an intricate game: he is trying to escape from time into eternity. And if this, baldly stated, does not sound very intelligible, neither does the mystic's account of his timeless moments of ecstasy sound intelligible to anyone who has not the capacity for mystical experience. Note how Proust describes the sensation that came over him when he tasted the little cake: an exquisite pleasure invaded his senses and

at once the vicissitudes of life had become indifferent to me, its disasters innocuous, its brevity illusory. I had ceased now to feel mediocre, accidental, mortal. Whence could it have come to me, this all-powerful joy? What did it signify? How could I seize upon and define it?

Then when all the Combray memories came back, he no longer felt that the past was a shadow; it was existing in the here and now; must always have existed in the here and now; "memories such as these were no longer memories at all— they were the past not only come back, but come back in a form which no longer evolved and dissolved as events taking place in time must do." Several such moments are described in the last volume, moments bringing with them strange joy and peace along with the memory of a past scene evoked by a chance sensory impression. These were

fragments of existence withdrawn from time; but this contemplation, although of eternity, was fugitive. Yet I felt that the pleasure which it had given me at rare intervals in my life was the only one which was fecund and real . . . And I had decided to devote myself to it and to fix it; but how, by what means? The method which seemed to me the only one, what was it besides that of creating a work of art?

Thus Proust's Great Enlightenment, recorded in this last volume, was the discovery

that for him there was possible a kind of memory not identical with the ordinary sort; a vision of the eternity in which even the most completely forgotten experience had already taken its place.[68]

Proust represents his hero, then, as planning the work that Proust has as a matter of fact completed. In the light of the explanation of his purpose and his philosophy given in these seventy pages in the last volume, we glance back over the story which has been unrolling itself in the many preceding volumes.

It is as though Proust brought up out of the secret hold of his life's vessel a wonderful poop lantern of transparent glass, just discovered as the ship is entering the harbor. Hung triumphantly now at the stern of the boat, this lantern casts a clear stream of unblurred light over that long foam path left by the vessel's keel, which stretched back to the receding horizon.[69]

A lucid summary of *Remembrance of Things Past* has been given by Edmund Wilson in *Axel's Castle,* and both he and Joseph Wood Krutch (in *Five Masters*) have convincingly analyzed the relation between Proust's life and character and his monumental novel. There is no need to attempt what has been much more than competently done. What is offered here is merely a note on what we feel is a somewhat neglected aspect of Proust's masterpiece—its healthy, normal aspect. Mr. Krutch points out that Proust belongs with the artists who are set apart by some peculiarity of temperament or some exceptional experience. Such an artist, compelled to live a life different from the normal life of his contemporaries, regards events from an unfamiliar angle and

perceives relationships to which the rest are blind; cut off from the satisfactions permitted to most, he is compelled to seek others whose very existence is unsuspected. And when his work appears, it appears as a kind of revelation.

Proust had been from childhood cut off from ordinary satisfactions, and had to construct values of his own, or find himself in a vacant world. Mr. Wilson is even more insistent on Proust's over-cultivated sensibility, his neurotic temperament, his valetudinarianism—all those elements in him that make him a perfect case for psychoanalysis. And Mr. Wilson goes on from the decadence in Proust's work to the decadence of the society which it reflects—"the society of the dispossessed nobility and the fashionable and cultivated bourgeoisie, with their physicians and their artists, their servants and their parasites." (It is that whiff of decay again—welcome to the Left Wing critics.) Proust, Mr. Wilson concludes, "is perhaps the last great historian of the loves, the society, the intelligence, the diplomacy, the literature and the art of the Heartbreak House of capitalist culture." Of course both critics do full justice to the superb qualities of objective dramatic imagination in Proust's work, the strength of his character portrayal, and the strange beauties in that inner world of contemplation which is peculiarly his. What, however, we wish in our turn to insist upon is this: that Proust's moods and observations and feelings, his values and his satisfactions, often come to us as recognitions, not as revelations. And we shall give some examples, leaving it to the reader to pass upon their normal and healthy character.

The hero, who had adored his grandmother, remains in a curious state of apathy for months after her death, unable to see her face clearly or feel his love and grief. This distresses him, as a similar numbness has distressed most of us who have lived long enough to lose people we loved. One night, in the same seaside hotel where he had often stayed with his grandmother and suffering from one of his old heart attacks, he bends cautiously down to take off his boots; as he touches the top button, he bursts into tears. He sees, bending over his weariness, as she had bent years before in a moment of identical distress and loneliness, "the tender, dejected, preoccupied face" of his grandmother. He remembers then

how, an hour before the moment at which my grandmother had stooped down like that . . . to unfasten my boots, as I wandered along the stiflingly hot street, past the pastry-cook's, I had felt that I could never, in my need to feel her arms round me, live through the hour that I had still to spend without her. And now that this same need was reviving in me, I knew that I might wait hour after hour, that she would never again be by my side. I had only just discovered this because I had only just, on feeling her for the first time, alive, authentic, making my heart swell to breaking-point, on finding her at last, learned that I had lost her for ever.[70]

Most of us are incapable of making the intricate analysis of this experience that Proust makes—we do well if we follow it—but how many of us have had a similar experience!

Often when we have been shocked by some bad news, a detail of landscape, a face, a gesture, an arrangement of colors—something from the world around us—leaps out at us with startling distinctness. Proust's hero has just learned from an indifferent doctor that there is no hope for his grandmother, who has suffered a stroke while they were in the park. He is taking her home in a carriage.

The sun was sinking. It burnished an interminable wall along which our cab had to pass before reaching the street in which we lived, a wall against which the shadow cast by the setting sun of horse and carriage stood out in black on a ruddy background, like a funeral car on some Pompeian terra cotta.[71]

To see the shadow, and to see it that way, gives the stamp of authenticity to the young man's shock.

One more example from this relationship of the youth to his grandmother. He comes home unexpectedly from an absence and enters the room where his grandmother, who does not yet know of his return, sits reading and meditating, absorbed in thoughts she never allows herself to dwell on when he is with her. For a moment, he sees her as a stranger would see her, his eyes mechanically taking a photograph. Usually we see the people dear to us in the light of our love. Every casual glance at their faces is "an act of necromancy"; we read there the delicate and permanent qualities of their minds. Each face that we love is "a mirror of the past." But now and then by chance, our intelligent and pious affection is forestalled by our eyes, which set to work mechanically like films and register a likeness that places the one we love among those outsiders of whom we say, "He's begun to age a good deal." So the young man sees instead of his grandmother, for a moment only, "a dejected old woman" whom he did not know, "red-faced, heavy and common, sick, lost in thought, following the lines of a book with eyes that seemed hardly sane." [72]

This is one of the passages in Proust that immerse us in reveries of our own. We are likely to be lost in them before we reach the concluding sentence of a paragraph so long and involved that we can only yield ourselves to its embrace and hope all will be well. It is the surprise of at last coming to the surface that may prevent us from realizing how familiar the experience is.

Turn for contrast to some of his portraits of people who are known to us all—such as the perpetual invalid. Aunt Léonie, after her husband's death, had declined to leave, first Combray, then her house in Combray, then her bedroom, and finally her bed, and lay perpetually in an indefinite condition of grief, physical exhaustion, obsessions, and religious observances. Sometimes she was overheard talking quietly to herself:

She never spoke save in low tones, because she believed that there was something broken in her head and floating loose there, which she might displace by talking too loud; but she never remained for long, even when alone, without saying something, because she believed that it was good for her throat.

One of her claims to distinction was that she couldn't sleep.

In the morning Françoise would not "call" her, but would simply "come to her"; during the day when my aunt wished to take a nap, she used to say that she wished to be quiet, or to rest; and when in conversation she so far forgot herself as to

say "what made me wake up," or "I dreamed that," she would flush and at once correct herself . . . At one side of her bed stood a big yellow chest-of-drawers and a table which served at once as pharmacy and as high altar, on which, beneath a statue of Our Lady and a bottle of Vichy, might be found her service books and her medical prescriptions, everything that she needed for the performance in bed of her duties to soul and body, to keep the proper time for pepsin and for vespers.[73]

Or take Françoise, another person we all know, who is moved by distant sufferings and indifferent to those right under her nose. "The sufferings of humanity inspired in her a pity which increased in direct ratio to the distance separating the sufferers from herself." She dislikes the kitchen-maid, who has loved unwisely. One night, after the girl's confinement, she is seized with appalling pains, and her mistress wakes Françoise and sends her in haste for a medical book in the library, which contained first aid instructions.

An hour elapsed and Françoise had not returned; my mother . . . grew vexed, and told me to go myself to the book-case and fetch the volume. I did so, and there found Françoise who, in her curiosity to know what the marker indicated, had begun to read the clinical account of these after-pains, and was violently sobbing . . . At each painful symptom mentioned by the writer she would exclaim: "Oh, oh, Holy Virgin, is it possible that God wishes any human creature to suffer so?"

But, dragged back to the kitchen-maid's bedside,

she had nothing to offer but ill-tempered mutterings, mingled with bitter sarcasm . . . "Well, she need never have done what she must have done to bring all this about! She found that pleasant enough, I dare say! . . . He must have been a god-forsaken young man to go after *that*." [74]

Then see in Madame Verdurin ourselves, enjoying the morning coffee and the morning horrors in the newspaper. Madame Verdurin suffered from a headache if she did not have *croissants* with her coffee, and during the War she had to get special permission to have the bakery make them for her.

She started her first *croissant* again on the morning the papers announced the wreck of the *Lusitania*. Dipping it into her coffee, she arranged her newspaper so that it would stay open without her having to deprive her other hand of its function of dipping, and exclaimed with horror, "How awful! It's more frightful than the most terrible tragedies" . . . [But] while she indulged in these saddening reflections, she was filling her mouth, and the expression on her face, induced . . . by the savour of the *croissant*, precious remedy for her headache, was rather that of placid satisfaction.[75]

Nothing, we must all confess, is more normal and healthy than these breakfast emotions. The enumeration of examples of the "normal" in Proust could be continued indefinitely, but one more must suffice.

At some time or other, most of us have strolled at night through dark streets in some unfamiliar town, detached completely from our own concerns, released into contemplation of alien lives that can never mean anything to us beyond the glimpses of the shadowy moment. Proust's hero takes such a stroll in a garrison town, where the streets have not yet become for him what they are in the place one lives in— merely means of communication between one part and another.

The life led by the inhabitants of this unknown world must, it seemed to me, be a marvellous thing, and often the lighted windows of some dwelling-house kept me standing for a long while motionless in the darkness . . . Here the fire-spirit displayed to me in purple colouring the booth of a chestnut seller in which a couple of sergeants, their belts slung over the backs of chairs, were playing cards, never dreaming that a magician's wand was making them emerge from the night, like a transparency on the stage, and presenting them in their true lineaments at that very moment to the eyes of an arrested passer-by whom they could not see. In a little curiosity shop a candle, burned almost to its socket, projecting its warm glow over an engraving, re-printed it in sanguine, while, battling against the darkness, the light of the big lamp tanned a scrap of leather, inlaid a dagger with fiery spangles, on pictures which were only bad copies spread a priceless film of gold like the patina of time or the varnish used by a master, made in fact of the whole hovel, in which there was nothing but pinchbeck rubbish, a marvellous composition by Rembrandt. Sometimes I lifted my gaze to some huge old dwelling-house on which the shutters had not been closed and in which amphibious men and women floated slowly to and fro in the rich liquid that after nightfall rose incessantly from the wells of the lamps, to fill the rooms to the very brink of the outer walls of stone and glass—the movement of their bodies sending through it long unctuous golden ripples.[76]

Each reader of Proust will feel the stir of his own mem-ories of such night wanderings. To this reader, it is a mem-ory of Antwerp on an evening when an accident had cut off all electric light; a memory of dark side-streets; of people sitting on door-steps, chatting in low voices, the babies in shapeless nightgowns asleep in their mother's arms; of glimpses into little shops and family living-rooms and cafés, lighted by candles stuck into steins, amber glasses of beer in the candlelight, working men and women sitting at the tables; a memory of a watchmaker busy at some late job, and of three bearded faces bending over the parts of a clock spread out on a table under an oil lamp . . .

So, in innumerable ways, Proust, remembering things past, recovers for us our own "lost time."

D. B.

XIII

THOMAS MANN: JOSEPH AND HIS BROTHERS

IN an article on "Literature and Hitler" in *The Modern Thinker* for August, 1934, Thomas Mann writes that he has tried to strike a balance "between what is essentially German and what is essentially European and cosmopolitan"; that he inclines "towards the European rather than towards the specifically German"; and that this European bias derives from his mother's influence. Discussing *Buddenbrooks* in an earlier chapter, we referred to that mingling of racial strains in Mann's heritage which throws light on certain recurrent patterns in his work. One of five children, three boys and two girls, Mann passed a protected and happy childhood in Lübeck, far less interested in the career of a merchant, for which he was intended, than in writing. The death of his father, when Thomas was fifteen, was followed by the liquidation of the century-old grain firm and the departure of his mother and the younger children to Munich.

Mann tells in *A Sketch of My Life* how he finished his school course in Lübeck, worked for a year in an insurance office in Munich, attended courses at the university with the idea of preparing himself for journalism, and then spent a year in Rome with his brother, where he "devoured Scandinavian and Russian literature and wrote." When he returned to Munich he had the "fearfully swollen bundle of manuscript" which was his first novel, *Buddenbrooks*. The fortunes of his own family had given him the central conception of the book. He speaks of his attitude toward life at this time as "compact of indolence, bad civic conscience, and the sure and certain feeling of latent powers." He joined the staff of the magazine *Simplicissimus* in Munich; was released after three months from compulsory military training because of an injury to his ankle; was assigned to the category of "last resorts"; and when the Great War broke out was not called upon, partly because the first doctor to whom he was taken had read his books, and declared, "You shall be left alone." *Buddenbrooks* (1901) had had an unanticipated success; the short stories *Tonio Kröger* and *Death in Venice* and the novel *Royal Highness* had strengthened his reputation. Of *Tonio* he says:

Here perhaps for the first time I learned to use music to mould my style and form. Here for the first time I grasped the idea of epic prose composition as a thought-texture woven of different themes, as a musically related complex—and later, in *The Magic Mountain,* I made use of it to an even greater extent.

He married in 1905, and there are pleasant glimpses of his family life in *A Man and His Dog* and in the most charming of his later stories, *Early Sorrow.* During the War, when he "shared to the full the pangs of intellectual Germany in the clutch of destiny," he wrote *Reflections of a Non-political Man,* regarding it as a War service with the weapon of thought.

Mann had begun *The Magic Mountain* before the War, but found it impossible to go on with it amidst the misery and confusion of the years that followed. Yet the novel profited by the War, which drove him to a general revision of his principles and to painful and conscientious searching of his own mind. The direct result of these meditations was recorded in the essays, and thus what he calls "the worst of the introspective burden" was lifted from the novel.

But the problems dealt with in the narrative, like those in the volume of confession and struggle, were all present and alive in me before the war; everything was there before the war—it was only actualized and bathed in the lurid and desolate light of the conflagration.

In 1912 Mann's wife had had to spend some months in a sanitarium at Davos; he himself spent several weeks with her, and there "accumulated—the word but ill describes the extreme passivity of my stage—the fantastic impressions" out of which he planned to make a short tale. "The fascination of death, the triumph of extreme disorder over a life founded upon order and consecrated to it—these were to be reduced in scale and dignity by a humorous treatment." There was to be a simple-minded hero and an easy and amusing narrative manner. And so *The Magic Mountain* was begun.

At bottom I hardly concealed from myself the possibilities for expansion, the propensities of my material. I was early conscious that it belonged to a dangerous concentration of associations . . . For me that which is full of associations is quite precisely that which is significant . . . I shall never fathom . . . why every working idea of mine presents itself to me in a harmless, simple practicable light . . .

then begins to develop according to a law of its own, and presently a short and humorous tale grows into a two-volume philosophical novel. *The Magic Mountain* appeared in 1924, having had Mann under its power for twelve years. Mann was astonished at its success, for its subject matter was certainly not by its nature of the popular sort.

But [he says] the national crisis had produced in the general public precisely that alchemical keying-up in which had consisted the actual adventure of little Hans Castorp . . . The German reader recognized himself in the simple-minded but shrewd young hero of the novel.

Recognition abroad was rapid and in 1929 Thomas Mann was awarded the Nobel Prize for literature.

From the tuberculosis sanitarium among the snows, where time seems to halt and where the whole atmosphere is feverish, Mann views the problems of man's destiny through the eyes of the simple but receptive Hans Castorp, who comes for a few weeks and stays enchanted for seven years. Castorp passes through physical, intellectual, and spiritual adventures; he spends "the long undistinguishable time intervals by taking stock of himself, his derivations, his significance in the world, and the meaning of the world to him." It is a novel of ideas, seen through a temperament, dramatized in concrete characters and incidents. It is the sickness of European society, on the brink of the catastrophe of the War, that is diagnosed. There—down below the enchanted mountain— a life and death struggle is going on among forces that can only be given such elusive names as humanitarianism, liberalism, democracy, mysticism, pragmatism, nationalism, communism, science, charlatanism, sickness and health.

Far along in the book, Hans Castorp, lost while out skiing in a sudden snowstorm and half delirious from exposure, has a dream of a beautiful seacoast and islands bathed in the light of some golden age, peopled by human beings, children of sun and sea, so graceful, courteous, and dignified in their work and play, that he feels a thrill of ecstasy in watching them. But when his eyes follow the direction of the gaze of one lovely grave boy, he sees the moss-grown façade of an ancient temple, and he is drawn against his will through gateways, up long flights of steps, along pillared corridors, until at length he faces the bronze door of the innermost temple. Within this sanctuary obscene old hags are celebrating a horrible human sacrifice. With the sound of dreadful whispered brawling in his ears, he struggles out of his nightmare, and there in the snow by the little hut where he had found shelter, he tries to spell out the meaning of the dream.

"Now I know that it is not out of our single souls we dream . . . The great soul of which we are a part may dream through us . . . its own secret dreams, of its youth, its hope, its joy and peace—and its blood-sacrifice . . . I have dreamed of man's state, of his courteous and enlightened social state; behind which, in the temple, the horrible blood-sacrifice was consummated. Were they, those children of the sun, so sweetly courteous to each other in silent recognition of that horror? It would be a fine and right conclusion they drew. I will hold to them, in my soul."

This dream, rich in suggestions that can be only hinted at in a brief summary, has a central place in *The Magic Mountain* in the evolution of Hans Castorp's—and Mann's—thought. And when one begins to read *Joseph and His Brothers,* the dream plays in one's memory like an overture to the new novel, where we find again the themes of the vision: the morning glow and freshness and grave beauty of a pastoral life in the ancient world, and the dark and sinister hints of a still more primitive past, stained with blood and with monstrous superstition. It is a congenial if far-fetched fancy to think that the dreamy Hans Castorp, who is lost in the mists of the battle-field at the close of *The Magic Mountain,* has reappeared as young Joseph, in moonstruck meditation by the well near Hebron.

It was by an accident that Mann's thoughts were turned in the direction of the Biblical narrative. Some time in 1926 or 1927 a Munich artist showed him a portfolio of illustrations depicting the story of Joseph, and asked for a word of introduction; and this request sent Mann to the old family Bible to read "the graceful fable of which Goethe said: 'This natural narrative is most charming, only it seems too short, and one feels inclined to put in the detail.'" The story took possession of his mind.

The tendencies of the time, the tastes of my early days united to make the theme alluring to me . . . We have pushed forward our knowledge, whether into the darkness of prehistoric times or into the night of the unconscious; researches that at a certain point meet and fall together have mightily broadened the scope of our anthropological knowledge, back into the depths of time, or—what is really the same thing—down into the depths of the soul; and in all of us there is awake a lively curiosity about what is earliest and oldest in human things: the mythical, the legendary, the time before the dawn of reason . . . Myth and psychology [he goes on in *A Sketch of My Life*], the anti-intellectual bigots would prefer to have these two kept far apart. And yet, I thought, it might be amusing to attempt, by means of a mythical psychology, a psychology of the myth.

He was fascinated, too, by the idea of contributing to human tradition in drawing his material from an ancient realm of civilization and fancy, "a favorite subject of all the arts, hundreds of times elaborated in the east and the west in picture and poesy." His work would take its historic place in the line. Finally, these dreams had their roots far back in his childhood, when he had had a passion for the land of the pyramids and for archeological and Oriental reading. He planned a triptych, of which the Bible story should be one wing, the other two dealing with Spanish and German subjects, "the religious-historical theme running through the whole." But—an old story with Mann—as he began to work, the narrative expanded; Jacob took up a commanding position; the ancestral history grew in importance; Joseph, at the end of the first volume, hasn't yet been sold into slavery by his jealous brothers. A second volume has already appeared in Germany, and he is at work on the third volume. "I shall require about another year for its completion. If I may be permitted a personal opinion, I believe that *Joseph and His Brothers* is my best work." [77]

Almost every reader who can find a Bible around the house will refresh his memory before embarking on an adventure in which he will need to hold fast to the thread of the story in Genesis.[78] "A psychology of the myth" creates complications. The episodes in Genesis follow a straightforward time sequence. Mann mixes them all up. The order in Genesis can be indicated by ABCDEFGHIJ; the order in

Joseph and His Brothers is JEBCFGIADH. This looks confusing; but it isn't at all, as one reads. Yet after coming out from under the spell of delight in which the book has held the imagination, one wonders why Mann arranged the incidents as he did. To try to analyze the effects secured by this puzzling time order throws an interesting light on esthetic problems, and vastly increases one's admiration for Thomas Mann as an artist.

The opening scene between Jacob and young Joseph is, chronologically, the last. In that beautiful picture of father and son in conversation by the well, we gain a clear impression of their temperaments, the resemblances between them, and the deep love that binds them to each other—a love amounting to idolatry on Jacob's part. The incidents that follow develop the sharply contrasting relationship between Jacob and Esau, their bitter rivalry and their antithetic traits of character. The story of the stolen blessing is reserved for a later place; what we have at this point is Jacob's flight after the blessing, the pursuit by Esau's vengeful son, and the meeting of the estranged brothers many years later, when Jacob is returning from his long sojourn with his uncle Laban. Woven in with this narrative is Jacob's relationship with his God—his vision of Heaven, his wrestling with the angel—experiences separated in time by twenty-odd years, but both intimately connected with the humiliations he suffers at the hands of his twin brother. The first vision lifts up his spirit after his escape from his nephew—an escape bought at a heavy sacrifice of pride; the second experience prepares him to meet Esau by filling him with confidence in God's favor.

And then comes the Shechem episode, of which the reader should by all means taste the full barbaric flavor in Genesis. Dramatic, bloody, grotesque, this story of the rape of Dinah and the hideous vengeance of her brothers—even when

toned down by Mann's historical speculations—is repellent
and all but incredible to the modern reader. Suppose it were
placed where it belongs in the time order: it would then
interrupt the long narrative of Jacob's love and service for
Rachel, and would come just before the birth of Benjamin
and Rachel's death. It would hopelessly shatter the mood of
sympathy for Jacob which is created in us by Mann's telling
of the Jacob-Rachel idyll—in many ways so modern in feeling. Mann gets the Shechem treachery safely out of the way
before Jacob meets Rachel. Then he disposes of old Isaac—
whose death really occurs after Rachel's. And the death of
his father sends Jacob's mind back to brooding over the past,
and particularly over that little matter of the stolen blessing. So we now have this incident related as Jacob recalls it—
not in its bald detail, but colored by his reflective mood. And
at length comes the sustained narrative of Jacob, Laban,
Leah, and Rachel. We are left with the dominant impression
of Jacob's love and grief, and so are carried at the end of
the book back to the beginning, understanding deeply now
why Jacob adored Rachel's son.

It is an involved narrative movement, but there are no
jolts, and there is no weariness for the reader. As we begin
to tire of mere "story" or come to events hard for us to
regard with other than alien eyes, Mann pauses for speculation on myth and history and time. He plays skilfully upon
our emotions. The sympathy that is aroused when we see
the imposing old patriarch in the moonlight, leaning on his
staff, and anxious with a touching solicitude for his beautiful
son, carries us safely through the humiliation of his cringing
before Eliphaz and the cowardice revealed in his meeting
with Esau. Then we are given the heavy dose of his con-
nivance in the Shechem affair and his theft of the blessing.
By this time our tolerance for Jacob has worn a little thin,
and some of our old convictions about him, that made us feel

how odd it was of God to choose Jacob, are coming to the top. Whereupon we are recaptured by his love-at-first-sight for Rachel, by the hard dealing he gets from Laban, by his joy over the birth of Joseph and his grief over Rachel's untimely death—and we are drawn back (with greatly increased knowledge and understanding) into the sympathy awakened at the beginning.

But how—for the analysis may as well be thorough—are the transitions effected in this weaving back and forth? In the opening scene of talk between Jacob and Joseph, intimations are casually introduced of events to come or events in the past, to be more fully told later in the volume. Joseph, seeking to entertain his father with fancies about names, throws him into one of his brooding reveries; memories connected with names rise out of the past; he sees again the ford of Jabbok and lives over the strange heavy dream of the wrestling match with the man-angel who bestowed upon him the name "Israel." Jacob comes out of his musing, and he and Joseph take up an antiphonal chant, a matching of tales, such as must have been customary in days of oral, not written, tradition: "Well I know . . ." followed by "That know I as thou knowest it." Out of this evening antiphony Mann picks the name Eliezer and falls to speculating on the probable identity of the servant-teacher of Joseph and the messenger sent by Abraham in quest of a bride for his son Isaac. This leads Mann on to reflecting about other confusions of time and identity, the recurrence and the telescoping of stories: Abraham told some King Abimelech that Sarah his wife was his sister; Isaac told the same tale about his wife Rebecca to some other King Abimelech—or was it the same king? Other stories stretching back into a past far behind Jacob are woven in. And humorously enough, after planting us among these confusions, Mann observes, "I do not conceal from myself the difficulty of writing about people who do not know precisely who they are." At one moment he makes these people seem very solid and very close—the next, they are dissolved in the mists of a remote antiquity. He is psychologizing the myth. He works around again to the name "Israel," which had been the name of a robber tribe of the desert, faithful to a troublesome hobgoblin of a god, Yahu, for whom was reserved "an extraordinary theological career." Some of Yahu's followers had contact with Abraham, and Yahu was thus drawn into the orbit of the wanderer's spiritual speculations. "The name which Yahu's Bedouin warriors gave themselves was to become the name of Abraham's spiritual seed . . . precisely because Jacob had had it whispered to him in that pregnant night by Jabbok ford." A bold and lawless title—Israel—"God fighteth"—a title, when applied to Jacob, that aroused the private mirth of Simeon and Levi, those roughneck sons of Jacob who had carried through the Shechem outrage. They knew their father was no fighter; so did he. But his memories of defeat did no violence to the dignity of his soul, for always in such states of physical depression had come from the depths some powerful revelation of grace. So it had happened after the encounter with Esau's son—and of that we are now told. It is a dramatic episode, quite different from the musical, reverie-drenched scene at the well; and so a pleasing modulation of the narrative movement. And it is followed by the vision itself, built up in more fantastic, sumptuously Oriental detail than in Genesis.

Thus Jacob had triumphed over Esau's son. How had it been—the transition seems inevitable—in the similar encounter with Esau, many years later? This meeting has already been referred to, in connection with Jacob's fears of harm to Joseph, lingering at night by the well; he remembers other anxieties about Joseph—how he had hidden the child and his mother in the rear of the company, when he saw Esau and his troop approaching. Now the same episode recurs, but in a new relationship—recurrence with change, a sound esthetic principle. The scene with Esau gives us brilliantly contrasted portraits of the two brothers: the subtle Jacob and the tactless Esau, always forgiving Jacob for the filthy wrong done him, never forgetting to remind his brother whom he loved of their twin entry into this world— Jacob after Esau, holding fast to the heel of Esau, the stronger. (When this encounter comes properly into the chronological sequence, it is merely referred to and dismissed: "Next came the Red man.")

"Since next, after parting from Esau," Jacob came to Shechem—thus we are led, as by the hand of a naïve teller of simple tales, into the Shechem episode. And after it is over, we are told: "These are grievous tales. And Jacob the father was weighty with them, stately and bowed down as by his manifold possessions." Jacob muses; and Thomas Mann muses; and the two strains of reverie blend and separate and blend again almost imperceptibly in the section which follows, where Isaac's grotesque death—he falls into a bleating confusion of himself with the ram which was caught in the bushes and saved him so many years before from sacrifice at his father's hands—and the hoaxing of Esau are embedded in a matrix of meditation on history and myth. The soul of Jacob was deep sunk in musing, yet mightily uplifted, in those days when his father was dying, and it was as if the ground beneath his feet were transparent,

consisting of crystal layers going down and down without any bottom and lighted up by lamps which burned between the layers. But he walked above them among the experiences of his proper flesh, Jacob, present in time, and gazed at Esau, who likewise walked again with him according to his archetype and was Edom the Red.

As Jacob's reveries give place to Mann's, we go further and further back into legend and myth: "our tale issues into mysteries and our signposts are lost in the endlessness of the past, where every origin betrays itself as but an apparent halt and inconclusive goal." Jacob-Esau, Osiris, and Typhon-Set, the red huntsman . . . Mars the red, the fire planet . . . Mann awakens in us a passionate interest in mythology and comparative religion that almost sends us rushing off to a library—but Jacob draws us back just in time. With the hoaxing enters, of course, Rebecca, brilliantly portrayed, and a reconstruction of what really happened after Esau discovered how he had been tricked; Genesis, here, is too sketchy. Rebecca knew that Esau, brooding on revenge, had gone into the wilderness to consult his uncle Ishmael; she knew they were hatching murder. Ishmael, whose hold upon primitive ideas was much more secure than Esau's, made proposals that sent Esau running away in horror, "with his fleeces standing on end." Killing Isaac and eating of his flesh was the one way by which Esau could be sure of incorporating into himself the Abram-blessing. That was more important than a simple little fratricide for revenge. Esau ran away, but he came back, and the murder drama was planned. But meantime Rebecca had a chance to act. Her scheme to send Jacob off to Laban meant that she might never see her favorite again. "So it turned out. But Rebecca had no regrets, either then or later."

"We know what happened to the traveller on the first day out, his shame and his great exaltation"—and since we do know that, and the other incidents that would break discordantly into the story of Jacob and Rachel, Mann can launch himself on the full tide of Jacob's passion. During the twenty-five years of his life with Laban, Jacob changes from the frightened youth of the stolen blessing to the stately, subtle, profoundly experienced elderly father of the

opening scene. Mann's dexterity has placed all Jacob's least
admirable doings in the narrative before he meets Rachel.
Such ruses as he practices on Laban are justified by the overwhelming deception Laban practised upon him, which had
inflicted "a defeat so devastating to his senses and so humiliating to his feeling that his soul for long could not shake it
off."

The narrative movement we have been analyzing is that
of memory association, governed by moods rather than by
the logic and the time order of events. But whose memory
is it? Thomas Mann's or Jacob's? Throughout there is a
subtle mingling of Jacob's reverie by the well near Hebron
and Mann's reverie over Jacob. A long philosophical prelude
before the curtain rises on the moon-lighted landscape in-
itiates us into the mind of Mann, gazing down into the
fathomless well of the past. Then as the story develops, the
interludes of reflection and interpretation keep us not only
in touch with this mind, but steeped in its atmosphere—an
atmosphere created by the "blending of reason and sympathy
in a gentle irony that is not profane." [79]

But there is established, too, at the outset, a memorable
picture of Jacob, musing; and casually, from time to time,
this is recalled to our minds, so that always in the background is this suggestion of memories passing through the
mind of Jacob.

Here is the picture. Joseph is spinning fancies under the
moon, spreading out his little knowledge in the hope of
pleasing his father. He pauses: " 'but alas, I see that the
father hearkeneth not, but that his ears are sealed up by his
thoughts, and he is in deep musing.' " And when Jacob
mused, "it was the highest degree of emotionally absorbed
absence of mind"; it was a proper musing, "recognizable at
a hundred paces," and inspired awe—this sight of

the old man leaning on his staff which he grasped with both hands, the head bowed over the arm; the deep, dreamy bitterness of the lips in the silver beard; the old brown eyes, boring and burrowing into the depths of memory and thought—eyes whose gaze was cast up so much from below that it almost got caught in the overhanging brows . . . His soul was played upon by chords and correspondences, diverted and led away into far-reaching considerations which mingled past and to come in the present moment, and made his gaze blurred and broken as in deep introspection.

His way of coming out of his reverie was no less expressive than his absorption in it: "with a deep sigh, with weighty dignity, he straightened up and shook it from him and with lifted head looked about him widely in space as one who wakes."

After Isaac's death, "deep-sunk in musing, yet mightily uplifted, was the soul of Jacob in these days when he with his brother Esau buried their father; for all past events stood up in him and became present to his spirit." As Esau blubbered and howled and rambled on about the past, naïvely reconstructing it in the image of his desire, Jacob's dim and blurring gaze rested upon the huntsman his twin,

and all the events of the past rose up again in him and became the brooding present: their childhood, and how the long-awaited decision had at last been made, with the curse and the blessing and all that these involved. He mused dry-eyed, only now and again his breast heaved with the heaviness of his thoughts, and he gave an inward gasp.

It was while tending Laban's flocks, serving through his years of waiting, that Jacob developed his gift for contemplation. His soul was tranquil then, and waiting formed the ground bass of his life. He thought much of Rachel

as he lay propped on his elbows with his cheeks in his hands, or with his hands folded in the back of his neck, one leg supported on the other knee, in the shade of rocks or shrubbery;

or leaning on his staff in the wide plain with his sheep grazing around him. And not alone of her, but of God, and all the tales he knew, the near and far, his flight and wandering, of Eliphaz, and the proud vision of Beth-el; of the feast of the cursing of Esau; of Yitzchak the blind, of Abram, of the tower, the flood, of Adapa or Adama in the garden of paradise . . . which reminded him of the garden which he had helped his clod of a father-in-law to plant, through his blessing, and which had meant such increase of prosperity to the man.

The scene of the wedding with Leah—who should have been Rachel—is introduced as if recalled by Jacob, for that defeat was often the theme of his brooding. And after the tale is told, we see again a picture that recalls that of the opening:

Such then are the tales of Jacob, written in the mien of the gray-haired man, as they passed before his swimming gaze, that got entangled in his eyebrows; when he fell into his solemn musing, either alone or with other people—and his look gave them a start, so that they nudged each other and whispered: "Hush, Jacob is thinking of his stories!"

They took care to check their own manifestations "in reverence for this many-layered burden of life and history."

So with this and that touch upon the visual sense we are kept in mind of the musing Jacob, and inattentive to the moment when he becomes the musing Thomas Mann. Towards the end, as in the prelude, Mann steps frankly forward in his own person. He stands with Jacob on the wooded heights of the mount of Gilead, watching for the pursuing Laban.

The scene, the unchanging landscape, river, sea, and misty mountain range are silent witness and sworn warrant for the truth of these stories which made Jacob's thoughts so weighty and his mien so awe-inspiring when he mused. I relate them in detail, circumstantially, as they can be proven to have happened here, in abiding harmony with mountain and valley. Here it was, it all fits; I myself went down into the depths and looked from the western shore of the evil-tasting sea of Lot, saw all with my own eyes, and that it is in order and agrees one part with another. Yes, these bluish heights in the east, beyond the lye, are Moab and Ammon . . . [and so on through the details of the landscape] Yes, it all agrees in itself, and bears evidence in the long run to the truth of the shepherds' songs.

Only a deep identification in spirit with certain qualities Mann found or imagined in Jacob could have carried him so smoothly through this perilous mingling of reverie streams. And of one aspect of this identification he speaks in the prelude. He has been commenting on Jacob's restlessness, his way of living, despite his wealth, "as though from hour to hour he must be awaiting the word which would make him take down huts and stalls, load poles, blankets, and skins on the pack-camels, and be off." Young Joseph knew why he lived thus: so it must be

because one served a God whose nature was not repose and abiding comfort, but a God of designs for the future, in whose will inscrutable, great, far-reaching things were in process of becoming, who with His brooding will and His world-planning, was Himself only in process of becoming, and thus was a God of unrest, a God of cares, who must be sought for, for whom one must at all times keep oneself free, mobile and in readiness . . . As for me [Mann goes on] I will not conceal my native and comprehensive understanding of the old man's restless unease and dislike of any fixed habitation . . . To me too has not unrest been ordained, have not I too been endowed with a heart which knoweth not repose? The story-teller's star—is it not the moon, lord of the road, the wanderer, who moves in his stations, one after another, freeing himself from each? For the story-teller makes many a station, roving and relating, but pauses only tentwise, awaiting further directions, and soon feels his heart beating high, partly with desire, partly too from fear and anguish of the flesh, but in any case as a sign that he must take the road, towards fresh adventures which are to be painstakingly lived through, down to their remotest details, according to the restless spirit's will.

It would be unfortunate if an impression were left of a book overweighted with speculation and reverie. For to look back over the experience of reading it is to retrace one's steps through a gallery of scenes and portraits precise and sharp in outline and glowing with color. The slender Rachel, walking in the midst of her flock—looking for the first time at Jacob with her short-sighted, faintly slanting eyes; Rebecca the matron, who might have stepped out of a Flemish triptych; the ill-starred Dinah, with the long narrow eyes of sticky black and a fatal sweetness; Esau, the goat-man, dancing up with pipe and tabor to welcome his returning brother; blind Isaac, eating the blessing feast, or dying in his strange reversion to the ram; the beautiful Joseph, with the quaint posturings of his moon-worship. And the scenes: the first meal at Laban's; the vintage feast on the vine-clad terraces of Garizim; the bridal chamber in the fatal dawn of Jacob's awakening to the sight of Leah, not Rachel, in his bed; the market place in Shechem, with the guardsmen running in crouching quickstep through the press of camel and donkey riders—a living Egyptian frieze.

And the superb portrait of Jacob. It is incredible that this Jacob, preserving as he does all the unlovely traits and tricks set down in Genesis, should be found at the end of the book so deeply rooted in our sympathies that we almost fear to take with him the road that stretches ahead, knowing what tribulations lie ambushed there. Jacob, without losing his own legendary identity, has strangely grown into the likeness of our own soul on its wanderings.

D. B.

THE SHORT STORY AND THE NOVELETTE: ANTON CHEKHOV, KATHERINE MANSFIELD, A. E. COPPARD, AND OTHERS

To complete our survey of fiction by some attention to the briefer forms, we are going to discuss first three writers who have been versatile and original in their handling of the short story, and have found this form of fiction adequate to express their wide experience and deep insight. Chekhov, of course, wrote plays as distinguished as his stories, and Katherine Mansfield and A. E. Coppard have written poetry. But they have left the novel alone, though perhaps the first two, had they not died before middle age, would have carried through plans they had for longer works. Many of the modern novelists have used the short story as a subsidiary form of expression: John Galsworthy, for example, and Conrad, and Hardy. But it is interesting to see just how completely life and character can be interpreted by fine artists who keep within the limits of story and novelette.

Nothing better could happen to anyone looking for adventurous life than to have his categories taken by surprise, for categories are perilously convenient. Our natural tendency is to account for people and all the relations between them in the accepted conventional way, to place them in pigeonholes and then to deceive ourselves with the idea that we have got hold of the truth about people. We are told that there are six (or two, or five) psychological types, and forthwith sort out our acquaintances. Chekhov, who distrusted categories, remarks that Tolstoy, in *Resurrection,* divides all the convicts into five classes. Why not ten, he asks? H. G.

Wells has for years had his eyes so fixed on "constructive-minded" and "muddle-headed" people that he has gradually lost that fine capacity to realize imaginatively a muddle-headed person, which he had when he conceived Mr. Polly. And so he is capable of lumping together most of humanity as people who just should not have been born. " 'The world swarms,' " he has his Sir Richmond say in *The Secret Places of the Heart,* " 'with cramped and undeveloped lives, which amount to nothing.' " Someone interjects, " 'I suppose they have a sort of liking for their lives.' " " 'Does that matter? They do nothing to carry life on. They are just blurred repetitions of one common life. All that they feel has been felt, all that they do has been done better before.' " To think in this way of undeveloped lives in the mass is convenient for the sociologist, who plans by reorganizing society to increase the opportunities for development. But the fiction writer—even one like Wells, who is preoccupied with social problems—must, as Wells himself wrote some years ago, recognize that at the root of every one of our social problems lies a psychological problem, "one in which the idea of individuality is an essential factor." To penetrate to the sources of individuality demands the open-minded warm curiosity and interest with which Chekhov approaches each human being.

The best writers let nothing, neither previous reading nor any preconceptions, stand between them and their viewing of life. If their vision is extensive and if they have sympathy they communicate to their readers deeper understanding, enrichment, and an added zest for life. Much of this effect in Chekhov is due precisely to his refusal to place people in categories of any sort. He was criticized for not being more dogmatic and definitive about some of his characters, for not solving their problems. In a letter to his friend A. S. Souvorin, he said:

It seems to me that a writer of fiction should not try to solve such questions as those of God, pessimism, etc. His business is but to describe those who have been thinking about God and pessimism, how, and under what circumstances. The artist should be, not the judge of his characters and their conversations, but only an unbiassed witness.

Chekhov had ended his story *Lights* by saying, "Yes, there's no understanding anything in this world." It is a story which reports the desultory conversation between two Russians about pessimism in which nothing was solved. But his critic had said that an artist must be a psychologist and a psychologist must be able to resolve and clarify what the layman cannot. Chekhov is firm in his conviction:

The time has come for writers, especially those who are artists, to admit that in this world one cannot make anything out, just as Socrates once admitted it, just as Voltaire admitted it. The mob think they know and understand everything; the more stupid they are, the wider, I think, do they conceive their horizon to be. And if an artist in whom the crowd has faith decides to declare that he understands nothing of what he sees—this in itself constitutes a considerable clarity in the realm of thought, and a great step forward.

The youthful Merezhkovsky in 1888 had written an article about Chekhov's stories in which he had called one of Chekhov's heroes a failure. Again Chekhov wrote to Souvorin:

How is he a failure? God grant us all a life like his. He believed in God, and he had enough to eat, and he had the gift of composing poetry . . . To divide men into the successful and the unsuccessful is to look at human nature from a narrow preconceived point of view. Are you a success, or not? Am I? Was Napoleon? Is your servant Vassily? What is the criterion? One must be a God to be able to tell the successes from the failures without making a mistake.

Perhaps he dreaded generalizations because of the dull insensitiveness that results from dealing with people in that way. This insensitiveness is typified by two of his characters that come to mind: the doctor in the play *Ivanoff*, and the landowning husband in the story *The Wife*. The doctor is, in Chekhov's words:

the embodiment of a program, a walking tendency. He looks through a narrow frame at every person and event, he judges everything according to preconceived notions . . . It is not enough that all men are sinners, he wants saints and villains.

This man is the foil for Ivanoff, whom the doctor cannot understand, and classes as a scoundrel because, although he has a sick wife, he goes to see a rich lady neighbor. " 'Of course he is a scoundrel.' " It is this stupidity of the doctor in placing him in a category and treating him as if he belonged there that helps to drive Ivanoff to suicide.

And the landowning husband is a similar person. His wife, whom he has made thoroughly miserable, admits that he is well-educated and well-bred, honest, just and high-principled, but that wherever he goes he brings suffocation and depression. All life is summed up for him under principles; and he has so many of them, and they are of such unyieldingly high standards, that he finds himself obliged to hate everything on the basis of one or the other. He fails to drive his wife to suicide only because of his enlightening contact with an intelligent doctor:

"I listened to the doctor and after my invariable habit tried to take his measure by my usual classification—materialist, idealist, filthy lucre, gregarious instincts, and so on; no classification fitted him approximately; and strange to say, while I simply listened and looked at him, he seemed perfectly clear to me as a person; as soon as I began trying to classify him, he became an exceptionally complex, intricate, and incomprehensible character, in spite of all his candor and simplicity."

Chekhov has an amusing story of a "man in a case," who might be taken as a symbol of the spiritual condition of

people who shut themselves up in theories and formulas.
This man was remarkable for

always wearing goloshes and a warm wadded coat and carrying
an umbrella even in the finest weather. And his umbrella was in
a case, and his watch was in a case made of grey chamois leather,
and when he took out his penknife to sharpen his pencil, his
penknife too was in a little case; and his face seemed to be in a
case too, because he always hid it in his upturned collar. He
wore dark spectacles and flannel vests, stuffed up his ears with
cotton wool, and when he got into a cab always told the driver
to put up the hood. In short, the man displayed a constant and
insurmountable impulse to wrap himself in a covering, to make
himself so to speak a case which would isolate him and protect
him from external influences.

With his distrust of easy simplifications, Chekhov pro-
tested against being himself placed in a category. He feared
those who looked for tendencies in his work; as we have
seen he was skeptical and mildly indignant about the critical
pronouncements that the young Merezhkovsky had made
about his stories:

When people talk to me of the artistic and the anti-artistic, of
tendency, realism, etc., I become confused, consent irresolutely,
and answer with platitudinous half-truths that are not worth a
penny. I divide all literary works into two classes: those that I
like and those that I do not like.

And that is all that Chekhov would have to do with classifi-
cations.

He feared or distrusted also those who were determined
to claim him as a liberal, progressive, or what not. He had
reason to be afraid. Later critics, impressed by the dreariness
and disillusion of the Russia of the twenty years before the
revolution of 1905 have tended to regard Chekhov as the
spokesman of this spirit—and of little else. Gorki, for instance, likens the tone of his work to a melancholy day of
late autumn,

where everything is strange, lonely, motionless, helpless . . .
The author's mind, like the autumn sun, shows up in hard outline the monotonous roads, crooked streets, the little squalid
houses in which tiny, miserable people are stifled by boredom
and laziness, and fill the houses with an unintelligible, drowsy
bustle.

Gorki imagines Chekhov passing in front of this dreary gray
crowd of helpless people like a sort of melancholy Christ,
murmuring with anguish in his heart, "You live badly, my
friends."

That Chekhov, like everybody else, experienced moods of
depression there is no doubt, and these moods may have
been occasioned by his sense of inadequacy as a writer. He
had the very highest regard for great writings; and if, especially at first, he did not take his own work too seriously it
was because he did not think of himself as a great writer. He
felt that the minor writers of his day were very minor indeed,
by contrast with such a great writer as Tolstoy; and he was
right. In a letter to his friend Souvorin he says:

Let me remind you that the writers who we say are for all time
or are simply good, and who intoxicate us, have one common
and very important characteristic; they are going towards something and are summoning you towards it, too, and you feel not
with your mind, but with your whole being, that they have some
object, just like the ghost of Hamlet's father, who did not come
and disturb the imagination for nothing.

The best of them, he goes on, have immediate objects, the
abolition of serfdom, etc., or remote objects like immortality, the happiness of humanity, and so on. These paint
life as it is, but their realism is so transmuted that you feel
there is, besides, the awareness of the life that ought to be.

We have no politics, we do not believe in revolution, we have no
God, we are not afraid of ghosts, and I personally am not afraid
even of death and blindness. One who wants nothing, hopes for
nothing, and fears nothing cannot be an artist.

But this mood is by no means consistently reflected in Chekhov's work.

Or again, there is Mr. Kaun, who explains Chekhov's apparent indifference to local, partial, temporary evils, as the result of his regarding all life as fraud and folly. Both views of Chekhov seem absurdly at variance with the spirit of such stories as *The Privy Councillor, Home, The Incident, Grisha, The Darling,* where, as in many other tales, he is quietly mirthful, even gay. We have his own words in a letter, "I am more often merry than sad." He made contacts with ease; he kept friends, he found great satisfaction in the society of other people, and they in his. One is fairly safe in assuming that Chekhov was by no means a depressed or depressing person. In his work he interprets convincingly the mood of pessimism, as well as other moods. It was a part of the spectacle of life around him, but to call him pessimist is to commit the old naïve blunder of identifying the artist with some phase of his work. Souvorin's wife read *The Black Monk* and feared that Chekhov because he wrote so vividly about mental disease might be in danger of going out of his mind. Chekhov amusingly reassures Anna Ivanovna in a letter to her husband:

I believe I am mentally sound. It is true I have no special desire to live, but that is not, so far, disease, but something probably passing and natural. It does not follow every time that an author describes someone mentally deranged, that he is himself deranged. I wrote "The Black Monk" without any melancholy ideas, through cool reflection. I simply had a desire to describe megalomania. The monk floating across the country was a dream, and when I woke I told Misha [his brother] about it. So you can tell Anna Ivanovna that poor Anton Pavlovich, thank God! has not gone out of his mind yet, but that he eats a great deal at supper, and so he dreams of monks.

But Chekhov denounces more seriously this sort of labeling in another statement:

I regard trademarks and labels as a superstition. My holy of holies is the human body, health, intelligence, talent, inspiration, love, and the most absolute freedom—freedom from violence and lying in whatever form they may take.

And what he demanded for himself he demanded for his characters, so that you will find no labels on Chekhov's characters. His people cannot be easily classified. Each human being has for him a uniqueness, affects him with wonder. Chekhov must have felt this about hundreds of people; this accounts for the curious freshness of his perceptions. Of a village priest who used to pay him long visits at his country-house, he writes: "He is a very good fellow, a widower, and has some illegitimate children." Is this humor, or naïveté— or merely delighted comprehension? All these things were true about the priest; make what you can of them. Gayef, in *The Cherry Orchard,* somewhat apologetically admits that his sister hasn't led a virtuous life, but adds: "She's a dear, kind, charming creature, and I love her very much." There is apparently indifference in this attitude—but is it the indifference of a moralist or of an artist?

Chekhov the man, the doctor, could not be in any true sense indifferent to the morality of the society in which he moved. He was obliged, like other men, to make concessions, to adapt himself to his environment. All this is clear from his words; when he is speaking as moralist, he assumes at once that one does not lie, or steal, or bear false witness. Minor sins are a personal matter, and bring their own discomforts, such sins as he refers to in a letter: "It is true that I have waxed wanton and slothful, have laughed heedlessly, have eaten too much and drunk too much and been profligate."

But Chekhov presents life as he finds it, and if he finds it not conventionally moral, he keeps his vision clear by his attitude of indifference. He was anything but insensitive to

the agonies of life, but the indifference of the artist was one way of controlling his feelings.

Only those who are indifferent are able to see things clearly, to be just and to work. Of course I am only speaking of intelligent people of fine natures; the empty and selfish are indifferent enough anyway.

Chekhov was often enough charged with writing stories that had a bad influence. Because he didn't point out how wicked horse-stealing was, he was accused of condoning the offence.

You want me to say that horse-stealing is an evil [he replied to one of his critics]. But that has been known for ages . . . It would be pleasant to combine art with a sermon, but for me personally it is extremely difficult and almost impossible, owing to the conditions of technique . . . To depict horse-stealers in seven hundred lines, I must all the time speak and think in their tone, and feel in their spirit.

There is something very ironical in accusing the artist of exerting an immoral influence by his work, because he is more interested in understanding his characters than in judging them according to a predetermined moral code.

Other critics called him an immoral influence because he drew his material now and then from "muck-heaps": these, he declared, play a very respectable part in the landscape; "the evil passions are as inherent in life as the good ones." Realism is demoralizing, you say? That is just another dubious generalization:

Everything in this world is relative and approximate. There are people who can be demoralized by children's books, and who read with particular pleasure the piquant passages in Psalms and Solomon's Proverbs, while there are others who become only the purer from closer knowledge of the filthy side of life . . . No literature can outdo real life in its cynicism; a wineglassful won't make a man drunk when he has already emptied a barrel.

No artist was ever less enclosed "in a case" than Chekhov. Take his attitude towards religion. His early training was strictly orthodox—with singing in the church choir, reading of the Apostles, psalms, regular attendance at matins, assisting at the altar, and ringing the bells. As he grew older, he released himself from the formulas of orthodoxy—with its pigeonholes of elect and damned—without losing his delight in the beauty of church ritual. He loved Moscow because of the many churches and the bells, and on Easter Eves he passed from church to church all night long, coming home in the dawn to sing hymns with his father and brothers. The very spirit of the festival lives in the story *Easter Eve,* in the beauty of the setting and in the soul of the monk.[80]

To escape the letter and retain the spirit—that was all a part of the process by which Chekhov "painfully squeezed the slave out of himself, drop by drop." Gorki, who knew him in his later years, says that he lived on his own soul and was "always himself, inwardly free"; and that everyone in his presence involuntarily felt a desire to be simpler, more truthful, more genuine.

He knew how to lead his visitors away from making pompous, pretentious, prepared speeches, to talking naturally and unaffectedly in their own manner.[81]

These were the visitors with claims to culture. By the simple people with whom he came in contact—servants, messengers, porters, beggars, tramps, postmen—he was regarded, writes Kuprin in his *Reminiscences of Chekhov,* "with a great and heartfelt love, and not only with love, but with subtle sensitiveness, with concern and with understanding." And he relates an anecdote about a Tartar porter at Yalta, who used to watch for Chekhov's figure as the steamer docked, and scramble on board ahead of the rest to take charge of his luggage. Once an ill-tempered mate struck the man for getting in his way. The Tartar threw down the luggage, beat his breast with his fist, and shouted: "What? Are you striking me? Do you think that you struck me?" And pointing at Chekhov, "It is him—him, you struck!" Chekhov, very pale, came up to the mate, and said quietly and distinctly, but with an unusual expression, "Are you not ashamed?" The mate murmured something and promptly disappeared.[82]

Chekhov's contacts with people—and they were many and varied—must have been full of such revealing moments, especially if we remember that a physician has the advantage of seeing people in crises of one kind or another. The author himself says:

I have no doubt that the study of medicine has had an important influence on my literary work; it has considerably enlarged the sphere of my observation, has enriched me with knowledge the true value of which for me as a writer can only be understood by one who is himself a doctor. It has also had a guiding influence, and it is probably due to my close association with medicine that I have succeeded in avoiding many mistakes.

In his art he tends to fasten upon certain moments, certain moods, certain apparently trivial incidents as possessing a special significance—moments that he knows will reveal not the stereotyped but the unique personality.

It has been said of Katherine Mansfield, and is equally true of Chekhov, that she knew

that when people marry, or make money, or die, very little may really be happening to them; and in her stories these and other important events happen seldom, and are never at the center of the stage . . . The truth is in minutes rather than in years, in the emotion not of a day, but of a second, in the chill or warmth of a sudden mood, in the tunes played on the mind by anything, by nothing at all.[83]

Whether or not the "truth" is in these instants of realization rather than of action, the sense of being alive is in them. That sense breaks in upon our course of habit and routine in the brief pauses of sensitive awareness. We have a heightened consciousness of physical well-being, of love or hate or intimate understanding, of esthetic delight, of ironical insight or comprehension; or we glimpse some intellectual or spiritual horizon. Chekhov and Katherine Mansfield isolate such moments and disengage their significance.[84]

Consider Chekhov's *Lottery Ticket,* which presents an extended moment in the consciousness of two people. A man and his wife have for years bought lottery tickets without ever drawing a lucky number. For a few minutes one night, they think they have won. They begin to wonder what they shall do with the money. Their conversation is intermingled with their unspoken reveries. Both think of going abroad. He visualizes the journey with his wife: her preoccupation with the children, parcels, baskets, bags, lunches, tea, headaches, tips. Why should *she* want to go?

And for the first time in his life his mind dwelt on the fact that his wife had grown elderly and plain, and that she was saturated through and through with the smell of cooking, while he was still young, fresh, and healthy, and might well have got married again.

All sorts of dormant resentments crop up until they begin to look at each other with glances full of hatred . . . When they discover that theirs is not the winning number after all, hatred and hope die down, and it seems to both that their rooms are dark and small and low-pitched, and that their supper has disagreed with them, and that the floor is littered with scraps.

The fleeting dream of wealth has so intensified their latent desires that they realize just what they actually feel about each other—and what they feel in that moment is not love.

Or consider another moment. A theological student, returning from hunting through the cold and gloomy evening mist one night in early spring, is oppressed by the poverty

and hunger and desolation of the people and the countryside. It must have been like that, he thinks, for a thousand
years. Coming upon a campfire, he falls into talk with two
peasant women. At just such a fire, he reflects, the Apostle
Peter warmed himself. And he tells the story of Peter's
denial so dramatically that the women are moved. One
weeps. As he goes on his way, he thinks that what had happened to Peter must have some relation to her, since she had
wept; what had happened nineteen hundred years ago had
a relation to the present; Peter was somehow near to her,
because her whole being was interested in what was passing
in his soul.

When he crossed the river by the ferry boat and afterwards,
mounting the hill, looked at the village and towards the west
where the cold purple sunset lay, a narrow streak of light, he
thought the truth and beauty which had guided human life
there in the garden and in the yard of the High Priest had continued without interruption until this day, and had evidently
always been the chief thing in human life . . . and the feeling
of youth, health, vigor . . . and the inexpressible sweet expectation of happiness, of unknown mysterious happiness, took possession of him little by little, and life seemed to him enchant-
ing, marvellous, and full of lofty meaning.

The sixteen-year-old Nadya in *After the Theatre,* experiences a sense of youth, but with a less reflective emphasis.
Returning from the opera—*Onyegin*—she dramatizes herself
as the heroine who loves in vain, and sits down to write a
letter to one of her admirers. " 'I love you, but you do not
love me!' " She laughs. To be unloved and unhappy, how
interesting, beautiful, touching, poetical. And presently she
is crying over her imagined sufferings, until "little rainbows
are quivering on the table, on the floor, on the ceiling, as
though she were looking through a prism." So she stops
writing and thinks: " 'My God, how interesting, how fascinating men are!' "

There was a stir of joy in her bosom for no reason whatever;
. . . Her shoulders quivered with subdued laughter, the table
and the lamp chimney shook too, and tears from her eyes
splashed on the letter.

Her reverie flows into irrelevant images of her mother, and
the street, and the pencil, and the life in the country. Everything is good, but would be better still in the spring.

She had a passionate longing for the garden, the darkness, pure
sky, the stars . . . it seemed to her that there was the scent of
wormwood in the room, and that a twig was tapping at the window.

She sits down on her bed, not knowing what to do with the
immense joy which fills her with yearning; she looks at the
holy image and says: " 'O Lord God.' "

Laura, in Katherine Mansfield's *The Garden Party,* is as
touchingly young as Nadya; but she is awakening to deeper,
more realistic apprehensions of life. It is a much more complex moment; beginning with a mere awareness of joy, it
ends with puzzled wonder and questioning of the very nature
of existence itself. Through the emotions of this seventeen-
year-old girl we feel the joyous excitement of preparations
for a garden party. There is to be a band, and a tent on the
lawn, and the house is full of canna lilies. Laura "crouched
down as if to warm herself at that blaze of lilies; she felt
they were in her fingers, on her lips, growing in her breast."

When cook urges her to have a cream puff in the kitchen,
Laura is carried back to her childhood. Being grown up,
she at first refuses.

Oh, impossible. Fancy cream puffs so soon after breakfast . . .
All the same, a few minutes later Josie and Laura were licking
their fingers with that absorbed inward look that only comes
from whipped cream.

Into the midst of this joyousness someone comes to the
kitchen door with the news that a man in one of the

cottages just below had been accidentally killed. A mere accident to everyone but Laura: to her the intrusion of death. " 'How are we going to stop everything?' " she cries. And they are all mildly upset—at the idea of stopping everything. Laura, talked down, tries to put the death out of her mind. " 'I'll remember it after the party,' " she thinks.

"The perfect afternoon slowly ripened, slowly faded, slowly its petals closed." And with the end of the party the death of the poor man intrudes again; and her mother, at leisure now, feels some compunction, and to assuage her conscience, or to conciliate Laura, decides to send a basket of food to the striken family. This idea does not appeal to Laura—this taking the scraps from their house to the poor people. But in the end she carries the basket; and in a daze she is led into the cottage, into the room where the dead man is lying. Death *is* the solemn terror she thought it would be; but the face of the dead man gives her the feeling of a certain peaceful beauty. When, afterwards, outside, her brother asks her, Was it awful? she sobs:

"It was simply marvellous. But, Laurie—" She stopped, she looked at her brother. "Isn't life," she stammered, "isn't life—" But what life was she couldn't explain. No matter. He quite understood. *"Isn't* it, darling?" said Laurie.

What could be more unpromising than to interpret moods that terminate in such acts as the crushing of a cockroach or the torturing of a fly? Both Chekhov and Katherine Mansfield have used such moments to probe below the surface, with the idea of stirring the devils that lie waiting there. It is like poking into a hornet's nest, and finding, when you pull out the stick, a swarm of angry hornets buzzing at the end.

A discontented clerk, in Chekhov's *Small Fry,* is spending Easter Eve on extra duty in the office. Nobody is around but the porter in the hall—and a cockroach that wanders in and out of the circle of the lamplight on the table. The Easter bells give him no pleasure.

The din of the bells grew louder and louder . . . And the better he could hear the bells and the louder the roar of the carriages, the darker seemed the muddy walls and the smutty cornice and the more the lamp smoked.

There is a sort of gnawing at his heart for a better life, with more color and excitement. He idly canvasses ways and means to get on, finds none feasible, even considers stealing, stares at a letter he has just written in cringing terms to a man whom he hates but who has power to get him a post worth eighteen instead of sixteen roubles; grows more and more disgusted. And he ends by viciously slapping at the cockroach, which has the misfortune to scuttle into the lamp-light again.

The cockroach fell on its back and wriggled its legs in despair. [He] took it by one leg and threw it into the lamp. The lamp flared up and spluttered. And he felt better.

In *The Fly,* by Katherine Mansfield, the Boss locks himself in his inner office to think of his son who was killed in the war, and of whom he has just been reminded by a long conversation with a former clerk. It has troubled his senti-mental soul to realize that he has almost forgotten his sorrow. He has withdrawn because "he wanted, he intended, he had arranged to weep . . . 'My son!' groaned the Boss, but no tears came yet." This is really the first time that he has been unable to weep when he pressed the button. He tries to work up his emotions by recalling details about his son's life and death . . . Then his attention becomes idly centered on a fly which has fallen into his broad inkpot, and idly he picks it out and puts it on a blotter. He watches it shake itself laboriously free of the ink. "But just then the Boss had an idea. He plunged his pen back into the ink, leaned his thick wrist on the blotting-paper, and as the fly tried its wings, down came a great heavy blot." Again the fly shakes itself clean, and again comes the blot of ink. He likes its pluck so much that he continues the game . . . Finally he leans over the fly and says to it with a kind of tenderness, " 'You artful little b . . .' " and he has the brilliant notion of breathing on it to help the drying process . . . the Boss decided that this time should be the last, as he dipped the pen deep into the inkpot. It was the last. He flung the fly into the waste paper basket. "But such a grinding feeling of wretchedness seized him that he felt positively frightened . . . He fell to wondering what he had been thinking about before . . . For the life of him he could not remember."

Both stories reveal the spiritual aridity of these men whom we have seen in moments of casual cruelty. But they reveal something more deeply profound and universal—the lower depths filled with devilish impulses and desires, hatreds, frustrated affections that lie just beneath the surface of socialized consciousness. It is a terrible business, this stirring of these impulses from their quiescent state to a condition of active frenzy. Chekhov's *Enemies* shows you something of the monsters which lie just below the surface. The only child of Dr. Kirilov has just died of diphtheria. The mother is kneeling at the bedside, her arms flung across the body. The doctor feels a kind of numbness. Everything is suddenly still after the storm has passed. In the wondering expression on the dead child's face, the attitude of the mother, in the quiet, there is the "subtle, elusive beauty of human sorrow, which men will not for a long time learn to understand and describe, and which it seems only music can convey."

A gentleman in great excitement comes to take the doctor to his wife, in a town eight miles away; a matter of life and death, he insists. The doctor scarcely comprehends, and is bewildered to think that anyone would drag him away from the deathbed of his child. But he goes—still in a stupor of grief. When they arrive at the gentleman's home, the gentleman discovers that his wife has played a trick upon him with feigned illness, and has eloped with another man. He breaks out into passionate, theatrical lamentations, pours out his secrets, relieves his heart, until he is interrupted by the furious words of the doctor, who is aroused to a sense of deep insult. Has he been brought by this well-fed, well-dressed gentleman, from a dead child and a grief-stricken wife, only to play a part in a vulgar farce? He resents the wealth around him, the good looks of the gentleman. " 'You look on doctors and people who work and don't stink of perfume and prostitution as your menials.' "

They fling undeserved insults at each other, in the egoism of unhappiness. All the way home, the doctor thinks not of his wife or child, but of this gentleman and all the wealthy like him, and his thoughts are unjust and inhumanly cruel. He hates and despises all who live in rosy subdued light among sweet perfumes; and a conviction is born that will outlast his sorrow.

Now if this can be done so effectively for isolated single moments of existence, one would suppose that theoretically several such moments could be linked together to form a more extended picture, to give the sense of greater scope. And this is precisely what Chekhov and Katherine Mansfield have done. In the light of this possibility, let us examine Chekhov's *The Steppe* and Katherine Mansfield's *At the Bay*.

Of *The Steppe* Chekhov wrote in a letter to Korolenko:

I have attempted to describe the steppe . . . Each page turns out a compact whole like a short story, and pictures accumulate, are crowded, and, getting in each other's way spoil the impression as a whole. As a result one gets, not a picture in which all the details are merged into one whole like stars in the heavens, but a mere diagram, a dry record of impressions . . . The reader will be bored or curse.

But Chekhov was mistaken about the reader.

The Steppe tells of a little boy who takes a long trip with the wool wagons from his uncle's farm to the town where he is to go to school, and of the steppe itself and the people who live there—and the little boy's response to all of it: especially the impregnation of his youthful spirit with the mystery and beauty and terror of the steppe. Nothing very unusual happens. There is a little fishing, swimming, sunshine, rain, and a violent electrical storm. And the little Yegorusha gets sick. The lad is thrown for companionship during the greater part of the journey with the peasants who drive the wagons. We experience with the boy the new sensations; share his loneliness when night comes over the steppe; feel the chilly dew on his body; know the unhappiness that brushes his soul. With him we see the stars as he lies on his back on the top of the bales of wool and calls softly to his mother. For nearly everything along the journey comes to us as part of the boy's impressions. In the heat of the afternoon the caravan stops along the river bank and the men go in swimming. Then they fish. At night they fry the fish over the open fire.

The heat has been intense, the day sultry, and a storm has been gathering near the horizon. Chekhov, who uses description very sparingly, perfectly realizes the menacing storm, and the effect of it upon the peasant drivers and upon Yegorusha:

there was a sense of overwhelming oppression over everyone. It was sultry; they all drank a great deal, but could not quench their thirst. The moon was intensely crimson and sullen, as though it were sick . . . All were dreary and spoke listlessly and without interest. Panteley did nothing but sigh and complain of his feet, and continually alluded to impenitent death beds.

The mood is built up through tautened nerves and ruffled tempers.

This mood is dramatized with great beauty in the handsome peasant bully, Dymov. Over the campfire, in the presence of Yegorusha, he picks a quarrel with Emelyan, another peasant. And the poor little lad suffers. We remember that earlier in the day, when they were all swimming, Dymov, in the exuberance of his energy, ducked Yegorusha. The lad had resented it violently, and had sworn at the peasant. Now, when he sees Dymov treating the weak Emelyan with even greater cruelty, he defies and curses him. " 'You are the worst of the lot; I can't bear you . . . In the next world you will burn in hell! Don't you dare insult Emelyan!' " Then he bursts into tears and runs back to the wagons. "Lying on the bales and twitching his arms and legs, he whispered: 'Mother, mother!' " And then comes one of the most moving moments in the tale, when Dymov climbs up on the wagon, and by way of repentance says softly: " 'Yera! here, hit me!' "

Occasionally Chekhov himself interprets the steppe, but this pushing the boy out of the immediate foreground of the story, this shift from character to author and back again, is skilfully done. He says of a feeling of loneliness that comes to us when we look intently at the stars: "One is reminded of the solitude awaiting each one of us in the grave, and the reality of life seems awful . . . full of despair . . ." Then he shifts back easily to the little boy:

Yegorusha thought of his grandmother, who was sleeping now under the cherry-trees in the cemetery. He remembered how she lay in her coffin with pennies on her eyes, how afterwards she was shut in and let down into the grave; he even recalled the hollow sound of the clods of earth on the coffin lid . . . He pictured his granny in the dark and narrow coffin, helpless and deserted by everyone. His imagination pictured his granny suddenly awakening, not understanding where she was, knocking upon the lid and calling for help . . .

Take another variation of this method. In Katherine Mansfield's story, *At the Bay,* the curtain is lifted, not on several moments in one person's consciousness, but on one or two moments in the consciousness of several people, so that the ensemble of a whole family emerges. It is a will-o'-the-wisp sort of fancy that Miss Mansfield plays over these people, lighting up what Stanley Burnell thinks about his friend and neighbor, Jonathan Stout, who has beat him into the surf for his morning swim; what is going on in Stanley's mind when at the breakfast table he confronts Beryl, his wife's sister, who has forgotten to put the sugar in his tea; how he expects the exclusive attention of everyone in the household until he has located his stick and caught the coach which Beryl has held for him. And then, "Oh, the relief, the difference it made to have the man out of the house." Then we see what goes on in the minds of Beryl, of the wife Linda, of her mother, of the servant-girl Alice, who

washing up the dishes in the kitchen, caught the infection and used the precious tank water in a perfectly reckless fashion. "Oh, these men!" said she, and she plunged the teapot into the bowl and held it under the water even after it had stopped bubbling, as if it too was a man and drowning was too good for them.

Or Linda Burnell dreams the morning away as she sits in a steamer chair, under a manuka tree on the lawn. We know how she feels about this childbearing business; that she doesn't love her children—not even the infant boy who lies on the ground near her and seems to be saying in answer to her grudging mood:

"Don't like babies?" . . . The boy couldn't believe her. "Don't like *me?*" He waved his arms foolishly at his mother . . . Linda was so astonished at the confidence of this little creature . . .

Ah, no, be sincere. That was not what she felt; it was something far different, it was something so new, so . . . The tears danced in her eyes; she breathed in a small whisper to the boy, "Hello, my funny!"

Or we go to the beach with Beryl and see her under the charm of Mrs. Harry Kember, who puts ideas into her mind that at once attract and repel her. "Beryl felt she was being poisoned by this cold woman, but she longed to hear."

Or we take a rest in the afternoon with the child Kezia, in her grandmother's room. Her grandmother says that she has been thinking about Uncle William, who has died in Australia.

"Why did Uncle William have to die? . . . Does everybody have to die? . . . Me? . . . But, Grandma, what if I just won't? But, Grandma, you're not to die. You couldn't leave me, you couldn't not be there. Promise me you won't ever do it, Grandma . . ."

Kezia jumps down, clasps her grandmother, and begins kissing her. " 'Say never, say never,' she gasped between the kisses." In a moment death is forgotten in the excitement of the game. But the significant thing is that the idea of death has come to the child.

Although the stories we have been discussing are not, according to conventional definition, short stories, something does happen in them by way of finality or climax. Yegorusha comes to the end of his journey; Harry Kember tries to seduce Beryl Fairfield. But what of the stories where absolutely nothing comes off?

Some things in life happen as they ought to, and some very much as they ought not to, and others just do not happen at all. Situations call for the gesture of understanding, the act of friendship, the offer of sympathy, the avowal of love. These possibilities are latent, but something prevents their realization. We may be aware of what has slipped past only after it is all over, or we may be acutely aware of it at the moment. External things intrude: the telephone rings, the waiter presents the bill; or internal things inhibit, and we say, "I've got an engagement at six o'clock," instead of "I'm in love with you."

These moments are distressing to reflect upon. We can relieve the strain of non-fulfilment by daydreams of what might have come off and didn't, or seek the solace of art, whose function it is to round out and fulfil the incomplete.

What possible satisfaction, then, can we derive from being confronted in literature with these moments of frustration? As a matter of fact, some readers don't derive any. But others enjoy stories like this, because life has so often appeared to them in that way that they cannot believe in neat endings. Their "credulity has been weakened by intelligence or self-awareness," as Conrad Aiken says. To be sure, they want escape. But they do not want to escape through being duped. They desire art to confront these moments honestly, and either account for them or give beautiful expression to their peculiar quality; either tell us why they come or what they feel like when they do come. And this second achievement, this finding expression for an undramatic, elusive emotion, is perhaps the more difficult of the two.

What is Katherine Mansfield's *Psychology?* A few moments in the lives of a man and a woman whose even, placid friendship is troubled by the hope each has that the other may make an avowal of love. But nothing happens. Why didn't they give way to the impulses they both felt? And why is the story sultry and oppressive, like a storm that doesn't break?

Why didn't they speak? There is a vague suggestion that they knew their friendship was in danger, and that it was she who would be destroyed, not he. But the hint is left shadowy and undeveloped. So it is not comprehension of causes that the story offers.

He wanted to murmur, "Do you feel this too? Do you understand it all?" Instead to his horror he heard himself say—"I must be off; I'm meeting Brand at six." What devil made him say that instead of the other? And she instead of saying: "You've hurt me, you've hurt me—we've failed,"

hands him his hat and stick and smiles.

The secret drama never comes to the surface. They meet in her studio, as they have done many times, have tea, talk of the novels of the future, have pauses in the conversation—somehow different from other pauses. He leaves, the bell rings, an old spinster calls, gives her a faded bunch of violets, she experiences a release of emotion in her warm greeting of the little old lady, goes back, and begins a note to him about the psychological novel.

How does Katherine Mansfield contrive to make this story so tense? By her handling of the silences that fall between these two. Perhaps only music can convey the unspoken emotion, but she uses imagery that weaves the spell of music . . . The man has been speaking of the charm of her studio:

"Often when I am away from here I revisit it in spirit—wander about among your red chairs, stare at the bowl of fruit on the black table—and just touch, very lightly, that marvel of a sleeping boy's head . . . I love that little boy."

And then they are both silent.

A new silence came between them. Nothing in the least like the satisfactory pause that had followed their greetings—the "Well, here we are together again, and there's no reason why we shouldn't go on from just where we left off last time." That silence could be contained in the circle of warm, delightful fire and lamplight. How many times hadn't they flung something into it just for the fun of watching the ripples break on the easy shores. But into this unfamiliar pool the head of the little boy sleeping his timeless sleep dropped—and the ripples flowed away, away,—boundlessly far—into deep glittering darkness.

And then both of them broke it. She said: "I must make

up the fire," and he said: "I have been trying a new . . ." Both
of them escaped.

But presently it happens again.

They faltered, wavered, broke down, were silent. Again they
were conscious of the boundless, questioning dark. Again, there
they were, two hunters, bending over their fire, but suddenly
hearing from the jungle beyond a shake of wind, and a loud,
questioning cry . . .
She lifted her head. "It's raining," she murmured. And her
voice was like his when he said: "I love that little boy."

Verotchka presents two moods of Ognev, a young statis-
tician—just before Vera tells him she loves him, and just
after. These moods are saturated with the imagery of the
warm, moonlit August night, the garden, the country road,
the bridge at the edge of the wood where they stop and
where Vera speaks, and Ognev, to his own bewilderment,
fails to respond. The first feeling is agreeably sentimental,
arising out of his leave-taking of the family that has enter-
tained him during his stay in the district. "His heart,
warmed by the wine, was brimming over with good-humor,
friendliness and sadness." As he walks away through the
garden, he recalls all the pleasant episodes of his stay, and
reflects vaguely on life and the niceness of people and the
loveliness of this night with its transparent floating mists.
Vera, the daughter of the house, is waiting at the gate to
walk a little way with him. She is in the grip of an emotion
that Ognev, absorbed in his comfortable mood, fails to notice, until to his amazement he finds himself listening to her
declaration of love. "The sad warm sentimental mood induced by leave-taking and the home-made wine, suddenly
vanished and gave place to an acute and unpleasant feeling
of awkwardness." Vera was enchantingly beautiful; all that
she said, half-laughing, half-crying, had music and passion.
"Rebellious feeling whispered to him that all he was hear-

ing and seeing now, from the point of view of nature and personal happiness, was more important than any statistics and books and truth . . . 'My God, there's so much life, poetry, and meaning in it that it would move a stone, and I . . . I am stupid and absurd.' " When Vera suddenly understands, and goes away abruptly, he feels miserably that he has lost something very precious, that he has crossed a shadow-line, leaving certain possibilities irrevocably behind him. But why, he wonders, couldn't he respond as he wanted to? And in a flash of sharp self-realization, he is aware of his impotence of soul, his incapacity to be moved by beauty, his premature old age, brought on by his education in "facts," his casual existence, his struggle for a livelihood, his homeless life in lodgings.

We are left with the clear impression of these two revealing moods; with a lovely sense—gained wholly through Ognev's perception—of Vera's pure passion and courage; and with the same wonder that Ognev feels about this thing that should have happened and didn't. His self-analysis offers at least a small measure of comprehension. But it may be that, as Chekhov says, "there is no making out anything in this world," and the mystery of temperaments is left unsolved.

Dissatisfaction with a story like *Verotchka* may result from a critical preference for certain established forms. And if one insists on these forms, one can find satisfaction in the stories of Chekhov and Katherine Mansfield where things do "come off"—things like the strangling of the baby in Chekhov's *Sleepy-head*. And of his *Grasshopper,* Dr. Blanche Colton Williams says, "As to plot . . . one of the most carefully wrought pieces of narrative in the collection, *The Kiss.*" When these writers set their hands to it, they can do the plot thriller. They employ the technical devices of suspense, complication, just about as often, perhaps, as life employs them.

In Katherine Mansfield's *Pictures,* we have Ada Moss, ex-contralto, with her struggle looming large in the first paragraph. If she doesn't secure a job in the movies today, she cannot pay her insistent landlady, and she will be on the street. The struggle might be staged as Virtue versus Bread. There is suspense, and rather grim humor, in the narrative of Ada Moss's job-hunting journey from A, through incidents B, C, D, E, to the dénouement at Z. The moment the heroine walks into the restaurant with the conscious purpose of spending her last sixpence for coffee, and the subconscious hope of picking up a man, the struggle is ended. And ordinarily Miss Mansfield would have stopped here, leaving us to divine any conclusion we like.

But a short story should have not only struggle, but complication, and a snappy ending. How can we have complication without two lines (or more) crossing? And here we have the lines. One is that of Ada Moss, of course; and the complication occurs when it crosses that of "a very stout gentleman wearing a very small hat that floated on the top of his head like a little yacht . . ." and we have reached Z when Ada "sailed after the little yacht out of the café."

A similar excellence is found in *Bliss,* the story of Bertha Young, who, at the instant of her realization that she is in love with her husband as never before, discovers that he loves another woman. Viewing the story from the angle of the short-story formula, we trace the crossing and recrossing of the three lines of action—those of Bertha, of her husband, and of Pearl Fulton. The apparent indifference of the husband to the woman who has so strangely attracted his wife gives to the revelation at the end the impact of a shock.

Most stories would begin where *Bliss* ends—with Bertha's glimpse of Pearl Fulton in her husband's arms—and then proceed through complication and suspense to a solution of the triangular problem. But in *Bliss* it isn't this obvious problem that is solved, or that we care to have solved. What excites our curiosity and demands a solution is the unexplained mood of bliss in which we find Bertha when the scene opens. The first sentence sounds the mood of bliss, which deepens, extends and mounts. It moves relentlessly, colored by a quality of joyousness, tinged increasingly with excitement, lifting itself up in Bertha's heart to a mystical ecstasy. Something outside the story, something the reader brings to it—the common experience of distrusting such an unusually happy mood—intervenes, and we carry over, as we watch Bertha's emotion, a slight doubt. The interaction of story and reader creates a suspense which rushes us onward to the end. When this mood of bliss is dissipated, and Bertha's emotion is frozen into an unearthly silence, we experience a shock that leaves us stunned. This climax is a solution. Who cares what they do afterwards, whether they were all happy or unhappy?

Certainly Katherine Mansfield has here in a highly sophisticated art expressed a deeply perplexing impulse in the human soul. Bertha dimly attributes her unexpected happiness to her newly formed friendship with the wonderful Pearl Fulton who is coming that night with others to dine. The author meant us to believe that it is this friendship which makes a light of spiritual ecstasy to shine in Bertha. In its radiance her home takes on new colors, her love for her baby is more acutely felt, her dinner guests are more delightfully odd, she is more drawn to her husband. Everything about her is incredibly lovely—the blue bowl of fruit, the jade color of the evening sky, and the flowering pear-tree in the garden.

After dinner that night she is quiet, but quivering with joyousness. She waits for Pearl Fulton to give a sign. A sign of what? That they understand, without naming it, this friendship which has so suddenly, so miraculously sprung into life. "At that moment Miss Fulton 'gave the sign.' 'Have you a garden?' said the cool, sleepy voice." Bertha is so excited she can only obey. She pulls the curtains aside and points to the tree in the garden.

And the women stood side by side looking at the slender, flowering tree. Although it was so still it seemed, like the flame of a candle, to stretch up, to point, to quiver in the bright air, to grow taller and taller as they gazed—almost to touch the rim of the round, silver moon.

How long did they stand there? Both, as it were, caught in that circle of unearthly light, understanding each other perfectly, creatures of another world, and wondering what they were to do in this one with all this blissful treasure that burned in their bosoms and dropped, in silver flowers, from their hair and hands?

Because Bertha is thrilled with the strange emotion, she does the most natural thing in the world—she gropes for an outlet. To whom should she turn except to her husband? "For the first time in her life Bertha Young desired her husband." And she remembers their intimate life. She had been cold; that had troubled her at first. But he too had been different. They had talked it over with great frankness; they had been such good pals. But it is not as a pal that she desires him now.

But now—ardently! Ardently! The word ached in her ardent body! Was this what that feeling of bliss had been leading up to? But then then. . .

We feel like exclaiming "Then, what?" But we immediately know what the flashing thought was; and feel how it must rock Bertha's heart . . . Pearl Fulton was not cold . . . What outlet was Pearl seeking? She too knew this feeling of bliss. Bertha's questions are answered when a few minutes later she sees Pearl Fulton in her husband's arms.

In the end, about all there is to say of this story is that a dissonant, climactic chord is struck, with overtones making analysis as baffling as life itself.

Chekhov and Katherine Mansfield offered a new literary form. They outraged the sanctities of the short story by rarely having either plot or climax. Kuprin records an interesting remark of Chekhov's on technique: "When one has written a story I believe that one ought to strike out both the beginning and the end. That is where we novelists are most inclined to lie." It has been the experience of not a few intelligent people devoted to Kipling, de Maupassant, Stevenson, that, after reading them and subsequently thousands of stories patterned less skillfully upon them, the manner became more obvious than the matter. These discontented readers feel duped; for they see how often formulated fiction distorts character to fit a mould. As soon as the story is concluded, the characters cease to exist. They go out like moving pictures.

Mr. Canby, writing in the New York *Evening Post,* comments: "A few years ago it was boasted that here more than in any other country in the world the technique of the short story had approached nearest to perfection." And he observes with approval that

if that was at all true at the time, this "mastery of technique" seems to us lately to have slipped a number of cogs . . . That is why [he adds] we bless the memory of the late Katherine Mansfield. At the lowest possible estimate she lifted the contemporary short story again to a certain dignity—to a dignity the modern magazine editor tacitly disallows—to a dignity to which the short story as an artistic medium is certainly entitled.

Mastery of formula has been too often interpreted as "mastery of technique." The formula is useful in helping a poor workman to a market; it supports him with an external scaffolding of rules; it hides his ignorance of life, his blurred observations; it encourages him to provide for much action concentrated in a short space of time—action concluding with an inevitable optimistic ending—like life.[85] By the pioneering of Katherine Mansfield and Chekhov a taste has been stimulated; and writers who have long felt dissatisfaction with the kind of tale they were forced to write (if they wanted to sell) have a better chance to secure a hearing. We can gather quite a formidable body of this new literary material, where, of much deeper import than plot, are true observation, skillful selection, and accurate recording of human behavior; where a few moments are given us, and "from these brilliantly spot-lit points the whole life of the characters before and after spreads in the reader's imagination like ink on blotting-paper." [86]

It is not just any moment that reveals the unique subtle quality of a particular human being; it is only this moment or that of deep significance. The writer who goes in for this kind of story needs to possess exquisite intuition. And these writers have it. They move through a story gathering mood unto mood, until they end with a cluster that is exactly right. One of the means to this quietly spectacular result is the amazing use of imagery. This is particularly true of Katherine Mansfield. Chekhov tended to distrust the use of images and figures of speech. He wrote to Gorki to say how much he liked Gorki's descriptions of nature—except for one blemish:

Only the frequent personification . . . when the sea breathes, the sky gazes, the steppe barks, nature whispers, speaks, mourns, and so on—such metaphors make your descriptions somewhat monotonous, sometimes sweetish, sometimes not clear; beauty and expressiveness in nature are attained only by simplicity, by such simple phrases as "The sun set," "It was dark," "It began to rain," and so on . . .

Yet in each writer there is a richness, an economy in their expressions which is not only a reconstitution of the external world, but a spiritual interpretation of the mood induced in man. These expressions meet not merely the eye of the sense but the eye of the soul as well; they are magical touches suggesting relation with another world.

An artist seeking to fix a likeness on canvas or in clay, or to catch the spirit of a landscape, watches for the moment when something in the human being and something in the surroundings leap forth to meet each other and in a flash reveal the peculiar inner quality of person or external world. The artist may have looked at the landscape again and again, yet its spirit has eluded him. Then one day a bent figure crosses the field, and the flash comes. Or he may have studied a woman in all sorts of conditions and against many backgrounds, without penetrating the secret of personality—until some stormy day on the beach a greenish light in her eyes and the greenish-black of the waves flash a message to each other, and the human being springs to life—to a new one for the artist. Thomas Hardy was aware of the brooding, sinister spirit of Egdon Heath, its watchful intentness, when at dusk the reddleman and his van, splashed with crimson, crossed its expanse. The distinguishing mark of such moments of insight is the reciprocal relation of the inner and the outer—what we might call a kind of chemico-mystical synthesis that occurs. Chekhov and Katherine Mansfield have caught these flashes; always in their most illuminating revelations is this association of subject and object. What would *Psychology* be without that room? *Bliss* without the sky of jade and the pear tree? *Yona* without the snowy streets, cab, and little mare? *Ma Parker* without the sink and the sardine tails and the literary gentleman's flat? *Easter Eve* without the ferry, the bonfires, the bells? These are not just effective settings, nor are they merely the pattern which results from weaving sense impressions into the texture of thought. They are the integration of subject and object.

It may be that only certain temperaments find a special satisfaction in all of this: those people, for example, who shrink from the world outside them and flee into themselves, and adjust with difficulty and delay to the outer reality. Other temperaments—those who, in action and in feeling, respond easily and promptly to whatever the reality may be in their environments, who in a sense dominate that reality—may not find such writers as Chekhov and Katherine Mansfield sympathetic. To the subjective reader they mean much. They plunge him into the familiar stream of his reveries; but through their concrete imagery they keep him in touch with the world of sense. They may lead him, for the time being, more deeply, by identification, into the morass of isolation; but, because the characters are like himself, he is drawn out of his own loneliness by sympathy. And if these characters—as sometimes happens—make a satisfactory adjustment to their reality, he is encouraged in his own efforts to reconcile the inner world of fantasy which he prefers, with the outer world of obstacles.

By contrast, the fiction of outer action and movement— even if it as expert as O. Henry's or Kipling's—is rarely plausible to him. He does not find his own world there, save in the standardized patterns of feeling which he scorns. It gives him nothing but a temporary escape; the other kind of fiction points him toward a solution.

One of the most frequent and painful experiences of all subjective natures is that of loneliness; they feel alien to the world and the people about them. It is amazing, when one thinks over the characters in Chekhov's and Katherine Mansfield's stories, to note how many of them realize for us this isolation. Ma Parker, the charwoman; Yona, the "cabby";

Laura, the sheltered, indulged young girl; the "man with-out a temperament"; the dying Bishop; the busy lawyer; the little shoemaker's apprentice; the old professor: the list suggests the range of people. They are not all deeply intro-spective by nature; perhaps life has forced them to turn in upon themselves for the first time, or for only a brief space. Their emotion appeals to us in subtly varied forms. Like Ma Parker, we may have wanted to weep over cumulative mis-eries, but have found no place to go; to tell someone of our peculiar grief, but have found no one to listen. We may have been set apart in our eminence, like the Bishop; or in our perception of some social iniquity, like the student in Chekhov's *Fit*. We may have sought for some link of under-standing with a person dear to us, and have felt only a dull sense of impotence, or have achieved a momentary or acci-dental success that leaves us more bewildered than before.

Chekhov's old professor (*A Dreary Story*), daily drawing away from his family, his friends, and his work into a spir-itual remoteness, feels this strange alienation most when the young woman who has been nearest to him appeals des-perately for his help and understanding in some crisis of her life; and he can say nothing but, " 'I don't know, what am I to do? Let us have lunch.' " And he is utterly at a loss and confused, touched by her sobs, quite unable to reach across to her, dully conscious all the time that he is near his death, that he will never see her again.

The professor is hopelessly shut in. But little Vanka, the shoemaker's boy, is just going through the agonizing loneli-ness of homesickness, which will wear off in time. One Christmas Eve, while master and mistress and workman are at the service, he writes a letter to his grandfather. His com-position is broken throughout by his reveries. He sees his grandfather—nimble and lively, with an everlastingly laugh-ing face and drunken eyes, and the two dogs that follow him on his rounds as night watchman. Vanka awakes from his memories of the village to the reality of his hard life—beatings, teasing, overwork, rocking the shoemaker's wretched brat—and he writes: " 'Take me away. I will powder your snuff for you, I will pray for you, and if I do anything you can thrash me like Sidor's goat.' " Then, childlike, he tells his grandfather all about Moscow, the things in the shops, breaking off to ask him to get a gilt walnut for him from the Christmas tree at the big house. Staring out of the window, he remembers how he always went with his grandfather into the forest for the tree, and how, before chopping it down, the old man smoked a pipe, slowly took a pinch of snuff, and laughed at frozen Vanka. He sees the fir tree, the hoar frost, and the hare flying like an arrow over the snowdrift. It is as if Chekhov had thrown a pebble into Vanka's consciousness and the ripples were spreading. The letter grows more incoherent:

"Do come, dear grandfather . . . For Christ's sake, I beg you, take me away . . . My life is wretched, worse than a dog's. I send greetings to Alyona, one-eyed Yegorka, and the coachman, and don't give my concertina to anyone."

He addresses the letter to "Grandfather in the Village," drops it in the postbox, and falls asleep dreaming of grandfather on the stove, swinging his bare legs, reading the letter to the cooks.

The cruel isolation that results from the feeling of being shut out from the group is portrayed in Katherine Mansfield's *The Doll's House*. The two little Kelveys, grotesquely dressed, daughters of a washerwoman and a jailbird, snubbed by all the respectable children in the school, have no share in all the excitement over the Burnell children's doll's house —that wonderful house, with its plush furniture, its stove and tiny plates, and the irresistible little lamp on the dining-room table. Everybody has been taken to see it but them.

One of the little Burnells, following a sudden impulse, and disobeying the strictest commands invites them into the back yard to see the wonder: "like two little stray cats they followed across the courtyard." Scarcely time for a look before Aunt Beryl, furious, rushes out to scold her niece and shoo the little Kelveys away like chickens. "Burning with shame, shrinking together, Lil huddling along like her mother, our Else dazed, somehow they crossed the big courtyard and squeezed through the white gate." But the strange little Else, the tiny wishbone of a child, with cropped hair and enormous solemn eyes, who never smiled, who went through life holding on to Lil—Else nudged up close to her sister, and smiled her rare smile—" 'I seen the little lamp,' she said softly."

And there is the monk Ieronim in Chekhov's *Easter Eve*, the ferryman plying back and forth over the dark river all night long, grieving for the dead friend who composed the beautiful hymns of praise, which no one in the monastery appreciated but Ieronim. The great bell rings, there are bonfires at the river's edge, a rocket zigzags in a golden ribbon up the sky, people are restless and happy.

"They'll begin singing the Easter hymn directly," said Ieronim, "and Nikolay is gone; there is no one to appreciate it . . . There was nothing written dearer to him than that hymn . . . You know, in our monastery, they are all good people, kind and pious, but . . . there is no one with softness and refinement . . . They all speak loudly and tramp heavily when they walk; they are noisy, they clear their throats, but Nikolay always talked softly, caressingly, and if he noticed that anyone was asleep or praying he would slip by like a fly or a gnat. His face was tender, compassionate . . ."

Ieronim found someone to listen to him, at least, as he ferried his passanger over to the monastery. Yona in Chekhov's *Grief* was less fortunate. This peasant cabby, picking up fares on a snowy night in the city streets, grieving over the death of his son back in the village, tries to tell his customers, one after another, of the terrible thing that has happened to him. They break in on his halting words with impatient commands to drive faster, to look where he is going. No one even in the tavern will listen. So he goes out to the stable, and while his little mare munches her hay, he pours out his story: " 'Now suppose you had a little colt . . . And all at once that same little colt went and died . . . You'd be sorry, wouldn't you?' " [87]

The reader of fiction, wondering how the writer chooses his material, understands readily enough that a romantic sailor, elaborately tattooed, whom one sees in a foreign port, may not be unworthy of a Conrad tale. Or, in front of a theater, a grotesque old lady in antiquated clothes, lace and tattered red roses on her hat, cheeks and lips painted, who asks us through toothless gums, with a ghost of a solicitous smile, to buy a package of chewing-gum—O. Henry, he thinks, could do her perfectly. But he feels more surprise when a writer chooses a drab, colorless charwoman. He has seen a Ma Parker a hundred times, but never as a subject for a story.

We have all known a Ma Parker. If we have seen her on the street, in the wind, we may have been touched momentarily to think that she must have had a hard life. This hard life Katherine Mansfield presents. Ma Parker goes on with her work at the literary gentleman's flat, and the story of her life at home goes on within her mind, as she washes dishes, scrubs, and makes the bed. Ma's little grandson has just been buried. The literary gentleman thinks that " 'she does look dashed, poor old bird,' " and so in the effort to be consoling, he hopes the funeral went off well—" 'these people set so much store by funerals.' " But Ma Parker scarcely heeds him. This last blow has made very present to her the sordid and pitiful facts of her long hard life: her first place in London, where the cook was cruel to her; her marriage to a baker—that, thought the literary gentleman, must be a pleasant sort of job, handling the fresh loaves and all. But she had been too busy with the ghastly misfortunes of childbearing and child-burying to enjoy the fresh loaves. She lives again through the long illness of her husband, who had "flour on the lungs"; her son's going off to India. " 'Then young Maudie went wrong and took her sister Alice with her.' " Ethel married a good-for-nothing little waiter who died of ulcers the year Lennie was born. And now little Lennie! [88] . . . Intimate memories of Lennie keep coming up into Ma Parker's mind—so vivid that she feels his arms around her neck, hears him begging his "gran" for pennies, watches him suffer in his last fever. She can no longer bear it. She had never broken down—no one had ever seen Ma Parker cry. But now with overwhelming force the consciousness of her long hard life bears in upon her. In a daze she puts on her battered hat and in a daze walks out of the flat. She must give way to it somehow. She can't go home—it would frighten Ethel to see Ma break down. She can't cry on a bench—she might be arrested.

Wasn't there anywhere in the world where she could have her cry out—at last? Ma Parker stood looking up and down. The icy wind blew out her apron into a balloon. And now it began to rain. There was nowhere.

This realization of isolation is not always deeply melancholy. In Chekhov's *Home,* a lawyer, a widower, tries to make his delicate seven-year-old son realize the iniquities he has been guilty of. The governess tells him that the little boy has been smoking and must be reprimanded. After dinner, in his study, the father takes the child on his knee to talk to him, make him aware how bad it is for him to smoke, how wrong to take other people's tobacco. In words of one syllable he talks about the laws of property. Seryozha should not take what belongs to his father; his father doesn't take Seryozha's things.

"Perhaps I'd really like to take your toy dogs and pictures, but I don't—for they are not mine, but yours." "Take them if you like [exclaims Seryozha] please don't hesitate, papa, take them! That yellow dog on your table is mine, but I don't mind."

The child's attention keeps straying to some object on the table, or some little happening of the day, or he catches just enough of his father's talk to awaken his own reveries, into which his father cannot follow him. And the father strays off into reveries, too—fragments of ethics or philosophy. To reach the child, he reflects, one must be able to think as he does, to feel with him. Seryozha plays with his father's beard, talking half to himself.

He felt the child's breathing on his face, he was continually touching his hair with his cheek, and there was a soft warm feeling in his soul, as soft as though not only his hands but his whole soul were lying on the velvet of Seryozha's jacket.

Absurd that an experienced advocate should be at a loss with his own son! At last, after exacting from the child his word of honor not to smoke—and he gives it readily, with clearly no sense of its meaning—the lawyer abandons his efforts. Seryozha demands a story, and the father improvises what seems to him an incredibly naïve fairy tale about an old tsar whose only son died from too much smoking. Seryozha is touched at the desolation of the old tsar:

his eyes were clouded by mournfulness and something like fear; for a minute he looked pensively at the dark window, shuddered, and said, in a sinking voice: "I am not going to smoke any more."

And he goes to bed leaving his father completely bewildered at the process by which this happy result was wrought.

For the reader in his lonely moods, these realizations of the moments of isolation have the effect, paradoxically, of breaking down the spiritual barriers separating him from his fellows. Since some of the pain of such moments lies in inarticulateness, there is profound satisfaction in having them made beautifully articulate.

If one were asked what Mr. A. E. Coppard's sketches and stories and tales are about, one might for the moment be at a loss for an answer, so varied is his range of interest, and then one would say, "They're about life." That's what Mr. Coppard presents—life. This is, theoretically, what all writers do; but of many story writers one feels that their province is a little world of their own; that they have invented a much too pleasant and orderly garden and have attempted to fit life into these confines; and that their portrayal of life is debased and falsified. We are aware of a monotonous subject matter and an even more monotonous treatment. With Mr. Coppard we feel neither. We are astonished by his versatility, and delighted with his fresh and sometimes unusual handling. It is this wide variety of Coppard's interests that gives the impression of an unrestricted use of a very great range of the experiences of life.

His imagination plays over the human scene selecting all kinds of subjects. He is almost equally convincing whether he is writing of tragedy, melodrama, fantasy, high comedy, or low comedy. Perhaps what delights him most and what he presents with the greatest reality are the simple peasants of England, the farmers, the poachers, and their women. But he is equally skillful when he writes about more sophisticated men and women, old or young. He knows very odd people, some of them characters that remind one of Dickens. He writes of stage and circus people, of Cockneys, of artists and ex-artists, and of gypsies. And some of his most successful sketches are about children.

It is true that in his one hundred and more published tales there is a rather high percentage of stories shockingly tragic. They are not pleasantly tragic—remote and vitiated like so many contemporary stories of casual killings. Coppard provides no shock absorbers with his tales; for he too surely knows that one of the values of a story of this kind is its power to move the reader. He does not soften; he does not modify. What he does, at his best, as surely as Conrad (and in a much shorter space) is to make clear the motives for these tragic deeds. He makes them understandable, he accounts for them. But to make this point bear too much stress would be to do an injustice to Coppard. For in his work you will find stories that are mellow and pleasant and humorous.

He recounts a very absurd dream in *Big Game*. Old Squance is an undertaker. But in the pleasant and healthy little village where he and his wife live very few people die, and to supplement his undertaking business he has the "more vital occupation of builder." But the cottages have been very well built in Tamborough, and so Mrs. Squance has to keep a little shop where she sells all sorts of notions. Mr. Squance is a mild man, yet he had gained for himself the reputation of being very heroic. It had to do with Mrs. Squance's dream.

It seemed to be morning in her dream, early; it must have been early. She and Squance were at breakfast when what should walk deliberately and astoundingly into the room but a lion. Mrs. Squance, never having seen a lion before, took it to be a sheep dog, and she shouted, "Go out, you dirty thing!" waving a threatening hand towards it.

But Mr. Squance recognizes the animal and shouts " 'Lion! lion!' "

It had a tremendous head and mane, with whiskers on its snout as stiff as knitting needles, and claws like tenpenny nails; but its tail was the awfullest thing, long and very flexible, with a bush of hair at the end just like a mop, which it wagged about, smashing all sorts of things.

Mrs. Squance asks her husband if he has a pistol and when he says he has not, she says, "Then we're done." But she decides they're not done yet, and she tells her husband to hold him whilst she goes out for a pistol. The dream continues with the usual absurd dream difficulties. And when Mrs. Squance returns much later with the pistol, she finds that Mr. Squance has thrown the lion out of the window.

But that is not the end of the story. There is a moral, a charming modern instance of the "application" of the stories in the *Gesta Romanorum*. Mr. Coppard says that Mrs. Squance awakened "startled to find the window of their room actually smashed." She related these circumstances so many times as the years went on that "she herself at last vividly believed in the figure of old Ben as a lion-slayer." [89]

His little sketch *Luxury* is a delightful and ingenious turning to literary account of a little incident that one feels has the true autobiographical touch. There are other sketches also, both of them dealing with children, *Weep Not, My Wanton* and *Communion*. The first tells of a tinker, slightly drunk, walking along an English down with his little boy, upbraiding him for having lost a sixpence. The opening paragraph is a perfect setting of an English twilight summer evening. The only sounds are those of "anguish" from "a score of young boar pigs . . . being gelded by two brown lads and a gypsy fellow." The father's litany continues.

What the father saw when he looked at his son was "a thin boy, a spare boy, a very shrunken boy of seven or eight years, crying quietly. He let no grief out of his lips, but his white face was streaming with dirty tears." The little boy does not speak, "and lifting his heavy hand the man struck the boy a blow behind with shock enough to disturb a heifer.

They went on, the child with sobs that you could feel rather than hear."

Behind are the mother and their little daughter. The mother seemed "to have no desire to shield the boy or to placate the man." And soon they change places: the father takes the little girl, and when the mother joins the little boy and cries out, " 'What's 'e bin doin' to yeh? Yer face is all blood!' " the little boy explains that it's nothing, it's only his nose, and gives his mother the sixpence. That is all, except the final paragraph of description of the countryside which finishes the picture.

They went together down the hill towards the inn, which had already a light in its windows. The screams from the barn had ceased, and a cart passed them full of young pigs, bloody and subdued. The hill began to resume its old dominion of soft sounds. It was nearly nine o'clock, and one anxious farmer still made hay although, on this side of the down, day had declined, and with a greyness that came not from the sky, but crept up from the world. From the quiet hill, as the last skein of cocks was carted to the stacks, you could hear dimly men's voices and the rattle of their gear.

Of his story, *Willie Waugh,* Miss Lillian Gilkes has written: "He can make the conversation of two English villagers over the loan of a saw convey a whole history of manners."

Sometimes Coppard gives us a story written in the conventional form that we are accustomed to, as in *Fifty Pounds* and *Alas, Poor Bollington,* in each of which there is the surprise ending. But we read neither of these stories so much for the form as for the very fine characterization and the imaginative invention achieved. Merely to outline the plots would give no sense of the qualities the stories possess. And the same may be said of many of Coppard's best tales: *The Angel and the Sweep, The Ballet Girl, Judith, The Old Venerable, The Handsome Lady, Dumbledon Donkey,* and many others.

There is in Coppard's volume *Nixey's Harlequin* one long piece of fiction, *My Hundredth Tale,* that because of its personal interest we might discuss at some length. To say that this tale is strictly autobiographical would be very unsafe, yet in reading it we cannot help feeling that Coppard is treating himself as though he were one of his own characters. Fact and fiction are no doubt hopelessly intermingled; and perhaps Coppard is himself not always sure where fact stops and fiction begins, any more than Sherwood Anderson is in his *A Story Teller's Story.*

In *My Hundredth Tale* are some unforgettable pictures of a writer, Johnny Flynn by name; of his father, his mother, his friends, his loves. The story develops Flynn's later life, his troubles, uncertainties, reflections, and his sharply accented despair due to his inability to love with any peace. On this note he concludes, fearing that he is not a personality at all. He has lived in and with the passions of his characters so faithfully that now he can only counterfeit passion and no longer has any clear and definite personality. In his earlier sketch, *Luxury,* Coppard had given what one senses to be thinly disguised autobiography, but the man in that piece is clearly a fictionalized character. It is told in the third person, not, like *My Hundredth Tale,* in the first person. Where the mood of *Luxury* was light and bantering, Johnny Flynn's story is told in dead earnest . . .

I am going to be garrulous [Flynn says], to say what I like, just anyhow. It will mean nothing to you, it may be tiresome to you, but to me it will be life, and my only heaven.

Johnny is going to lay bare his inner substantiality.

When Johnny was ten he had a friend, Bill Brown, and Bill had a sister, Carlotta.

She was shy and slender, with pale cheeks and pale hair that hung as beautifully from her crown as a waterfall from a rock.

Whenever I kissed Carlotta she would turn her face gently away and not look at me, never look at me.

As a boy he visited the caravan of the gypsies, and was a special friend of the king and the queen. No wonder the fine figures of gypsies play frequent rôles in Coppard's tales. Johnny Flynn remembers the queen, a magnificent woman, "with a lovely brown Romany face and black curls as long and stiff as candles."

He was put to work helping a street vender, but that did not last long, though it left many impressions that he no doubt used later in his life as a writer. Then his father began to die, and an uncle, a "monumental mason" wanted to help him.

At the back of his mind there was also the idea, dim but audacious, of arraying me as a child mute, in black, with gloves and a tall hat flounced with crêpe, for use as a special and novel attendant at infants' funerals.

There follows a magnificent narrative of the writer's recollection of his father's funeral.

For his South Downs he has such a passion as Emily Brontë had for the moors:

I learned to run wildly up on these uplands, where the heart was never known to tire nor the limbs to fail; or I would lie and gaze at the lovely land, my mind flowering with thoughts that have borne no fruit. Fluid tender hours!

His friend Bill Brown excelled him in everything.

I do suspect now that I did not love him at all, and that my emotion was but a reflection of another I indulged in, the timid silent worship of his timid silent sister, Carlotta.

He fell in love with other girls one after the other, "or with some together—it is so easy; fancy turns you round and about like a cock on a church, this way, that way." In each love affair his mother's divination toppled his idols. "How did she know that I had a queasy mind and was terrified by ugliness or vulgarity? I did not know it myself, then!" Very delightful reading it is—the way his mother does her toppling. There were Myra Stogumber, Violet Mutton—"Sacred Caesar, what a name!"—Honor Clapperton. And there was Rose Tilack, neat and clean, "but with a scatological mind that would have shamed a monkey."

Then John Flynn finished a book and

its creation had been a tortuous delight. I had fashioned a group of people, imaginary persons, and filled them with passions and humours, with virtue, vulgarity, and laughter, with blood, bones, tears, bad temper, and love. Their emotions were not my own, they were spurious, and yet I had lived with these figments so closely, brooded over them so long, that I myself helplessly assumed the protean dooms I inflicted on them, suffering the foul and rejoicing at the fair when I permitted them a respite from my slings of outrageous fortune.

Flynn says that of all human characteristics he divined most keenly the thing called vulgarity. He had lived in it, he sprang from it. And the danger of one turned prig through reading and writing poetry was that, out of false shame, vulgarity might be denied. But with this quality of vulgarity, which Coppard uses very extensively, which he makes almost a business, he has done what he has done for melodrama. He came to know that vulgarity is the nourisher of existence, that in this soil flourished the emotions that impel human beings in every conceivable direction— toward low and vile exhibitions, but also toward piety and sacrifice, kindliness, and decency itself. It could lead to strength and health, as with Rabelais; and rarely did it lead to decay. Flynn (it is so difficult not to confuse him with Mr. Coppard) had felt of the herd, "hideous were their faces and forms and minds, vulgar their clothes and habits, their amiable jokes, their tears at funerals, their passions for food, politics, and propriety." From all of this he at first escaped to the fairer worlds of hills and imaginative dreaming. But there was too much health, too great vitality and sanity in Johnny Flynn to mope away his life and waste his gifts. A child of vulgar inheritance, he had two-fold the strength of its virtues. We find him casting off his shame and turning his distress to account; Johnny Flynn turned the light of his art upon hobgoblins that were his snobbish shames and he suddenly saw his own people as decent, kindly, no longer hideous. "I saw that those who ignorantly live may yet profoundly die." He reflects about the forest where he lives— "a floral bastion that leans and dreams in unimaginable beauty against the void." What is the purpose of the trees? To make chairs, "on which the vast buttocks of the world may be seated to drink its tea or nurse its weeping child." And what is the purpose of the whole vulgar world? For the artist to record with fidelity and compassion and humor, so that a beauty emerges. Still Flynn was lonely because his world could not read his books.

He went for human companionship to London, where he found a desert; suburbs "that were as blank as the mind of Lot's wife." After some years, back to his town, and when he returned to his house in the forest he brought a woman with him. From this point the tale records three episodes of Johnny Flynn's love life, each thrilling, and each, in the end, unsatisfactory. Johnny finally takes stock, and then it is that he must believe he has lived so long with his characters that he has no clearly recognizable character of his own.

His life with Dove was wrecked by her jealousy of his writing. How well Coppard knows the vagaries of the heart! He hopes Dove will go away. "But there were other times that I thought I should die if she ever left me, just as I thought I would kill her if she did not, so incalculable are our wretched passions."

A fleeting episode with Carlotta and then she married her

affianced tape manufacturer, though Johnny and Carlotta loved each other. His despair was largely mixed with wounded pride that Carlotta could give him up for a vulgarian. He was conscious of his superior quality, though he made never a claim to superiority of class. Thus for him Carlotta is another vulgar woman, as Dove had been. He vows to have no more traffic with such women; and the cry from his heart is that surely not all women are merely low.

In his unhappy examination of conscience, he believes he understands himself:

I had lived so intently in my world of fictitious shadows, writing of people who had no existence, aping emotions and postures that had no real play, counterfeiting violence and imitating peace, that when I touched this real thing of my own, imagination twirled up like a cloudy witness and warned me that I was lost indeed, that I was but a fiction-monger, a dealer in illusions and masquerade. I had lost myself in these shadows. I was a nonentity, my being was a myth. I had no love, I could only *pretend* a passion that had never stirred a ripple in my blood.

But this realization gave him a shock that produced a real emotion indeed, and then this realization and this emotion were digested and he spent five years writing books, until he came to a kind of valley of the shadow. This boredom and despair did not crush him; his great energy, his love of life were fighting for him. "If only the earth itself would burst like a rocket; if the sea would but leap into the sky and become a new Niagara, or the hills upheave their bosoms and twirl upon their own paps!"

Nothing happened. He went to London. There he met Livia, wealthy, perfumed, upper-class; they loved, and Livia returned to his forest with him. Livia turns out to be no cook and thoroughly untidy, with a passion for buns which Johnny hates. She goes away from time to time and gives Johnny breathing space. He thinks about love, that it is

"mysterious, unprincipled, tender, fierce, sublime, brutish, delicate, and devastating, all fire and frailty, with less substance than a rainbow and eternally desirable."

Then Johnny, still miserably class-conscious in spite of his success as an artist, grows jealous. Livia is eluding him; he feels the cleavage in his heart. His fierce jealousy reaches a climax when he reads a letter about himself that Livia had written. There he finds himself called a vulgar, uncivilized man. A brief sharp quarrel and Livia leaves him. He says: "With the women of my own class love had been nipped by *their* deficiencies, with Livia it was ruined by my own . . . I am a lost ship waiting for a wind that will never blow again."

A young writer of a successful first novel told her publisher that she was at work upon a theme calling for a treatment shorter than that required for the usual novel and longer than for the longish short story. But he said, "Oh, don't do that! Not a novelette—" because of the state of the market and the taste of the public and the caprices of the book trade and this and that. So she went away, resolved not to expand or contract her novelette theme—having, though young, or because she was young, an artistic conscience—but to look for another that would require 100,000 words. The experience of Thomas Mann, he being a German, would probably have been considered irrelevant by the publisher, but it interested the young author when she was reminded of it. Mann wrote *Buddenbrooks,* a long novel, when he was young, and *The Magic Mountain,* a very long novel, twenty-five years later. And after *Buddenbrooks* he wrote *Tonio Kröger* (25,000 words or so), having conceived it while working on the novel; and before *The Magic Mountain* he wrote *Death in Venice* (30,000 words), which he calls a "petit roman." He has said how it pleased his orderly mind, as he looked back on his work, to note the relationship of the two short novels to the two long ones: *Tonio* corresponding to *Buddenbrooks,* and *Death in Venice* to *The Magic Mountain.* It would have been unfortunate for Mann's development to be told that he must follow up *Buddenbrooks* with another long novel. But happily the German public has somehow or other become trained to appreciate the "petit roman," and that makes a nice receptive atmosphere for a writer like Mann, who takes twelve years for a *Magic Mountain* and meanwhile finds refreshment and growth and preparation in the briefer forms. The French public is trained, too, and a novelette of 25,000 words such as Antoine de Saint Exupéry's *Vol de Nuit* receives the Prix Femina, is published in book form—paper cover, of course, at a price of about sixty cents, and is translated and sold here for three times as much. For the American public will accept translations of French and German novelettes by Schnitzler, Mann, Arnold Zweig, Stefan Zweig, Gide, and others. Yet the novelette is a form with which "in the English-speaking world neither editor nor publisher seems ever to know what to do, trying to palm it off now as a short story and now as a novel."

Ludwig Lewisohn (*Expression in America*) makes this comment in speaking of Henry James, whom he calls the "undisputed master of the novelette in English." But James had little encouragement until in the eighteen-nineties Henry Harland founded the Yellow Book and told him to go ahead and pursue "our ideal, the beautiful, the blest *nouvelle*"—defined in the French dictionary as "une composition littéraire qui tient le milieu entre le conte et le roman"—which keeps the middle (to be literal) between the short story and the novel. Put aside the question of why the English-speaking public is, or is supposed to be, cool to the novelette. Put aside, also, the ungracious diversion of showing how much more satisfactory certain 100,000 word novels would be, if they were one-half or one-third as long, and let us take several novelettes and examine the themes and see how they would suffer from expansion or compression. In that way we can emphasize the desirability of the form, with its fine qualities of "isolation of material and depth of tone, restraint upon over-elaboration, and yet the final effect of brimming fulness."

Henry James's *Washington Square* (60,000 words) has a single line of interest, the one and only love affair of Catherine Sloper, of Washington Square in the eighteen-fifties. It is a complicated affair, involving an antagonistic father and an actively friendly and scheming aunt. It could be disposed of in a short story—leaving, however, no space for development of background. But the age and place need development, for they not only give a delightful antiquarian flavor to the story, but they explain Catherine's behavior and lend it significance because of its typical quality. Suppose an editor had said, "We must have 100,000 words." What could James have done, if he still wanted to tell about this particular girl? He could have put in more background easily enough. There are lots of curious details about the way they lived in Washington Square that he has omitted; he could have told us about the china and the silverware: some modern novels leave no cocktail glass undescribed. And the result would have been top-heavy—too much Washington Square for a lightweight like Catherine. For, comparing her with the heroine of James's long novel, *The Portrait of a Lady,* we note at once how much more interesting Isabel Archer is—a girl who can inspire and sustain several full-sized love affairs, who has capacity for more profound emotion than Catherine and more zest for experience. Catherine would tire us in a long novel. James could have multiplied her love affairs, of course, and so turned the novelette into a novel. But since she is a placid person, whom we leave in her parlor at the end, seating herself with her morsel of fancy-work—"for life, as it were"—that would seem improbable. It would be the expansion of a mildly interesting person, who would then become merely bulky, not significant, like some other expanded persons in and out of fiction. She and the background that explains her are both necessary, in a neat balance, as we now have them.

In Willa Cather's *A Lost Lady* (about 40,000 words) the main theme is the personality of Mrs. Forrester, expressing itself in an inhospitable environment—that of the railroad builders' frontier in the Middle West, with all its opulence of gesture in a crude setting. Mrs. Forrester is not the product of this half-baked civilization, as Catherine Sloper is of the gentilities of Washington Square. She is a perennial type, this woman whose special gift is a personal charm which she cannot help exercising upon any male within its radius. In societies with established traditions in the art of love, she could have followed one of several accepted patterns. But the interest lies in watching her seek fulfillment where there are no accepted patterns, and the pathos in the spectacle is that this exquisite charm is so largely wasted on cheap people and in incongruous situations. The novelette affords space for adequate development of this environment and for a full-length portrait of Major Forrester, whose perception of his wife's weakness and whose shielding of her form one of the moving themes of the story. Mrs. Forrester is presented to us by indirection and in retrospect. This kind of reporting —as by messengers in Greek tragedy—becomes (to quote Mr. Lewisohn, still on the subject of the novelette) intolerable in narratives of novel length, but is fitting in the novelette

with its quiet initial assumption that all cannot be told nor every subject exhausted, that glimpses and fragmentary reports, which the imagination can weave on more largely, must suffice.

As for *Death in Venice*, Mann could have compressed within short-story limits the parallel progress, with its sym-

bolism, of the hero's moral disintegration and the plague in the city. But this disintegrating hero is an artist, and Mann has pondered for many years over the problem of the artist, his place in society, his peculiar temptations and his dubious justifications. So he enriches the story with philosophical speculation, with lovely far echoes from Plato; and for these there would have been no room in the short story. Only after his mind and his art had grown ripe for profound and extensive exploration into the sickness of society did he give us *The Magic Mountain.*

The length of André Gide's *Strait Is The Gate*—about 45,000 words—permits him to throw into relief the temperaments of Alissa and Jérôme and the problem of the curiously frustrated relation between them. There is need to follow the development of the two lovers from childhood more fully than a short story could do, for it is an under-the-surface drama, not so easy to comprehend as dramas that burst out in vivid explosions. The reasons for the failure of their love remain ambiguous to the end—implied in Gide's devious way. Suppose the narrative were lengthened by elaboration of minor characters or introduction of more episodes: either the intimations that intrigue us would seem too faint, their delicate tracery lost against a more crowded background; or else Gide would have had to come out into the open and state plainly what can be more subtly and effectively implied.

Night Flight (Vol de Nuit) has a theme: the happiness of men lies not in liberty but in the acceptance of a duty; man does not find his end in himself but subordinates himself and sacrifices to something that dominates him and lives upon him. We act, reflects Rivière, chief of a network of air-mail services in South America, as if something were of greater value than human life. Three air routes, from Chile, Patagonia, and Peru, converge on Buenos Aires, whence the air mail departs for Europe. The pilots must fly by night to effect the saving of time that gives the air service the advantage over earth and water routes. Rivière is responsible for the inauguration of night flights, long resisted by his superiors as unreasonably dangerous. He is laconic and inflexible. You do the job or you don't; and if you don't, you pay the penalty, though it may be an evil chance working against you and it is unjust to blame you. We see Rivière in several minor actions and gain a sense of the spirit that animates the service. The pilot from Chile arrives, dazed by an odd experience crossing the Andes, when the peaks beneath him seemed to come alive in a tempest. But he is not encouraged to dwell on this experience; Rivière frowns upon imagination and introspection in his pilots. The pilot from Peru arrives on time after a safe and clear flight. But Fabian, the pilot from Patagonia, runs into a cyclone—a strange and unearthly encounter that terrifies and exalts and finally kills. The suspense of his ordeal is heightened by shifts of scene from the plane to headquarters, with his young wife telephoning as his return is delayed, and the radio messages coming in broken and half-intelligible and finally ceasing altogether. The crisis for Rivière is: shall he send off the pilot for Europe on this night when one pilot and plane have been lost? Fabian, his relation to his wife of six weeks, his battle, his strange exaltation in the region of stars into which he penetrates before his fall—all this by itself would make a beautiful and dramatic short story. But the shorter treatment could not show the branching pattern of the destinies controlled by Rivière. On the other hand an elaboration of several other suggested themes would make a novel. We could then learn perhaps how Rivière came to hold the philosophy that influences fatefully the lives under his direction. We should also become more deeply involved in the individual lives, in the suffering of Fabian's wife, for instance. In

the novelette she exists primarily to represent another world
of values impinging on this world of the night flights. What
the novelette does is to create the atmosphere of an impersonal force, working through men and calling forth in them
qualities they did not know they had.

Stefan Zweig, in his *Episode in Early Life* (30,000 words),
introduces us to a distinguished professor on his sixtieth
birthday, musing over a book just presented to him by his
colleagues and pupils. It is the story of his own career, complete down to details that he himself had forgotten; a biography and a bibliography as well. But he smiles as he turns
its pages; the index with its two hundred names does not
contain the name of the one man who had imparted to his
life its creative impulse, who had decided his fate for him,
and who now summons him back into his youth. And he
feels that he must now perform a service for this man who
was more real to him than any other. He must write some
pages dealing with matters he has always kept hidden, and
add them to the account of what is publicly known; lay a
confession of feeling beside the learned volume that is a
history of his thought-life.

The story follows of his relationship with a teacher in a
provincial university, the teacher who had first awakened
his mind and fired his enthusiasm for the work that became
his life interest. It was an ambiguous relationship, though he,
an unsuspicious youth, was slow in realizing the nature of
the emotion he had aroused in the teacher and was experiencing himself. The situation is complicated by the
teacher's wife. It is developed through several dramatic incidents, culminating in a poignant interview between teacher
and student, when the teacher tells the story of his life and
its secret passions and despairs. After that revelation the separation of the two is inevitable. But the impulse the young
man had received during this bewildering and agonizing

experience is strong enough to launch him on his career.

Could this "episode" have been told in fewer words—within the limits of the short story? Easily. But Zweig has chosen to do what few writers would risk, and by doing it successfully has deepened the force of the narrative. This teacher had the gift of eloquence. When he talked or lectured of the Elizabethan dramatists who were the theme of a great book he had been writing for years—and never completed—he communicated his own passionate enthusiasm to his hearers. Most writers would be content to state the fact; and perhaps describe the effect of this eloquence upon the listeners. But Zweig tells us what the teacher said—there are pages of these discourses—and they are brilliantly convincing. We, like the young man, fall under the spell. And we are persuaded of the authenticity of his intellectual awakening. That was harder to do than to persuade us of the emotional impulses that led into the relationship; and it required more than the space of the short story.

So one could go on ticking off masterpieces in this form: Edith Wharton's *Ethan Frome,* Conrad's *End of the Tether,* James's *Turn of the Screw* and *Aspern Papers,* Constant's *Adolphe,* Anatole France's *Thaïs.* Why not more hospitality to the novelette, to save us from the inflation or the compression or the neglect of beautiful themes, which belong in that *milieu entre le conte et le roman?*

FICTION AS EXPERIENCE

WHEN we finish reading any of the novels we have been discussing, we feel depressed or exhilarated, bored, interested,
sympathetic, satisfied, antagonistic, confused—or perhaps
merely glad, like the tourist in the art gallery, that that will
never have to be done again. We can pass on to the next
novel without any further reflection. But we may wish to
come to some conclusion about the book or ourselves, and
the relation between them. The first step is to disengage this
emotional response or impression of ours and hold it off
from us, if we can, and look at it. What has been happening
to us while we were reading?

Here we are, complicated organisms, with all sorts of impulses, all sorts of attitudes and incipient promptings to
this or that kind of action; with a good many possible selves.
A self is no longer regarded as a hard kernel somewhere inside of us, but as a coördinated group of tendencies to act in
certain ways in certain contingencies. Our self keeps on
growing and changing because we are in ever-shifting relation with surroundings that compel control and adjustment.
This environment, physical, social, economic, and so on,
both hems us in with restrictions and offers us possibilities of
expression. At best, it frustrates some of our interesting potentialities, and at worst forces us into distorted or stunted
development. Such of our impulses as find no employment
in our ordinary activity have to be released in other ways.
One of the ways is sheer daydreaming—such daydreaming as
we have shared with Leopold Bloom, Mrs. Dalloway, the
patriarch Jacob, and a host of other people in the novels
that explore the stream of reverie. Like them we play at sat-

isfying wishes of all sorts, we let neglected impulses slip out on the stage and imagine what it would be like if they acted out their rôles. If we have the talent, we may take hold of some of these unorganized daydreams and shape them into a painting or a fugue, a story or a poem or a song. If we lack this skill, some one more gifted has probably done this shaping for us, and by good luck or through deliberate seeking, we find that expression of our desires, and feel almost as released and freed of tension as if we had created the picture or poem or novel ourselves. Experience gradually makes us more and more intelligent in the search for what will satisfy us. We know when it is the Love-Death music of *Tristan* that we want, and when it is what Aldous Huxley calls the "mathematical merrymaking" of a Bach fugue; when our criminal impulses can fulfill themselves in an Agatha Christie tale, and when nothing short of a Karamazov tragedy will quiet them.

The psychologist will usually say that our healthy growth lies in facing the conditions that are impeding the harmonious play of our impulses and altering them. It is true that to escape in daydreams, however beautifully organized by ourselves or others, may become a dangerous habit. The hero of Schnitzler's *Road to the Open,* a talented musician, uses his music to avoid dealing with the situations that his own irresponsibility has created. His is a technique not merely of escape, but of cowardly evasion. But the problems we face may be insoluble at the moment; we must wait for some new development. Our restlessness may become intolerable and prevent us from doing anything else. A few hours with music, books, paintings, an escape into an imagined world, give us the respite we need, and reconcile us to a temporary suspension of the decision about our problem. Relaxation of pressure when it becomes too great, stimulation of an unused set of impulses when another set is tired out, awakening of the senses when routine has dulled them, interludes of contemplation when calls for action have been too insistent: all this is implied when we say of an artist—he takes me out of myself, he creates the illusion that enables me to escape.

So we carry further the suggestion in the first chapter about the need of mastering our personal perspective. The nature of the interplay between life and literature becomes clearer. A few simple things can be said about it; as for example the following comment on the difference between youthful and adult relationship with novels: "I explain things that happen to me in terms of what I have read, while my mother explains events in books by the personal experience she has had of such events." Most adult readers are familiar with this alteration in point of view. But back of the simple general statements that can be made lies a very intricate and obscure process, as any one will realize who looks back over years of reading and living and attempts to trace the connection between them. Only this effort—again a part of the task of mastering our personal perspective—can change psychological and esthetic theories from intellectual playthings to tools we can use in our living. Here is the experience, typical enough to be quoted, of a mature reader who made this effort:

I became absorbed in uncovering early trails, long buried under traditions and habits, and in discovering others as unfamiliar to me as roads travelled in my sleep. I weeded out traces of my youthful convictions and dreams, of my pain in the face of reality and my fear of life. I unearthed memories of books which had pleased, shocked or comforted me, and of others which had led me into paths so new that the earlier ones had been forsaken. When my weeding was done, I was amazed at the pattern which the paths of my life revealed. I realized that there had been a constant interplay of my natural needs and of books. I saw impulses and influences of which I had been entirely unconscious.

Some I respected, others I regretted. But there they all were, spread out before me, and none of them could be ignored or denied. I felt as though I had met myself and life face to face, and though each was both better and worse than I had realized, each was richer. Then I experienced an unusual feeling of freedom and exhilaration. I was no longer afraid of the patterns my life might trace, for I had gained some understanding of its motif. New paths stretched out before me which I was eager to follow; and I knew that those which I could not take literally could, as in the past, be reached through books.[90]

The moralists and would-be censors, whom we have always with us, would like to sum up the complicated process revealed in this experience by the question: will people act upon the suggestions of fiction and drama? They often risk an affirmative answer, relying on their own intuitions or on some convenient, easily manipulated psychological theory, or perhaps on statistics collected at great expense by some foundation—statistics, for example, about the effect of gangster movies on selected groups from orphan asylums. Something of what is really involved in answering that simple question is made clear by Mr. I. A. Richards in his *Principles of Literary Criticism*.

In trying to set some standard of value for the art experience, Mr. Richards assumes that the most valuable states of mind are those which involve the widest and most comprehensive coördination of activities, and the least curtailment, starvation, and restriction. A work of art coördinates a number of our impulses; no overt action may take place; but incipient or imaginal action is as important as overt action, though its results are not immediately apparent. These incipient activities or tendencies to action he calls attitudes. An experience may be made up of incipient promptings, lightly stimulated tendencies to acts of one kind or another, faint preliminary preparations to do this or that. Emotions are the signs of attitudes; but it is the attitudes themselves that are the all-important part of any experience.

It is not the intensity of the conscious experience, its thrill, its pleasure, or its poignancy which gives it value, but the organization of its impulses for freedom and fulness of life. There are plenty of ecstatic instants that are valueless; the character of consciousness at any moment is no certain sign of the excellence of the impulses from which it arises . . . A more reliable but less accessible set of signs can be found in the readiness for this or that kind of behavior in which we find ourselves after the experience.

Novels and stories and plays and moving pictures have done much to develop conventional, stereotyped, "stock" attitudes toward friendship, country, love, self-sacrifice, and toward such types as the gangster, the gentleman crook, the big-hearted prostitute, the bomb-throwing Red, and so on. Such attitudes tend to become fixed at certain levels of development, unless the pressure of experience or an unusual capacity for critical reflection operate to change them. When art or literature helps to fix immature attitudes, it may leave the adult worse, not better, adjusted to the possibilities of his existence than a child; for he is facing fictions projected by his own stock responses. Such art and literature Mr. Richards calls bad. "Against these stock responses the artist's internal and external conflicts are fought, and with them the popular writer's triumphs are made."

It is true that people seldom imitate directly what they see in the moving picture or read in the best-seller. If they did, the effects would be obvious and easily dealt with. But there may be no discernible resemblance or connection between the experience due to a work of art and the later behavior and experience which is affected by it. The influence may be overlooked or denied, but not, insists Mr. Richards, by anyone "who has a sufficient conception of the ways in which attitudes develop." So even when we seem to ourselves to be merely "escaping," we are developing attitudes that may have a profound influence later on our behavior. When a novel or poem or play has given more than usual order and coherence to our responses, has organized our impulses more completely and on a higher level than we usually achieve, we have a feeling of relief, freedom, increased competence. "We seem to feel that our command of life, our insight into it, and our discrimination of its possibilities, is enhanced, even for situations having little or nothing to do with the subject of the reading." If on the other hand our organization is depressed, forced to a lower and cruder and more wasteful level, we feel dissatisfied or baffled.

Here is an interesting analysis of the way a great novel, *Crime and Punishment,* coördinates for one reader a complex set of impulses.

There is a distinct relation between good literature and an intricately developed psychological equipment both in the author and the reader. Dostoevsky himself was a man of deep-seated instinctive and emotional equipment, with a highly developed nervous organization, fine intelligence and wide social and philosophical interests. Therefore his work should and does draw upon a bewildering source of material and elicits a bewildering reaction. *Crime and Punishment* plays on the theme of murder, the motives of murder, play thoughts of murder, the desire to murder, the fear of murder, murder in its effect on the murderer, murder in its social effect. Murder is probably based on the self-assertive instinct, and the underlying idea of the book, that a superman may commit murder and escape its consequences, also appeals to the assertive impulse. Raskolnikov's self-surrender during the course of the book and his ultimate acceptance of the futility of the theory he held at first appeals strongly to the submissive impulse, the balance wheel of the assertive. But these two instincts and their emotions are so involved with other instincts and emotions acting and counteracting that one could never say they were the dominant reactions elicited. Some readers may be attracted to the murder theme because it satisfies the curiosity motive, curiosity as to what it would be like to commit murder; some may enjoy it because it has the elements of a detective tale and satisfies another form of the mastery impulse— planned murder and escape. The sex motive appears in Raskolnikov's love for Sonia and her trade of prostitution. These are some of the instincts at play in the book, but so counterbalanced and complicated by others that a real semblance to the complexity of life is attained. Feeling tones, likes and dislikes, emotions, interests, tendencies and counter tendencies, are woven in and out in a vast close fabric. Murder is the theme, but the whole of life comes to support it, to play upon it, to light it up, to explain it, to present it with verisimilitude. Almost the whole catalogue of human impulses is drawn into it. And the skill, which arouses the critical, intellectual motive of mastery and manipulation, is its crowning glory to the acute and well-trained. Dostoevsky epitomizes life to the full, life lived that way, longed for that way, reproduced that way. That is why he is so bewildering, so fascinating, so excruciating, and withal so satisfying; because he packs into one moment a multitude of reactions and his novels cover months and years of those moments; because all of these native desires are satisfied not only in the person of one but of many characters, each exhibiting and eliciting reactions in every possible phase and nuance. And so we "play" with Dostoevsky.[91]

If we accept Mr. Richards's theory, that a work of art is valuable in proportion to the value of the experience it gives us; and if we test that value by our readiness for this or that sort of behavior after the experience; we are then faced by a question not discussed in *The Principles of Literary Criticism:* what is the test of value, of good and bad, in behavior? The answer depends on our philosophy of life, our ethical standards, our conception of the desirable form and development of society—and on about everything else. We may share Mr. Richards's prepossession in favor of "freedom and fulness of life," and think we are moving in that direction and are developing finer and finer attitudes; and an observer with a different ethical code may think we are going to the dogs and taking society with us. One can easily see—to take only one example—how opinions would differ about the value of the religious experience recorded by a reader of *The Brothers Karamazov,* who for a long time had been troubled and confused, working her way through a maze of baffling problems. Then she came to the chapter called "The Grand Inquisitor":

the scales fell from my eyes, and religion, as it is presented to and practised by the weak, stood forth in all its ugliness. The traditions of years crumbled away like the Palace of Beauty in *Parsifal,* and the stones still lie where they fell. My landscape and horizon grew more distinct; what had been blurred was clarified. Ivan gathered up all my vague attempts at a philosophy of life and crystallized them. It was like stepping out from a darkened room into a spring morning with its teeming possibilities.

And apparently Ivan's ultimate disasters did not destroy the effect of this enlightenment.

In our discussion of fiction, we have tried not to separate it from the human conditions under which it was brought into being and the human consequences it engenders in life experience. For to make that separation—as we quoted Professor Dewey in the first chapter—is to build a wall around artistic objects, that renders almost opaque their general significance, with which esthetic theory deals. A novel grows out of an experience of the author; it may—or may not— grow into an experience for the reader. Criticism, doing its best with the available facts to analyze both experiences, should lead us back to the author and forward to the reader; back to conditions of origin and forward to operation in actual life. The difficulties of such analysis have been sufficiently indicated, and we have raised more questions than we have tried to answer. The problem of an esthetic evaluation has been implied in parts of our discussion, and we think we have made such an evaluation now and then. But before we leave the whole subject we must give our practise the support of a little theory. For this theory we have drawn heavily on John Dewey's *Art as Experience*, especially Chapters I, III, VII, VIII, and XIII, summarizing ideas freely, but we hope scrupulously.

And first, what is an experience? We have used the word without definition again and again, well aware that volumes have been written and will continue to be written, to explain its meaning. We shall take Professor Dewey's definition, in *Art as Experience*, because we like it and think we understand it. He distinguishes thus between "experience" in general and "an experience" in particular: Experience in general is the interaction between the living creature and its environment; it is always going on; but when the material experienced runs its course to fulfillment, it is integrated within and demarcated in the general stream from other experiences; it is "an experience." In an experience, the flow is from something to something; one part leads into another; each part carries on what went before; the enduring whole is diversified by successive phases; there is continuous merging; there are no holes, mechanical junctions, dead centers. There are pauses and places of rest, but they merely punctuate and define the quality of the movement. An experience has a unity that gives it a name: that meal, that game of chess, that storm, that friendship; the unity is constituted by a single quality that pervades the entire experience. The close is a consummation, not a mere cessation; when the experience stops, it is because it has reached the end for the sake of which it was initiated. Every integral experience moves towards a close and ceases only when the energies involved have done their proper work.

An experience may be continuous in time, like the perfect

meal or game of chess. But it may complete itself only after many years, with many interruptions. A relationship among three people, say, may begin, develop, be broken off or lapse for a time, start up again between two of the three, exhibit entirely new aspects, lapse again, bring in the third person in a new relation, and suddenly, after twenty years fulfill itself in some culminating act, round itself out in some harmonious moment. At any point in the twenty years, one of those concerned might say—this is broken, incomplete, confused; I don't understand it. Then at long last he sees how motives and emotions and efforts and accidents have been working through an intricate, yet coherent scheme. In a novel or play, all that would in actual life hinder the perception of unity and continuity in an experience is cut away. And we are helped thus to recognize an authentic experience in our own lives, or else are given the satisfaction of seeing fulfilled in imagination what has been inchoate and disrupted and uncompleted in actuality.

In every experience there is an element of struggle and conflict arising out of the very conditions of life. For life consists of phases in which the organism falls out of step with the march of surrounding things and then recovers unison with it, either through effort or through chance. And in a growing life this recovery is not a mere return to a prior state, but an advance to a new state enriched by the phase of disparity and resistance through which it has passed. Because of the falling-out and the reëstablishment of balance, we have symmetry and rhythm in an experience. Rhythm occurs when movement is spaced by places of rest; there is no rhythm without recurrence; esthetic recurrence is that of relationships which sum up and carry forward. When our attention is focused on movement, we are aware of rhythm; when it is focused on the intervals that define rest and relative fulfillment, we are aware of symmetry.

Esthetic quality—as suggested by such terms as balance, rhythm, symmetry—is implicit in every normal experience, but generally fails to become explicit. It becomes explicit in the work of art. In two sorts of possible worlds, esthetic experience could not occur: in a world of mere flux, where change would not be cumulative and move to a close and where there would be no stability and rest; and in a finished world, where there would be no traits of suspense and crisis and no opportunity for resolution. The actual world combines movement and culmination, breaks and reunions. "The live being recurrently loses and reëstablishes equilibrium with his surroundings. The moment of passage from disturbance to harmony is that of intensest life." [92] "Equilibrium comes about not mechanically and inertly, but out of and because of tension." [93]

The artist cares in a peculiar way for that phase of experience in which union is achieved. He does not therefore shun moments of resistance and tension. "He rather cultivates them . . . because of their potentialities, bringing to living consciousness an experience that is unified and total." There are elements of pain in conflict and tension. That is the phase of "undergoing" in an experience. It is a matter of particular conditions whether this undergoing phase is in itself pleasurable or painful, although few intense esthetic experiences, as Professor Dewey says, are "wholly gleeful."

Let us finally consider the critic and especially the critical reader; for that is surely what the person who reads books about books is trying to become, though he may not be taking the best way.

The critical reader will do the following things by turn, as he can. He will keep a wary and inquiring eye on his own immediate perspective: the mood, the circumstances of the moment, his state of mind and body. He will also establish in

his own mind, with such clarity as he can manage, his larger
perspective—that formed by his prejudices, his background,
his beliefs, likes and dislikes, the order of his preferences.
Thus he will be able to make allowance for all these things
in his intellectual and emotional response. He will read,
also, with an open mind for the author's perspective, picking up such outside help as he can from interpreters and
biographers. He will watch, as Virginia Woolf says, how the
author places his tree there and his man here, and so on. And
he will set his own perspective and the author's off against
each other.

At the end of his reading he will have some sort of dominant impression—if, that is, the book has been an experience
for him, not a mere adventure, a passive undergoing. This
first total impression in the face of a work of art is most con-
spicuous in music. It is an impact that precedes all definite
recognition of what it is about. So that the impression
directly made by a harmonious ensemble in any art is often
described as the musical quality of that art. It is impossible
to prolong this stage of direct seizure. The only way to know
whether it is at a high level, or whether it is one of those
intense moments that are valueless, of which Mr. Richards
speaks; whether it has been induced by a product of high
quality or by a cheap and meretricious one—is to pass on to
the stage of discrimination. Mr. Richards would have us now
consider our readiness for this or that kind of behavior as a
test for the value of the experience. That is discrimination
of a psychological and moral sort. Esthetic discrimination involves referring the impression back to the grounds upon
which it rests. The reader may discover that these grounds lie
in his own temperament and personal history, rather than
in anything in the novel; the seizure was the result of factors adventitious to the object itself. That discovery is in itself a contribution to his esthetic education, and his next

impression will thereby be lifted to a higher level of discrimination. But if he finds he has been relatively disinterested, he will examine the novel in the light of the meaning of "an experience," looking for the elements of rhythm and symmetry, testing its conclusion to see whether it is consummation or mere cessation. He will try to relate technique to substance, asking why Conrad or Mann mixes up his time order, why Gide introduces a novelist into his story, why Mrs. Woolf relies so much on reverie and Mr. Hemingway so much on dialogue, why Dostoevsky confronts Ivan and Smerdyakov at this particular stage of the plot and not at another, and so on, following any of the numerous lines of inquiry that interest him, and may develop his capacity for discriminating enjoyment.

In our own living we have periods of equilibrium, followed by new struggles and adjustments. But "through the phases of perturbation and conflict, there abides the deep-seated memory of an underlying harmony, the sense of which haunts life like the sense of being founded upon a rock." [94] When we realize that an experience has reached its consummation, we are poised between the past and the future, living in a moment in which "the past reënforces the present and in which the future is a quickening of what now is." [95] These are the moments that art celebrates with peculiar intensity. And these moments, vicariously experienced, haunt our lives no less than those directly experienced, with the memory of underlying harmony . . .

Such moments of equilibrium as that when Philip Carey in *Of Human Bondage* realizes that he may weave the pattern of his life as the weaver the pattern of his rug, and make of its events, of his feelings, thoughts, and deeds, a design that would be no less beautiful because he alone knew of its existence . . .

The moment when Mrs. Ramsay in *To the Lighthouse,* in her constant effort to draw together the separate and constrained individualities of her family and friends, succeeds in making of the dinner in the candle-lighted room "one of those globed, compacted things over which thought lingers and love plays . . ."

The moment of insight won through conflict, which cames to Stephen when at the sound of his name Dedalus, shouted by his companions—the name of the fabulous artificer—"he seemed to hear the noise of dim waves and to see a winged form flying above the waves and slowly climbing the air . . . His heart trembled in an ecstasy of fear and his soul was in flight . . . He would create proudly out of the freedom and power of his soul . . ."

The moment in the tavern when Ivan Karamazov's long smothered emotion flares up in that burning arraignment of the universe that marks the temporary triumph of one set of forces in his desperate inner struggle—a temporary triumph only, but with the effect of a consummation . . .

The moment of Hans Castorp's awakening from his snow dream of humanity to a perception of the meaning of his experience on the Magic Mountain, and to the determination that death henceforth should have no mastery over his thought . . .

The moment by the Ionian Sea when Gissing's mood corresponded perfectly to his intellectual bias, when alone and quiet he saw the evening fall on cloud-wreathed Etna, the twinkling lights come forth upon Scylla and Charybdis, and wished it were his lot to "wander endlessly amid the silence of the ancient world, today and all its sounds forgotten . . ."

And finally that moment in the Guermantes library when Proust (or his hero) opens the volume from which his mother used to read aloud to him in his childhood, and suddenly across the years hears the ringing of the bell that announced

M. Swann's departure and the coming of his mother up the stairs to indulge him in his nervous fears; and he is terrified to realize that it must ring in his mind forever, for from that night, when his parents first indulged him, dates the decline of his will; only by making of his life a book could he retrieve that past he must always carry with him—a moment of terror passing into exaltation as he sees his path before him.

None of all these moments marks more than a temporary equilibrium between the close of one phase of conflict and the beginning of a new one. As such we cherish them—and all the more, if we are Platonists and believe that at such moments the veil is withdrawn from the fixed and eternal beauty.

NOTES

1. *The Common Reader: Second Series,* pp. 52-53.
2. John Dewey, *Art as Experience,* p. 3.
3. Pages 29 ff.
4. Stefan Zweig, *Three Masters.*
5. "Dostoevsky, posing as a sort of Jesus, but most truthfully revealing himself all the while as a little horror." *Studies in Classic American Literature,* p. 3.
6. *The Dial,* June, 1922.
7. Janko Lavrin, *Dostoevsky, a Psycho-critical Study.*
8. J. M. Murry, *Fyodor Dostoevsky: A Critical Study.*
9. *Yale Review,* December, 1933.
10. Marcel Proust, *Remembrance of Things Past: The Captive,* p. 515.
11. *The Captive,* p. 518.
12. E. H. Carr: *Dostoevski: A New Biography,* p. 112.
13. By contrast, the French players of the Vieux Colombier, stressing the action, the crime and its preliminaries, created the sinister and incredible atmosphere of the lunatic asylum. Nothing the characters did seemed "natural." The book lends itself dramatically to both interpretations. *Hamlet,* too, could be played as a bloody revenge tragedy.
14. Pages 39-40.
15. Edwin Muir, *Latitudes.*
16. Aimée Dostoevsky in her book, *Fyodor Dostoevsky,* says that the family persuaded Dostoevsky's literary friends who knew the circumstances of the murder not to speak of it in their reminiscences of her father.
17. Aimée Dostoevsky, *Fyodor Dostoevsky.*
18. *The Diary of Dostoevsky's Wife.*
19. It will be remembered that Smerdyakov is the natural son of old Karamazov and the village idiot Lizaveta, whom one night in a drunken orgy he embraced as a perverse sort of practical joke.
20. His daughter writes that, according to a family tradition, "it was when he heard of his father's death that Dostoevsky had his first epileptic fit." (Page 33.) Mr. Carr sees reason to doubt this, as well as some other statements of Aimée Dostoevsky, and holds to the traditional view that Dostoevsky

had the first attack in Siberia. Dostoevsky said himself of his attacks: "The depression which in my case succeeded the epileptic fits had this characteristic: I feel like a great criminal; it seemed as if some unknown guilt, a criminal deed, oppressed my conscience." Dr. Stekel (*Conditions of Nervous Anxiety and Their Treatment*, pp. 340-57) discusses Dostoevsky's epilepsy.

21. Percy Lubbock, *The Craft of Fiction*.

22. Thomas Mann, *Past Masters*.

23. John Dewey, *Art as Experience*, p. 105.

24. "Preface" to *The Nigger of the Narcissus*.

25. Professor Lamont of Rutgers University, who has made a detailed study, *Isolation in the Life and Work of Joseph Conrad*, soon to be published, of the isolated characters in Conrad's work, thus defines them: An isolated character in the work of Conrad is one who is shut off, either consciously or unconsciously, by some barrier, either external or internal, from the people with whom he wishes to associate or from the life which he wishes to live. Professor Lamont has classified the types of isolation in a most illuminating manner.

26. *The Last Twelve Years of Joseph Conrad*.

27. "Preface" to *A Personal Record*.

28. Conrad, *Last Essays*.

29. E. F. C., *Manchester Guardian*, June 23, 1923.

30. *The Twentieth Century Novel*.

31. "Preface" to *The Nigger of the Narcissus*.

32. A guess, of course, but based on comments from many students.

33. *Of Human Bondage* was published in 1915; *The Old Wives' Tale*, in 1908; *Nostromo*, in 1904; *Buddenbrooks*, in 1901.

34. W. L. Myers, *The Later Realism*.

35. See Max Eastman, *The Literary Mind*.

36. C. P. Fadiman, in *The Nation*, February 27, 1929.

37. *Human Nature and Conduct*.

38. *The New Republic*, October 12, 1921.

39. Once it was made clear that Joyce had Homer's *Odyssey* in mind whilst writing his own *Ulysses*, this analogy was given an importance that it seems to me not to deserve. Constant insistence that angle A in Joyce is analogous to angle A' in Homer is so far-fetched that I find myself saying: "Even if it is true, or partly true, what of it?" Pointing out these similarities is an amusing pastime and little more. This game detracts from an examination of Joyce's work on its own merits.

There seems to me no need for Joyce to be both propped and propelled by the Homer epic.

Furthermore, this tracing of design leads to absurdities. Odysseus was shrewd, crafty, cunning—these words state his dominant characteristics—and, in the end, Odysseus was successful. I fail to see that Leopold Bloom, Joyce's chief hero (if not his chief glory) was either shrewd or crafty or cunning. And, certainly, in the end, Bloom has achieved very little that we feel to be success.

If Molly Bloom, the wife, is the faithful, chaste, long-suffering modern Penelope, then I cannot read. But the chief absurdity in this cross-reference and very literary game, is Gerty MacDowell in the modern role of Nausicaa. As for the other analogies, Mr. Edmund Wilson writes of them sensibly in his essay on *Ulysses* in *Axel's Castle*. Their chief importance is to show what a "bite" Joyce has when he sets himself to do a vicious satire.

40. Winifred Holtby, *Virginia Woolf,* p. 18.
41. *Ibid.,* p. 20.
42. Article on Virginia Woolf in *The Dial.*
43. J. W. Krutch, review of "Mrs. Dalloway," *The Nation,* June 3, 1925.
44. Holtby, *op. cit.,* p. 22.
45. *Monday and Tuesday,* the Hogarth Press, 1921. Miss Holtby considers briefly in her book the possible indebtedness of Mrs. Woolf to other writers who employ the "stream of consciousness" technique. Dorothy Richardson's novel *The Tunnel,* not quite new in technique, resembling Sterne a little, was published in 1919, and Mrs. Woolf probably had read it. She had of course read Sterne. There is no evidence that she had read the portions of *Ulysses* that had appeared in *The Little Review;* the book itself was published in 1922. M. Delattre, "who seems to know," says in *Le Roman psychologique de Virginia Woolf* that she did not read Proust till 1922. "It does not seem important. At certain times particular forms of style present themselves to different writers, and quite independently of each other, they begin to work on similar lines," he concludes (p. 108).
46. *Mr. Bennett and Mrs. Brown.*
47. *Jacob's Room.*
48. Winifred Holtby, *Virginia Woolf,* p. 61.
49. *Ibid.,* p. 147.
50. Holtby, *op. cit.,* p. 160.

51. R. D. Charques, *Contemporary Literature and Social Revolution*, p. 108.
52. R. D. Charques, *Contemporary Literature and Social Revolution*, p. 114.
53. John Strachey, *The Coming Struggle for Power*.
54. *Point Counter Point*, pp. 294-95.
55. *The Bookman*, November, 1924.
56. *Point Counter Point*, pp. 293-94.
57. Appendix to the *Journal of The Counterfeiters*.
58. See Thomas Craven, *Modern Art*.
59. *New Republic*, April 21, 1917.
60. *New Masses*, July 3, 1934.
61. *The Daily Worker*, January 29, 1934.
62. See, for example, Maxwell Bodenheim's article in *The Daily Worker* for July 3, 1934.
63. From Miss Lumpkin's address at the Writers' Club, Columbia University.
64. *New Masses*, July 3, 1934.
65. Malcolm Cowley in *The New Republic*, July 4, 1934.
66. Albert Hirsch in the *New Masses*, July 3, 1934.
67. "Literary Wars in the U.S.S.R.," *New Masses*, July 10, 1934.
68. J. W. Krutch, *Five Masters*.
69. J. C. Powys, in the *New York Herald Tribune Books*, May 13, 1928.
70. *Cities of the Plain*, I, 217 ff.
71. *The Guermantes Way*, II, 8.
72. *The Guermantes Way*, I, 186 ff.
73. *Swann's Way*, I, 66 ff.
74. *Swann's Way*, I, 166.
75. *Time Regained*, p. 92.
76. *The Guermantes Way*, I, 124-25.
77. Thomas Mann, in *The Modern Thinker*, August, 1934.
78. The chronological order of the main incidents in the Genesis narrative, used by Thomas Mann in the first volume of *Joseph and His Brothers*:
   A. Isaac, Jacob and Esau: the stolen blessing.
   B. Jacob flees to his mother's brother, Laban.
      (The pursuit by Eliphaz, Esau's son, with intent to kill his treacherous uncle, and the way in which Jacob escaped death, seems to be an elaboration of the Bible story by Mann.)
   C. Jacob journeys east, has his vision of Heaven, and sets up his commemorating stone.

D. He remains for 25 years with Laban, serves for Rachel, is put off with Leah, finally marries Rachel, has born to him by wives and handmaidens all his sons, except Benjamin, and one daughter, Dinah, increases his wealth by his cleverness at cattle and sheep breeding, departs secretly with all his household and his goods, is pursued by Laban, but effects a reconciliation.

E. He wrestles with the angel for the name—Israel.

F. He is met by Esau, reconciled with him, and settles for a time at Shechem.

G. The affair at Shechem; the rape of Dinah and the ruse of Jacob's sons in avenging her, and the sack of the town.

H. Flight again, the birth of Benjamin and death of Rachel.

 I. The death of Isaac.

J. The scene of Joseph and Jacob conversing by the well, which opens the novel, is an elaboration by Mann.

79. In *A Sketch of My Life*, Thomas Mann writes that such an atmosphere would, he felt, be the right one in which "to incubate the problem" he had in mind at the beginning of his work on this novel.

80. Chekhov is buried in the old cemetery within the walls of a famous monastery on the outskirts of Moscow. The visitor there in August, 1923, found workmen from the near-by factory living with their families in many of the houses occupied before the Revolution by the Sisters. Those Sisters who were left—about two hundred of the pre-revolutionary three hundred—were crowded together in the row of little houses along one of the walls, supporting themselves precariously by filling private orders for embroidery, quilts, and the like. Individualistic industry had replaced the old religious communism of the pre-Soviet era. Chekhov would have savored the irony of that. And no one could have interpreted like Chekhov the lives of some of these women, derelicts of the great upheaval: the meek gatekeeper, who came out to greet us from a little cell-like recess under the great archway, over which some workman had scrawled in chalk—"Death to Mussolini, the bandit!" Or the austere old Sister, a black kerchief tied about her head, peasant fashion, who sat in a tiny vaulted room on a high stool before a lectern, with ikon and lamp above it, absorbed in reading a beautifully illuminated religious book. Or the placid, unworldly Sister, working at a quilting frame in a quiet spot in the

cloisters, close to the cell where she was living as a recluse in solitary communion with God.

81. A. Kaun, *Freeman*, March 1, 1922.

82. This peculiarly attractive quality of Chekhov's personality must have been due partly to his own sense of inner freedom. This he had won only at a painful cost. "Write a story," he says in a letter (Jan. 7, 1889) with a clear reference to himself, "of how . . . the son of a serf, who has served in a shop, sung in a choir, been at a high school and a university, who has been brought up to respect everyone of higher rank and position, to kiss priests' hands, to reverence other people's ideas, to be thankful for every morsel of bread, who has been many times whipped, who has trudged from one pupil to another without goloshes, who has been used to fighting, and tormenting animals, who has liked dining with his rich relations, and been hypocritical before God and man from the mere consciousness of his own insignificance—write how this young man squeezes the slave out of himself drop by drop, and how waking one beautiful morning he feels that he has no longer a slave's blood in his veins but a real man's."

83. Robert Littell, in *The New Republic*, February 28, 1923.

84. Whether Katherine Mansfield consciously modelled her technique upon that of Chekhov is unimportant. But we have the word of her husband, J. M. Murry (*The Dial*, February, 1924), that she had a deep instinctive understanding and a passionate love of Chekhov.

85. "Films often show life as it is, but never with vice triumphant." Will H. Hays, quoted in *The New Republic*, February 20, 1924.

86. Raymond Mortimer, in *The Dial*, May, 1922.

87. Gorki (*My University Days*) refers to this story when he tells of his grandmother's death, and how he longed to tell someone about her, and how kind and clever she was: "I carried about that desperate longing with me for a long time—but there was no one to confide in and so it burned out, unsaid. I recalled those days many years after, when I read the wonderfully true story of A. P. Chekhov, about the coachman who spoke to his horse of his son's death. And I bitterly regretted that in those days of sharp misery I had neither a dog nor a horse at my side and that I did not think of sharing my grief with the rats."

88. Ma Parker's Lennie grew out of the memory of a little

German slum boy whom Katherine Mansfield took care of for a time after her own child was born dead. The story of her unhappy marriage and separation and her stay in Bavaria, 1909-10, is told in *The Life of Katherine Mansfield,* by Ruth Mantz and J. Middleton Murry, pp. 316 ff. The man she married is said in this book to have been "of the type afterwards depicted with subtle understanding in *Mr. Reginald Peacock's Day."*

89. Cf. Anatole France, *Putois.*

90. From a paper by Miss Jennie L. Thomson.

91. Quoted from a paper by Mrs. Emily M. F. Cooper.

92. *Art as Experience,* p. 16.

93. *Art as Experience,* p. 14.

94. *Art as Experience,* p. 17.

95. *Art as Experience,* p. 18.

BIBLIOGRAPHY

A selected list of books is given for each chapter: other works by the novelists discussed, interesting to read after those taken up in the text; critical and biographical studies and essays; books of general criticism in the field. Since the bibliography had to be strictly limited in length, the list is highly selective.

Chapter I

On the relation between an author and his work the following studies are of interest: Helen E. Davis, Tolstoy and Nietzsche (New Republic Inc.); Matthew Josephson, Zola and His Time; C. J. Jung, Modern Man in Search of a Soul (especially chapter 8, "Psychology and Literature"); J. W. Krutch, Five Masters; Janko Lavrin, Tolstoy: A Psycho-critical Study; V. G. McGill, August Strindberg: the Bedeviled Viking; André Maurois, Aspects of Biography; Alexander Nazaroff, Tolstoy the Inconstant Genius; Avrahm Yarmolinsky, Ivan Turgenev: the Man, His Art, and His Age; Stefan Zweig, Three Masters; Stefan Zweig, Adepts in Self-Portraiture.

On the relation between the reader and the novel, see Q. D. Leavis, Fiction and the Reading Public; Virginia Woolf, The Common Reader, Second Series.

Chapter II

Works by George Gissing (1857-1903), in good modern editions, are: The Nether World, 1889 (Nash, 1930); New Grub Street, 1891 (Modern Library, 1926); The Crown of Life, 1899 (Methuen, 1927); By the Ionian Sea, 1901 (Travellers Library Edition, Jonathan Cape, 1933, has an introduction by Virginia Woolf); The Private Papers of Henry Ryecroft, 1903 (Dutton, 1927); Veranilda, 1904 (Oxford, 1929); Letters to Members of His Family, collected and arranged by A. and E. Gissing, with a preface by his son (Constable, 1927).

There are essays on Gissing by J. W. Cunliffe, in English Literature during the Last Half Century; and by P. E. More, in Shelburne Essays, Fifth Series.

See also Morley Roberts, The Private Life of Henry Maitland, and May Yates's small but important book, George Gissing, an Appreciation (University of Manchester, 1922).

428

BIBLIOGRAPHY

Chapter III

Novels by Fyodor Mikhailovitch Dostoevsky (1821-81) are: The House of the Dead, 1862; Crime and Punishment, 1866 (edition published by Macmillan in the Modern Reader Series has an introduction by Dorothy Brewster); The Idiot, 1868; The Possessed, 1872; The Brothers Karamazov, 1880. The Macmillan edition of Dostoevsky's novels, in the translation by Constance Garnett, is recommended. Macmillan publishes Letters of F. M. Dostoevsky to His Family and Friends, and The Diary of Dostoevsky's Wife. Smith publishes Dostoevsky's Letters to His Wife.

Among critical and biographical works on Dostoevsky are the following: E. H. Carr, Dostoevski, a New Biography, 1931; André Gide, Dostoevsky; Hermann Hesse, In Sight of Chaos (The Brothers Karamazoff . . . Thoughts on Dostoevsky's Idiot); Janko Lavrin, Dostoevsky and His Creation; Dmitri Merezhkovsky, Tolstoy as Man and Artist: with an Essay on Dostoevsky, 1902; J. M. Murry, Fyodor Dostoevsky: a Critical Study, 1916; Stefan Zweig, Three Masters (essay on Dostoevsky).

Chapter IV

Fictional works by Joseph Conrad (1857-1924) are: The Nigger of the Narcissus, 1897; Lord Jim, 1900; Nostromo: a Tale of the Seaboard, 1904; Chance: a Tale in Two Parts, 1913; Victory, 1915; The Shadow-Line, 1917; Youth: A Narrative and Two Other Stories (Heart of Darkness and The End of the Tether), 1902; Typhoon and Other Stories, 1903.

Autobiographical works are: Some Reminiscences, 1912 (American edition, A Personal Record); Notes on Life and Letters, 1921.

Critical studies are: W. L. Cross, Four Contemporary Novelists; F. W. Cushwa, An Introduction to Conrad; Richard Curle, Last Twelve Years of Joseph Conrad; G. Jean-Aubry, Joseph Conrad, Life and Letters; Virginia Woolf, The Common Reader, First Series.

Chapter V

Works by W. Somerset Maugham (1874-) are: Liza of Lambeth, 1897; Of Human Bondage, 1915 (Doubleday, Doran, 1928); The Moon and Sixpence, 1919 (Grosset, 1928); Cakes and Ale; or, The Skeleton in the Cupboard, 1930; The Trembling of a Leaf: Little Stories of the South Sea Islands, 1921; East and West, 1934 (collected stories: English edition, Altogether).

See also F. T. Bason, A Bibliography of the Writings of William Somerset Maugham (London, Unicorn Press, 1931).

Maurice Guest, 1909, the fine novel by Henry Handel Richardson, deals with a variation of the theme "of human bondage" and is very interesting to compare with Maugham's novel. Maurice Guest is wholly dramatic in type, covering about a year's time.

Enoch Arnold Bennett (1867-1931) is the author of: The Truth about an Author, 1903 (Methuen, 1928); The Old Wives' Tale, 1908 (Modern Library, 1931); Clayhanger, 1910; Journal (3 vols., Viking Press, 1932-33).

There are essays on Bennett in W. L. Cross, Four Contemporary Novelists, and S. P. Sherman, On Contemporary Literature.

Thomas Mann's Buddenbrooks was published in 1901, and the English translation appeared in 1924. Other books by and about Thomas Mann are listed under Chapter XIII.

CHAPTER VI

Novels by May Sinclair are: The Divine Fire, 1904; The Three Sisters, 1914; Mary Olivier: a Life, 1919; Mr. Waddington of Wyck, 1921; Life and Death of Harriett Frean, 1922.

Compare with The Three Sisters Miss Sinclair's study The Three Brontës, 1912. The edition of 1914 contains a note on some newly discovered letters of Charlotte Brontë.

CHAPTER VII

Novels by David Herbert Lawrence (1885-1930) are: Sons and Lovers, 1913 (Modern Library, 1923); The Rainbow, 1915 (Modern Library, 1927); Women in Love, 1920 (Boni, 1922); Aaron's Rod, 1922 (Boni, 1922); Lady Chatterley's Lover, 1928. Short stories: The Prussian Officer and Other Stories, 1914 (Martin Secker, 1931); England, My England, 1922; The Woman Who Rode Away and Other Stories, 1928. Essays: Etruscan Places, 1932. Letters: Letters of D. H. Lawrence, edited with an introduction by Aldous Huxley, 1932 (Viking Press).

Among the many critical and biographical books on Lawrence are the following: Catherine Carswell, The Savage Pilgrimage; Horace Gregory, Pilgrim of the Apocalypse; Ada Lawrence and G. S. Gelder, Early Life of D. H. Lawrence, together with hitherto unpublished letters and articles (Martin Secker, 1932); Frieda Lawrence, "Not I, but the Wind . . ." (unpublished letters and material by D. H. Lawrence and memoirs by his wife), 1934; Mabel Dodge Luhan, Lorenzo in Taos; Edward D. Mc-

Donald, Bibliography of the Writings of D. H. Lawrence (Centaur Press); Rebecca West, D. H. Lawrence.

Essays on Lawrence in Aldous Huxley, Music at Night; John Macy, Critical Game; Edwin Muir, Transition; S. P. Sherman, Critical Woodcuts.

CHAPTER VIII

Books by James Joyce (1882-   ) are: Dubliners, 1914 (Modern Library, 1926); A Portrait of the Artist as a Young Man, 1916 (Modern Library, 1928); Ulysses, 1922 (Shakespeare and Co., Paris; Random House Edition, New York, 1933); Fragments from Work in Progress: Anna Livia Plurabelle, Haveth Childers Everywhere, Tales Told by Shem and Shaun, 1931.

Among books and essays on Joyce are: Charles Duff, James Joyce and the Plain Reader, 1932; Édouard Dujardin, Le Monologue intérieur, son apparition, ses origines, sa place dans l'œuvre de James Joyce, 1931 [Les Lauriers sont coupés, a short novel by M. Dujardin, published in 1887, read by Joyce 1901-3, was acknowledged by Joyce in 1921 as influencing his conception of "le monologue intérieur."]; Max Eastman, The Literary Mind; Stuart Gilbert, James Joyce's Ulysses; H. S. Gorman, James Joyce: His First Forty Years; Edwin Muir, Transition; Rebecca West, The Strange Necessity; Edmund Wilson, Axel's Castle.

CHAPTER IX

Novels by Virginia Woolf (1882-   ) include: The Voyage Out, 1915; Night and Day, 1919; Jacob's Room, 1922; Mrs. Dalloway, 1925; To the Lighthouse, 1927; Orlando: a Biography, 1928; The Waves, 1931.

Essays by Virginia Woolf, critical and biographical, include: Mr. Bennett and Mrs. Brown, 1924; The Common Reader, First Series, 1925; A Room of One's Own, 1929; The Common Reader, Second Series, 1932; Flush, a Biography, 1933.

Books on Virginia Woolf and her work include: Floris Delattre, Le Roman psychologique de Virginia Woolf (J. Vren, Paris, 1932), which contains a bibliography of French and English reviews and articles by and about Mrs. Woolf; Winifred Holtby, Virginia Woolf (Wishart and Company, London, 1932), which contains a bibliography of the articles and sketches written by Mrs. Woolf for periodicals.

Dorothy Richardson's novels—a series dealing with the spiritual adventures of the young Englishwoman, Miriam Henderson, as presented through the medium of her own mind—should be mentioned here. The whole work is entitled Pilgrimage, the volumes being Pointed Roofs (1915), Backwater, Honeycomb, The Tunnel, Interim, Deadlock, Revolving Lights, The Trap, Oberland, Dawn's Left Hand (1931). See J. W. Beach, Twentieth Century Novel, and J. C. Powys, Dorothy M. Richardson.

CHAPTER X

Aldous Huxley (1894-) has written the following novels: Crome Yellow, 1921; Antic Hay, 1923; Those Barren Leaves, 1925; Point Counter Point, 1928 (Modern Library, 1930); Brave New World, 1932.

Huxley's short stories include: Limbo, 1920; Mortal Coils, 1922; The Little Mexican, 1924 (American edition, Young Archimedes); Two or Three Graces, 1926; Brief Candles, 1930.

There are essays on Huxley in R. D. Charques, Contemporary Literature and Social Revolution; J. W. Krutch, The Modern Temper; Edwin Muir, Transition; John Strachey, The Coming Struggle for Power.

André Gide (1869-) has written: The Immoralist, 1902 (English translation, 1930); Strait Is the Gate, 1909 (English translation, 1928); Isabelle, 1911, and The Pastoral Symphony, 1919 (English translation, Two Symphonies, 1931); The Counterfeiters, 1925 (English translation, 1927). The Modern Library edition of The Counterfeiters has an introduction by Raymond Weaver.

An English translation of Gide's autobiography, Si le grain ne meurt, has been announced for publication in 1934 by Random House.

For a critical biography of Gide, see Léon Pierre-Quint, André Gide (English translation).

CHAPTER XI

For Émile Zola, see Henri Barbusse, Émile Zola; Henry James, Notes on Novelists; and Matthew Josephson, Zola and His Time. For Zola's theories of fiction, see his Le Roman expérimental, 1880.

For Maxim Gorki, see Alexander Kaun, Maxim Gorki and His Russia; and the volumes of Gorki's autobiography, My Childhood, In the World, and My University Days.

For the background of Russian proletarian fiction, the following books are instructive: Prince Peter Kropotkin, Memoirs of a Revolutionist; M. J. Olgin, The Soul of the Russian Revolution. (These deal with the period before 1917.) For the period after 1917, see William Henry Chamberlin, Soviet Russia; Ralph Fox,

Lenin: a Biography; three books by Maurice Hindus: Humanity Uprooted, Red Bread, and The Great Offensive; Leon Trotzky, The History of the Russian Revolution.

For a general survey of modern Russian literature, see Prince Mirsky, Contemporary Russian Literature.

Other Russian proletarian novels of recent date (out of a long list) are: V. Ilyenkov, Driving Axle; Leonid Leonov, Soviet River; Boris Pilnyak, The Volga Falls to the Caspian Sea.

For the Chinese background of Malraux's Man's Fate, see Agnes Smedley, China's Red Army Marches; also Victor A. Yakhontoff, The Chinese Soviets (1934).

For Scandinavian proletarian fiction, see: Gösta Larsson, Our Daily Bread, 1934, which deals with the Swedish working class, and is to be continued; Martin A. Nexö, Pelle the Conqueror (one-volume edition published by Peter Smith).

For American proletarian fiction, consult Granville Hicks, The Great Tradition, an interpretation of American literature since the Civil War, from a definitely radical standpoint; current issues of the weekly, New Masses, which tracks down and analyzes proletarian novels.

Chapter XII

The titles of the volumes in the English translation, by C. K. Scott-Moncrieff, of Remembrance of Things Past (A la Recherche du temps perdu) by Marcel Proust (1871-1922) are: Swann's Way (2 vols., Henry Holt, 1922); Within a Budding Grove (2 vols., Thomas Seltzer, 1924); The Guermantes Way (2 vols., Thomas Seltzer, 1925); The Cities of the Plain (2 vols., A. and C. Boni, 1927); The Captive (Knopf, 1929); The Sweet Cheat Gone (A. and C. Boni, 1930); Time Regained (Chatto and Windus, 1931, translation by Stephen Hudson). Random House published in October, 1934, a four-volume edition—4,300 pages—of the entire novel.

For biography and criticism of Proust, see Léon Pierre-Quint, Marcel Proust: His Life and Work. There are essays on Proust by Clive Bell (Proust); by J. W. Krutch (in Five Masters); by a number of authors in the volume Marcel Proust: an English Tribute by Various Authors, collected by C. K. Scott-Moncrieff; and by Edmund Wilson (in Axel's Castle).

Chapter XIII

Thomas Mann (1875-   ) has written the following novels and stories: Buddenbrooks, 1901 (English translation, 1924); Tristan,

1903 (English translation, in Death in Venice volume, 1925); Royal Highness, 1909 (English translation, 1926); Death in Venice, 1912 (English translation, 1925, including Tristan and Tonio Kröger); Tonio Kröger, 1914 (English translation, in Death in Venice volume, 1912); The Magic Mountain, 1924 (English translation, 1927); Children and Fools, 1928 (including Disorder and Early Sorrow, and a number of earlier stories); A Man and His Dog, 1930; Mario and the Magician, 1930; Joseph and His Brothers, 1934.

Mann's essays include: Three Essays, 1929; Past Masters, 1933. He has also written the autobiographical A Sketch of My Life, 1930.

A biographical and critical study of Mann is: James Cleugh, Thomas Mann: a Study (Martin Secker, 1933). This contains a bibliography, with titles and dates of German publication, and the more important translations. There are interesting pages on Thomas Mann's work in Arthur Eloesser, Modern German Literature. Hermann J. Weigand is the author of Thomas Mann's Novel Der Zauberberg: A Study.

Other modern novels which, like Joseph and His Brothers, attempt the re-creation of the past with distinguished success, are: Robert Graves, I, Claudius, 1934; Naomi Mitchison, The Corn King and The Spring Queen (Greece, Egypt, and the Black Sea settlements about the third century B.C.), 1931; George Moore, Héloïse and Abélard, 1921; Sigrid Undset, Kristin Lavransdatter, consisting of The Bridal Wreath, The Mistress of Husaby, The Cross, published in Norwegian, 1919, 1920, 1922, and in English translation, 1929; Sigrid Undset, The Master of Hestviken, a tetralogy, consisting of The Axe, The Snake Pit, In the Wilderness, and The Son Avenger; Helen Waddell, Peter Abelard, 1933.

CHAPTER XIV

The Macmillan Company publishes in thirteen volumes a complete edition of the stories of Anton Chekhov (1860-1904), translated by Constance Garnett. There is a good one-volume selection in the Modern Reader Series. Chekhov's letters, his Letters to His Wife, his Letters on the Short Story, and his plays—The Cherry Orchard, Uncle Vanya, Ivanov, The Three Sisters, and The Sea Gull—are all necessary for a complete impression of his literary personality.

Katherine Mansfield (1888-1922) wrote: Bliss and Other Stories, 1920; The Garden Party and Other Stories, 1922: The Dove's Nest and Other Stories, 1923. See also the Journal of Katherine

Mansfield, 1927; The Letters of Katherine Mansfield, edited by
J. M. Murry, 1929; and R. E. Mantz and J. M. Murry, The Life
of Katherine Mansfield, 1933.

The writings of A. E. Coppard (1878-) include: Adam and
Eve and Pinch Me, 1921; Clorinda Walks in Heaven, 1922; The
Black Dog, 1923; Fishmonger's Fiddle, 1925; The Field of Mus-
tard, 1926; Silver Circus, 1928; Nixey's Harlequin (containing
My Hundreth Tale), 1931.

Among novelettes may be listed the following: Willa Cather,
A Lost Lady (1923), My Mortal Enemy (1926), Obscure Destinies
(1932); Joseph Conrad, Heart of Darkness (1898), The End of
the Tether (1902), The Shadow Line (1914); John Galsworthy,
The Apple Tree (1916); André Gide, Strait Is the Gate (1909),
Isabelle (1911); Henry James, Washington Square (1881), The
Aspern Papers (1888), The Lesson of the Master (1892), The Turn
of the Screw (1898); Thomas Mann, Death in Venice (1912),
Tonio Kröger (1914); Jules Romains, Death of a Nobody (1914);
Antoine de St. Exupéry, Night Flight (1931); Arthur Schnitzler,
Casanova's Homecoming (1922), Fräulein Else (1925), Daybreak
(1927), Rhapsody (1927); Edith Wharton, Ethan Frome (1911);
Arnold Zweig, Claudia (1930); Stefan Zweig, Conflicts (1927).

Chapter XV

Among books on the criticism and the technique of fiction are
the following: J. W. Beach, The Twentieth Century Novel; Pel-
ham Edgar, The Art of the Novel from 1700 to the Present Time
(deals only with the art of the novel in English; contains an extensive bibliography, especially of articles in periodicals on such
novelists as Bennett, Conrad, Huxley, Woolf, and some of the
American novelists); E. M. Forster, Aspects of the Novel; John
Greig (John Carruthers, pseudonym), Scheherezade, or the Future of the English Novel; R. M. Lovett and H. S. Hughes, History of the Novel in England; Percy Lubbock, The Craft of Fiction; Edwin Muir, Latitudes; Edwin Muir, Transition; Walter
L. Myers, The Later Realism, A Study of Characterization in the
British Novel; Edith Wharton, The Writing of Fiction.

Among books on the general problems of literary criticism are
the following: John Dewey, Art as Experience; Henry Hazlitt,
The Anatomy of Criticism: A Trialogue; Matthew Josephson,
Portrait of the Artist as American; Joseph W. Krutch, Experi-
ence and Art; Ludwig Lewisohn, Expression in America; I. A.
Richards, Principles of Literary Criticism.

For information about the field of English and American literature the two handbooks by J. M. Manly and Edith Rickert are indispensable: Contemporary English Literature (revised 1928), and Contemporary American Literature (revised 1929).

Consult also for general information the following books on German, French, Russian, and Scandinavian literature of the modern period: Arthur Eloesser, Modern German Literature; René Lalou, Contemporary French Literature; Prince Mirsky, Contemporary Russian Literature; Toplöe-Jensen, Scandinavian Literature from Brandes to Our Day.

For information about translations of contemporary fiction, see The Literary World, a Monthly Survey of International Letters.

AMERICAN FICTION

American fiction is represented in this book only by a novelette of Henry James and one of Willa Cather, and by several proletarian novels. Novelists like Sinclair Lewis, Sherwood Anderson, Theodore Dreiser, Ernest Hemingway and John Dos Passos have been treated rather fully in several of the recent books on the American novel—those by J. W. Beach, Granville Hicks (The Great Tradition) and Ludwig Lewisohn, in particular. We append a short list of novels by American writers; some of them promising first novels, others rather neglected or inadequately recognized—all published within the last twelve years: Conrad Aiken, The Blue Voyage; Jane Culver, So Stood I; E. E. Cummings, The Enormous Room; Frank B. Elser, The Keen Desire; Vardis Fisher, In Tragic Life; Helen Hull, Islanders; Isabel Paterson, Never Ask the End; Raymond Weaver, Black Valley; Thomas Wolfe, Look Homeward, Angel.

COURSES IN MODERN FICTION

For instructors conducting courses in modern fiction in colleges, it may be of interest to know the kind of topic suggested to students writing papers or reports in the courses given by the authors in Columbia University. Such topics brought out statements of experience in the reading of fiction that have been drawn upon for illustration in Chapters I and XV.

Virginia Woolf's essay in The Common Reader, Second Series, from which the quotation on page 10 is taken, is the basis for the following suggestion: You have probably had some difficulty in mastering the perspective of one or several of the novelists in the course; have felt some inclination to make it resemble your own, and some distress or annoyance if you have not succeeded. Select several novels, each by a different author, define the per-

spective of each, and compare these different perspectives with each other and with your own.

A quotation from an article by J. W. Krutch (The Nation, December 2, 1931) furnishes the text for some extended comment by the student: "What we ask of a novel is an arrangement of the facts we know in accordance with an intellectual and emotional scheme acceptable to our minds. We expect it to read some sort of order into the bewildering complexity of phenomena; to show how a sequence of events may be interpreted in a way which justifies our attitude towards life; and to find a place for those standards and judgments and preferences which we cherish."

A topic that may bring out the difference between mere adventure in the reading of fiction, and experience, is the following: A critic has said that for many people art is the chief avenue of approach to new experience. He meant probably experience in the sense of contact with life, not escape. Confine the discussion to the art of fiction, and test the validity of the critic's statement from your own reading history. Can you trace any influence, due to fiction, upon your relations to people and problems?

And this question explores the meaning of such expressions as convincing or real or life-like characterization: You have probably had the experience, in re-reading a novel, of finding characters you thought very convincing at first reading turning into sawdust in your hands—or vice versa. You seek reasons in analysis of the novelist's technique; but some of them probably lie in your own temperament and changing experience. Select several novels: some in which the characters seemed life-like and convincing to you, and others in which they seemed the reverse; and make as careful analysis as you can of both yourself and the author's technique.

INDEX

COLUMBIA UNIVERSITY PRESS
Columbia University
New York

———

FOREIGN AGENT
OXFORD UNIVERSITY PRESS
HUMPHREY MILFORD
Amen House, London, E. C. 4